SoulCollage® Evolving

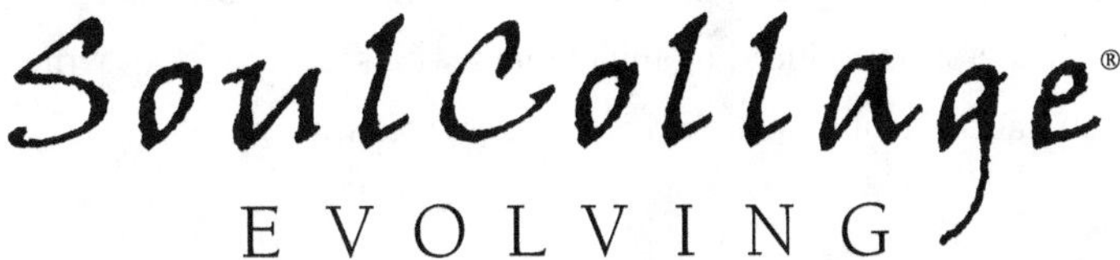

SoulCollage® Evolving

An Intuitive Collage Process for Self-Discovery and Community

Seena B. Frost

Hanford Mead Publishers, Inc.
Desert Hot Springs, California USA

For information address
Hanford Mead Publishers, Inc.,
12650 Reposo Way,
Desert Hot Springs, CA 92240
info@hanfordmead.com
hanfordmead.com

Kylea Taylor, Editor
Covered by Kerry LLC, Designer

ISBN 13: 978-1-59275-050-4
ISBN 10: 1-59275-050-4

THIRD EDITION

10 9 8 7 6 5 4 3 2 1

The official SoulCollage® website and global community is at https://soulcollage.org

Acknowledgments

I want to thank all the SoulCollage® Facilitators and Trainers who offered their stories and those who submitted cards for this book. Each one of them is unique and communicates, far better than my words, the power and fun of this process.

I am grateful to Daniel Cook, SoulCollage® Facilitator and graphic designer, who did a beautiful job of organizing and designing this book and its cover.

I want also to thank Kylea Taylor and Jim Schofield of Hanford Mead Publishers, Inc., for their interest, help, marketing skills, and constant attention. I don't believe any of this would have come to pass without their hard work and continuing belief in the process of SoulCollage®

~ Seena B. Frost

Contents

Photographs

Foreword

As we bring forth this third edition of Seena B. Frost's English-language book, a circle of us—Seena's daughter Jennifer Frost, LeAnne Thomas of the nonprofit SoulCollage Institute, and my husband Jim Schofield and I, as publishers of Seena's work—felt called to add a Foreword. We wanted to offer readers a glimpse into the rich soil from which SoulCollage® has grown into a worldwide self-discovery practice.

For decades, Seena taught and refined this method, receiving letters and reflections from those touched by it. She distilled its mission into these words:

> *"The intention of SoulCollage® is to offer a creative practice for exploring, healing, and evolving our many-faceted Souls, so every Soul is able to manifest its unique SoulEssence in increasingly balanced and joy-filled forms."*

This book, *SoulCollage® Evolving*, contains everything you need to begin. Chances are, you already have the materials at home, and anything else you might need is inexpensive and easy to find. Seena explains it all with her signature blend of humor, simplicity, and heart.

...deeply knowing oneself, and listening to our intuition, can reveal what is uniquely ours to offer the world.

SoulCollage®, like all living practices, has grown and transformed over the years. In this Foreword, I want to share a little about its psychological roots, its origin story, and the extraordinary example Seena gave us: how deeply knowing oneself, and listening to our intuition, can reveal what is uniquely ours to offer the world.

Seena was always multidimensional. But something shifted when she turned 71 in 2003—a fullness of expression emerged as she began to train the first SoulCollage® Facilitators. Her life had already been richly lived: she held an M.Div. from Yale Divinity School, had been a minister's wife, a mother of four, a licensed therapist, and director of a family counseling center. She wrote haiku, swam with whales, and brought humor into every space—whether classroom, therapy session, or sacred circle.

Yet, for a long time, a certain calling remained unnamed. In a 1987 journal entry, Seena wrote:

**"My 'project'! Can I call it that? More an idea that needs juicing, needs ideas, needs support. It must become a passion... A project needs to grasp me and shake me and say, 'Do me. I must be done. The world needs me done.'"*

That "project" remained quiet but persistent, waiting for the right season. And eventually, it found its form. Through Seena's persistent inner work, intuition, and courage, SoulCollage® emerged—a practice that has since touched the lives of thousands around the world. It has helped people hear their inner voices, decode their personal callings, and live more authentic lives. Today, there exists an archive of stories by Facilitators who have blended SoulCollage® with therapy, coaching, education, writing, ceremony, and more.

[SoulCollage®] has helped people hear their inner voices, decode their personal callings, and live more authentic lives.

SoulCollage® is rooted in respected psychological traditions: Jung's concept of Active Imagination, Virginia Satir's parts therapy, Gestalt Therapy, Humanistic and Transpersonal Psychology, Narrative Therapy, and Psychosynthesis. What Seena did so brilliantly was to synthesize some of the concepts from these systems and add a missing element: imagery. While many therapeutic methods overlooked the visual, SoulCollage® placed it at the center. Through choosing, arranging, and interacting with images, SoulCollagers create cards that embody parts of their inner world. Each card becomes a tangible doorway into intuition and self-understanding.

The process is physical as well as emotional: cutting, shifting, and placing images into a new form allows buried insights to rise to the surface. As one's deck of cards grows, so too does one's ability to reflect, integrate, and respond to life's questions with clarity and depth. It is, in every sense, a lifetime practice.

What moves me as much as the method itself is the way Seena lived its principles. She wrestled with uncertainty, followed intuition, and stayed open to surprise. She kept doing the next right thing—trusting that her unnamed project would someday ask to be born. And when it did, she welcomed it fully.

We each have callings. Some are quiet, some bold. Some emerge early, some late. Many of us, especially women and others in marginalized groups, face both external and internal barriers to hearing and honoring our gifts. Often, when we look back, we see that our callings were there all along—woven into what we love, what we are drawn to, and what we long to give.

Seena, born in 1932, came of age after WWII and during the conservative 1950s. In the radical 1960s, she began to experiment with new expressions of self—including attending clown school and developing two clown personas! Her creativity and curiosity never waned.

In Jean Houston's three-year Human Potential course, Seena intuited an archetype for each of her more than 100 classmates and wrote a Haiku for each one. Though this initial process used no images, it was the seed of what would become the SoulCollage® Community Suit.

She began making cards and drawing them to "read" during her daily journaling and using this "Neter Card process" with therapy clients. Soon, small groups formed.

One day in 1998, a client brought their cards into a therapy session with me. I was fascinated. My husband Jim and I, already running a publishing company, attended one of Seena's workshops. I had the deeply moving experience so many describe when making a first card. I knew this method needed a book.

As one's deck of cards grows, so too does one's ability to reflect, integrate, and respond to life's questions with clarity and depth.

At the end of the workshop, I spontaneously asked Seena if we could publish her book. As Seena loved to recount later, she was taken aback and retorted, "*What* book?" But she said yes. For three years, we worked closely editing and organizing. She invited her circle to contribute sample cards. Jim came up with the name "SoulCollage" to replace "Neter Card Process," and we trademarked SoulCollage® to protect the standards of work done under that name. Jim and I worked with designers for the website and the book. In 2001, *SoulCollage*® was born.

The book found readers. People who read the book showed up. They wanted training. They wanted community. And so, the SoulCollage® organization grew. Seena and I held the first Facilitator Training in 2003. In 2007, some experienced Facilitators were invited to apprentice as Trainers. Seena's friend and early protégé Mariabruna Sirabella became SoulCollage®'s master trainer, traveling the world and expanding the reach of the work. Mariabruna and the other Trainers, helped refine and evolve the training program.

Seena continued to participate until shortly before her death. In 2016 she was diagnosed with ALS and entered hospice care surrounded by family. Three days before she passed, she wrote to me:

"I am now starting on my final chapter of life. The doctors don't know for sure how much time I have, but we have contacted Hospice and leave it to God and the Great Spirit to call me home."

I shared her message with the SoulCollage® community, who responded with love, blessings, and cards. Seena's legacy lives on in the practice she created and the lives it continues to touch.

When the pandemic began in 2020, the SoulCollage® organization faced new challenges. All trainings had been in person. Within six weeks, we had made two major transitions. LeAnne Thomas created a global, online community. She set up the World of SoulCollage® and many other structures to meet current and future needs. Mariabruna Sirabella reviewed and transformed the entire contents of the SoulCollage® Facilitator Training, and she and

LeAnne collaborated in transferring that content to World of SoulCollage®, so that it could be delivered online. Post-pandemic options include both online and in-person trainings.

The SoulCollage Institute was established in 2024. It is a nonprofit entity established to steward the future of SoulCollage®: its trainings, research, and community programs. As I write this in 2025, there are over 6000 trained SoulCollage® Facilitators in over 60 countries.

From a spark in Seena's journal to a vibrant, global practice, SoulCollage® has evolved—and continues to evolve. Seena loved this book's title: *SoulCollage® Evolving*. She was always eager to see what would emerge next. I believe she would be smiling now, inviting you warmly to turn the page, stay curious, and let yourself be surprised.

—Kylea Taylor

Desert Hot Springs, California, USA
June 2025

What moves me as much as the method itself is the way Seena lived its principles. She wrestled with uncertainty, followed intuition, and stayed open to surprise. She kept doing the next right thing—trusting that her unnamed project would someday ask to be born. And when it did, she welcomed it fully.

CHAPTER 1

What Is SoulCollage®?

Come, let's sit down together for an hour or so and each of us will create a collage! What? You are not an artist? Not true. Using the SoulCollage® process everyone becomes an instant artist, and we also become explorers of Soul.

Stir together the ingredients of your *imagination* and *intuition* with a few powerful, cut-out *images*, and you can create your first SoulCollage® card. After that you will probably want to make a second, a third, and, over time, many more. Gradually you can create your deck of very personal cards. Hand and hand with the fun of creating these simple cards are the surprising ways they help you explore your Soul, your Shadow, and your inborn gifts. I once listened to a very wise woman describe the beauty and value of a "hand-crafted life," a life that is consciously assembled from pieces that you yourself select and craft together. Such a life is not one "pulled off the rack," having been put together by others or by a culture. The SoulCollage® process of selecting images and making personal cards will serve as a daily reminder to handcraft your own life, to choose pieces that fit together meaningfully and with joy—both for you and for the planet.

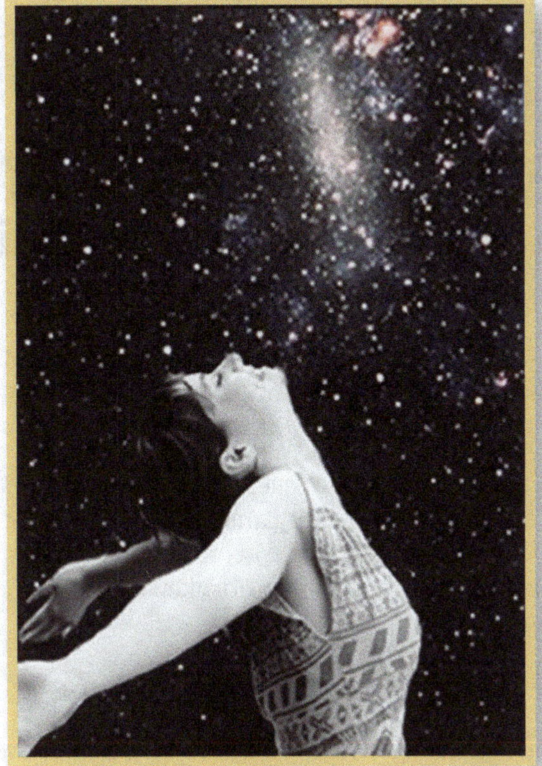

TITLE: **Gratitude**
SUIT: **Committee/Council**
CREATOR: **Pam Renner**

"I Am One Who soaks up grace like dry ground receives rain."

This book is designed to offer a flexible structure for creating your SoulCollage® deck. In it you will find "how-to" suggestions about creating cards and pictures of cards made by many "SoulCollagers." In addition, the book describes different ways to use the cards individually and in groups. You will find a way to listen to your intuitive wisdom bubbling up through the images on your own cards. I know from experience that you will be amazed by your own wise insights. Others will be amazed too, for this process is doubly powerful when shared with a community of people who are also creating cards and consulting their images.

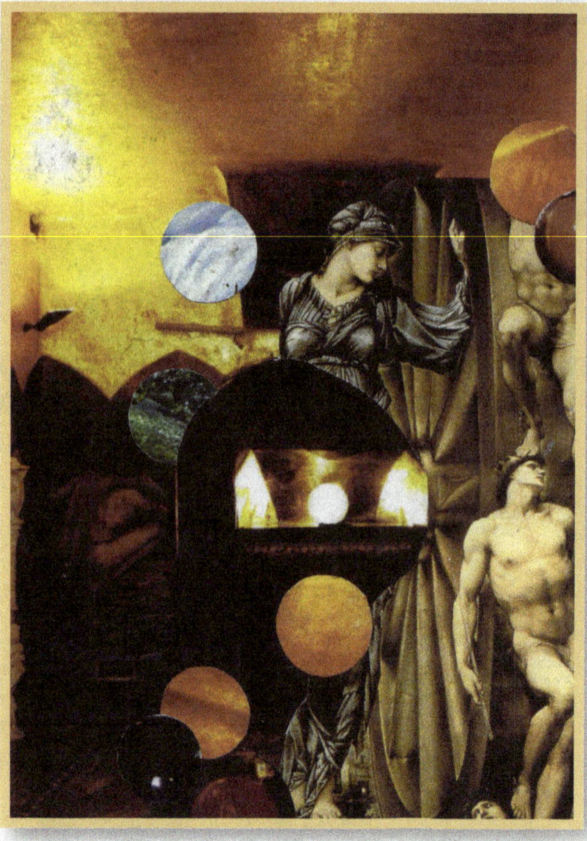

TITLE: **Transmission**
SUIT: **Committee/Council**
CREATOR: **Mariabruna Sirabella**

"*I Am One Who* embraces the transmission of wisdom, from living teachers and from the Beings beyond. Seeking and searching, I climb on your shoulders and you on mine. I receive and transmit the chain unbroken on the wheel of time."

Anyone can make SoulCollage® Cards

Anyone who wishes, men and women, young through elderly, can create SoulCollage® cards. You may make ten cards or a hundred. Either way you will cherish your cards and, I imagine, will want to find ways to share them. Your deck will become a visual journal, one with beauty and meaning and also with flexibility, so it evolves with you. You may decide to glue new images onto old cards, or make several cards for a special energy as that energy changes and grows in your Soul. I guarantee that you will cherish your cards, even the shadowy and fearsome ones. When you hold them all together in your hands, you will be holding a symbolic reflection of your one, many-faceted, evolving Soul. The longer you work with the images, the more power they have to reveal and change patterns in your life.

Clarissa Pinkola Estes, in her wonderful book, *Women Who Run with the Wolves*, tells a story that is a perfect metaphor for SoulCollage® work. The story, very briefly, tells about an old Indian woman, La Loba, who painstakingly gathers the bones of a wolf from the desert sands, being sure to find every one. She carefully arranges them on the floor of her cave, and then she sings over them. At last, as she continues to sing, the bones come together and take on flesh and blood; the wolf leaps up alive once more, but now is transformed into a beautiful woman who joyfully runs from the cave, free to be herself. This story is essential SoulCollage®! When you gather images from magazines and other sources, when you cut them out, paste them onto cards, and then consult them, it is the same sort of miracle. You are gathering your various inner parts, conscious and less conscious, lovable and irritating, beautiful and shadowy, and then you "sing" over them so they can transform into a freer and more vibrant Soul.

Some of the images you choose will symbolize inner parts of your self, parts such as your *Nurturer*, your *Organizer*, your *Explorer*, or your *Lonely Inner Child*. Other images will be more mysterious, mythic, and harder to name. These often represent the Larger-Story energies that have chosen to work in you, and who are guiding or nudging you. Perhaps they are even dragging you forward along your path. These are the universal, eternal, and invisible ones who weave your local story into the Larger Story of all creation. Following the lead of C. G. Jung, I call these energies "archetypes." Gradually, as you work with your SoulCollage® cards, the ways in which your local life story weaves into the Larger Story of the planet become clearer. The patterns of your particular path begin to emerge. Then you will be able to see how your unique thread shines in the weaving of the whole fabric of creation.

There is more to come in these next chapters as I share many personal stories of people using the SoulCollage® process. I will discuss the four suits of a SoulCollage® deck, suits which distinguish groups of guides, allies, and challengers active in every Soul. I will also describe different ways to consult your cards and ways to journal from them individually and in community.

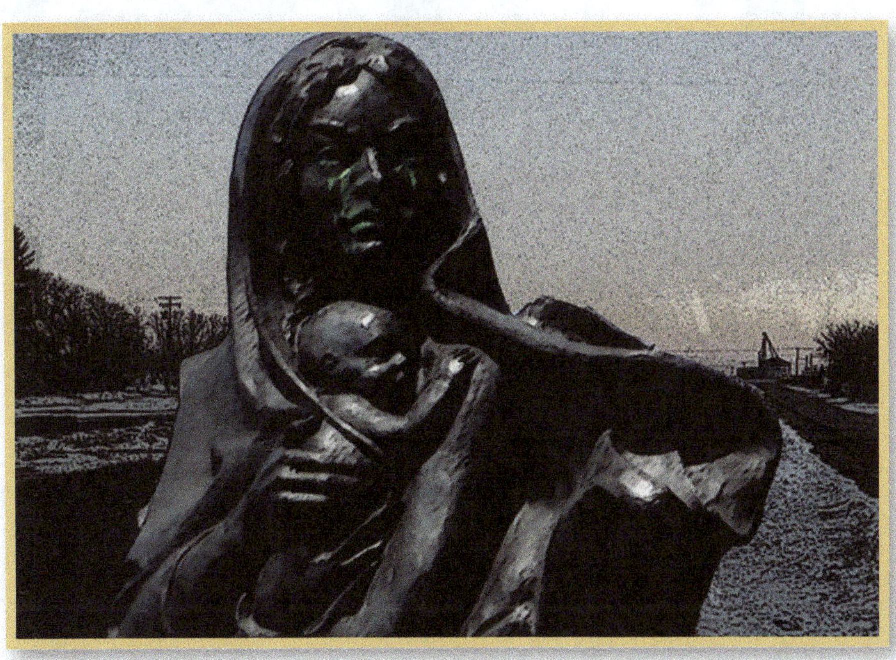

TITLE: **Pioneer Woman**
SUIT: **Committee**
CREATOR: **Lee Prouten**

"*I Am One Who* knows what it means to 'break trail' for those who follow."

The Cards in This Book

This book contains pictures of many SoulCollage® cards. Imagine them in color and larger in order to sense their full power. Some of these, and several others, appear on the website, soulcollage.org, in color, and you can zoom in to see their detail. Many others are elsewhere on the internet. Almost all SoulCollage® cards in this book are collages done with stock photos and graphics or personal art or photos. Should an artist recognize an original image of his or hers on a card somewhere, we want to assure

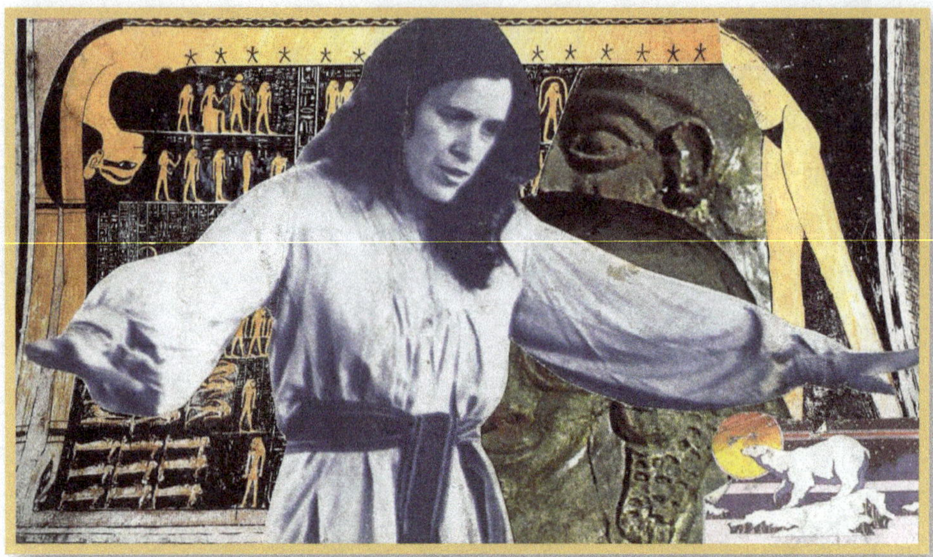

TITLE: **Jean Houston**
SUIT: **Community**
CREATOR: **Seena B. Frost**

"*I Am One Who* lives and teaches from mythic space. Cross the threshold into this juicy place and witness the Larger Story."

that artist that SoulCollage® cards are not made for resale, and that the recycled image is being cherished by someone instead of being thrown into the trash. Because the SoulCollage® cards you make are entirely for your personal use and not to sell, trade, or publish, you can create your own cards with any image that appeals to you. In your heart you will thank the photographers who took the pictures and the subjects in them.

Because the cards in this book are published as examples of the SoulCollage® process, we have been careful in this case to include only images from SoulCollagers' photographs, or images whose rights the card maker has bought. These are images for which we have the permission of the original artist or are otherwise copyright free. This is an unavoidable limitation we faced in order to publish the book. Many poignant cards are excluded because the powerful images they contained were obviously copyrighted. We thank all artists whose work is shown here as examples of the process, including the creators of SoulCollage® cards who share them here.

How SoulCollage® Began

The SoulCollage® process originated in a program I attended led by Dr. Jean Houston from 1986 to 1989. It was an incubating womb that immersed me in the world of myth, archetypal psychology, and various spiritual practices. During these same years and for the years after, I have been doing psychotherapy in a private practice. The work with collaged cards evolved over time in the context of my ongoing therapy groups. As people made cards and shared them with each other in these groups, this SoulCollage® process evolved. I pass on to you, in this book, what we discovered. In this new SoulCollage® book, I am sharing what many SoulCollage® Facilitators have discovered in their ongoing work with the process.

Collage is a metaphor for any discovering, gathering, and reweaving of energy-bits already formed and present in the universe. A new and personal creation can be made from the ever-present divine chaos of images all around us. Just choose, assemble, name, and then inhabit your SoulCollage® cards.

CHAPTER 2

Three Key Words in SoulCollage®

As you read through this book you will see that I adopt concepts and words often found in mystical and personal growth literature. However, I may define these words in ways that are a little different from what you are used to, so I will briefly go over them here. Then, when you meet these three words, you will understand what I mean. They are *Neter, Shadow,* and *Soul.*

Neter: An Ally, Guide or Challenger

When you begin the SoulCollage® process you will first select images and then create personal cards that represent different parts of your individual and unique Soul. Soon I will list and describe some of these parts, and I will show how the images on each card symbolize one of your *Soul's guides* or *allies* or *challengers*. However, instead of using these neutral sounding words, I will sometimes simply use the little word *Neter*. (It rhymes with "better" but has only one "t".)

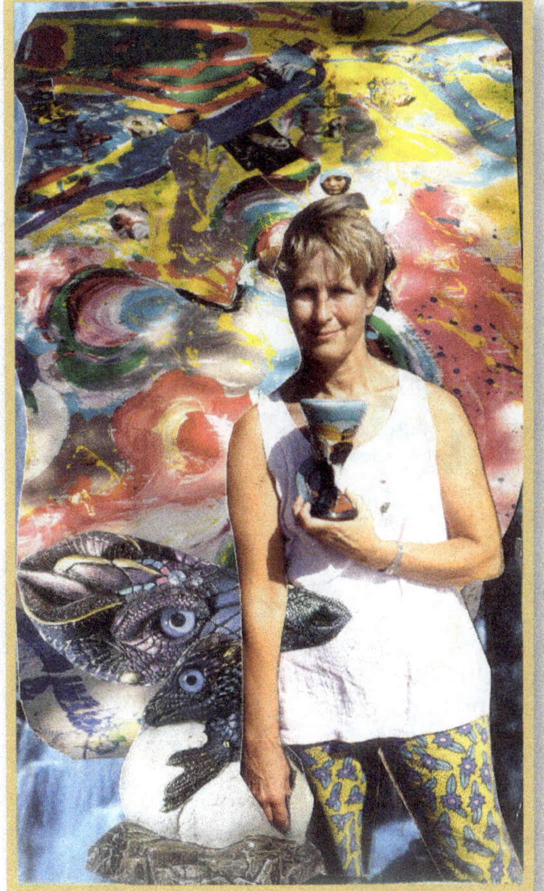

TITLE: **Sarah**
SUIT: **Community**
CREATOR: **Seena B. Frost**

"I Am your friend and I love you. I teach you that you are lovable."

Neter is my favorite substitute word for *energy, presence, guide, ally,* or *challenger*. The word, *Neter,* comes from ancient Egypt. It was a word uncovered in their hieroglyphs, and its meaning is mysterious and paradoxical, which is one reason I like it. It seems that

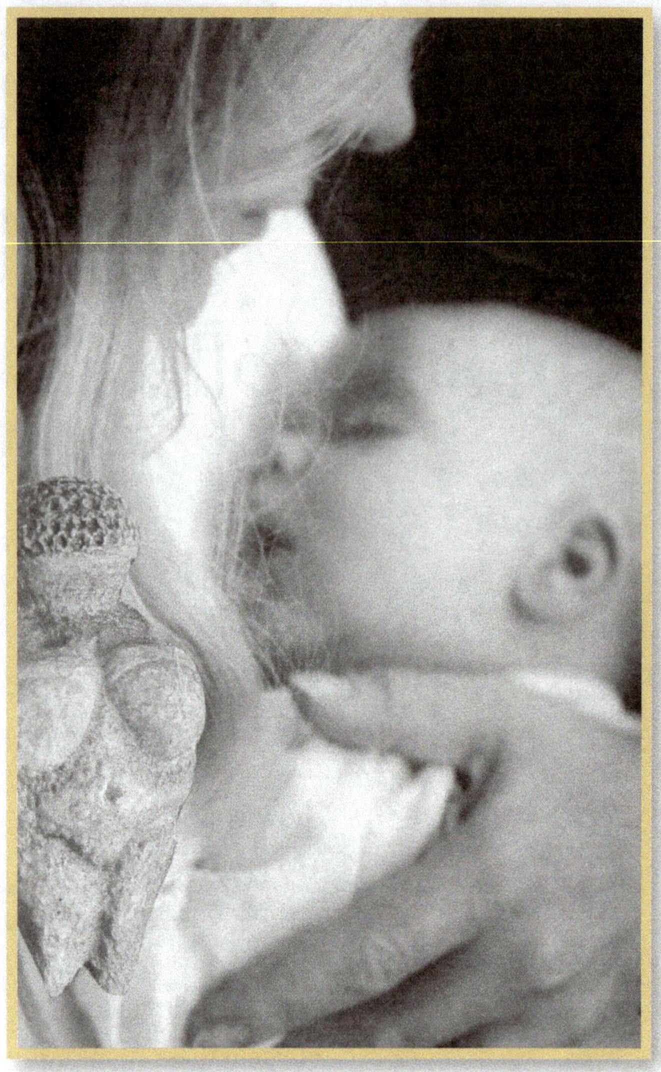

TITLE: **Great Mother**
SUIT: **Council**
CREATOR: **Pam Gonsalves**

"*I Am One Who* holds the Universe in my womb." [This is an actual photo of Pam and her second baby. ~Ed.]

the word *Neter* pointed to God beyond God, or what in SoulCollage® work we call *Source*. Neter meant *the One from which all that exists arises*. But—and herein lies the paradox of this word—Neter meant, at the same time, *the Many*. Ancient Egyptians were greatly in awe of the many divine forms manifested from this one Source Neter, and they named these forms as a group using a plural of this same word—*Neters* or *Neteru*. These Neters were the invisible archetypal forms that entered history and acted in space and time. They were individually named as gods and goddesses, and they acted as guides, helpers, and challengers to the beings on earth. These *Neteru* were revered and worshipped and talked about in stories; and, at the same time, they were understood to be manifestations from one formless Source Neter that underlies everything.

> *"The Shadow of a Neter is either an exaggeration of its best energy—too much of it—or the absence of it."*

What Egyptians meant by the plural word *Neters* would be the same as the archetypes of the Council suit in SoulCollage.® However, *I have expanded my use of the word Neter to include all the guides and allies and challengers of all four suits.* This means that inner personality parts, physical energies, community members, and archetypes are all Neters of our Souls. We have many, many Neters, and they all come from the one Source.

Another reason that I like the word Neter is because the little word *net* is embedded in it. A net is a paradoxical symbol with different "energies", just as our Neters are. A *net* can save us if we fall. A *net* can protect and hold us as we rest. Yet a *net* can also restrict us and prevent us from being free. *Nets* can feel wonderful or they can feel threatening. Your Neters are the same.

You will be amazed at the host of visible and invisible Neters who are present and active in your evolving life story and in the evolving story of this planet. Some will make themselves known to you if you decide to work with images and create SoulCollage® cards.

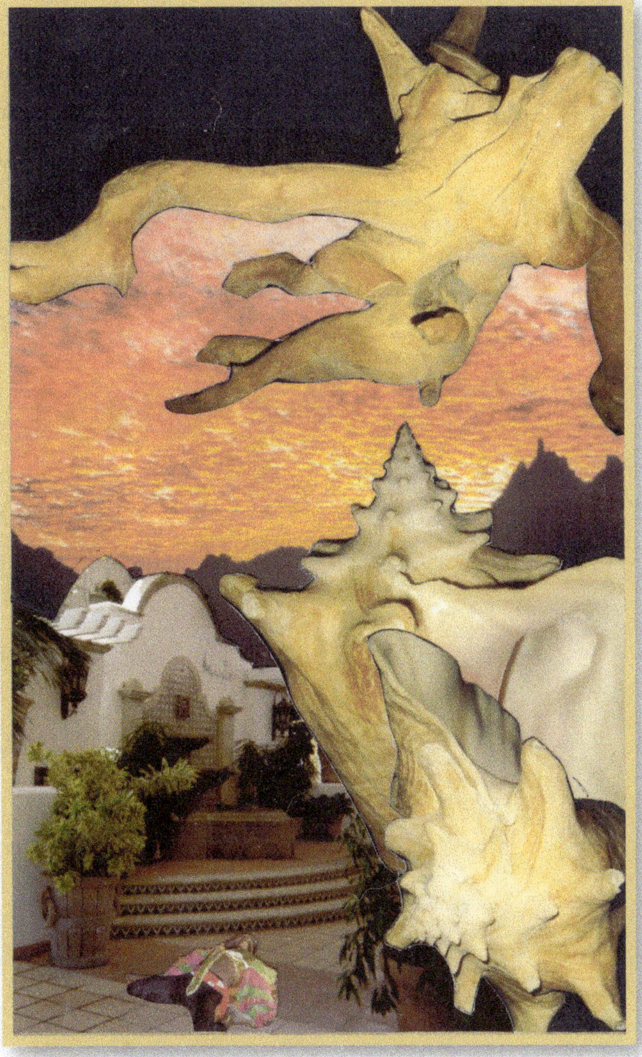

TITLE: **Facing Pluto**
SUIT: **Committee**
CREATOR: **Johnny Dillard**

"*I Am One Who* is struggling to relinquish my attachment to that which I am and to embrace that which I am becoming."

Shadow: Too Much or Too Little

When I use this word, *Shadow*, I am using it as C. G. Jung did, and it is important that you understand what the word means. Let me define it briefly here, and later I will devote a chapter to it.

One basic premise in SoulCollage® work is this: *every Neter exists in a form.* It may be visible or invisible, but still there is a form. It may be an energy form, it may be a physical form, and it may be a mental or conceptual form. But it is form nonetheless. And *every form by virtue of existing has the potential to cast a shadow.* Some Neters cast very dense Shadows, some very light ones, and every gradation in between. A key word here is balance; a Neter in perfect balance casts no Shadow. However our Neters easily lose their balance, and when they do, and we notice it, we recognize that their Shadow is present and showing.

In SoulCollage® work we don't draw a sharp line between good and evil, between positive and negative. The Shadow of a Neter is not the opposite of its most balanced and perfect energy manifestation. Rather, Shadow is either an *exaggeration* of its best energy—too much of it—or it may be the *absence* of its best energy—too little of it. I will give you many illustrations of this as we look together at the Neters of the four suits. All of them have Shadow potential.

The work we do with the Neters of all the suits in SoulCollage® is to help us feel and understand how their energy is manifesting in our life story, and to help us move towards a

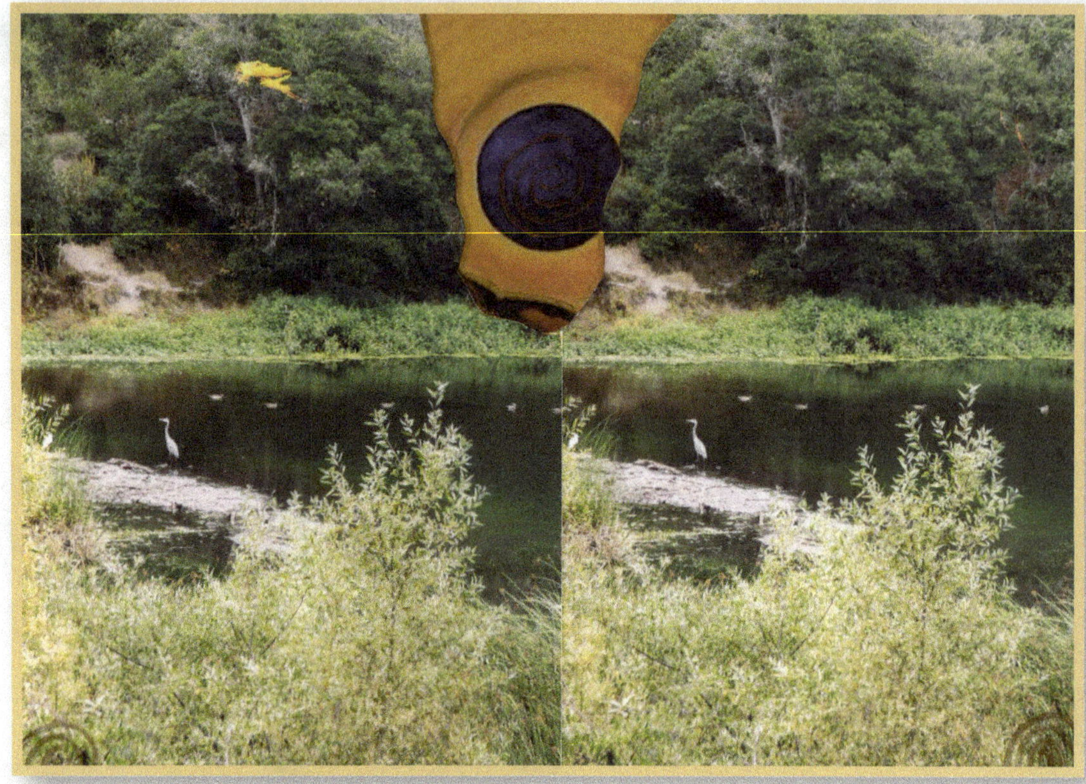

TITLE: **Time: Its Mystery**
SUIT: **Council**
CREATOR: **Mariabruna Sirabella**

"*I Am the One Who* is the Mystery of Time, the well of your eternity. I always lie in wait between moments."

balance where as little Shadow as possible is manifesting. And when Shadow does appear, we look for the value within it, for the "gold" in the Shadow, as Jung would say. There is more about Shadow in Chapter 9.

Soul

The word *Soul*, in SoulCollage® work, is inclusive. It includes all the Neters of the personal self: the personality parts, including the ego, and the energies of the physical body, and the archetypes that come from cosmic realms to influence us, and even other sentient beings. In other words, all the Neters of the four suits are included in *Soul*. This *Soul*, as I use the word in SoulCollage,® might also be called the *Whole Self*. And it is actually *holy* simply because it is a form manifested originally from Source. No matter how shadowed the Soul becomes through a lifetime, at its core there is a spark of the holy. I call that spark of Source which lies at the center of every Soul *SoulEssence*. This is not a Neter at all, as it has no form, and it may be what many people mean when they use the word *Soul*. I will go into greater detail about *SoulEssence* in Chapter Four which describes the Transpersonal Cards.

CHAPTER 3

A Brief Overview of a SoulCollage® Deck

The Transpersonal Cards

You can create three Transpersonal Cards for your SoulCollage® deck:

Source: A deck's central card points towards *Source*, the formless and infinite *Oneness* from which all forms are manifested, and back into which all forms return.

SoulEssence: A second card symbolizes *SoulEssence*, which is a *spark of Source* existing at the core of every Soul; *SoulEssence* contains the coding of this unique form, its life potential.

Witness: A third card symbolizes the Witness, which is the potential for consciousness in every human form. When developed, it enables us to step back and see ourselves, without judgment, as a many-faceted form. It is like a *mirror.*

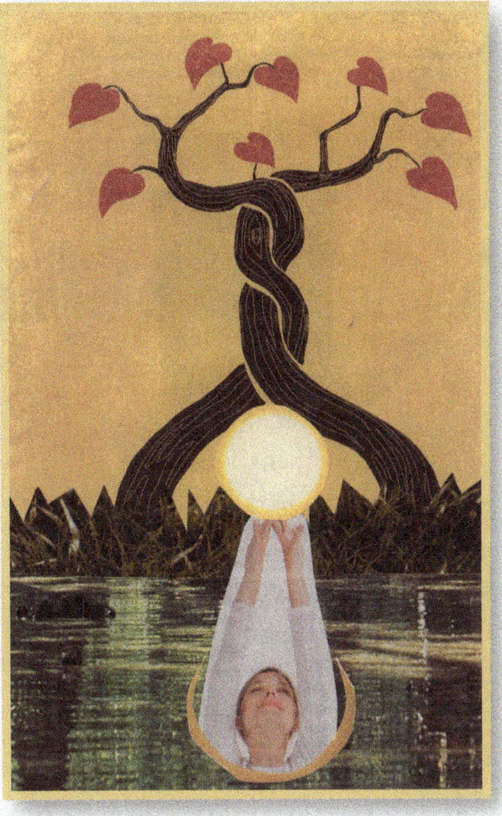

TITLE: **The Lightbearer**
SUIT: **Council**
CREATOR: **Glenda Rice**

"I Am the One Who shines the light on your path until your perspective shifts."

These three Transpersonal cards are described more fully in Chapter 4.

In addition to the three Transpersonal Cards, each deck can grow over time to contain SoulCollage® cards organized into four suits. Briefly these are:

The Committee Suit

In this suit of a SoulCollage® deck, the inner parts of your personality are identified, named, and imaged on separate cards. You will find images for the voices, or personality parts which fill your mind; these are the ones who advise and argue, cajole, threaten, and often drive you to distraction with their varying energies. This suit's name might also be *My Inner Family* because the personality parts are similar to members of a family who have lived together for a long time. In this suit the *psychological dimension of Soul* is addressed.

The Community Suit

In this suit of a SoulCollage® deck the images depict those external sentient beings whose energy is powerful and meaningful in your life, beings from both the past and the present. Over time you will identify and make cards for humans and pets that have loved you, taught you, and challenged you. Along with sentient beings this suit also can have cards for very specific places or things which have strong energy in your life, like a special tree, or house, or holy shrine. This suit's name might also be *My Local Allies*. In this suit the *communal dimension of Soul* is addressed.

The Companion Suit

In this suit of a SoulCollage® deck you imagine animals who reside in the seven energy centers of your body, centers that are often called *chakras*. These invisible Neters are discovered through a guided imagery process. Individuals will do visualizations, over time, to discover their personal set of seven animals, each one representing the energy of one chakra. This suit's name could also be *My Energy Guides*. In this suit *the energetic nature of Soul* is addressed.

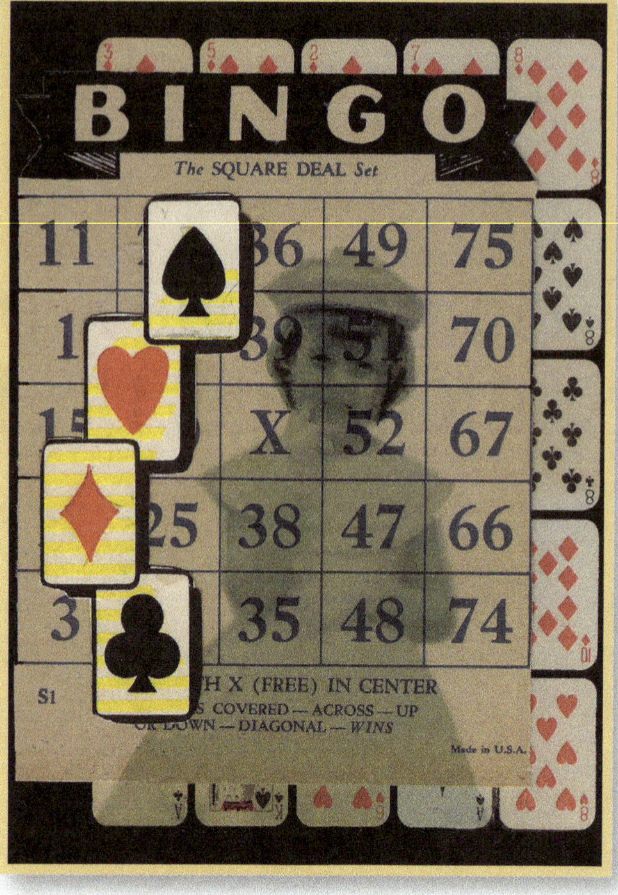

TITLE: **Thinks Too Much**
SUIT: **Committee**
CREATOR: **Pam Renner**

"*I Am One Who* complicates the simplest things by putting responsibility before play and accomplishments before play."

The Council Suit

In this suit of a SoulCollage® deck your cards will have images for the different archetypes who are actively guiding your life, and who are weaving it into the Larger Story of this planet. This suit honors the numinous, universal energies (such as *Death, Love, Courage, Reflection, Loneliness, Journeying*) which have always shaped human history, and which are shaping your life now. Neters in this suit may derive their names from mythology, from your religious or cultural traditions, or from your imagination. This suit could also be called *The Archetypes*. This suit reflects the entire weave of creation in which every created form is a thread and is intuited through images. Here we address the *spiritual nature of Soul*.

CHAPTER 4

The Transpersonal Cards

ONENESS BEYOND FORM

In the SoulCollage® process we spend most of our time creating cards with images symbolizing our many inner energies—the energies we call *Neters*. Then we listen as these Neters tell us about themselves and offer their perspectives on our life. As we do this work, our Soul becomes more balanced and will carry less shadow as it lives, and works, and plays in the world.

However, always on the edge of consciousness in SoulCollage® work is a deeper truth. Underneath the personal diversity of our Neters and the world's complexity "exists" Oneness, a Mystery out of which these forms arise and back into which they return. I suggest that you create these three cards to symbolize this Oneness, and that these cards have different backings from your other cards so they are easy to find in your deck.

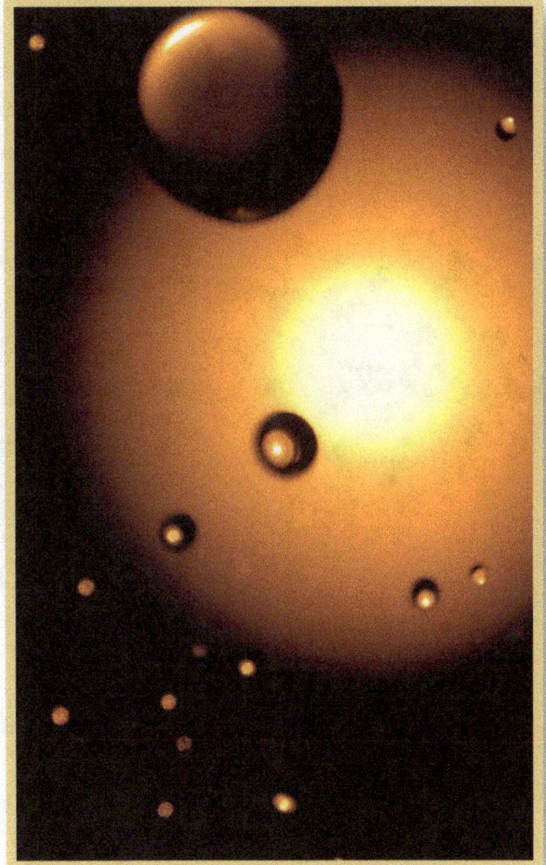

TITLE: **Source Card**
Transpersonal Card
CREATOR: **Catherine Anderson**

The three transpersonal concepts I have mentioned earlier are described in many mystical traditions and you will probably recognize them. Don't worry if the names I use are different from ones you know. The thing I want to underline is that the reality I will now write about is totally beyond description, is mysterious, holy, and without form. When we use images to represent this Mystery, we know they are just that, inadequate symbols pointing towards Oneness behind the Many.

Your three transpersonal cards will not represent Neters as your other cards do. These three have no form and therefore no potential for Shadow. *They also have no voice that we can intuit, so we do not speak from them in readings.*

Source

The primary Transpersonal Card in a SoulCollage® deck is your card for *Source*. In the early years of this process *Source* was the only Transpersonal Card; the second and third ones were added later to be clarifications of how Oneness underlies our existence. *Source* is a helpful name for this mystery, because it has less associations than many words of formal religious traditions. It carries no sense of "being-ness" or personality. *Source* is just that, the source of all that ever was, is, and will be. *Source* might also be called *Spirit*, if you prefer, or *Ground of Being* as Paul Tillich, the Christian theologian, named it.

So how do we represent *Source* on a card when there is no form? We find images to serve as symbols that, for each of us, uniquely point to this infinite reservoir of the possible. One person collaged a card with an actual egg-shaped hole in the center, symbolizing the vast *Nothing* out of which existence emerges, and back into which it flows. Others have chosen simple images of nature, images of flowers opening, or of light breaking through darkness. More than one person have imaged just the darkness, sensing *Source* as even before light and its forms. This card should not be a collage with many, complex images. It might well have just one image that shows great vastness and beauty.

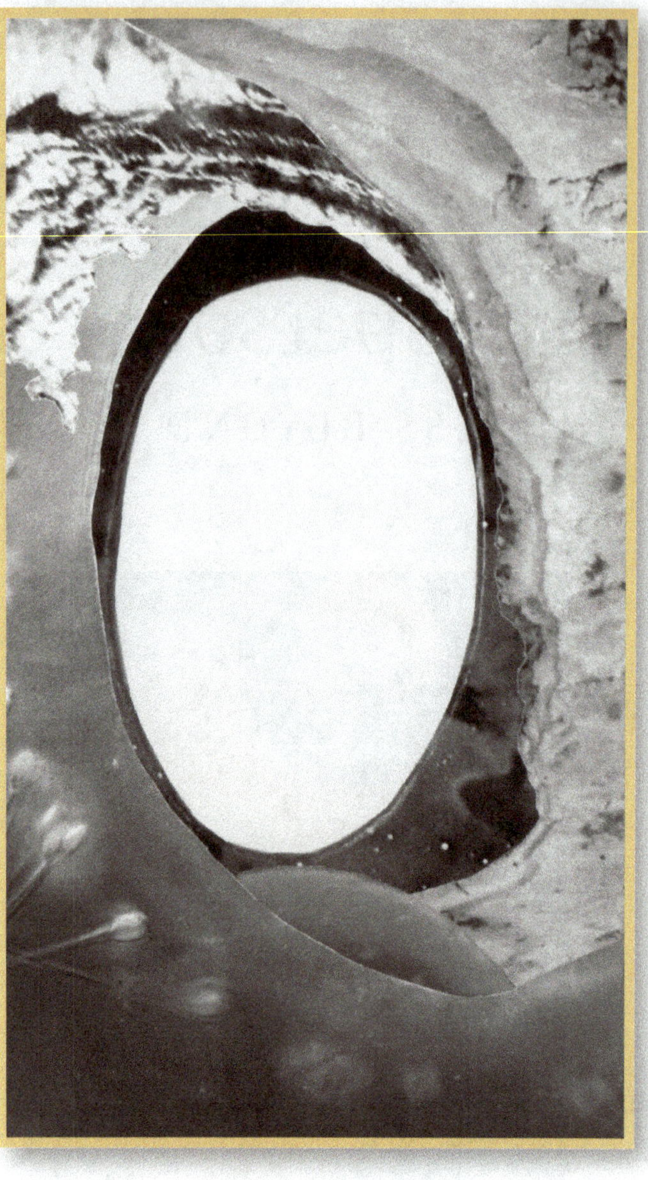

TITLE: **Source**
Tranpersonal Card
CREATOR: **Darien Payne**

You do not need to create your Source card first. Just collect possible images as you find them, and keep them in a special place. Eventually you will know which feels right, and then you can make this card. Put a special backing on it, different from the backings on your other cards. This way, when you lay your cards out face down, you can easily identify your Source card.

In the future, when you do readings with your SoulCollage® cards, you will place the Source card in the center, signifying that Oneness which unites all your diverse Neters. Metaphorically, one might say that Source is like the infinite net that I spoke of earlier. You, with all your Neters, are one of an infinite number of glittering jewels held in this divine Net, reflecting the beautiful and interesting patterns that your SoulCollage® cards will reveal to you.

SoulEssence

Your second Transpersonal card symbolizes your *SoulEssence*. This card points to that spark of Source that was in your individual Soul from your birth. Every human being has such a spark of pure and divine Oneness just by virtue of having come from the womb of Source, and it is the same for every living thing. Your *SoulEssence* is unique to you and is like a coding for manifestation into your many future forms. In other words it is your special potential. As beings grow there is a continual urge from within to fulfill this promise. For most living beings there is no consciousness or choice about it, and *SoulEssence* coding is manifested as fully as circumstances allow. A rose becomes a rose, an ant becomes an ant, and a redwood becomes a redwood.

Some teachers of mystical traditions call this immortal spark of Source in a being, the *Soul*. It inhabits the person through life, leaves the physical body at death, and moves on, perhaps to another body, perhaps to another realm. However, in SoulCollage,® we include much more than one's *SoulEssence* in the word *Soul*, as I described earlier. *Soul* includes all of our many inner parts who strive, over a lifetime, to translate our unique *SoulEssence* into myriad yet congruent forms. Referring back to my earlier metaphor, each Soul wants above all things to become a beautiful jewel in the eternal Net, living out what it was coded to be. When a Soul is on track, manifesting its *SoulEssence* coding in the world, the Soul feels balanced and happy. It somehow feels that it is manifesting in the way it was meant to manifest. So remember that in SoulCollage® the *Soul* includes the totality of a person's Neters, and the unique spark of *Source* within this Soul is the person's *SoulEssence*.

> *The SoulEssence card is the quintessential-ness of a being, is ever-present and immortal.*

A card for your *SoulEssence* may be more complex and have more images than your *Source* card. A photo of you as a child might be included, for SoulEssence is most transparent in our early years, before layers of *Soul* are developed that tend to obscure it. My own background image for this card is the same as my *Source* card, since it is directly from the Source that I feel this spark comes.

Be sure to back this card with its own backing, and place it, along with *Source*, in the center during a reading. It is another symbol of Oneness. It is formless potential and without Shadow, and therefore *SoulEssence* does not have a voice you can intuit to answer questions.

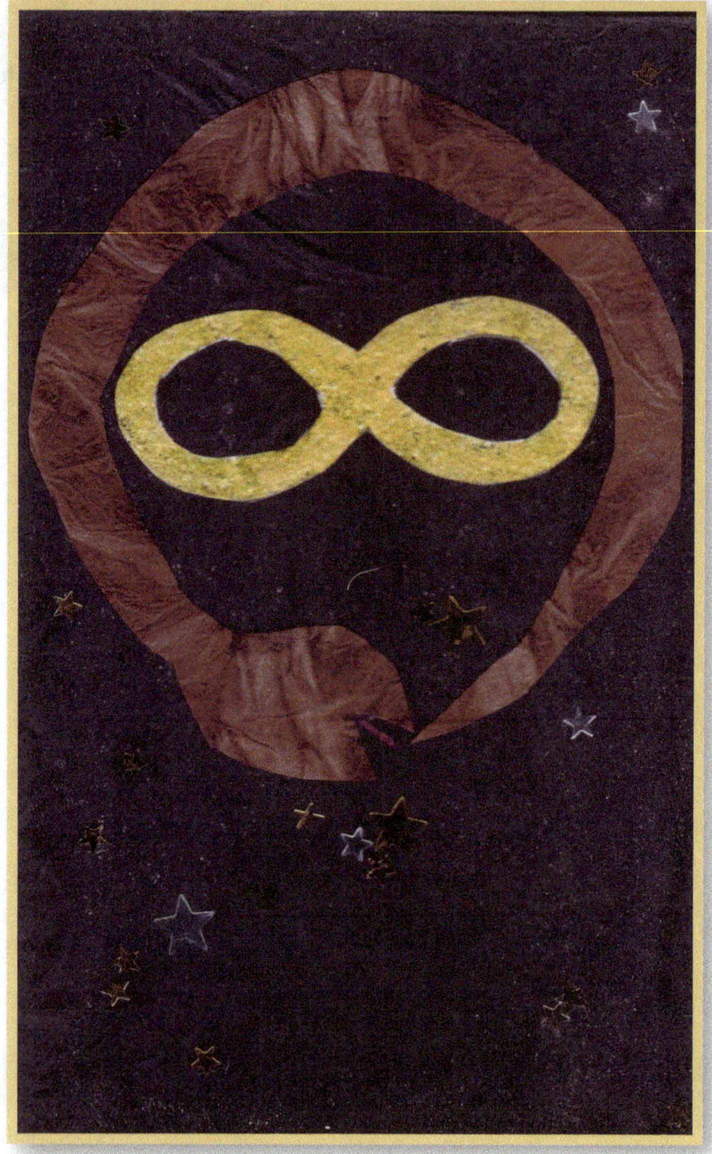

TITLE: **Witness**
Transpersonal Card
CREATOR: **Nancy Weiss**

Witness

Your third Transpersonal Card will have images to symbolize your *Witness*. Another word for *Witness* might be *Consciousness*, and it has huge importance in your ability to translate *SoulEssence* into beautiful forms. Without it, you would not realize that you can step away and identify your Neters. You could not recognize or make use of the transformative possibilities in the SoulCollage® process.

Witness allows you to develop an ability to move away from identification with your inner Neters and to begin to see them simply as parts of yourself, valuable and evolving workers in your life story. As far as we know, on this planet only human beings have so far developed this capacity for consciousness, and not every human being has chosen to do this inner work. Not by any means. Many are so caught up in their busy lives and are so identified with their ego Neters that they do not have the will to step back and take a look inside at who is helping and who is sabotaging. A life crisis may change that frantic and outer thrust. A world in crisis, like we have now, might be the catalyst. More and more, people are reading about *Witness* in books like Eckhart Tolle's *A New Earth*, and they are beginning to develop *Witness* in themselves. In SoulCollage,® as we create cards for our Neters, we are intuitively practicing this stepping back.

Witness is best compared to a mirror. We step back and see ourselves as if in a mirror. *Witness* is part of *Source* and is formless. It has no comment to make on what it reflects; it does not judge, it does not applaud. However, from the place of the *Witness* we may catch a glimpse of the patterns our Neters are making. We can also begin to recognize these parts of ourselves as Neters who change, and who will eventually dissolve. They are transitory forms—beautiful, or ugly, or ordinary. In this book, as I discuss the Neters of the four suits, you will see how the perspective of the *Witness* is essential to our exploration.

The *Witness* does not speak words in readings, for it is simply a potential and part of the Oneness of Source. Just like a mirror, it gives no evaluating feedback, except what we hear from our own limited Neters, as we look from this stepped-back perspective. It is Consciousness, a place to step into and detach. It has no form, it has no shadow, and it is silent.

Create a card for *Witness*. The images you find for this card may give some sense of the all-seeing eye of Consciousness and its reflecting nature. This card also has the special backing of the Transpersonal Cards, and, it too, is placed in the center during a reading.

You will undoubtedly discover that you have an inner Committee member who is able to function in the capacity of a witness. Name this Neter the *Observer Self* and make a Committee card for him or her. It will have valuable wisdom to give you as it refines its ability to step back and give you information from that place. However, like all Neters, this Neter is limited by form; limited by its language, its culture, its age, its gender, its prejudices, and its attachments. It has a shadow, maybe dense, maybe light, but it is not pure *Source* as your inner transpersonal *Witness* is.

This will all become clearer as you read Chapter 5, The Committee Suit, and Chapter 9, The Shadow in the Neters.

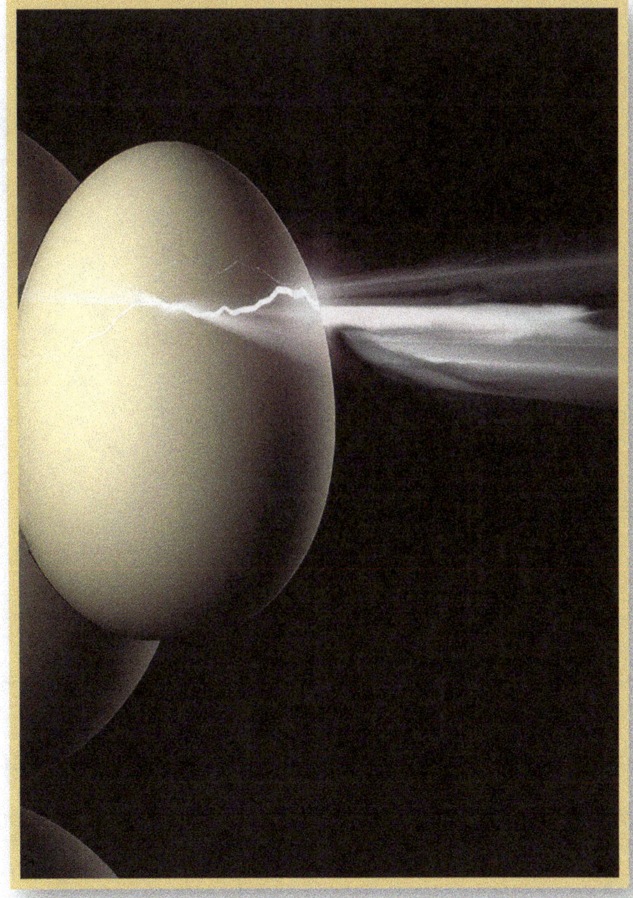

TITLE: **SoulEssence Transpersonal Card**
CREATOR: **Pam Renner**

Silence and the Transpersonal Cards

Some SoulCollage® workshops are organized around themes such as a particular suit, or the Shadow, or even the Transpersonal Cards. We have learned that when people gather with their primary focus on the three Transpersonal Cards, silence is a major ingredient. Participants will spend hours in silence, eating their meals, walking, meditating, and creating cards. When the silence ends, people have loved it so much that they often wish it would continue. A kind of shift seems to occur in the practice of silence, a movement into a place of vastness, wordlessness, and peace.

Most of us seldom allow ourselves this experience, and it is amazing what happens within a Soul when it quiets for a long period of time. Usually our minds slow down. The jabbering inner voices become less insistent, and, with practice, the present moment will begin to be the focus of our attention, without past or future diverting us. We begin to learn how to step into the realm of our *Witness* and remain there, simply watching, not hurrying to manifest our ideas into forms or to search for meaning in what we are doing. Mystics and meditators have known this for eons, but, for most modern westerners silence feels empty at first, boring, something that needs to be filled. When we are given encouragement and space to really enter and stay with it, silence can become filled with beauty, with gratitude, with life.

So, remember to integrate times of silence into your SoulCollage® practice, whether you are working alone with your cards or with a group. These periods can be quite short or much longer, whichever fits for your life.

I want to share a meditation practice offered by Miriam Goldberg, a SoulCollage® Facilitator from California. This is a way to meditate, using your SoulCollage® cards, on the Oneness and the "Many-ness" of your life and of all existence.

We first take a quiet moment to sit with our decks in front of us, cards partially fanned or spread out, facing upwards. We sense ourselves as a prism shining the light of our being onto and through each card.

The glowing mosaic of colorful images before us reflects the many ways we express ourselves to ourselves and in the world. We can see and feel how each of these luminous gifts arises from the ground of being between us and them, and how they are supported by it and held by the ever present mystery of it. As they shimmer together, an illumined reflection of our self, floating in the mystery, we can sense the ground of being beneath them expanding to include our self, sitting in this moment with our cards, all rising from and relaxing into the deep spacious mystery that holds us all.

Feeling a SoulCollage® Card with the Body

- When I sit with this card, where in my body do I feel a response, a sensation, warmth, energy, tension, "butterflies"?
- Would you [addressing the card and its Neter] share your wisdom about this sensation?
- Where in my body do you bring your gifts? Your vitality?
- How would you like me to use these gifts, this vitality?
- If I allow this vitality, this gift, to flow in my body, how will it nourish me and my life?

CHAPTER 5

The Committee Suit

THE PSYCHOLOGICAL DIMENSION OF SOUL

In the last chapter I talked about *Source*, that Oneness from which every form, including every Soul, is manifested. In this chapter we begin our exploration of the many forms that come forth from this unity, and specifically the forms in our *Committee*. This suit contains the diverse and often "out-of-balance" inner parts of a human Soul. By making SoulCollage® cards for them we are finding a way to step back and observe these personality parts, to name them, and get to know them. It is also a therapeutic way to balance and heal them, and to free them to evolve.

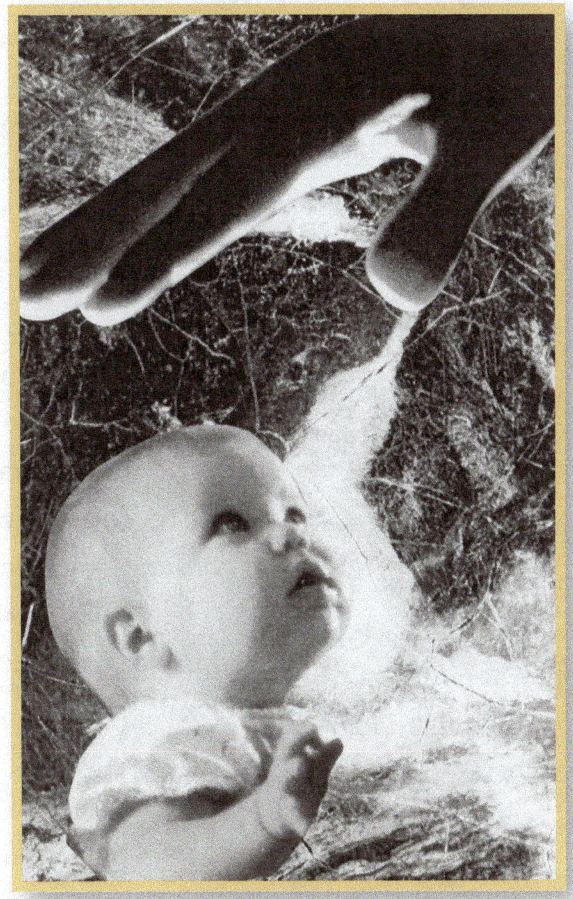

TITLE: **Distrustful Inner Child**
SUIT: **Committee**
CREATOR: **Cindy Cummings**

"*I Am One Who* wants you to love me, but I don't trust you."

Every Soul is both One and Many. We are whole, integrated human beings who, at the same time, contain strikingly different sub-personalities. These inner parts chatter in our minds day and night, each one seeming to have needs, prejudices, and goals. Some we know well because they are quite conscious. Others are more hidden, less easy to spot and name. Some have a lot of energy while others have soft or subtle energy. In SoulCollage® we call all these inner personality parts our *Committee*. We can imagine them sitting around a huge table inside our Soul, having long and short agendas, and sorting out the plans and actions of our daily schedule. Each one also has certain predictable reactions and responses to the words and actions of other human souls that we encounter.

Who of us has not engaged in inner conversations sounding something like this?

A. "We should really call Mother tonight and see how she's doing."

B. "O.K., but later."

A. "We always put things off and then don't do them. I'll feel better once we've taken care of it."

B. "O.K., in a few minutes."

A. "Why are you avoiding. It won't be bad."

B. "She'll scold us for not calling often enough."

A. "Which is true…"

B. "But I can't stand it when she scolds. I wish she'd just be glad…"

Etc., etc., etc!!!

Probably your word exchange is not this distinct, but the sense of two inner voices arguing is unmistakably present. *I want to/I don't want to. You should/ I won't.* These inner conversations are *normal.* Every one of us has a large cast of inner parts, and they act like characters in a dramatic script. Most of them repeat the same things over and over and are predictable in their worries, positions, and styles of reacting. If this sounds like some sort of mental illness, don't worry. We are all "multiple personalities" to some extent, and thank heavens for that. How boring we would be if there was only one character in our inner story!

Serious mental problems do sometimes occur with sub-personalities, particularly if one part separates totally and finds a way to run the show without the other parts having any control or even knowledge of it. Other serious problems occur when group cooperation literally breaks down, and certain ego parts become so exaggerated and out of line that the person becomes dangerous to herself or himself or to those around. If the separation of parts becomes abnormally extreme, then therapeutic treatment with a professional person and/or medication may be needed. However, for our normal, everyday "inner dialogues," a creative process like SoulCollage® can help with the work of balancing and educating our Committee.

Getting to Know Sub-Personalities

Psychologists have written volumes about how, why, and when sub-personalities develop, and how they work together and against each other. Nearly every model of psychotherapy aims, by one method or another, to help inner personality parts learn to cooperate. The work in personal psychotherapy is focused on helping clients become aware of their Committee, and to encourage these inner parts to work together more harmoniously.

Most people, when they begin making SoulCollage® cards, start with the Committee suit. This is normal, because most of us are interested in, and even concerned about, this constant drama inside our heads. We want to understand our inner characters, or *Neters* as we are calling them, so that we can encourage better cooperation between them.

The Observer

In a moment I'll describe several Neters you may recognize and want to include in your

Committee, but I'll begin with one that I mentioned earlier: the *Observer*. Simply because you've read this far in a book about SoulCollage® makes me believe your *Observer* is present and awake on your Committee! Eventually you will find the right image and create a card for it, because, in order to do this process, your *Observer* Neter needs to be on the job and in your deck. This is the Neter who steps back and looks at your whole self from a somewhat objective place. The *Observer* works to identify your unique inner parts, name them, and describe them. You might say it is your ability to be self conscious. This is the Committee's best attempt at developing a part that can step back and partially separate from all your other Neters in order to see them without judgment. I say "partially," because *your Observer, like all Neters, has form.* It has language and a history, and it has cultural limitations to its perspective. Undoubtedly it will have blind spots and prejudices, so its objectivity is partial. Still, we do our best with our personal and evolving *Observer* Neter, expecting it can learn to step even further back and become ever more objective. Because of the formless presence of our Transpersonal *Witness*, we humans each have this unique potential if we actually take the time to discover and develop our *Observer*.

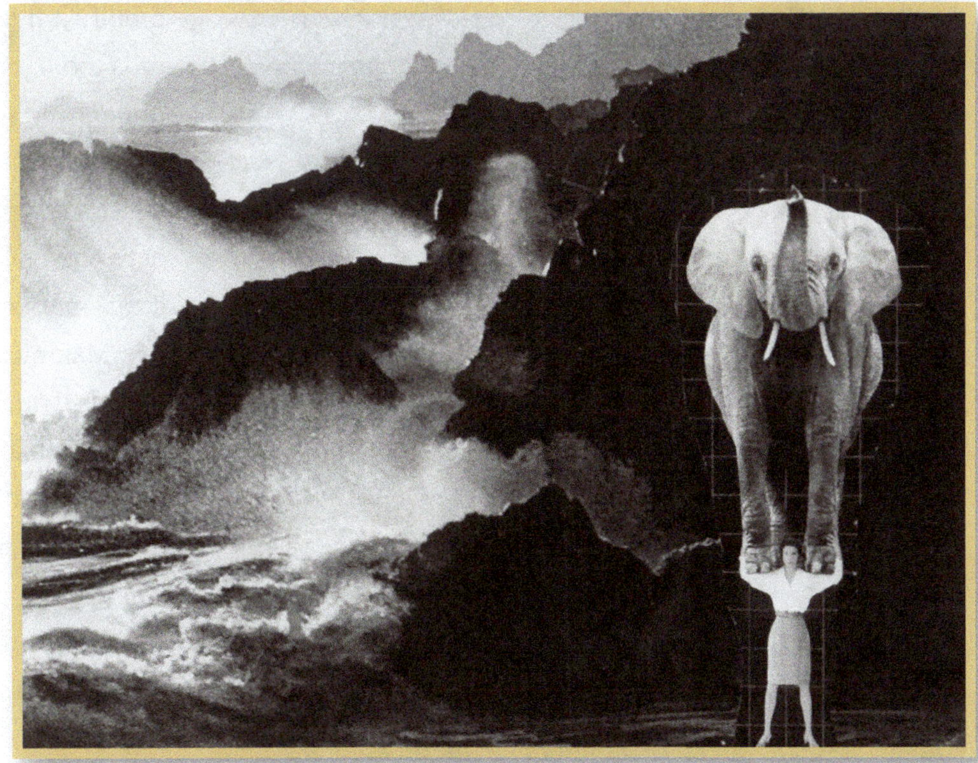

TITLE: **The Strong Self**
SUIT: **Committee**
CREATOR: **Debbi McDill**

"*I Am One Who* is strong enough to carry the life God has given me."

Other Committee Neters

I'll now give you examples of other Committee Neters. Hopefully this will nudge you to make your own personal list, because your cast of inner characters is different from everyone else's. First, most of us have a *Critic*, an inner voice that criticizes us for things we do or don't do. Sometimes this voice sounds like our parents' or a teacher we had. Sometimes it is loud and angry, with a finger-shaking stance. Sometimes it is quiet and just makes a disapproving face. Personal inner *Critics* take different forms and have different intensities, so it helps to get a modify it if it speaks too often or is too harsh. You can begin to understand its history, and what it wants to make happen in your life story. It probably wants to help you be better, even though it may not be doing a skillful job. Making a SoulCollage® card for this *Critic* Neter can help you detach and see it as one of many parts of yourself, just one manageable part. Perhaps you will learn to listen to it, and then consciously ask it to sit down and be quiet so some other member of the Committee, perhaps your *Nurturer* or your *Cheerleader,* has a chance to talk.

Another Neter that all of us have to some degree is the *Judge.* This Neter is related to the *Critic,* but it has a different target than yourself. It looks away from self and criticizes other people and external situations. We can have a very loud *Judge* and a very small *Critic*, or vice versa. Sometimes both are very exaggerated or *shadowed* as we would say in SoulCollage® work. Our egos are largely defined by the density of the Shadow in all of our Committee Neters, but particularly so in our *Critic* and our *Judge.* I will talk much more about the Shadow in Chapter 9.

What follows is a beginning list of many possible Committee Neters.

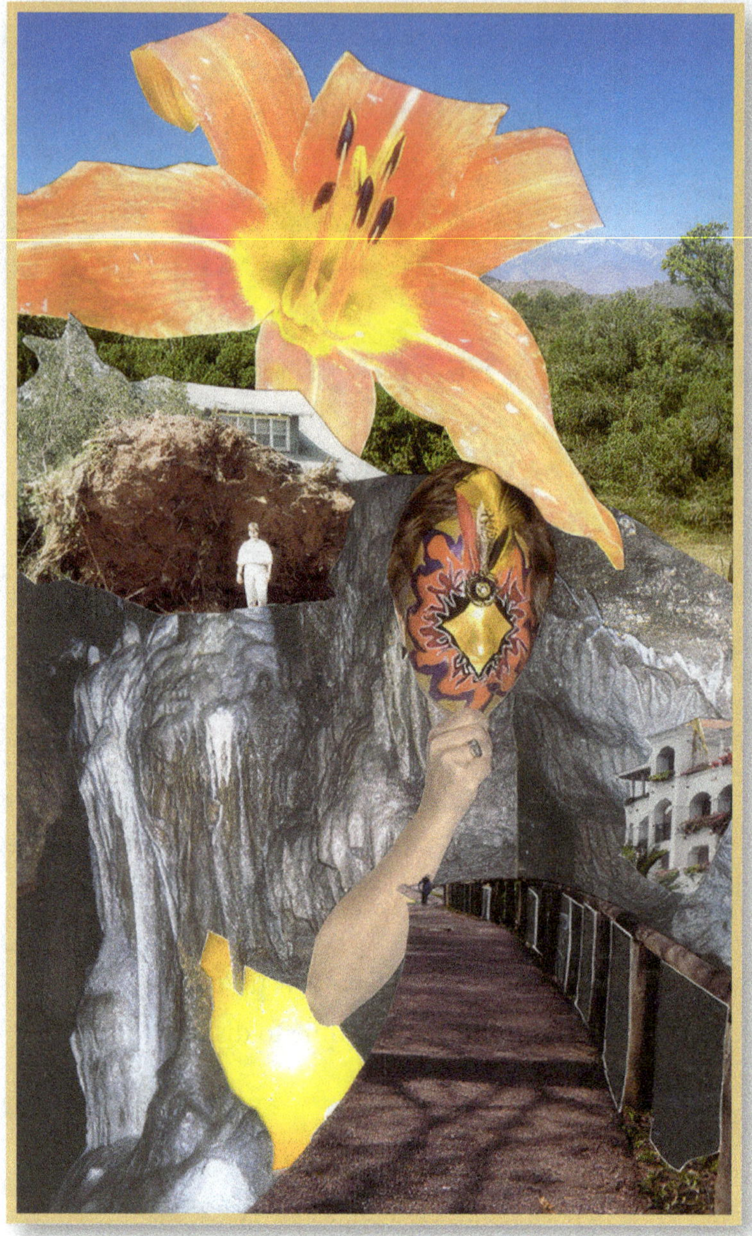

TITLE: **Descending to Transform**
SUIT: **Committee**
CREATOR: **Mili Dillard**

"Time after time, *I Am One Who* experiences showing up for myself by leaping into the deep earthen cauldron to descend and confront the demon."

sense of yours. Eventually you'll find an image to represent it, make a SoulCollage® card for it, and name it. This will help you recognize its voice when it nags you. It will help you

Neters Who are Usually Seen as Negative and Bothersome

The Critic (of self)* (We all have this one to some degree.)

The Judge (of others)* (We all, likewise, have this one.)

The Wounded Child

The Rebellious Child

The Raging Self

The Perfectionist

The Nag

The Bitch

The Bully

The Procrastinator

The Whiner

The Controller

The Jealous One

The Blamer

The Liar

Etc.

Neters Who are Usually Seen as Neutral

*The Observer** (Essential for doing SoulCollage® work)

The Organizer

The Teacher

The Caretaker

The Gardener

The House Cleaner

The Student

The Responsible One

Etc.

Neters Who are Usually Seen as Positive

*The Happy Child** (Make a card for this one as it is in there somewhere.)

*The Grateful One** (Make a card for this one too; it is absolutely essential for happiness.)

The Curious Kid

The Lover

The Loyal Friend

The Writer, Poet, Storyteller

The Volunteer

The Generous One

The Persistent One

The Comedian

The Hostess

The Artist, Musician, or Dancer

Etc.

All our parts have a need to be engaged in dialogue.

You will recognize immediately many of these Neters listed, because they are large in your personality, and you know them well. Already, you may have added a dozen more to your list.

There are other parts that may be more elusive, because they don't like to be brought into the light of consciousness. They will resist being named by your *Observer* or by someone else. Examples might be:

The One Who Fears Intimacy

The One Who Tries but Is Never Enough

The One Who Won't Accept Blame

The One Who Resists Growing Up

The One Who Stays on the Sidelines

The One Who Must Be Right

These names are simply suggestions to start you thinking about your own Committee members. We all have quite a few. One or two may stand out as dominators, taking the main stage more than you would like. They try constantly to run your show, so make SoulCollage® cards for them early on. Others may be on the fringe of your consciousness, seldom speaking, even hiding, but with a kind of simmering energy. They will actually reach out and choose images when you are browsing through magazines, but even then try to escape examination.

All our parts have a need to be named and engaged in dialogue, so, as they appear in inner conversations, add them to your list. You may put a question mark beside some when you are not yet sure what name best describes this energy.

If you are courageous enough, ask a family member or a friend to help you identify some Committee Neters. This takes fortitude because you may well be told that you are too

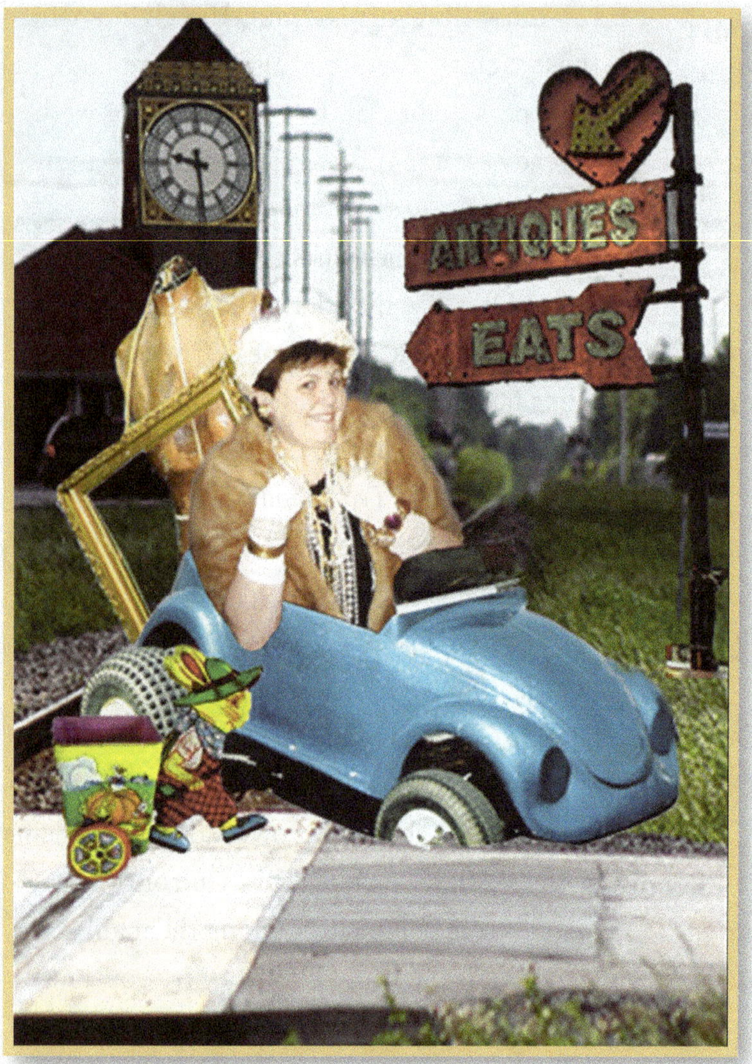

TITLE: **Garage Sale Goddess**
SUIT: **Committee**
CREATOR: **Pam Renner**

"*I Am One Who* believes that everything and everyone can be restored to purpose. My journey has proven that every desire has access to a resource. *I Am One Who* finds lots of resources at garage sales."

"controlling", or too "flighty", or "too" something else. There could be several "too muches" and "too littles".

On the other hand, you may be told about positive Neters, ones you have never recognized as being vital parts of yourself at all. One woman asked her husband to review her list of Committee members, and he asked, "Well, where's your Chief Best Cook? So, of course she made a card for The Chief Best Cook who was indeed a major Neter in her story.

If you are working with a SoulCollage® group, consider sharing lists. Listening to another's list will help you identify Neters you may have "forgotten" or chosen to ignore. When someone names what for you is almost unnamable, you gain courage and permission. One woman in a group confessed to having an Angry Child Neter who could get so out of control that she threw dishes across the room. It took courage to talk about this part because no one would ever have guessed this proper lady would have such a hidden Neter. She rarely let it out, and then only at home with her husband. She not only spoke of it in the group, but she also found images and created a SoulCollage® card for it. Others were empowered by her example to acknowledge and make cards for their own hidden and "unspeakable" parts.

When You Do Not Like Some of Your Parts

"But," you may be saying, "I hate those negative parts of me. I don't want to name them and make cards for them. That might just give them more energy. I want to be rid of them."

It would be nice if we could simply send certain ones to the recycling bin, but that's not the way our psyches work. Usually, if we ignore shadowed Neters, they grow stronger, and they may cause more serious trouble from their repressed position. Looking the other way is seldom the best solution. We need to recognize and work with these Neters, and making SoulCollage® cards is one creative way. It encourages us to look at our inner parts from the place of our *Observer.* We go into this stepped-back place and recognize each part as simply one of many parts. Just doing this helps us become less identified with it. We see that one obnoxious part, like our *Bossy Self*, is not our whole personality. We can listen to it more objectively now, and learn how and why in our history it originated. We discover what it fears and longs for, and why it acts the way it does.

Psychologists have found that each inner part has an energy it wants to contribute to the Soul, and each is trying in its own, sometimes twisted, way to help. The *Critic*, who may sound a lot like one of your parents, may hope to drive you to do everything really well so your life will be more successful. The *Judge* may hope its words will get some external person like a spouse or a child or an employee to wake up and attend to their life better. The *Raging Child* who lures a loved one into a fight may be covering for a *Fearful Child*, trying to protect that weaker part from being ignored or disappointed. And on and on it goes.

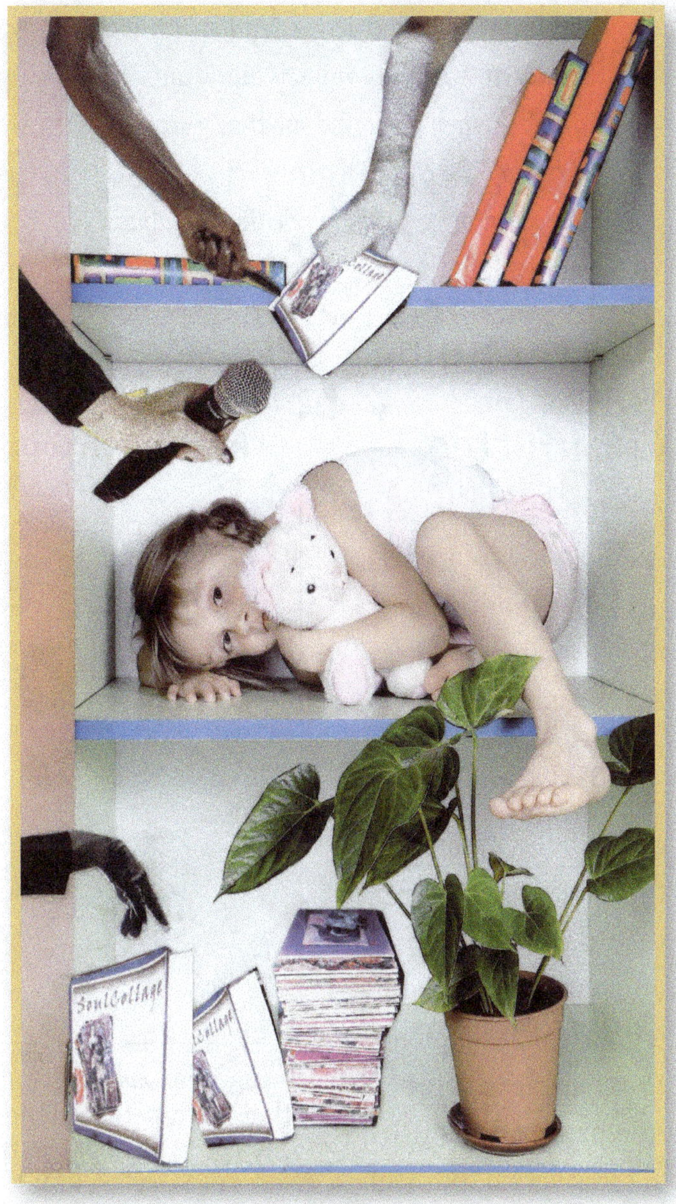

TITLE: **Scared Child**
SUIT: **Committee**
CREATOR: **Seena B. Frost**

"*I Am One Who* pleads 'Don't make me go out there and make that speech! There must be someone bigger who can do it. Please.....please.....please.'"

Here's what one woman wrote about this:

I have several Neters, whose cards I made thinking them all negative, and I hated looking at them. Then, in readings, they showed up and revealed their value in my life. One I had called My Destructive Tendencies card because it was about my self that wants to smoke; then it showed me that it was a Survivor Neter, and her rebelliousness was, at least in my growing up years, valuable. I was amazed.

Diagramming Your Committee

A helpful thing you can do with your list is this: draw your Committee as shown here. Make a circle to represent a central Committee table, and then draw circles around this table to represent the Committee Neters on your list. Start with big ones that dominate. Have smaller circles to represent parts that are less verbal, but still active. Perhaps there is a child part that is very large. Perhaps there is a child part that is hiding under the table and only a tip of it shows. Perhaps there are some Neters that have teamed up; *The Critic* and *The Perfectionist* often do this, and they can appear in your drawing as an overlapping unit. There may be some Neters that are sitting right by the door—barely in consciousness—with some even outside the door. These could be buried still, and, although they send energy up into the Committee meetings, their identity is yet a mystery. Don't forget to have circles for some of the large, but neutral, Neters and also, of course, for your joyful and creative Neters.

Who's who on your committee?

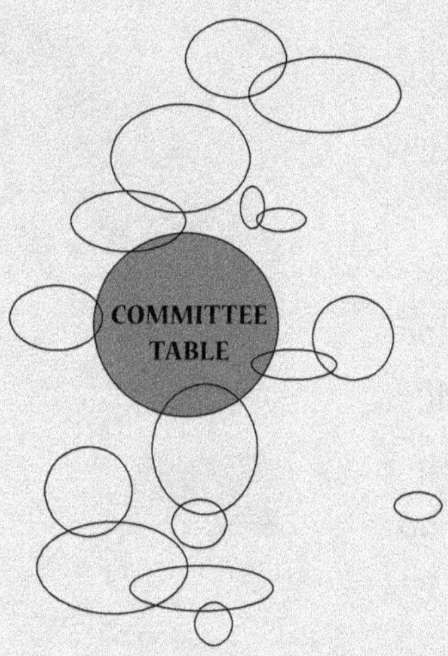

COMMITTEE TABLE

I was amazed to find out there were that many people in there. Talk about the Three Faces of Eve; this is the forty faces of Mary! — **RMFK**

Diagramming like this can be a fun exercise, especially as you begin working with the SoulCollage® process and are doing this left brain work of identification.

However, remember one thing: your Committee evolves and changes all the time whether you pay attention to it or not. Circles may grow and diminish and change their allegiances. Furthermore, as with all committees, change comes slowly, and change takes work and attention and patience. One hope is that by doing work with your SoulCollage® cards, your Committee will become more fluid, evolve faster, and find a balance that assists your SoulEssence coding to manifest more fully in your life story.

Do one beginning diagram like this, putting names in your circles, and then, after a few years of SoulCollage® work, do another one and see what has changed. See who has shown up, who has calmed down, and which ones have found balanced and useful places around your inner table. It may surprise you!

Browsing for Images: Right-Brain Play

When you begin doing the wondrous play of browsing in magazines and tearing out images or searching stock photos online, *put away your lists*. These lists are preliminary, a sort of seeding, and not essential to the real process. Don't go to magazines expecting to find the perfect image for a certain Neter, as for your *Critic* or *Judge* or *Shy Child* or your *Observer*. It almost never works that way. Browsing time is when that other part of you, your right brain and your intuition, reaches out and surprises you by choosing images that your thinking, left brain might never have picked.

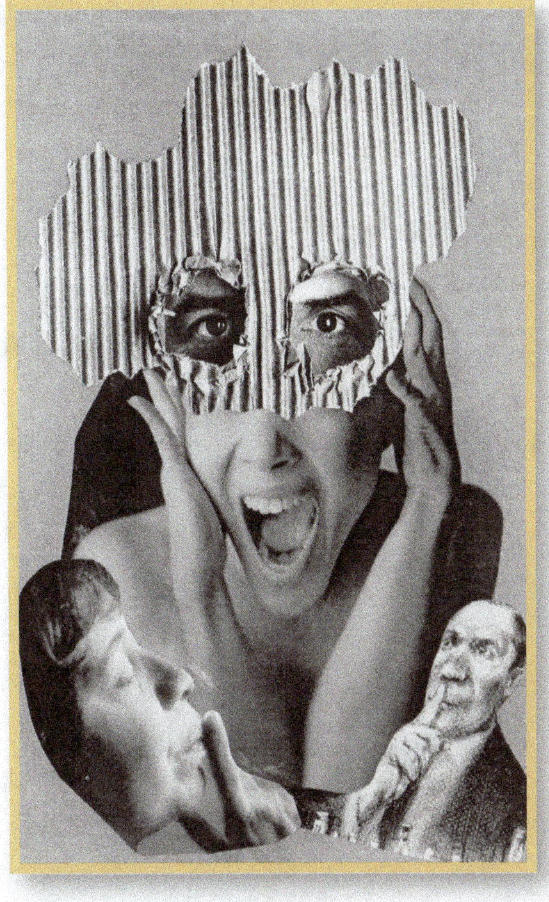

TITLE: **The Prisoner Self**
SUIT: **Committee**
CREATOR: **Cindy Cummings**

"*I Am One Who* is imprisoned by myself, and by others. I am afraid to be who I am."

It is in this mindless play with images that the value and the creative magic of using collage as a medium reveals itself. If you were to decide to draw or paint a part of yourself, you would need to be intentional about doing it, trying to get the right color, or dimension, or expression. You might worry about doing it well enough and then dismiss your effort as amateur. Not so with collage. As you browse in a meditative way, *powerful images will reach out and choose you*. No talent is needed except to stay open and watchful. There are hidden but strong, energetic Neters inside your Soul that will recognize images that express themselves. They will almost demand that you grab an image and tear it out. You may have no idea what part of you this is, and you may not like the image it demands, even to the point of not selecting it. However, it often keeps insisting, and you will have to go back and retrieve it. In this browsing time with images, you may easily collect a dozen or so, often ones with different energies from each other, so they will eventually go on separate cards. You will recognize some of the Neters they represent, while others remain a complete mystery. Certain images can be used as backgrounds or supporting images, while others you may never use at all. Images are abundant so allow yourself to tear out any with strong or enticing energy for you. Some will be scary and serious; some, hopefully, will be comical and make you laugh out loud. As you do this collecting, don't be in a hurry to interpret or name. Let your free-flowing, creative play extend into the process of creating the card.

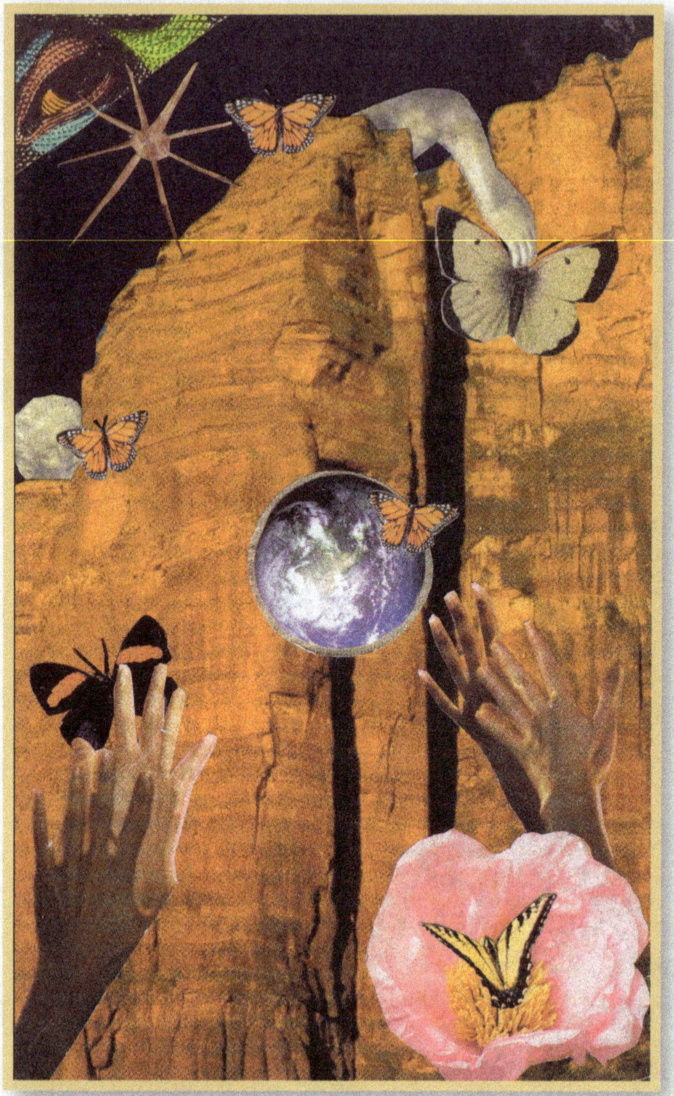

TITLE: **Released**
SUIT: **Committee**
CREATOR: **Nancy Weiss**

"*I Am One Who* lets go of the weight of the world, weight I have carried for eons, it seems, trudging on and on. *I Am One Who* trusts that other hands will hold the world upright, and so I will fly into my own blossoming. *I Am One Who* is free at last."

Assemble images that feel like the same energy for you and see how they want to piece themselves together. There will be time later, perhaps while doing the ***I Am One Who…*** exercise (see Chapter 11), for the part whose energy is represented to reveal its name and nature. You may be surprised later at how a small thing, hidden in one of the images, will turn out to be a key to the entire energy of this Neter.

Here is an example of a Neter who revealed itself and surprised its creator:

A woman shows the people in her SoulCollage® group a card she created called her School Girl card. It has three young girls in school uniforms, arms around each other, gaily dancing down the street. In the background, just barely visible, is the head of a watching man in dark glasses. Discovering this face was a complete surprise as it was not an image the woman had consciously included while making the card. It was just part of the background which had not been covered. At first glance the face seems ominous, a threat to the innocent joy of the carefree children in the card. However, as the woman read from the card, the man revealed himself to be a Divine Protector, a Watcher, and not threatening at all. He now takes on an archetypal quality in this Committee card.

Collaging Only One Energy per Card

I want to take a moment to underline a point I made earlier, one that is often forgotten as people begin creating cards. In the SoulCollage® process the point is to make many cards over time, so that each card is a separate Neter, a distinct energy that is present in your Soul. There is no set number, and some people have decks of over a hundred cards. If you have made a list of your inner personality parts, you can see that there are many different ones in the Committee suit alone, and I can guarantee there are others lurking that you have not put on your list. So, as you begin assembling a card, have it represent *one energy*. For example: if you are making an inner child card, don't include several different child energies on this one card. In time you can create several inner child cards, e.g., *Happy Child, Lonely Child, Scared Child*, etc. Keep cards focused and simple. Often those with just a couple of strong, related images are more powerful and easier to name and read than cards with a wide array of disparate images and symbols.

Neters Do Change

As you glue images on to a card, this question will naturally come up: *"What if this Neter changes?"* And, of course, they do change, especially these in the Committee suit. Neters are fluid and will grow and diminish in energy. Sometimes they behave well and sometimes they are exaggerated and out of line, or even absent when needed. I will discuss this Shadow nature of all our Neters more fully in Chapter 9. But the bottom line is this: although our parts do change, they seldom disappear completely. If they seem to, it is likely that they are waiting in the wings of the personality and may reappear again when the proper situation arises. Hence, we don't throw cards away.

Some people, sensing a shifting of energy in a Neter, have glued new images over the old ones, perhaps letting a bit of the old image show as a reminder of its original nature. Some have saved a card that no longer feels relevant in a "retirement community" box and made another one with images that are stronger and truer. The Neter's name may change, but somehow it is the same personality part evolving inside the Soul.

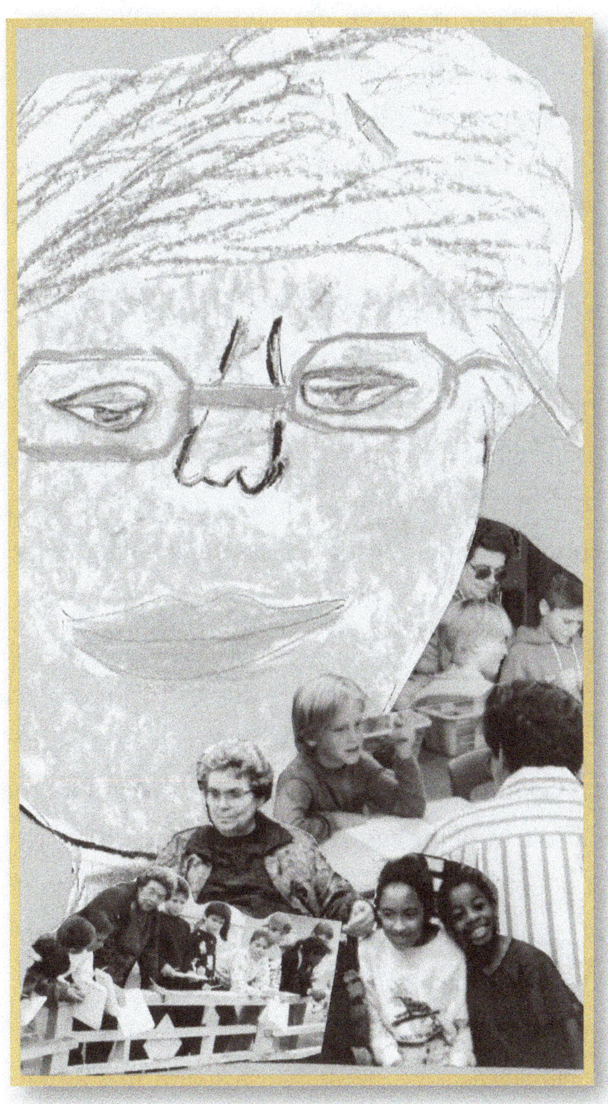

TITLE: **My Teacher Self**
SUIT: **Committee**
CREATOR: **Andrea Thelander**

It is very important to keep the SoulCollage® deck fluid, so we do not get "stuck" with any Neter, especially a negative one, as it first reveals itself.

Hold your cards lightly. Play with them. Love them. Change them. If they should all disappear one day, start again. This happened with one woman whose deck of a hundred cards was stolen from her car. She had been reading from this deck in an ongoing group for fifteen years, and one day her cards were gone. She mourned for a moment as we all did, but then she eagerly began making new cards. She created them without thought, not trying to replicate the missing cards, and the result was amazing. All of us in the group began to see the relationship of these new cards to certain of her old cards, but these Neters had changed. They had evolved. Some were more grounded, some more free. And yet a connection with the old Neters was still there. This is a lesson for us all about the transitory nature of our Neters, and, at the same time, about their enduring presence. Your SoulCollage® cards can be an ever evolving celebration of the transitory inner Neters of your Soul.

Your SoulCollage® cards can be an ever evolving celebration of the transitory inner Neters of your Soul.

Defending the Ego

What SoulCollage® calls the Committee suit contains many Neters that are also part of the ego. Unfortunately, this concept of ego has received a very negative spin in recent spiritual and self-help literature, and I want to underline here that an ego is not, in itself, negative. *An ego becomes negative by degrees when it is out of balance.*

Our egos are absolutely essential to our existence in this world, and the more balanced these Neters are, the better they work for us and for others. Remember, the Golden Rule tells us to love others *as* we love ourselves. Not *instead* of ourselves. However, it is true that this balance is difficult to find and keep. It is impossible actually, over the long run. It's part of human nature, especially unconscious human nature, to love oneself more than others, and to act in one's own self interest first. As we do this, the ego takes on density, a Shadow. It's also true that when we love the other more than we love our self, there is another kind of Shadow. But, again, more about all this in Chapter 9. The main thing to remember is that the ego is essential and does its work best when balanced. The more we work with our ego Neters, the better we become at maintaining this balance.

The Committee and the Larger Story

One more question I'll write briefly about is this: *How do our personal Committee Neters fit into the Larger Story of this planet, while they are manifesting simultaneously a Soul's individual story?*

Because the process of SoulCollage is based on the paradoxical truth of the One *and* the Many, our inner Committee Neters all need to be recognized as manifestations of the One, of Source. Therefore they have to be playing roles in the Larger Story of this planet, as well as in our local, personal stories. I will suggest a couple of ways to think about this.

First, remember that within each Soul is a spark of the Source. This spark is *SoulEssence,* and it is a like a unique "holy potential" within every Soul. Our SoulEssence is a gift that we can never lose no matter how covered over and hidden it becomes. And it is a coding we may gradually come to know when we do consciously work to live our personal life in harmony with this inner promise and direction. In the moments when we succeed in doing this we will probably experience our life as happy, no matter what the external circumstances.

Committee Cards Are Often Connected with the Council Cards

One other thing to remember in this question of the Larger Story includes the fourth suit, the Council Neters or archetypes. These archetypes are powerful, universal energies that enter our personal lives and direct Committee Neters in manifesting pieces of the Larger Story. Archetypes, although they are powerful energies, have less visibility in the natural world than humans, animals, and things. So, they must find particular and willing forms, often Committee members, to help them manifest their special energies in the world. Council Neters will recognize the unique coding of a particular SoulEssence, and they become active in that person's life. Sometimes this happens suddenly, but often the Council Neters are present from early childhood.

We will look at archetypes more deeply in Chapter 8, but remember for now that some of your Committee members are closely entwined with them. Images for both may appear on one card. Examples might be the archetypal *Creator* alongside your inner *Artist*; or the archetypal *Warrior*, working together with your inner *Political Activist*. If both Neters appear on one card then you decide which suit the card belongs in.

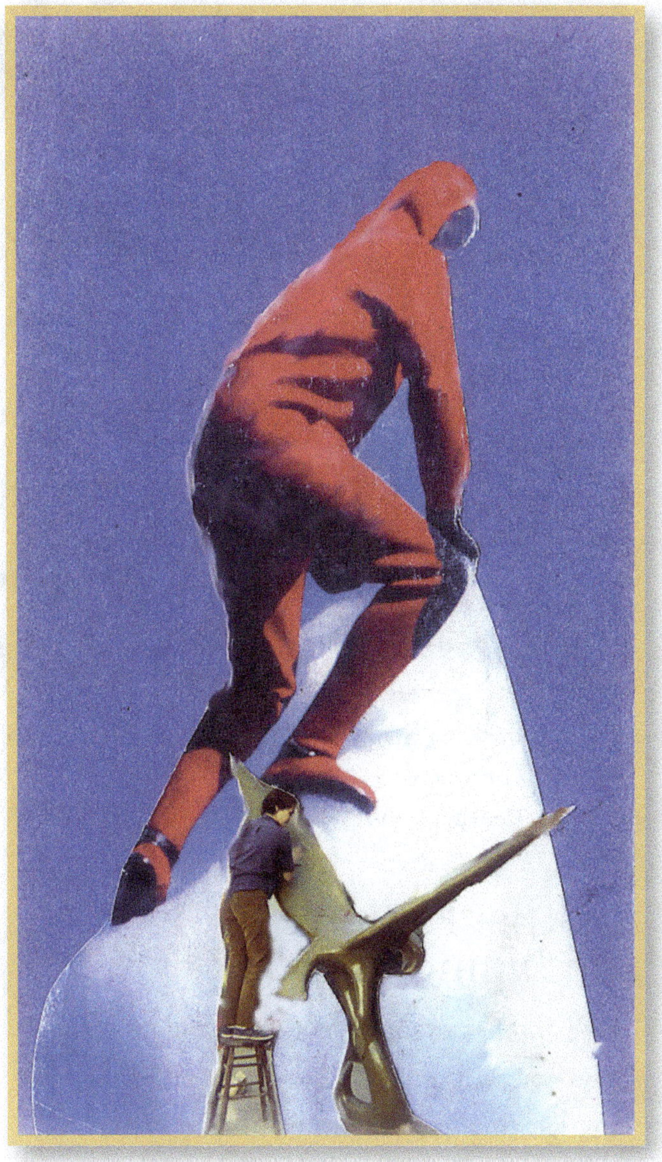

TITLE: **My Achiever Self**
SUIT: **Committee**
CREATOR: **Seena B. Frost**

"*I Am One Who* says, 'that was good fun, but how many more of these mountains do we need to climb?'"

You can always make two cards, a Council card with the image for the archetype as the central image, while in the Committee card it would be in the background with the personal image in the foreground. In the final analysis, it doesn't much matter to the Neters which suit you assign them; they simply want to be recognized and heard!

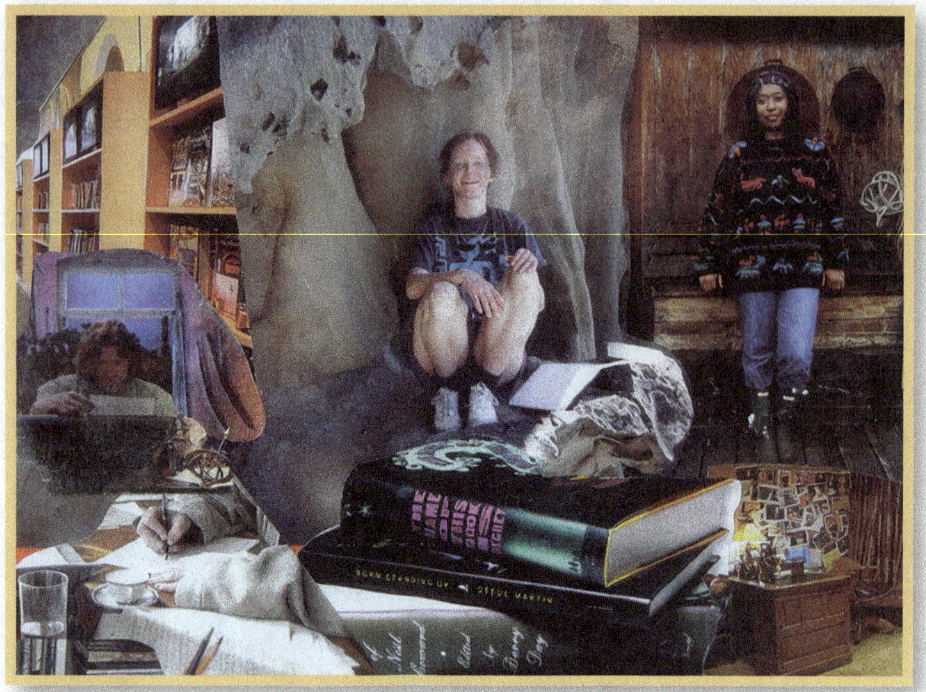

TITLE: **Inner Writer**
SUIT: **Committee**
CREATOR: **Heather Conn**

Alice Walker photograph in this card is by Anthony Barboza, photographer.

Another Example of Combining Suits

Here's another example of a combining of suits. Here is a card that SoulCollage® Facilitator, Heather Conn, from British Columbia, Canada created for her *Inner Writer*. It is a Committee card with a photo of Alice Walker as well as several other images. Here are Heather's own words:

> *As a professional writer, I cherish my Committee card* The Writer, *which includes an image of the Pulitzer-Prize-winning author Alice Walker. I had felt immediately drawn to this picture of her in a store [on a book cover] years ago, even when I was barely familiar with her work. Last year, while working temporarily in San Francisco from Canada, I was delighted to hear Walker read from her latest children's book. Her message of nonviolence, combined with her powerful presence and spontaneous, insightful words, inspired me deeply. She seemed like a kindred spirit to the SoulCollage® community. Later, I approached her and showed her my* Inner Writer *card, which I felt bore an element of tribute towards her. I explained the process of SoulCollage® to her. It seemed that as soon as she heard the word "Soul," she cried out: "Oh, I love that." She took my card and signed it on the back with a big heart and her signature. I was thrilled. This connection gave me a palpable sense of the strength and breadth of community in SoulCollage,® particularly since I was away from friends, loved ones, and my spiritual network while in California. Thanks, Seena, for sharing this process with so many and allowing it to reach out in man-y unimaginable ways.*

Many thanks to you too, Heather. This is a perfect example of including a Community figure on a Committee card. I did a similar thing on my *Inner Writer* card where I have a small picture of Shakespeare's face in the corner for inspiration. Now you could use this same photo as the primary image on a card just for Alice Walker, and have her in your Community suit as well.

CHAPTER 6

The Community Suit

THE COMMUNAL DIMENSION

The second suit in the SoulCollage® deck is the Community suit, and it is exactly what its name indicates. It contains cards for *those beings, that impact your personal story with their special energy*. You will probably create many cards in this suit and that is as it should be. Our community is a continual shaping presence in our Souls. These cards will be collaged with images of, and symbols for, historical people and pets in your immediate and extended community. These beings offer the "net" of their love and wisdom, but also may "net" you with their demands and challenges. They are guides, allies, and challengers just as our Committee Neters are, so we call all of them *Neters* as well. In readings we intuit their opinions and wisdom in answer to our questions.

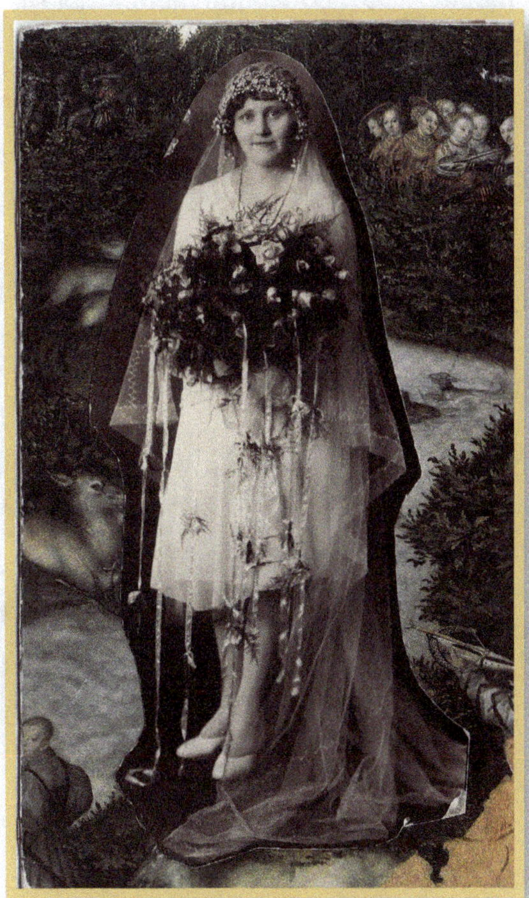

TITLE: **My Mother**
SUIT: **Community**
CREATOR: **Leta Delurgio**

"*I Am One Who* is a loyal, steadfast wife."

If you are wondering why I include these beings that are external to our physical bodies, this is the reason. The boundaries that separate us from each other—time and space—are very permeable, and the energy of other beings constantly crosses into our Souls and influences who we are. And we in turn influence others, constantly and often without our knowing. Think just of your ancestors, and how their genes were handed down to you, giving you talents, and tendencies, and shortcomings. Remember the teachers who inspired you and challenged you. Think of your parents, siblings, spouses, and children who are so integrated into your Souls that without them you would not be the same person. Even people who gave you negative messages about yourself are part of your Soul, and their messages may be internalized as part of your Shadow.

The Community suit was actually the initial suit of this process. In 1986, I began a three-year program led by Jean Houston, and, as a final project in 1989, I brought to our meeting over a hundred "Neter cards", one to honor each participant in the group. Over the six months between sessions, I had drawn one name each day, designating that person my Neter of the day. I then created a card to honor him or her. This practice became so much a part of my daily life that I needed somehow to keep going with it and so began the gradual development of the process now called SoulCollage.®

Who Should You Choose for this Suit?

Select your Community Neters from ancestors, family, friends, teachers, healers, even pets. You may know these beings personally, or you may know them through their art, writing, or special deeds. They may be alive or dead, but they should be historical and not mythic. Liking them is not the major criterion for choosing a Community Neter. What you are identifying and honoring is their special kind of energy and its impact on your Soul. It is this being's unique perspective which you will ask for when you draw its card for a reading.

I made a Community Neter card for an elderly woman whom I greatly admired. I had asked her, at one of her birthday parties,

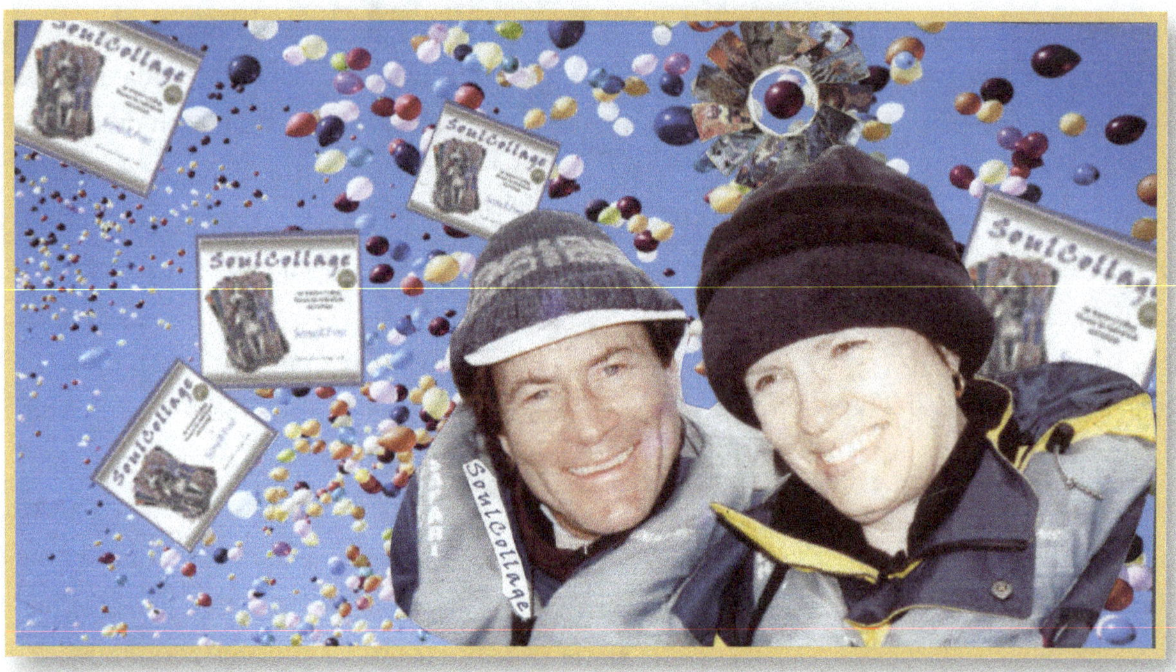

TITLE: **Kylea and Jim**
SUIT: **Community**
CREATOR: **Seena B. Frost**

"We Are the Ones who came into Seena's living room one Saturday years ago, and discovered this process now renamed SoulCollage®!"

to share the secret of her very long life with me. She replied without hesitation: "Cherish your interruptions!" This both surprised and worried me because I am not a person who cherishes most interruptions. Still, her words alerted me to a kind of goal-oriented rigidity in myself. Now, years later, when I draw Louise's card I am reawakened to her words and to the challenge it gives me.

One woman tells about the importance of a Community card that honors a dead family member:

> *My Dad has been dead now for four years and Seena kept telling me to make a card for him and I resisted and resisted. I had a lot of guilt associated with his death. We had taken a cruise, and had a very bad argument the day before we docked...and I was not very nice.... Two months later he was gone...I never got to say I was sorry to him and lived with that guilt...But once I made this card and put it out, I felt better and knew that it was okay... So that is how I use this card. I keep it out most of the time. It is very comforting to me."*

A SoulCollage® Facilitator, Julia Field of Washington state, tells of her experience with a Community card:

> *When we did readings, one of the cards that came up to guide me was one I'd made for my sister. This kind of annoyed me, because she is not someone I generally ask for advice — I've always considered us to be so different from each other in how we think and approach things. I wasn't surprised by what the card had to say to me (my sister always has ready answers), but I was surprised by how receptive I was to hearing it. Had my sister herself spoken the exact same words to me, my patterned responses would have kicked in and shut me down. I feel like the card served almost as a mediator between us, and our relationship has shifted since (or, I have shifted in how I am in our relationship). I can hear her better now. I have more appreciation for the quality in her that the card captures, and I can see that quality more clearly as a budding aspect of myself as well. Another SoulCollage® miracle!*

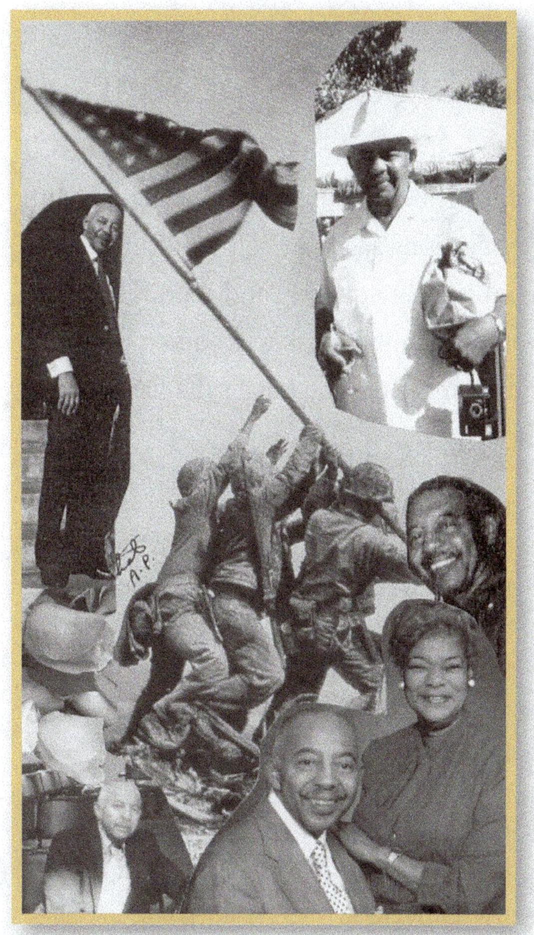

TITLE: **My Father**
SUIT: **Community**
CREATOR: **B. J. King**

"*I Am One Who* loved my father and knew he always loved me. I have been so proud of him and his loving, forgiving, accepting way of Being God in Form."

Making a List for Yourself

Create a list of some Community Neters who might be included in your deck. Here are questions that can help you start. Jot down answers quickly and without a lot of thought. Some names will come up again and again. After you create the list you can prioritize it, if you want.

- List fifteen people who feel very significant in your life. They can be alive or dead.
- Name three ancestors whose energy or personality traits you have inherited. Name one ancestor you might like to invite to be a special guide.
- Name three teachers who influenced your life in a big way.
- Of the great human beings of history name three you would like to consult about your life's direction.
- Who would you call if you needed to talk to someone in the middle of the night?
- Who would you want nearby when you are sad or depressed?
- Who might you call when you're in a mood to play?
- Name five people to be marooned with on a desert island?
- Who inspires your deepest dreams for yourself? Who encourages them?
- Whose challenges push you and also help you grow?
- Name some pets that have been precious to you in your life.
- Name two actual physical places where you love to go, places with special healing or uplifting energy.

This list is, of course, only a start. Names will come up as you look at books on your shelf, read newspapers, look back at photo albums, and talk with your family and friends.

Honoring Groups

I expect, after making this list, you have a sense of a dozen or more people to make cards for. Some of you may be thinking: "This is too big a group"; others may be thinking their group is too small. Either is fine as you get started, so let it unfold. There is no set number of cards that go in this suit, and you will add to your list over time. I belong to several groups that are important in my life, and it would be too cumbersome to make a card for each member. So I make collective SoulCollage® cards with several faces on them. When I draw this card in a reading the energy of the total group answers my question. In addition I may create individual cards for certain members of a group, those who are special friends. The groups on these cards should not be large or general groups but rather ones you meet with regularly and know the people.

Honoring Pets

A favorite Community card of mine is *My Pets over the Years*. For me there were too many pets to make a separate card for each one. Besides, I love seeing them all together on one card. Some of these pets are still alive; most are dead. I even found an ancient snapshot of myself as a child with my dog and cat. Whenever I draw this card I remember my various devoted pets and how they loved and amused and "companioned" me. I smile at the Basset Hound named

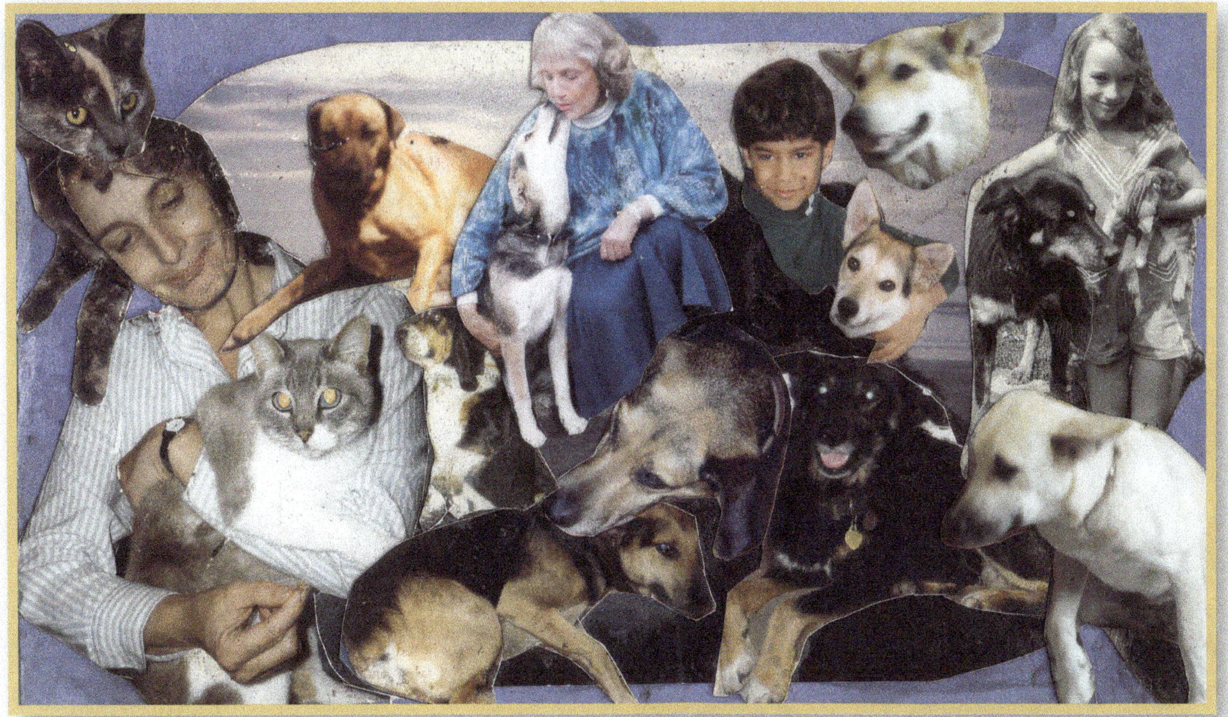

TITLE: **My Pets Over the Years**
SUIT: **Community**
CREATOR: **Seena B. Frost**

"We Are the greatly loved animals of your past and present. You have named and loved each one of us and we loved each other unconditionally."

Sugar Plum with her huge ears, and the old cat named Lucy who had at least nine lives and maybe more. This card speaks with the energies of warmth and loyalty and devotion when I draw it.

Honoring Special Places

Over years of doing SoulCollage,® we discovered that many people wanted to make cards for special places that were high in energy for them. Often they made a separate suit for these power spots. However, it seemed to me that they could easily be included in the Community suit, and that is where I recommend you put them. These "place cards" would not be general cards for trees or mountains, but would be for a special tree or a spot on a mountain that you love to visit. It could be a bench or a place you sit to meditate. It could be your childhood room, or a special and specific place at a vacation spot that has precious memories. I have a card for a post in an ancient fence that I pass on my daily walks, a post whose picture I took so I could put it on a card. So, for these cards especially, it is good to have an actual picture of the specific place.

Creating these Cards

The cards in the Community suit are the most intentional of the SoulCollage® cards, meaning that you won't just browse through magazines letting your unconscious choose images. Rather you will have an intention to create a Community card for someone who may be on your list. Select a photograph if you have one, reducing or enlarging it for your card, cutting away extra

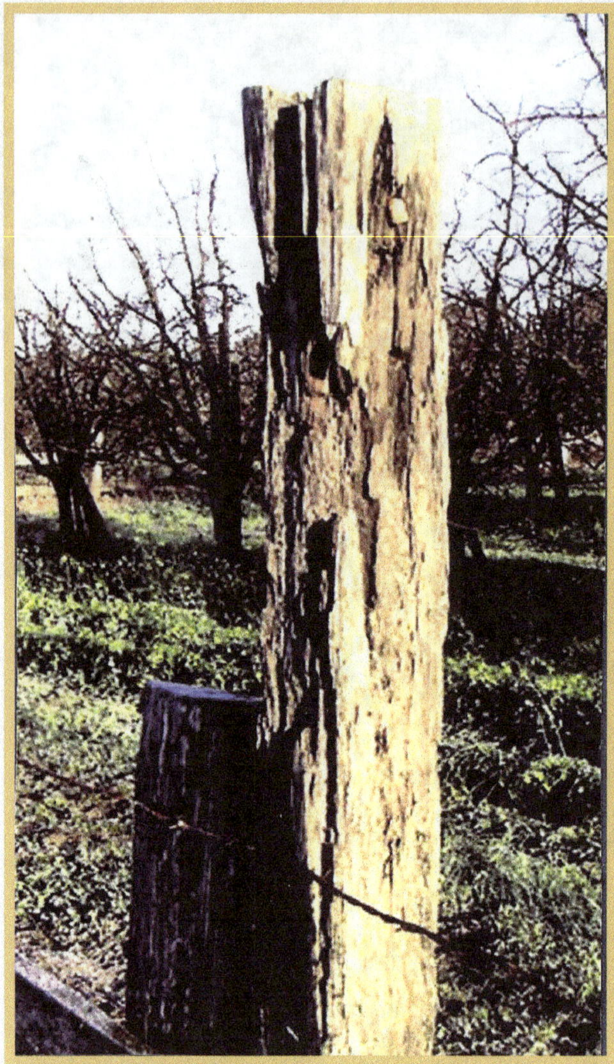

TITLE: **The Mystic**
SUIT: **Community**
CREATOR: **Seena B. Frost**

"I see you and bow to you as you walk by. *I Am One Who* reminds you that Love re-members us as one."

people, backgrounds and irrelevant things. You may even cut up a portrait from an old album knowing you will see this picture more on a card than in an album. Choose images for the background that reflect the person's energy whether it is a garden or books or a kitchen or some interest or creation or hobby. If you don't have an actual photograph, make the card with symbolic images that are suggestive of the person's primary energy for you. Often these cards are made in spurts after you have collected special images in envelopes, meaning to incorporate them into certain Community cards.

Some people have avoided this suit, thinking it too hard to find the "perfect" images to portray a loved one. Let me assure you that there's no need to represent every quality or interest of a person. Simply their picture carefully cut out and put on a new background, and a couple of supporting images will be good reminders of their energy.

> *You may even cut up a portrait from an old album knowing you will see this picture more on a card than in an album.*

Also, it's fine to have two people on one card, as Mother and Father, if you experience their energy as a unit (e.g., *Parents*). However, if their energy towards you is quite different, make two cards. Likewise a group of ancestors can be together on one *Ancestors* card if they would all tend to give you the same sort of advice.

As with all your SoulCollage® cards, I encourage you *not* to collage words on to a card as that limits what the Neter might say to you in a reading. But do cut the image of the person out of its background with special care and attention. Noelle Remington, a SoulCollage® Trainer from Washington state, remembers hearing another Facilitator, Jeri Bodemar, say this about the cutting out process:

As we cut an image out from its background, we are blessing it. When I cut out the images for Community cards, especially photos of my friends or loved ones, I remember this intention. As I cut around her fingers, arms, and the rest of her silhouette, I imagine that I am blessing her.

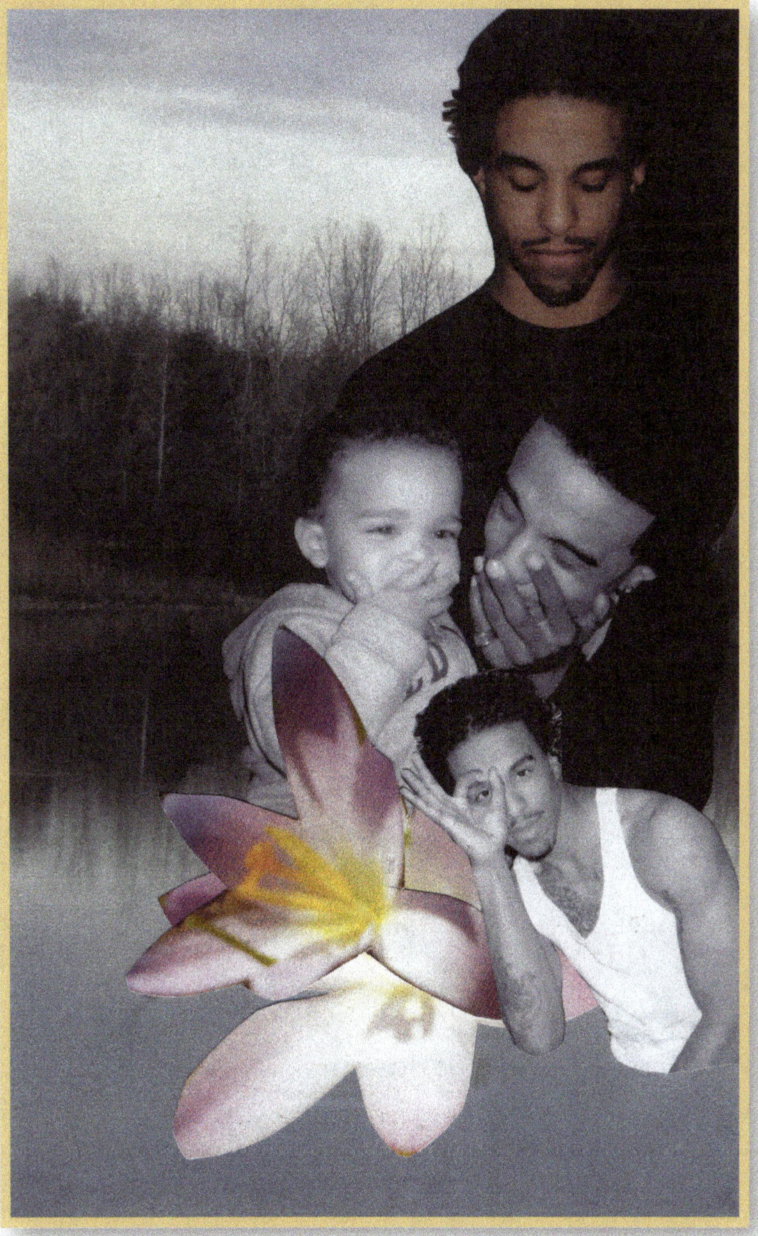

TITLE: **Darrin, Sr.**
SUIT: **Community**
CREATOR: **Jeannetta Holliman**

"I Am the courageous, sensitive and silly one, wise beyond my years, I Am an old soul with a bit of recklessness. Fire burns in my belly. Taking risks, I feel alive—trusting more than fearing the outcomes."

Using and Sharing Your Cards

Over and over in this book I will emphasize the value of using your cards in some sort of daily ritual. I have a daily practice that I've done for over twenty years: I draw two cards each morning from my deck which sits, face down, on a little altar. Always I draw one Community card which I recognize by its backing, and the second card I draw from any of the other suits. I turn them over and recognize them as my Neters for that day. I put them up where I will see them, and I also enter their names in my daily journal. This is really all that I do in this ritual so it does not take a lot of time. It is meaningful though, for in some odd way the energy of the Neters will stay with me. Once in a while I email or phone a person and let them know they are my Neter of the day. This practice has kept me in touch with some people that I might have lost over the years. The next morning I put those cards back in the stack, thanking them, and draw two more for the new day. This is just one idea for a daily ritual. Create one of your own.

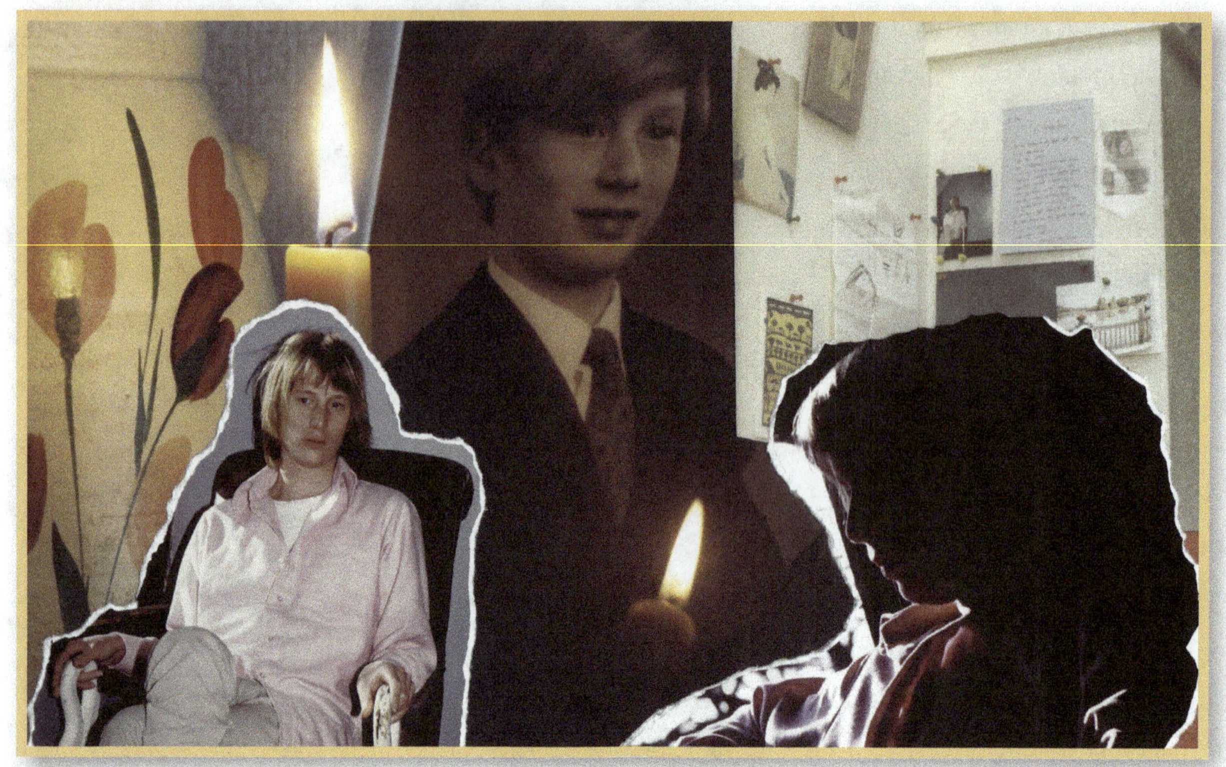

TITLE: **Honoring Tim**
SUIT: **Community**
CREATOR: **Pam Swing**

"*I Am One Who* has gone before you. I had to let go of life even though I fiercely loved it. *I Am One Who* teaches you about grief and the finality of loss. *I Am One Who* lives in your heart."

For my brother Timothy Gram Swing 1955-1983

Of course you will use these cards along with your other cards in readings, and I will describe these in more detail in Chapter 12. But, in brief, when you draw a Community card to answer a question, you will enter into the energy of the person or animal or place, and speak to the question *from the first person.* You will intuit what this person might give you as an answer, being true to this person's energy as you know it. With places and things, of course, your intuition becomes imagination which also is very wise.

Finally, let me encourage you to share the cards you create with the people you have chosen to honor. That is, if they are alive and available. These Community Neters will love to see their cards, and most likely will be interested in the SoulCollage® process and how you will be using their image. They will be pleased that you have included them as Neters of your Soul.

What if the Energy of a Card Changes?

This question comes up with the cards in every suit. Probably with the Community suit there is less sense of the Neter's energy changing very much, but if they do change in a significant way you can add a new image or make a new card. You can also put a card into the retirement box if there is no energy anymore for you from this being.

The Shadow in Community Cards

Another question often asked is this: "Who should I *not* put in this suit?" My answer here is: "Do not put a being into your deck who is totally toxic to you." What I mean here is that you should not consult a Neter who has nothing useful to offer you, not even a challenge that is motivating. There may be some people who challenge you or correct you, and, hard though it is, you actually appreciate their energy. You should probably include them even if you don't "like" them personally.

This is different from your Committee cards. In that suit you need to include Neters that are difficult, because these are more personally yours and you are working to bring them into balance. It is not your task to change and balance the energies of your external Community Neters, not unless they have become internalized through messages as from teachers or parents. It is more your job to *listen* to them, and, after listening, to sort, accept, or reject their input. When you do include a Community Neter whose energy is often out of balance, perhaps a loved one who is overly demanding or critical, be sure to recognize this Shadow part and perhaps represent it in some way on the card. There could be a small symbol included that only you will understand. And remember this basic principle of SoulCollage®: *all Neters, because they have form, have the potential of Shadow.* Every being in the Community suit is included in this. You may not indicate this Shadow on most cards, but remember that the potential is there, even in your saintly grandmother or the Dalai Lama. Sometimes in a reading this Shadow part will show up and give its input on a question; however in most readings the more balanced or positive energy of this same Neter will give the answer.

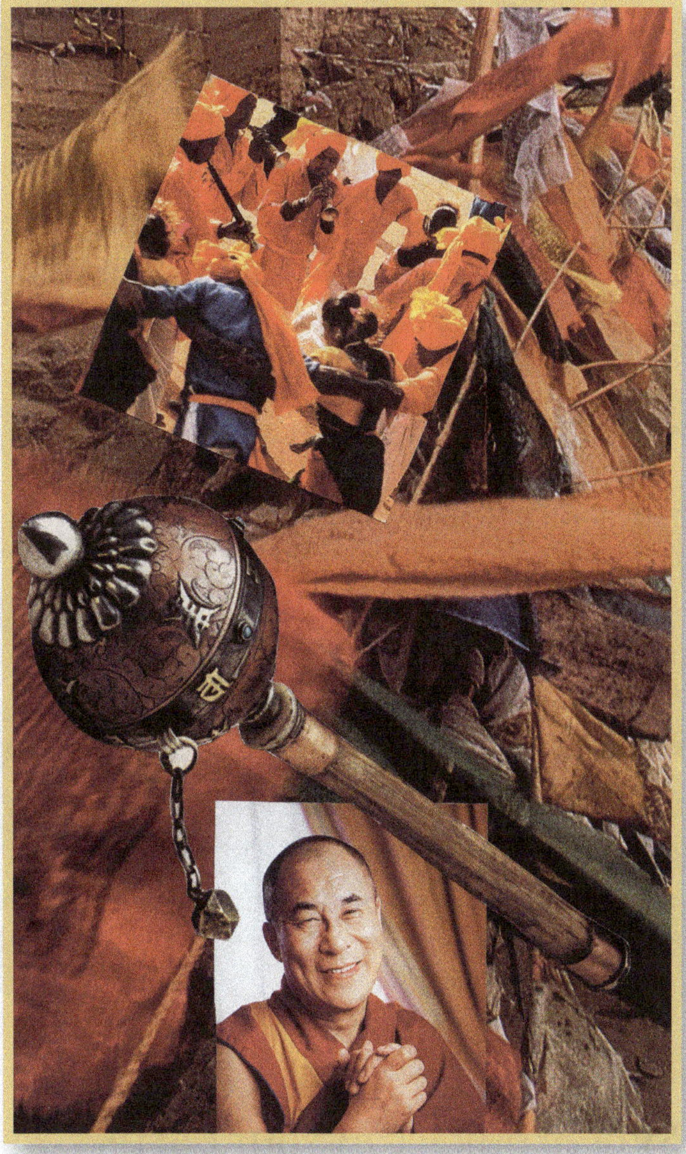

TITLE: **Dalai Lama**
SUIT: **Community**
CREATOR: **Jeri Bodemar**

"*I Am the One Who* says: 'The very purpose of our life is happiness — it is within our own hands. A challenging reminder.'"

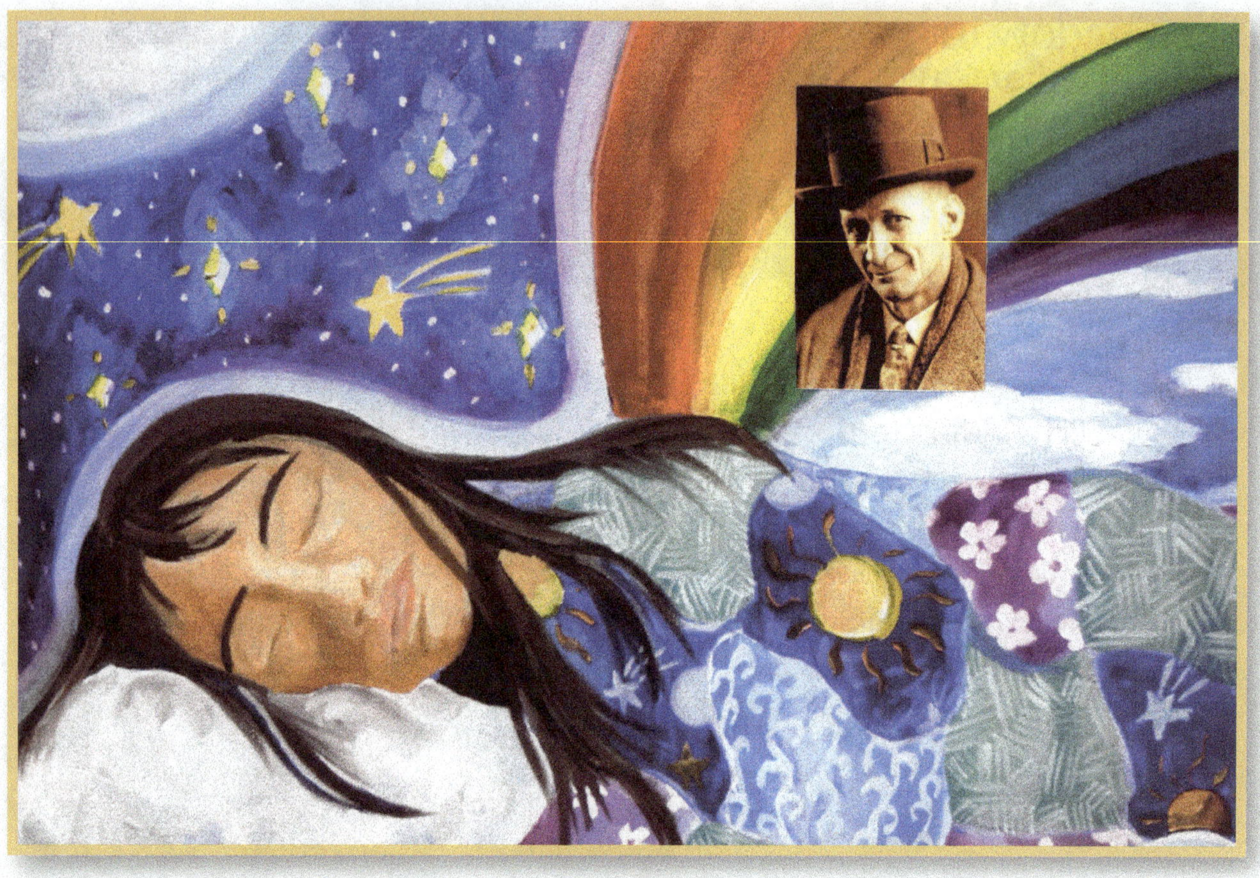

TITLE: **Grandfather Dreaming**
SUIT: **Community**
CREATOR: **Dori King**

"*I Am One Who* has been the gentle touch in troubled moments, the soft hugs in good times. I come to join you as you dream, with a whisper of words full of smiles. I Am One watching you shine."

Synchronicity in Your Cards

I want to talk briefly about synchronicity because it frequently shows up in the drawing and consulting of Community cards. *Synchronicity* was a word that C.G. Jung used, and a phenomena that interested him greatly. He defined it as "an acausal connecting principle" or, in easier words, "the meaningful coincidence of two events." Jung experienced synchronicity often, such as when he would have a dream and then a patient would come in who described the exact same situation. In SoulCollage® we experience it when we draw and turn over a Neter card in a reading, and it is the card we made for the very person or situation that we are asking about. It's like thinking about someone, and then they call on the phone. Only here it's like thinking about someone, and their card turns up, or an image exactly right for them shows up on a card. This is especially surprising when you have a lot of cards in your deck, and your hand seems to choose a card that turns out to be amazingly coincidental.

This is not really something unusual or weird. If we believe that all the many energies of the universe are deeply intertwined in the oneness of Source, then this can be expected.

However, most of us are not watching with enough attention and so miss most of the synchronicities around us. As we develop our *Observer* self through SoulCollage®, we will consciously notice how Souls are intertwined, and we will start to notice coincidences. They happen even as we reach out an energy finger towards another being—a reach not limited by time and space. We do this kind of reaching in the creating and reading of our SoulCollage® cards, and especially in the use of Community cards. So expect surprising synchronicities; watch for them and enjoy them!

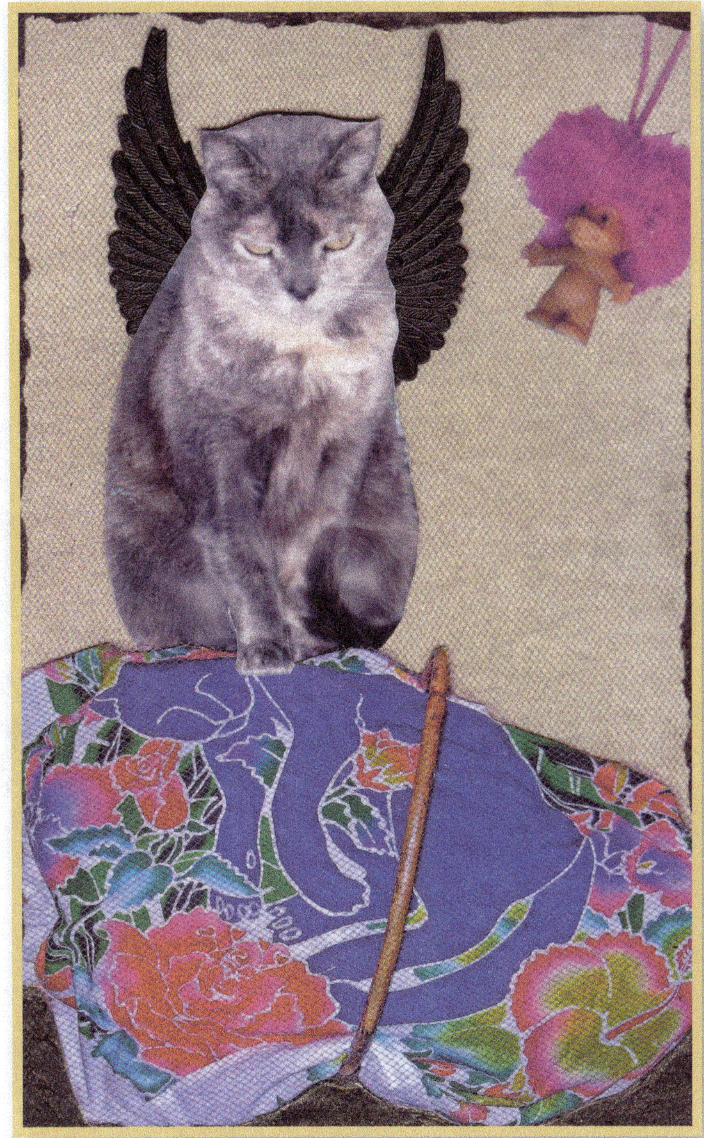

TITLE: **From Behind the Veil: Socks**
SUIT: **Community**
CREATOR: **Nancy Weiss**

"*I Am One Who* comes from behind the veil to tell you that love never dies. Find me in the cloth with which you cradled me, and in your turns on the labyrinth."

Community Suit Workshops

Some SoulCollage® Facilitators are doing specialized workshops, concentrating on one suit over a period of time. SoulCollage® Trainer Noelle Remington from the state of Washington has led five-week and weekend workshops which focus just on the Community suit. Here is part of a report she sent me about such an event:

> *On the last day of the workshop I invite participants to lay out all of their Community cards in a timeline in an exercise inspired by an activity in Deena Metzger's book,* Writing for Your Life (p. 199), *and then reflect on the following questions: What are the qualities these people have in common? How, together, have they impacted me? What specific heritage (strengths, gifts, and inheritance) emerges from the line? What is the legacy I am being called to carry on?* Noelle goes on to say: *What I love about this exercise is the basic premise that your Community reflects back to you who you are and so the gifts you see*

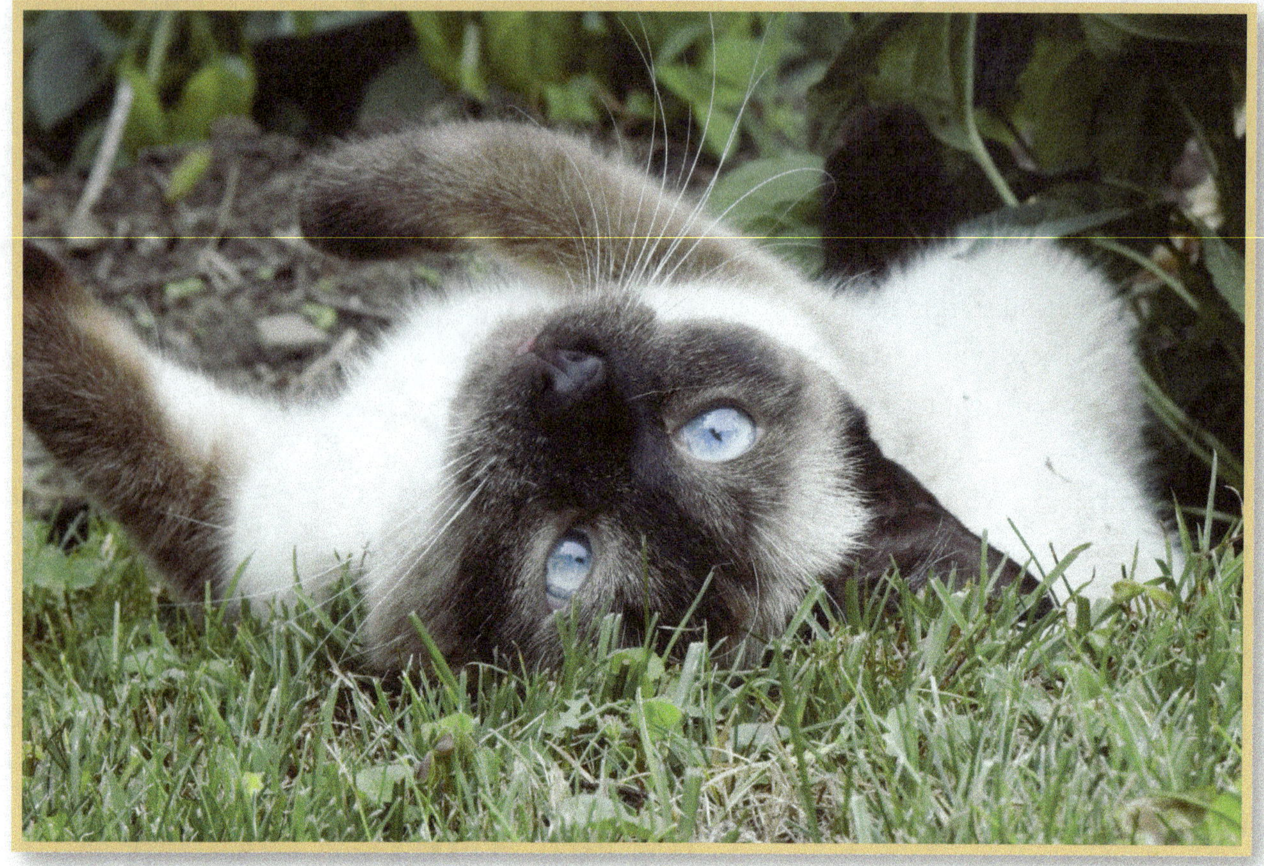

TITLE:	**Gracie**	"*I Am One Who* is curious stalking you in the garden."
SUIT:	**Community**	
CREATOR:	**Laren Leonard**	

in them are also present in you. It's especially powerful to do with cards you've created for your teachers, mentors, and others who inspire you in your life. It's a way of acknowledging and honoring your lineage and exploring the legacy you are being called to live.

"Your Community reflects back to you who you are and so the gifts you see in them are also present in you." ~Noelle Remington

CHAPTER 7

The Companions Suit

THE ENERGETIC DIMENSION

The third suit of a SoulCollage® deck is that of the Companions. You will discover your Companion Neters when you do several guided visualizations, and the Neters you find for this suit may seem stranger and more mysterious than in the first two suits. Imagination and intuition will be your best tools for finding them, and also in creating cards for them. Try not to set up expectations, and stay as open as possible when you visualize. Almost certainly you will be surprised by who appears and what they offer to you.

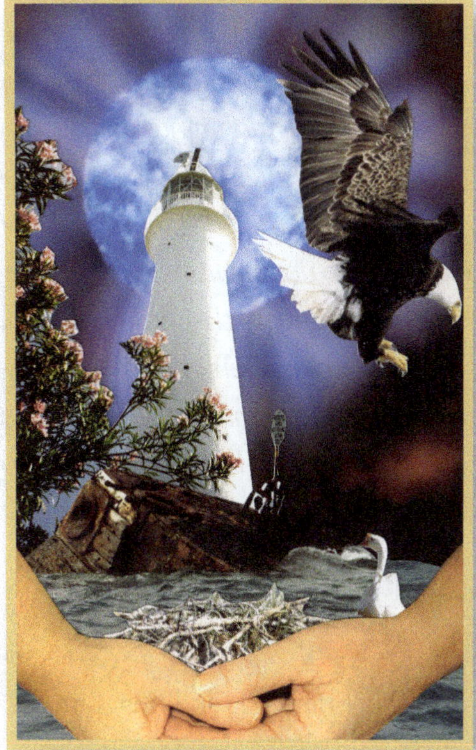

TITLE: **7th Chakra Eagle**
SUIT: **Companions**
CREATOR: **Mili Dillard**

"*I Am One Who* brings light and spirit into conscious awareness and form as I come to rest fully in my body and my emotions."

The Neters of the Companions suit are *mirrors for the energies of your physical and subtle bodies*, their flow, their blockages, and their changing ability to help and heal… or to hinder and hurt. Using the ancient yogic system of energy centers, called *chakras*, you will discover the Neter beings, primarily animals, living and working in each of your seven chakras. We do this with a guided visualization (a sample text is provided later) which you can record and use again and again. Or you can purchase the *Introduction to SoulCollage®* audio on which I have recorded it. Everybody imagines their own animals, so each person's deck is different in the combination of animals chosen for the seven chakras. Very often there is repetition of ones that appear to people gathered in a group, but the total collection of seven will be uniquely yours.

The concept of chakra energies comes from Eastern yogic philosophy, and is now widely accepted by Western healers who work with energy. Very basically it is this: vital energy moves up and down our bodies along the spinal column, concentrating in at least seven vortices along this route. Through many kinds of energetic work, including massage, meditation, yoga, acupuncture, breathwork, and visualization, this energy flow can be opened, balanced, and directed so it flows more freely through the body. Doing energy work enhances our physical health and also our mental and emotional health. As we work with our personal, energetic rhythms they come to be more in tune with the rhythms of nature. Your SoulCollage® cards in this suit can be used in many ways to help you towards this balance.

Why Look for Animals?

Later, in this chapter, you will find a listing of the seven chakras, with a brief description of each one's special attributes. It is helpful to read this before doing your first visualization. If you want more complete information there are many books available with diagrams and descriptions. I will recommend one book in particular, the one which has been most helpful to me in developing The Companions Suit. The author is Steve Gallegos and the book's title is *The Personal Totem Pole*. Gallegos pioneered the work of discovering personal animal totems in the chakras, and he describes his process in this book. He uses guided visualizations to access these animals, just as we do in SoulCollage,® and he describes powerful experiences in which people find their animal totems and dialogue with them.

We must reconnect our souls with the vitality of nature. and imagining animals in the chakras helps us to do that. As we work with our personal, energetic rhythms they come to be more in tune with the rhythms of nature.

Others have written about the importance of humans reconnecting with our primitive, animal energy. Here are the beginning sentences of Ladson Hinton's article, "A Return to the Animal Soul": *The future survival of humankind depends upon return to a right relationship to nature. The need is both inner and outer. In this endeavor the animal soul is our most dependable guide...Since we no longer hunt in lonely communion with animals, and since few of us feel called to go on formal vision quests, we have to seek ways of recreating meaningful connection with the animal realm.*"

I agree with Hinton's premise that we must reconnect our souls with the vitality of nature and imagining animals in the chakras helps us to do that.

Michael Harner, author of *The Way of the Shaman*, talks of encouraging animals to help us by "dancing" them. In SoulCollage® work this suggests that we not only find images and make cards for our animal Neters, but that we, at times, embody the particular energy of one of them, and *actually move as this animal might move*. Put on music after a guided visualization, and, if space permits, "dance your animals". Should there not be enough room, suggest that people imagine that they are moving in the energy of their animal. For some people this may feel awkward, even embarrassing. We spend so much time in our heads that getting into our bodies in a spontaneous and public way can seem strange. But in this suit the Neter animals are all about the movement of energy flowing through our physical bodies, so, allow this to happen if you can. If not, just do it in your imagination until you are comfortable moving physically as well. At the same time let your Observer notice what your various Committee Neters are saying as you move. Jot down their comments, positive and negative, so you remember them and can be conscious of their perspectives.

In SoulCollage® we want you to relax and find your animal Neters through guided imagery or visualization. Other ways might be through dreams where an animal appears as a guide, or in meditation or breathwork experiences. These are ways to imagine "becoming" and "communicating with" a numinous animal. We want to avoid having the logical mind choose an animal that it "thinks" would fit the energetic description. Our intuitive mind will have better wisdom in this selecting process and you will find your animal Neters through guided imagery or visualization.

Finding the Companions Through Guided Imagery

Now we'll imagine that you are about to relax and do a guided visualization to find *one* of your chakra animals. I recommend doing just one animal at a time so you will need to do this visualization several times. You may be in a group doing this, or you may be alone in your home using an audio you recorded of the following guided meditation.

— *Get very comfortable, but not so comfortable that you go to sleep.*

— *Be sure that you will not be disturbed by phones or other interruptions.*

— *Turn on the recording that contains this guided imagery journey.*

— *Breathe and allow yourself to drop into a very relaxed state or a light trance state.*

— *Let your mind follow the recorded words and your imagination will do the rest.*

— *In the visualization you will first journey from chakra to chakra, getting in touch with the various energies but not yet attempting to visualize an animal. This helps to give your body time to relax.*

— *After this period of general relaxation, you will be directed to return to one chakra and spend time there, feeling its particular energy and finally letting the animal or being, who lives in your body there, show itself. You will spend time watching this Neter, actually becoming it and moving with its energy; then you will dialogue with it internally.*

— *If no animal comes up for you, let that be all right and know that you can return to this chakra again. If many animals or beings show up, let them parade across your mind without judgment and see if one eventually claims this place as theirs. Sometimes two animals may be in one chakra, representing different energies that occur there. Usually there is just one.*

When you return to full awareness you can write for a few minutes or, better yet, before you write, begin to move as your animal Neter to help anchor the energy into your consciousness. If you are doing this process with a group, it is valuable to share your experiences, reporting on what animals appeared and how they were moving. Since this suit is one in which you will intentionally search for the right image of it for your card, other people can be on the lookout for you too. Accept images that others offer, but don't settle for one that is not really the right one. It needs to not only look like the animal you imagined, but even more, to express the energy of the animal whether it is running, flying, swimming, sleeping, or hiding. Perhaps you will put two images of the same animal on your card, showing its different energies, if you experienced something like that.

Sometimes a being that is not an animal shows up in the visualization. If this being, say an angel, or a unicorn, or a tree, is clearly the Neter of this energetic place, just go with it. I suggest focusing on animals, however, because they are a really good resource for getting back in touch with our elemental energies. However, if your unconscious chooses something else for one of the chakras, it is better to trust this than to force something else.

Surprising Animals

Trusting one's unconscious is a vital part of the SoulCollage® process; this is true in finding the images, in creating the cards and in doing readings. Very often this trust will lead to surprises, surprises that are fun and surprises that may be disturbing. This is especially so with guided imagery where we try to keep the thinking mind quiet, and to let deeper energies emerge to select our Neters.

In the Companions Suit you may experience that an animal will show up who not only surprises you but also dismays you. I won't tell you what some of the stranger ones have been. I don't want to seed your thoughts with them. But you can imagine! Do your best to keep your *Inner Critic* still, and accept the animal or being that appears. It most likely has a message about the energy of this chakra that is significant for you to understand and work with. Don't do any interpreting right away; just go ahead and find images and make the card. Stay open. Surprise is at the heart of the SoulCollage® process, and is a transformational catalyst because it moves us out of our normal channels of thought.

Change begins to happen with the entry of a surprising image, and after that with practice. Change does not usually arrive and stay with us, just because we have an "aha!" experience. In order to change the old groove in our brain, we must practice with the new energetic awareness. This is why we must continue on beyond finding our animals in the imagery session; we need to make cards for them, and then dialogue with them—daily, or at least often.

I want to share a story about a surprising and little appreciated being that appeared to a SoulCollage® Trainer from California in a visualization. Such a story of changing consciousness is not unusual. Perhaps it will encourage you to allow your wise unconscious to choose your chakra animals for you. I'll let Mariabruna Sirabella tell her story in her own words:

> *When I attended my first workshop with Seena she led the Companion visualization inviting us to focus on the heart chakra. I have quite a list of beloved animals I identify with, so I was excited at the prospect of meeting a familiar, cherished presence. Instead, in the*

profoundly relaxed state of the trance induction, I saw a swan. I shook my head. The swan was not on my list. Who wants a swan in the heart? Not me. I never felt an affinity with swans: too much of a show off in parks, not wild enough, just not my style. An eagle would have been more acceptable. I could have even settled for the mesmerizing salamander that visited me in dreams. No matter how much I shook my head, the swan came back. Seena's voice reminded us to be accepting and non-judgmental. The visualization was over and short of cheating –cheating whom? – I resigned myself to work on the image and symbolism of a swan for the next four hours and made my first SoulCollage® card: My Heart Chakra Companion.

A few years later I was reviewing my cards and playing with the idea of re-doing the heart chakra, the one with the swan, when all of a sudden I had tears in my eyes. With a flash of recognition I finally saw my early childhood "ugly duckling" in this beautiful swan. How could I have ignored it for so many years? An ugly duckling transformed into a swan is a most appropriate inhabitant of my symbolic heart. Its presence there affirms my heart as a place of transformation, and a place from which to support others' transformation. This card has become a very important reminder of how my own experience of aban-

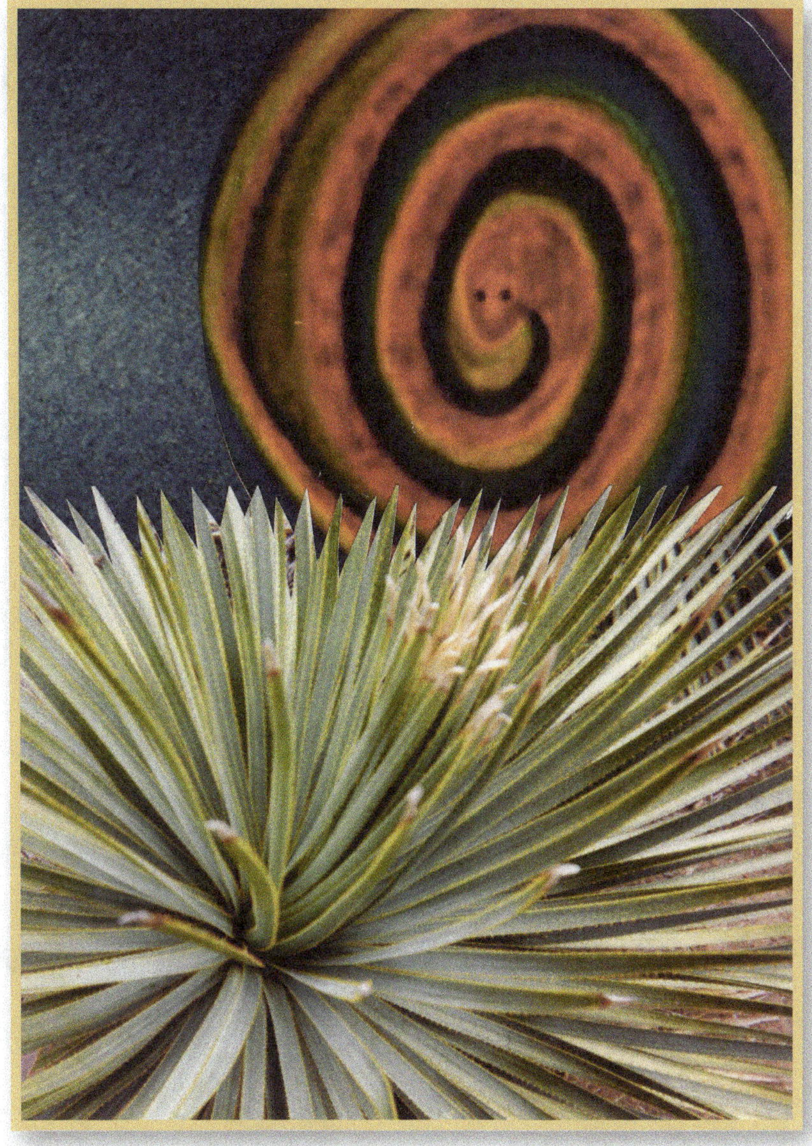

TITLE: **Fire Serpent – First Chakra**
SUIT: **Companions**
CREATOR: **Mariabruna Sirabella**

"*I Am One Who* sustains the fundamental necessities of Being: may you respect your instinct and vibrate with Life, remember how to grow food, shelter your body and tend the Waters."

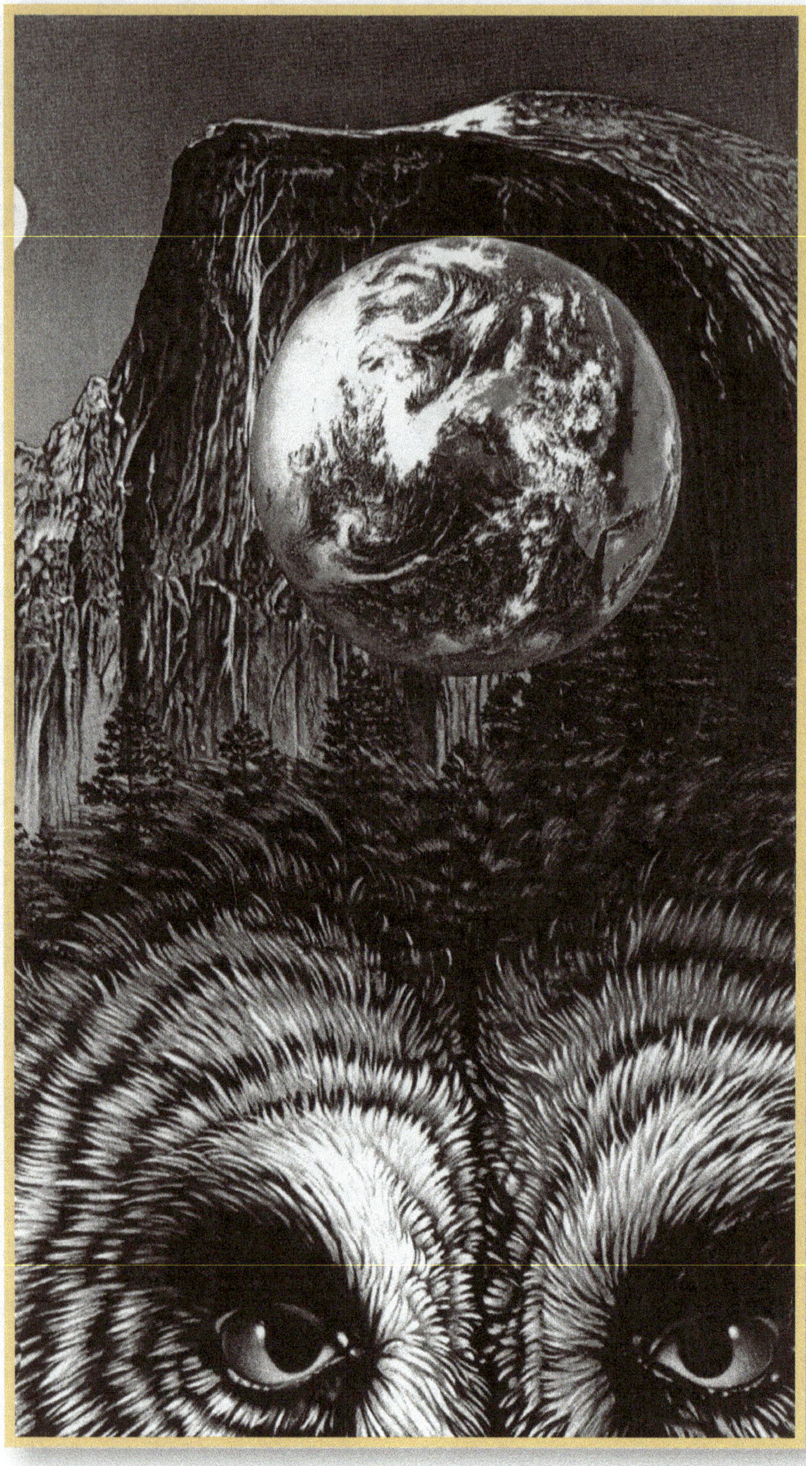

TITLE: **Sixth Chakra Owl**
SUIT: **Companions**
CREATOR: **Bobby Tucker**

"*I Am One Who* calls to you from the inner recesses of your Being. I see and understand all things. Trust my wisdom."

donment and non-belonging was transformed when I came closer to my true nature.

The Seven Chakras Described

I'll give you now brief descriptions of the attributes generally associated with the seven energy centers of the body, the chakras. As we journey up the spine they become increasingly refined. However all seven are important to the well-being of our physical body and to all the Neters of our Soul. If any one of the centers becomes compromised so the energy does not flow freely, the Soul will experience it in some physical, mental, or emotional way.

First Chakra: At the base of the spinal column is the first, or root, chakra. It is the foundation chakra, where the body's energies are firmly rooted in the flow of the earth's energies below. This chakra is associated with the material things of our life, with shelter and food and with having enough to sustain our lives. It has to do with our sense of security, our "groundedness", and is connected with our self-esteem at a very basic level. A free energy flow here will help us keep our balance and feel stability both physically and emotionally. Here, in this root chakra, is energy that begins in the earth and flows upwards. It flows all along the spinal column, to give our whole being a sense of natural vitality.

Second Chakra: In the curve of the sacrum in the lower back is the chakra associated with sexuality and sensuality. Some part of this energy is vital for procreation; however this is also the energy center that fuels our creativity, our passions, and emotions. Its energy, linking with the first chakra's vitality, thrusts upwards to activate and enliven the chakras above it. Here also, it is said, is the residual energy of our ancestors.

Third Chakra: On the spinal column, behind the navel, lies the fiery "jeweled lotus" chakra. This is the place of our personal power, of our strong ego. Here is our ability to firmly say "No" when a boundary must be set; it is also our ability to say "Yes", clearly and willingly, and to take action. From this place we often compete, from here we try to control, and from here we work to protect. In this center is the swirling, hot energy that can help us make our individual way in a difficult world. Without freely flowing energy here we can feel stuck and helpless. This is not a negative energy place; it is neutral and, when healthy, has strong vitality. The Shadows of excess and egotism can be traced to energy that is off balance in this chakra.

With guided imagery we try to keep the thinking mind quiet, and to let deeper energies emerge to select our Neters.

Fourth Chakra: The fourth chakra is centered on the spinal column, behind the area of the heart. At this point the rising energy is becoming more refined than in the three survival-oriented chakras. Here the second chakra energy of sexual love, which often is possessive and demanding, becomes less "I-centered" and moves towards the beloved with care and compassion. This is the agape center with energy that embraces the other as special and holy. Here we are moving towards a sense of the unity of the soul with all souls, with all nature, and with Source.

As heart energy is activated, thoughts and feelings of alienation and struggle begin to fade, and joy begins to bubble up. The degree of refinement in this chakra varies widely from being to being and needs continual attention and work.

Fifth Chakra: The fifth chakra is centered in the throat and is sometimes called the "bridge chakra." It is an entry place where we can receive nurturance and wisdom from outside our self, and also the center from which we can communicate what we feel and what we know. It is related to the second chakra where passion and creativity originate, and here in the fifth chakra they are manifested into forms in the world. It is understandable that this is called the communication chakra; it includes both the receiving and delivering of messages. This communication can have many different forms such as words or music or painting or even bodily movements that convey a message. Since this is a narrow physical place the energy here is more refined and more controlled than in the second or third chakras. How well these baser energies have been refined in the heart chakra will determine what degrees of refinement issue forth from this fifth chakra.

Sixth Chakra: The sixth chakra is found between the eyebrows behind the center of the forehead, and is often called "the third eye." Here, where the left and right hemispheres of the brain are joined, is the energy center which fosters and unites our intuition and our logical wisdom. Because of the integrating energy of the sixth chakra we are able to step back into our Observer self, and sense the Larger Story and our place within that story. Our chakras grow more and more refined as energy travels upwards in the body, and this sixth one can be a receptor for illumination that we may call mystical. It leads to and is linked to the seventh chakra of Unity.

Surprise is at the heart of the SoulCollage® process. It is a transformational catalyst because it moves us out of our normal channels of thought.

Seventh Chakra: The seventh chakra is just above the top of the head, and is sometimes called the "crown chakra". In Hindu traditions it is imaged as a "thousand-petaled lotus" and it is the locus of our experience of Oneness with the universe. All duality and separation fall away here, and a state of peace and sometimes ecstasy can be felt when one is able to spend moments breathing within this energy. We experience ourselves as one with all that is, was, and will be.

There are many interpretative books which can help you understand the energies of the various chakras, and some are listed in the Resources section at the end of the book. Use them to enlarge your cognitive understanding.

The animals that come up for you from your intuitive unconscious may seem to have little to do with the energies as described both above and in these resource books. Remember to trust your own process and your own deep wisdom. The symbols that bubble up for you in each of the chakras will have some unique and special meaning just for you.

Here now is the guided visualization which you can record for your own use and for the use of your groups. It is similar to the one recorded on my *Introduction to SoulCollage®* audio.

Guided Imagery for the Companion Neters

Prepare your space for a ritual by burning a candle, perhaps having some flowers, and putting on soft music. And begin…

Let your Critic Neter: *take a "time out". Send him or her to the kitchen for a cup of tea or outside for a walk. Good.*

Closing your eyes when you are ready and taking three deep breaths. With each breath relaxing more and more, deepening gradually into a light trance. (Pause)

Now breathing normally again, letting yourself feel any tension or tightness loosening and slipping away and out of your body. Breathing and relaxing. Deeper and deeper. (Pause)

Beginning with your toes and feet...then moving up to the calves of your legs and your knees...then on to your thighs.

So now feeling both legs becoming more and more relaxed. (Pause)

Moving on to your buttocks and your back...and also to your lower abdomen and stomach. Breathing and letting tension slip away.

Now moving up to your chest area and upper back and then to your shoulders...feeling the burdens you are carrying slipping off for the moment. Breathing and relaxing.

Now focusing on your arms beginning with your upper arms...and then the elbows and lower arms...and finally your hands... Again letting the tension drain away. Breathing and relaxing.

Now moving to your neck and to your face...relaxing all the little muscles around your mouth and around your eyes...Even feeling the muscles in your scalp, in the back of your head — all letting go. Breathing and feeling relaxation throughout your body. There is nothing you need to accomplish right now. Just staying aware and opening.

If there is any place in your body that still feels tight, tending to it for a moment more, breathing into that place and relaxing. (Pause) *Good.*

You are now entering a deep space within yourself, a relaxed space that your intuitive self recognizes and is happy to visit. Your wise inner self wants to give you a very special gift.... Staying alert and staying open to receive it.

Imagining now a warm, golden energy streaming down from above your head. This energy, in the form of golden light, streams into you through your seventh chakra, the energy center just above your head. The light is streaming down and around all of your body. Letting yourself feel it like a warm blanket or a cocoon; nestling into it.

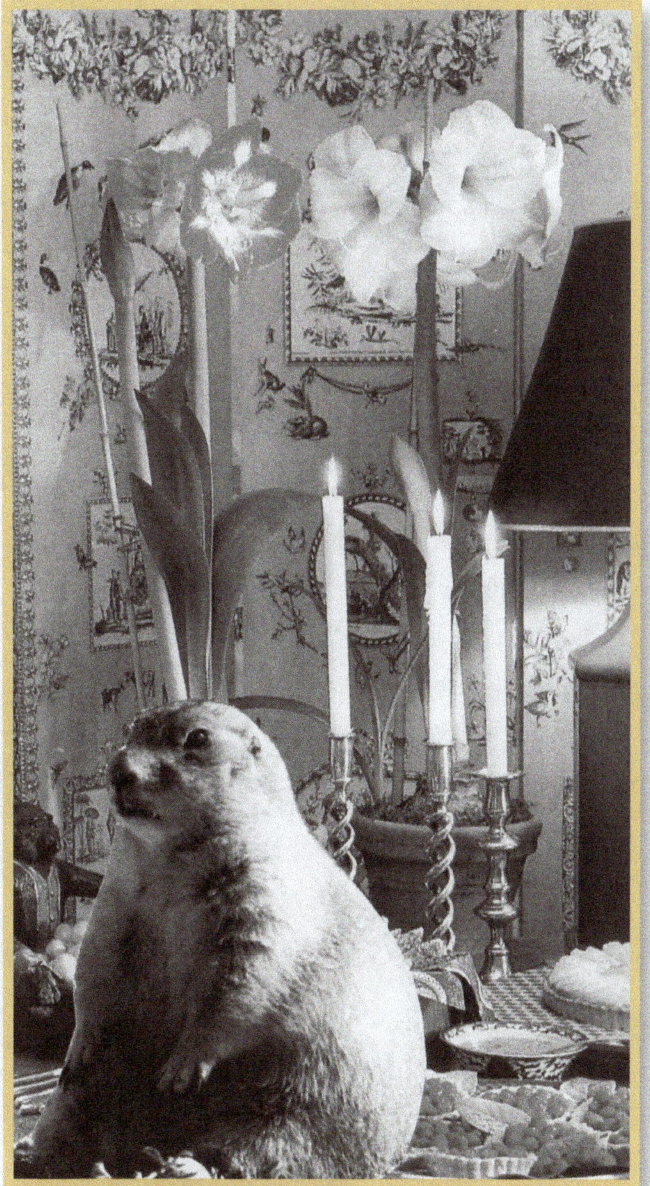

TITLE: **Second Chakra**
SUIT: **Companions**
CREATOR: **Lyda Lettunich Hayes**

"*I Am One Who* loves candles, flowers and colorful fabrics. I savor seasonal food and good wine."

Resting in this space, letting it widen and open into a vastness that connects you with all existence. Breathing and relaxing. (Pause)

Now the golden light is streaming down from this seventh chakra energy center into your sixth chakra, your third eye. Here is your intuition and your wisdom. This space contains your vision both into the future and back into the past. It is a far-seeing place. Breathing into this sixth chakra, feeling it open. (Pause)

Now letting the golden light stream down from this energy center into the fifth chakra in your throat. Feeling this place receive the vitality and warmth of this light and letting it open wide. Here is your ability to communicate what you deeply know; here is also your ability to receive what you choose to receive from outside yourself, and to let it serve you. Relax and breathe into this energy center in the throat.

Now allowing the golden light to stream down from this energy center into the fourth chakra, your heart. Feeling this place receiving the light and opening to it. Breathing and relaxing. Feeling the vast openness of your heart. This is your place of compassion. It is the place from which you both give and receive deep and abiding love. Breathing into this heart energy.

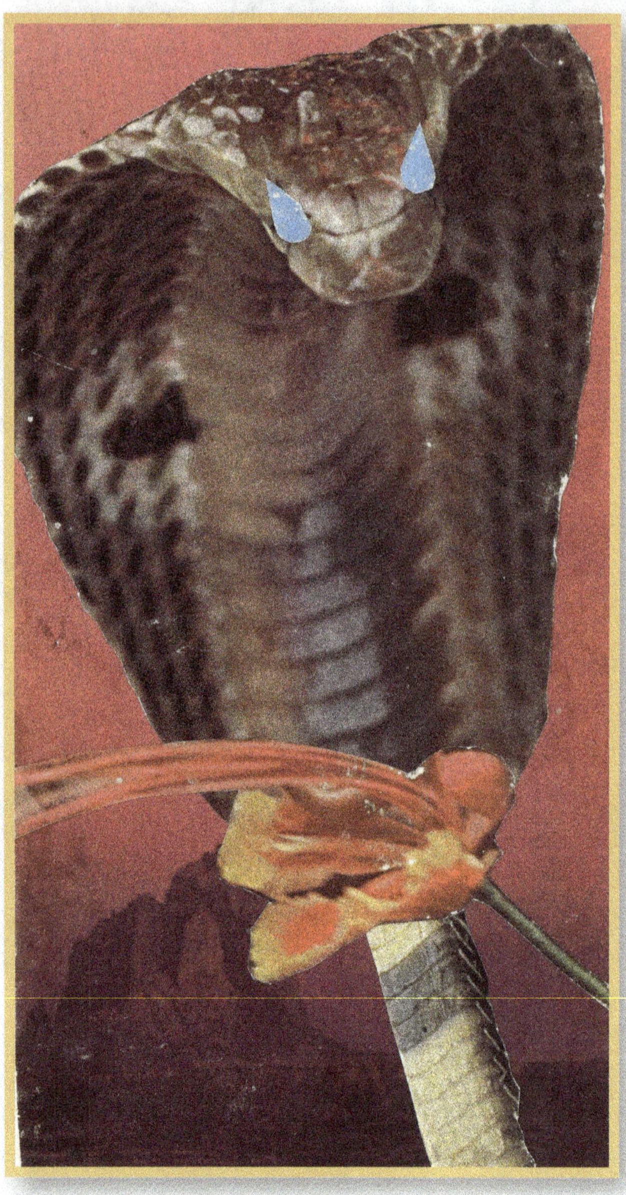

TITLE: **Sixth Chakra**
SUIT: **Companions**
CREATOR: **Meg Gorney**

"I Am your inner eye, the One that can see your life's invisible, unfolding themes and patterns Follow my lead as I point out the direction to go."

Now letting the golden light stream down from this energy center into the third chakra, your personality center. Feeling power and vitality swirling in this center and breathing into it. This is the place of your ability to set boundaries and maintain them as you need to. It is a powerful place from which to act and to compete when that is useful. Breathing deeply into the third chakra.

Now letting the golden energy stream down from this energy center into the second chakra, your place of creativity, your vital sexuality, and your passionate likes and dislikes. Here also are residual energies from your ancestors. Feel this chakra's energy flowing freely. Breathing into it.

Now letting the golden energy stream down into the first chakra, your root chakra. Here the energy from above meets the energy coming up from the earth; they are mingling and blending right here in your foundation center. This is the place of your material well-being, your ability to survive and thrive in this world. Breathing into this chakra and feel it opening.

From this first chakra imagine gazing up along your spinal column and seeing all your chakras glowing and opening. Breathing and relaxing. (Pause)

Now letting yourself ride this energy upwards until you come to the ____ chakra. [Here name the chakra you choose to visit this time unless you choose to explore the first chakra.] *Stopping here, entering into this energy center and being still in it for a few moments, looking around, watching, seeing what the landscape is like… breathing…waiting.* (Pause)

Now allowing the animal or being who lives in this chakra, for you, to make itself known. Staying alert and watching and listening. You may see it or you may hear it, or you may feel its presence. (Pause)

Letting the sense of this animal become clearer and clearer. (Pause)

If no animal or being comes right away, staying open, waiting and watching. If several animals come in, letting them show themselves until one of them seems to be the primary being living here. One of them will have more energy for you, so stay with this one even if it is surprising and not the animal you might have chosen. Trusting what comes in for you. (Pause)

If you are sensing or seeing an animal, if it feels right, gaze into this animal's eyes if it will permit you. Then, reaching out and touching it. Using all your senses. Smelling it, feeling it, hearing it, seeing it. (Pause)

Now allowing yourself to imagine actually entering the body of this animal and, through its eyes, looking back at yourself. (Pause) *Allow yourself to imagine moving within the actual body of this animal…if it runs, running with it, if it flies, flying with it, if it crawls, crawling with it, if it swims, swimming with it, if it walks, walking with it. Experiencing this movement as deeply as you can in the cells of your imaginal body.* (Longer Pause)

Now returning to your own body and again looking deeply into your animal's eyes, ask it three questions:

What do you have to give me? (long pause)

What do you want from me? (long pause)

What symbolic gift can you give me to help me remember? (long pause)

Now taking a moment and thanking the animal of this chakra for appearing to you. Blessing it and asking for its blessing. Saying goodbye, promising to make a SoulCollage® card to honor it. Promising to visit it again, and to nurture its energy and to use it.

If no animal or being has appeared to you during this meditation, allowing that to be all right. You can visit this chakra another time. Perhaps the being is not ready to reveal itself.

Now, beginning to return to full awareness and returning for a moment, to the first chakra, your root, and closing it down just enough so it is safe to return; then to the second chakra, your creativity, and closing it down just enough so it is safe to return; and then to the third chakra, your center, and closing it down just enough so it is safe to return; and then to the fourth chakra, the heart of compassion, and closing it down just enough so it is safe to return; and then to the throat, your ability to communicate, and closing it down just enough so it is safe to return; and finally spending a moment in your seventh chakra, feeling your oneness with all that is, breathing into that Oneness. Then closing this crown chakra just enough so it is safe to return.

Taking your time, come back to normal consciousness, stretching your arms and legs, opening your eyes and looking around. Taking all the time you need. Grounding yourself. Beginning to feel the energy of this physical place, and of the other beings around you.

After this visualization it is a good idea to write down what stands out from this experience, especially the answers to the questions if you have received them. If you are with a group doing this process, it is valuable to share together what animals appeared, what the experience was like, and some of the answers received. If the group is small enough, do it together. If it is large or time is limited, do this in partners.

Now you can call back your *Critic* who has been out having a cup of tea and a good time. Hopefully, it has not been bugging you about what was happening, or not happening, in this visualization.

Write down, or if in a group, share together what animals appeared, what the experience was like, and some of the answers received.

CHAPTER 8

The Council Suit

THE ARCHETYPAL DIMENSION

The fourth suit of a SoulCollage® deck contains cards for the Council of archetypes *who are actively at work and at play in your unique Soul*. The Council is the most mysterious of the four suits. Very often these Neters will show up energetically in powerful images you choose to collage together, but then they resist being pinned down with a name or with words. They may seem to resist containment on one card and require several to describe their aspects. This is especially true if the archetype has a major presence in your life story, if its energy ebbs and flows, and if it is sometimes shadowed and sometimes balanced. The magnetic energies of archetypes pull you beyond your little local story while weaving your story into the Larger Stories being played out in the world. Therefore, expect that the archetypal cards you create will have a mythic power that feels vaster and more compelling than your other SoulCollage® cards. This bigger-than-life quality helps you identify them as Council cards after you create them, and distinguishes them from Committee Neters whose energy may feel similar. It feels similar because these personal Neters are often your archetypes' willing or reluctant vehicles.

TITLE: **The Fool**
SUIT: **Council**
CREATOR: **Mili Dillard**

"*I Am One Who* leaps into life with child-like zeal and confidence."

When you work with your Council images in readings, you will want to do it with special reverence and also, again, with openness to surprise. These Neters have more power to bring transformation than other Neters; they generally speak in the subtle language of the heart rather than the language of the mind, the ego, or of other people. Don't expect them to be predictable and reasonable. When you do risk consulting them, they can help you with hints about the essential patterns of your life stories: their potentials, their changing plots, their primary directions. With attention and practice, you may catch glimpses of how your personal life patterns are being woven into the world's Larger Stories. Archetypes do the weaving of all mythic and universal stories, and we, each one of us, are the threads with which they weave.

Not only are archetypes metaphors, they are metaphors whose images grab us and direct us.

What is an Archetype?

Some of you are probably asking "what really is an archetype?" And it's not an easy question to answer. All definitions fall short because the word points to something indefinable and at the same time real. Archetypes are like *universal patterns* of energy, appearing in every culture across time, yet known by many different names. They are *invisible* energies until they take on some sort of form within a person or community's life story; they are *silent* until they express themselves in dreams, poetry, myths, music or intuitive voices from the unconscious. And they are *numinous* with a compelling and vital energy. C. G. Jung was one of the first modern thinkers to recover the concept of archetype, and to remind us of its once prominent place in ancient philosophies. He hesitantly defined it this way: *The concept of the archetype…indicates the existence of definite forms in the psyche which seem to be present always and everywhere… In addition to our immediate consciousness, which is of a thoroughly personal nature…there exists a second psychic system of a collective, universal, and impersonal nature….* Jung called this system *the collective unconscious* and believed that it consisted of many archetypes.

James Hillman, a master teacher of archetypal psychology, states that archetypes are *metaphors* rather than things, and that *they are best met and experienced with images.* He says "archetypes throw us into an imaginative style of discourse." Not only are archetypes metaphors, they are metaphors whose images grab us and direct us. Hillman says in his book, *Blue Fire:*

> *One thing is absolutely essential to the notion of archetypes: their emotional, possessive effect, their bedazzlement of consciousness so that it becomes blind to its own stance…An archetype is best compared with a god. And gods, religions sometimes say, are less accessible to the senses and to the intellect than they are to the imaginative vision and emotion of the soul.* (p. 24)

The One and the Many

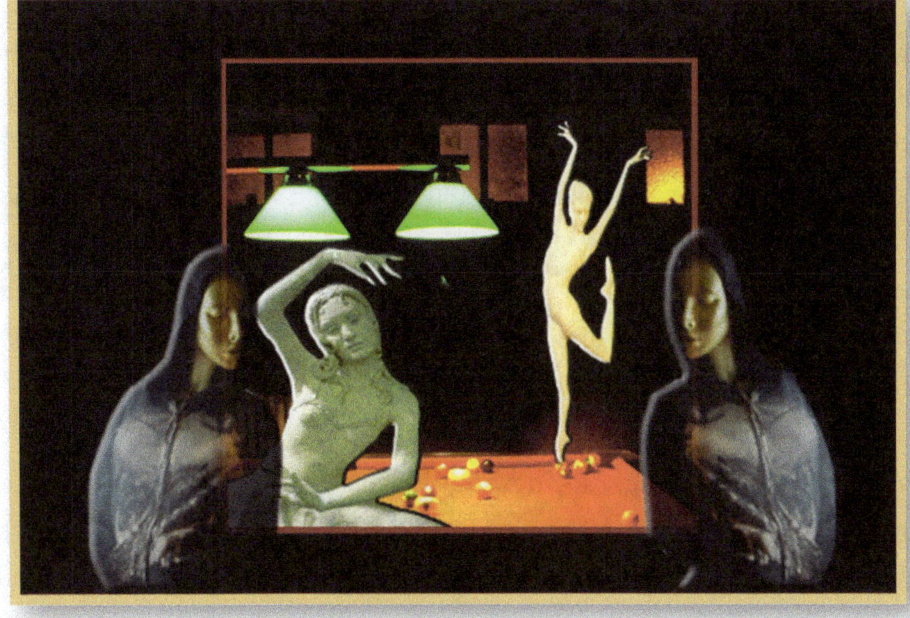

TITLE: **Night Child of Albert Street**
SUIT: **Committee**
CREATOR: **Lee Prouten**

"I Am One Who stands on the edges of society."

If the Council suit in SoulCollage® consists of archetypes, and if archetypes are comparable to gods, then how does this fit with the strongly monotheistic religions, Judaism, Christianity and Islam? Let me speak briefly to that question here because it may concern some of you.

I've already spoken of this, in the chapter on definitions, but I will say more here. In ancient Egypt there was a word, *Neter*, and this word meant, first of all, One Divine Source beyond all creation, formless, mysterious, and silent. A second use of the very same word, *Neter*, indicated the archetypal Neters who came forth from the Source, and were cosmic energies that took on many different forms, and had many names, in human history. These Neters were revered and feared and called upon by humans. They were known as gods and goddesses, angels or demons, who helped people, guided them and often challenged them. They were numinous and powerful beings and had energy and intention for the humans whom they chose to visit. These archetypal Neters also had the potential for Shadow if they got off balance, grew too intense or obsessed, or were absent when needed.

So, we see how, in the consciousness of this ancient Egyptian civilization, there existed *a middle realm* of many archetypes as well as the higher realm of One Source behind everything and beyond form. Here again is the paradoxical concept of the One and the Many. One Source and many Divine manifestations from Source.

Source is not one specific divine being with a gender, language, emotions, personality and laws. However such invisible beings do seem to exist in our world, and, in this book, I have chosen to call them "archetypes" which was the word C.G. Jung used to describe them. Others across eons have named them with other words: gods and goddesses, angels and demons, ghosts or simply divine guides. Such forms came into existence as soon as humans began asking questions about life and death, past and present, right and wrong. Intuited responses to these forever yearnings have been written down by philosophers, religious thinkers, prophets, mystics and poets for untold eons. Many civilizations named these archetypes individually and worshipped them as gods and goddesses, each with different attributes. When the Hebrews began their great experiment with monotheism, which continued on into Christianity and Islam, many of the archetypes or attributes of the gods were attributed to this one God. He alone was Creator, All-Powerful King, All-Knowing Wisdom, Judge, Punisher, Warrior, and also Forgiver and Merciful One. This God did have a gender, and many of the feminine attributes of the goddesses were not included in his personality such as fertility and the aliveness of nature. Also not included was the possible existence of Shadow.

C. G. Jung who was Christian and also a psychiatrist and a student of many cultures, reintroduced to Western thinking what he called the *middle realm* which is this realm of the diverse and powerful and sometimes destructive archetypes which are metaphorically like 'gods' and 'goddesses'. This realm lies between the realm of matter and physical forms which we all are familiar with, and the realm of Oneness, Spirit or Source, which is invisible and formless and without Shadow.

In SoulCollage® we make three cards for the Transpersonal realm, cards that point to the formless Source. In the Council suit each person creates cards for multiple archetypes from the middle realm. These are actual forms like invisible patterns; they move through history and within the consciousness of human beings. They may have Shadows and may lose their balance as do the Neters of the other suits, but on a grander scale. We probe our histories, our dreams, and our passions to recognize the ones playing roles in our personal stories, either as guides or challengers.

Selecting Your Archetypes

Who should you include in your Council suit? Because this is a personal deck and not a deck designed for everyone to use, you will make cards for the archetypes that compel you and guide you, ones your heart responds to most strongly. Right at this moment you may not know who they are, but your deep Soul knows. Trust your intuition.

You will make cards for the archetypes that compel you and guide you, ones your heart responds to most strongly.

You may feel gripped by the *Warrior* aspect of the divine, or feel held by the love of the *Mother* or *Father* archetypes, or inspired to teach by the *Lightbearer*, or drawn to medicine by the *Shaman Healer*, or be constantly searching for truth led by the *Pilgrim*. You may be a student of the laws of the *Law Giver*, or a *Penitent* who seeks to escape the wrath of the *Judge*. I will give you a list and more descriptions that will help you understand these mysterious Neters and how to recognize ones that have chosen you, chosen to energetically inhabit your personal Soul.

The list I am about to give you will be a prompting for your unconscious, but you will not make cards for all of them. Certain ones seem to choose certain Souls, most likely drawn by the coding of the SoulEssence in that Soul. Therefore you will develop your own constellation. Some may come into your life and bring strong energy and direction for a time and then move on; others may stay present, or in the wings, for a lifetime. Many lay claim to individuals through the family or community or religion in which they are born and raised. Yet there are always archetypes that act differently from the norm, and who enter through one person to disrupt the regular patterns of a family or community.

TITLE: **Fairy Queen Messenger**
SUIT: **Council**
CREATOR: **Wendy Grace**

"*I Am the One Who* appears through the elements of nature to tell you all nature is alive. I Am here to speak of the force and magic kingdoms of nature and help you bring this creative power into your life."

Since these archetypal patterns are constantly flowing through the cosmic unconscious, and, at a very deep level in personal psyches, we humans usually remain unconscious of which ones are working through us. Initially we have little choice about these powerful Neters; they choose us. But as we become more awake and conscious of the energies guiding us, we develop some intentionality so we can work *with* rather than against them. Also we can work to find balance when an archetype's energy threatens to consume us. It is a bit like surfing a vast ocean wave where balancing skill is needed to safely ride it, and also skill in getting off the wave before it hits a rock. As we become more conscious of our Soul's coding, we can learn to call in an archetype that we desperately need, one who is there in our depths but seems to be sleeping. *Forgiveness* might be an example. Or *Courage*. Or *Patience*. Consciousness brings degrees of selectivity, but not unlimited amounts for these are strong energies with directions of their own!

If the *Great Mother* archetype chooses to grab your Soul, you will be drawn to nurturing and caring for the young and for any being that needs nurturing. If the *Warrior* archetype is strong in your psyche you will be passionate for just causes and in protecting people and the planet. When the *Creator* claims you there will be the urge to manifest new forms, over and over, and let them go. When either the *Fool* or *Death* enters your life and interrupts the story which your Committee Neters may be constructing, you will not be able to say "Thanks but no thanks." In other words, our local Neters cannot command Council Neters. Still, with consciousness, moments of balance can be found. Again, it is like being a good surfer riding a big wave!

What you will do as you create Neter cards for your Council is *image, name, honor, and consult those archetypes* that you recognize in your life story. Often you will be drawn to images that represent deeper and more elusive archetypes—ones who live on the far fringes of your consciousness. These flit in and out, inviting you, or daring you, to engage with them more consciously.

Assume, as you begin working on Council cards, that you will make several. Some archetypes have always been present in your life. You will remember how they influenced you even in childhood. Others may have been active in one phase of your life and now, seemingly, have moved on. Still others may just be arriving to conduct a new chapter of your life story.

The archetypal images which leap out and grab you will be more mysterious than Committee images. They will have a universal quality with ancient symbols and mythic figures, less defined than the Neter beings of the other suits. Often images will be strange metaphors for these invisible forms.

As you collect these images and collage these cards you may not know who or what you are imaging, and the cards can remain unnamed for a time. You may suspect that an image is a Council Neter and is inspiring your life in a big way, but you still may not know its name. *Honor the unknowing* and do not force the Neter into articulated form too soon. Let the meaning incubate, change, unfold.

A Partial List of Archetypes

I will give you a list of names, simply to help you begin thinking in archetypal terms. Then I will speak more in depth about a few of them.

The Great Mother
The Loving Father
The Law-Giver/Judge
The Fool
The Wise Old Woman/Man
The Divine Child
The Creator
The Warrior
The Witch
The Dreamer
The Healer
The Pilgrim
The Seeker
The Teacher/Guru
The Savior
One Who Descends and Returns
The Tribal Chief

The Pattern Keeper
The Hearth Tender
The Lightbearer
The Waterbearer
Mother Earth/Gaia
The Hero/Heroine
Anima/Animus
Eros/Agape
Power
Greed
Death
Grief
Necessity
Patience
Forgiveness
Compassion
Gratitude

These and many more are universal archetypes that have been recognized and named by cultures and religions over centuries. Some you may choose to name with names from ancient myths like *Hestia* or *Penelope* for the *Hearth Tender*, *Cupid* or *Aphrodite* for *Sexual Love*, *Kwan Yin* or *Mary* for *Compassion*, *Inanna* or *Christ* as *One Who Descends and Returns*. You can certainly use names from your culture or faith, e.g., *Christ the Savior* or *Great Mother Mary* or *Buddha the Teacher*, or *Shiva the Destroyer*. The major Arcana of the Tarot deck will suggest archetypal names such as *Empress*, *Hierophant* and *Magician*. You can also use more general names like some of the ones listed above, *Grief*, *Forgiveness*, or *Gratitude*, and you might even make up names. However, personalizing your Council archetypes with the form and name of a mythic being will help you meet the energy it contains more personally, feel its numinosity, and receive its power to guide you. It is easier to participate intuitively in images of a Neter than using a collage that has no beinglike forms in it. Plus, very often the mythic story about the named being will help your life patterns in your own life Story.

There are many current books describing archetypes. Some that I especially recommend are suggested in the back of this book. However, I will spend a few paragraphs here describing some Council archetypes often found in SoulCollage® decks.

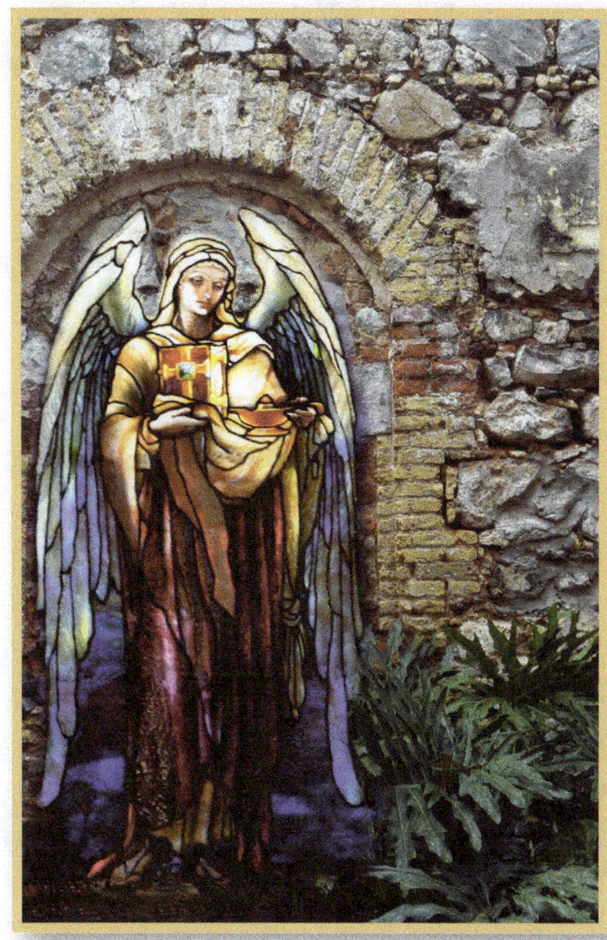

TITLE: **Angel of Compassion**
SUIT: **Council**
CREATOR: **Laren Leonard**

"I Am the One Who says, 'the cycle of the heart is to love, lose, and risk loving again.'"

The *Great Mother*

This may well be the oldest of all archetypal forms, appearing repeatedly in ancient agrarian cultures. She is fertility. She controls the cycles of nature, including the cycles of the human body. She is caretaker of the young and of those in need. She is patient yet sometimes very fierce. She sacrifices for her children, even her own well-being. She is unconditional love. In ancient Egyptian lore the goddess, *Sekhmet*, is a fierce and fiery Mother, the most powerful of their many gods. *Mary*, the Christian Madonna, is also an expression of this archetype, one much beloved and worshipped in many countries. For some Christian women and men, *Mary* is the most powerful and present archetype in their lives. She is the symbol of comfort, forgiveness, and compassion. Images of her abound, and she is often found in SoulCollage® decks.

The *Great Mother* has had many other names throughout the ages: *Demeter, Isis, Kwan Yin, Parvati*, and others. She has strongly influenced the lives of women and men of every culture, through eons. She is sometimes frightening in her fierceness as is *Sekhmet* (*The Terrible Mother*). But more often she is *Abundance* over-flowing. She is *Nurturance*. She is the *Giver of Life* itself.

The magnetic energies of archetypes pull you beyond your little local story, while weaving your story into the Larger Story being played out in the world.

History tells how male *Warrior* archetypes arrived in her peaceful and agrarian territories, brought by bands of migrating herders and hunters, and they conquered her territories and her devotees. Over time they forced *Great Mother* and other feminine archetypes underground, or reshaped them into consorts or daughters of their masculine deities. *Athena* is an example of a powerful female goddess that was later imagined as emerging from the head of *Zeus* and therefore subordinate to him. *Lilith* was the first, mythical wife of Adam who was wild, sexual and independent. She did not make it into the orthodox canon, but was reshaped into the archetype of *Eve* who was a somewhat more compliant wife and mother.

One SoulCollage® Facilitator, Suska Davis of Washington state, has created a large SoulCollage® deck. She writes this about an experience on a trip to Israel:

> *As an attempt to stay grounded I packed a few SoulCollage® cards, mostly Mother figures, for my trip to Israel. The journey, a peace-making mission, was intense. In between witnessing the severe conflicts between the Israelis and Palestinians, we visited sacred sites. There I felt pulled beneath the varied layers of history where the "Great Mother" awaited me in her beauty and her anger. She let me know both her love and her displeasure with the conflicts. Finally, she assisted me in a symbolic personal rebirth which left me with a sense of peace. I felt gratified about the depth of healing I received which perhaps was shared with the people of that torn land.*

The ***Witch***

This archetype needs explanation because of her bad press. "Witch" comes from the word *Wicca* which means *wisdom*. She is usually a feminine archetype, and she is a lover and protector of the earth. She is midwife to all births and deaths without sentimentality. She is at home traversing in the darkness of the underworld and relishes the mystery and power that she finds there. She knows how to recognize and also how to grow and administer healing herbs. Her wisdom includes magic, ceremony, and the health and well-being of the physical body. She uses her knowledge primarily to benefit the living beings of the earth including animals, which she especially cherishes. She is never squeamish about blood or vomit or excrement as these are part of nature itself. The depth of her wisdom of the earth's cycles is awesome, as are her vitality and fierceness in protecting the earth from abuse and neglect.

The *Witch* archetype, because of her native powers, her link with darkness, her fierceness, and her femaleness, was frightening to those men whose wisdom was of the mind and of light and spirit rather than of the body and the earth and of darkness. There have been several persecutions of the *Witch* archetype, and one began in the Middle Ages spearheaded by male heads of the Christian Church. She is still persecuted by fundamentalists of more than one faith. Women influenced by this archetype are not easy to keep within any church's ecclesiastical rules. Their practices may be outside of the strict dictates of scripture so women in touch with *Witch* energy may be considered evil and thought to be aligned with the demons of the underworld. Many have been put to death. Some still are.

Persecuted, the *Witch* archetype went underground. In the last century and currently, she is remerging in identifiable forms. Once more she is being named. Her energy is arising in many women and some men—people who cherish the earth, its wildness and special gifts. Her fierce, dark, feminine energy is rising to balance the light and wisdom of masculine archetypes that are closely associated with sky and Spirit.

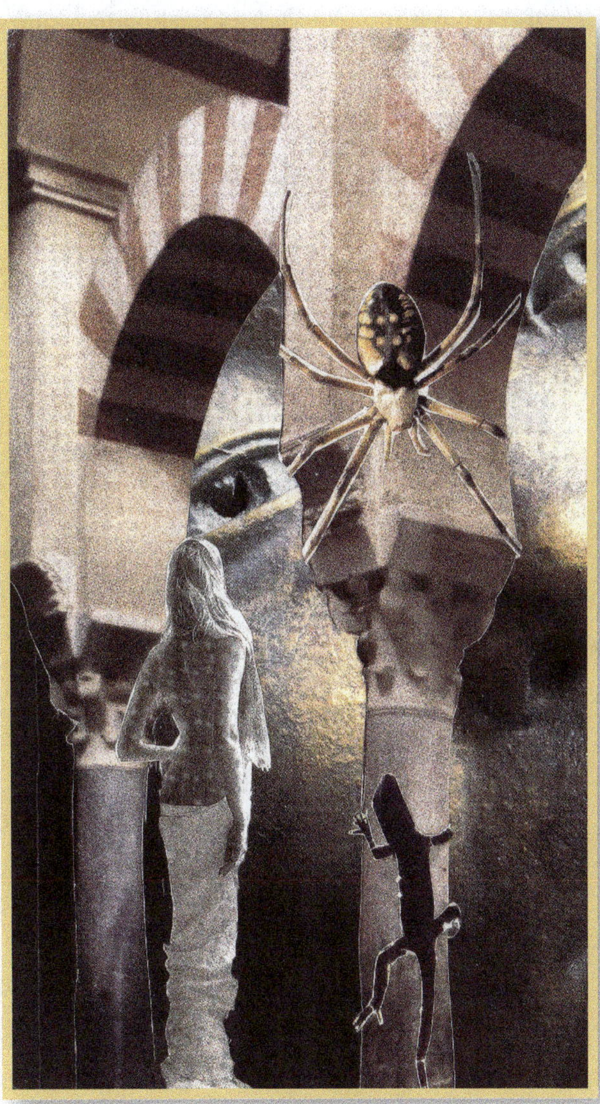

TITLE: **The Inner Feminine**
SUIT: **Council**
CREATOR: **Meg Gorney**

"I Am Meg's soft Feminine Soul peering out at her rough exterior self looking in."

The *Creator*

This archetype can easily be confused with *Source*, the Oneness that is the ground of all that is. Source does not exist in a form, but rather is the source of every form. One such form is the being we imagine creating the universe. Humans have always revered this archetype, so in most religions there is a central *Creator* archetype. In some it is imaged as male, in some as female, in some as animal. In all of them this Creator energy is manifesting. The male *Creator* of Genesis speaks words and the universe is formed out of the void. *Female*

Creator archetypes create from their bodies. They birth the universes. In some cultures there are myths in which *Creator* is an animal who drops pieces of itself and these form into parts of the universe.

The main attribute of the *Creator* archetype is action. He/She creates and creates, again and again, and each time lets go of the creation, sending it out and on its way. The *Creator* does not deliberate or worry or demand payment. The *Creator* cannot *not* create. Some humans (artists, musicians, dancers, decorators, writers, etc.) are caught by the energy of this archetype, often from childhood, and spend much of their time creating. It is as if their life connection depends on manifesting their ideas and feelings in some new form which others will see, hear, feel, and experience. When these artists get caught up in marketing their creations, or in holding them close for fear they will be copied or stolen, these are either signs of the shadow of this archetype, or they are signs of ego Neters working in these people and casting Shadow on the *Creator's* energy.

The Warrior

The *Warrior* is another universal archetype, known in every culture and one which is both revered and feared. The essence of the *Warrior* energy is "passionate protection". In every tribe there must be warriors who protect the tribe and especially protect the women and children because in them lies the future. However the *Warrior* archetype may show its Shadow or negative side by acting with unnecessary violence, or by aggressive rather than protective action. When the *Warrior* archetype grabs someone, and it grabs women as well as men, it is usually in the service of a cause. The *Warrior* is alert to danger, especially when it comes close to children, to the poor, to the earth, to animals, to the atmosphere. Then it marches forth to stop the violator. Imagine the man defending his wife and family against an invader. Imagine the teacher who risks her life in an inner city school. Imagine the ship that goes into hostile waters to stop the killing of whales. Imagine…and here you may fill in the space with your own just cause, one you are passionate about. Social activists are people possessed by the *Warrior* archetype. So are suicide bombers. One may or may not agree with the cause they embrace, but there is no denying the vitality and passion with which this archetype infuses those whom it claims. And there is no avoiding the Shadow when we become conscious and step back; then we can recognize the exaggeration of the *Warrior,* first in ourselves, and then in world leaders.

The Wounded Healer / The Lightbearer / The Shaman

These three archetypes are not exactly the same, but they overlap as archetypes often do. All three take the Souls they claim on journeys between the worlds. Although these people may be firmly grounded in this world as healers and teachers, at the same time they will travel out far beyond themselves, engaged in difficult quests. They go beyond the normal, sensible world to find the "light" whether it be a cure or wisdom or some other impossible dream, and then they bring light back to the world to benefit others. A symbolic physical posture might be with one hand stretching upwards to the sky while the other hand reaches downwards to the earth. They are, at the same time, dreamers and realists. And sometimes they are wounded in their journeying.

Jesus, when on earth as a human being, was inhabited by all three of these archetypes. First, he was *Wounded Healer* who healed others while he himself was wounded even to the point of death. Second, he was *Lightbearer* as he brought a new and special teaching to the people, light to "people who walked in darkness." Finally, he was seen as *Shaman*, as one who traveled safely between the worlds, dying and going even to the underworld and coming back alive to bring hope to the world.

Journeying between worlds is an often a repeated theme in the myths of the world.

This journeying between worlds is an often a repeated theme in the myths of the world. *Orpheus* was a mythic figure who traveled for love to the underworld and returned with wisdom to help others. However, he could never heal his own wounds. *Prometheus* was part god and part human, a *Lightbearer*, who stole fire from the Olympic gods and carried it to earth so humans would not perish. He was sorely wounded for this act by an angry *Zeus*. A female goddess, *Inanna*, Queen of Heaven in ancient Sumerian mythology, also left Heaven and descended through seven gates to the underworld where she was finally killed. After three days she was rescued, rose from the dead and returned to Heaven to rule with even more wisdom and power because of her journey.

There are many other myths and stories in world cultures showing the continuing presence of these three powerful archetypes.

Many of us who are teachers, therapists, doctors, nurses, hospice workers, and so on are held in the grip of one or more of these archetypes. We know them so well, and have known them for so long, we forget that archetypal energies are inspiring our life choices and weaving our stories deftly into the Larger Story. We are pulled by archetypes such as these towards the manifestation of our SoulEssence, that personal coding in our deep Soul.

The Waterbearer

I'll speak briefly of the *Waterbearer* archetype because she is especially powerful to me personally as a guide and ally. If you are intrigued and want more, check on the SoulCollage® website, soulcollage.org, and look for articles I have written. One is about the *Waterbearer* and a gallery exhibit that several of us mounted to honor this particular archetype, and to teach about her. Many people contributed their cards for this event because many are inspired by her, especially women. I say *her* because I believe this archetype is another of the rising feminine archetypes of this new age, rising to *balance* strong masculine archetypes such as *Lightbearer* and *Warrior*. The *Waterbearer* is the logo for the Aquarian Age, and although this being is often depicted as male, I believe this is inaccurate. After all, which gender has been the primary carrier of water in cultures over centuries? The energy of this archetype is

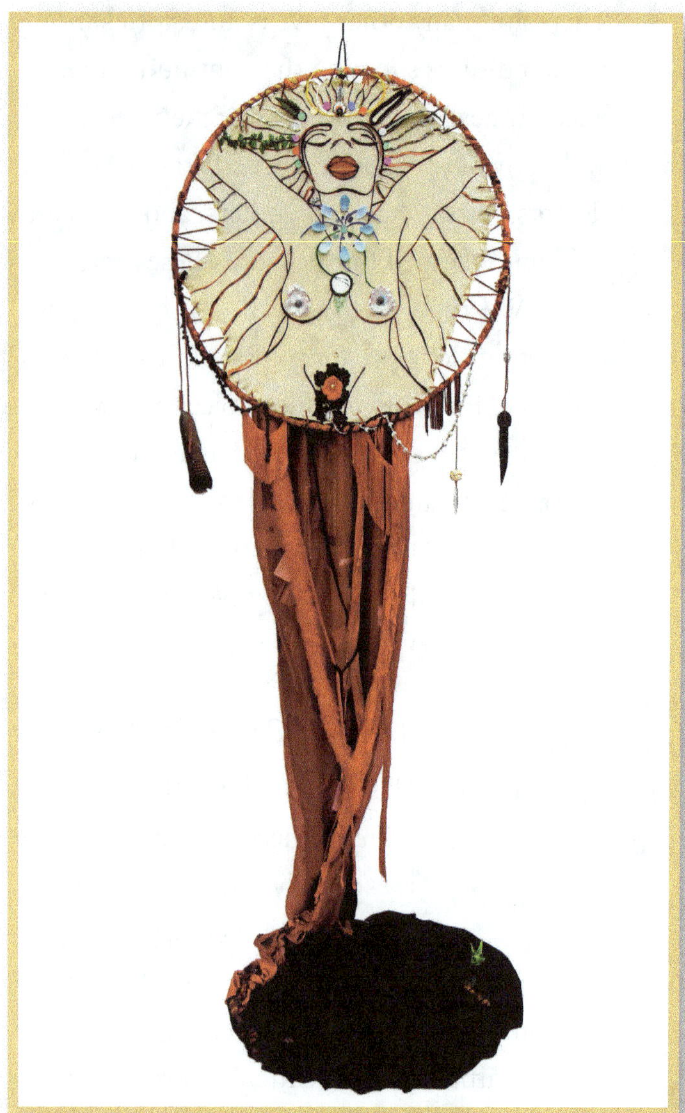

TITLE: **Celebration**
SUIT: **Council**
CREATOR: **Kira Jones**

"Celebration is my name. I release my joy into the world for all to see and feel!"

more of the earth than the sky, and she brings water to a thirsty land and a thirsty people. This archetype comes in to guard and protect the sources of water on the planet, physical and spiritual water, so beings can continue to live. She is passionate about water! In a sense she is a feminine version of Prometheus but bringing water instead of fire. For thousands of years now the *Lightbearer* archetype, descending from the heavens, has been prominent in cultures across the globe, perhaps so strong as to have become Shadowed. The earth is drying up from too much heat, and perhaps with too much light from the human mind; it is not balanced with water from the heart. And water on Earth is seriously threatened. The *Waterbearer*, as a feminine archetype, brings the water of compassion and of relationships and of caring for all thirsty life. Sometimes she teams up with the *Warrior* in the cause of protecting rivers and oceans around the globe. One goddess that has embodied this archetype for centuries is *Kwan Yin* who is often shown pouring water from a jar which she holds in front of her.

The Wild Woman and the Wild Man

These are two archetypes which have reemerged in the late twentieth century. Like the Witch they were forced underground for a time by science and by religion. Their essential energy is insistence on freedom, and innate wholeness. The *Wild Woman* and *Wild Man* insist that their humans are already whole beings and do not require another human being to complete them. They would say that living with a partner can be wonderful, but is not necessary to their happiness.

These archetypes seem more primitive and instinctual than some of the others. This energy, when it grabs a person, may bestow the experience of wild joy in nature, in dance and in traveling freely, without many possessions.

Clarissa Pinkola-Estes has described the *Wild Woman* archetype in her book, *Women Who Run with the Wolves,* and Robert Bly has described the *Wild Man* in his book, *Iron John*. In Greek mythology the virgin goddess *Artemis* is an example. The apocryphal *Lilith* is another.

The Fool

I strongly recommend that everyone make a Council card to honor the *Fool* archetype because he has made and will make many uninvited visits into your life. His usual purpose is to awaken a Soul, and usually he feels like an *Interrupter*. The *Trickster*, the *Court Jester*, *Coyote*, and the *Heyoka* are versions of the Fool archetype. He turns things upside-down in our lives, generally to our dismay and bewilderment. Most Committee members do not want to be interrupted when they are busy with their projects and plans. The *Fool* punctures our complacency when we are too sure, too proud, too pompous, and especially when we have gotten off track from our coding. Also when we've gotten lazy. This archetype is usually imagined as masculine in the history of cultures, just as the *Witch* is most often imagined as feminine. However, there may well be female *Fools* who grab and awaken people, so you are free to use images from either gender, whichever seems to fit for your *Interrupter*.

Pay attention to the Fool when he comes and spins you around. His usual purpose is to awaken a Soul.

One reason the *Fool* is associated with the masculine is because he is also associated with Spirit. There is a sense that this archetype enters a life from above. He descends and grabs us for a round of his special dance. He is never predictable, and he often has a sly humor which seems to imply, "Don't take yourself so seriously!" Usually the *Fool* enters a life quickly and leaves again quickly. We may be left flat on our backs, figuratively or literally, wondering what hit us and why. Later we may be able to look back and see how a seeming disaster gave us a needed gift or changed our direction. Then, if we are awake enough, we will appreciate it. So pay attention to the *Fool* when he comes and spins you around. Look for his truth. Remember that, of all the people in a King's court, only the *Court Jester* dared tell the King the truth and escape punishment—usually. And only a *Heyoka* dared to make fun of a Chief. The *Fool* is on your side, so make a SoulCollage® card for him, and learn to recognize him when he arrives in your life. Dance with him and laugh with him. Ignoring him is dangerous business.

Death

Your Council suit cannot be complete without acknowledging the archetype of *Death* and making a card for it. The essential energy of Death is transformation. Like the Fool it is an Interrupter. Unlike the Fool, it has little sense of humor, and the losses and changes experienced in this transforming experience may be greater than those the Fool initiates. This, of course, is true whether you are experiencing

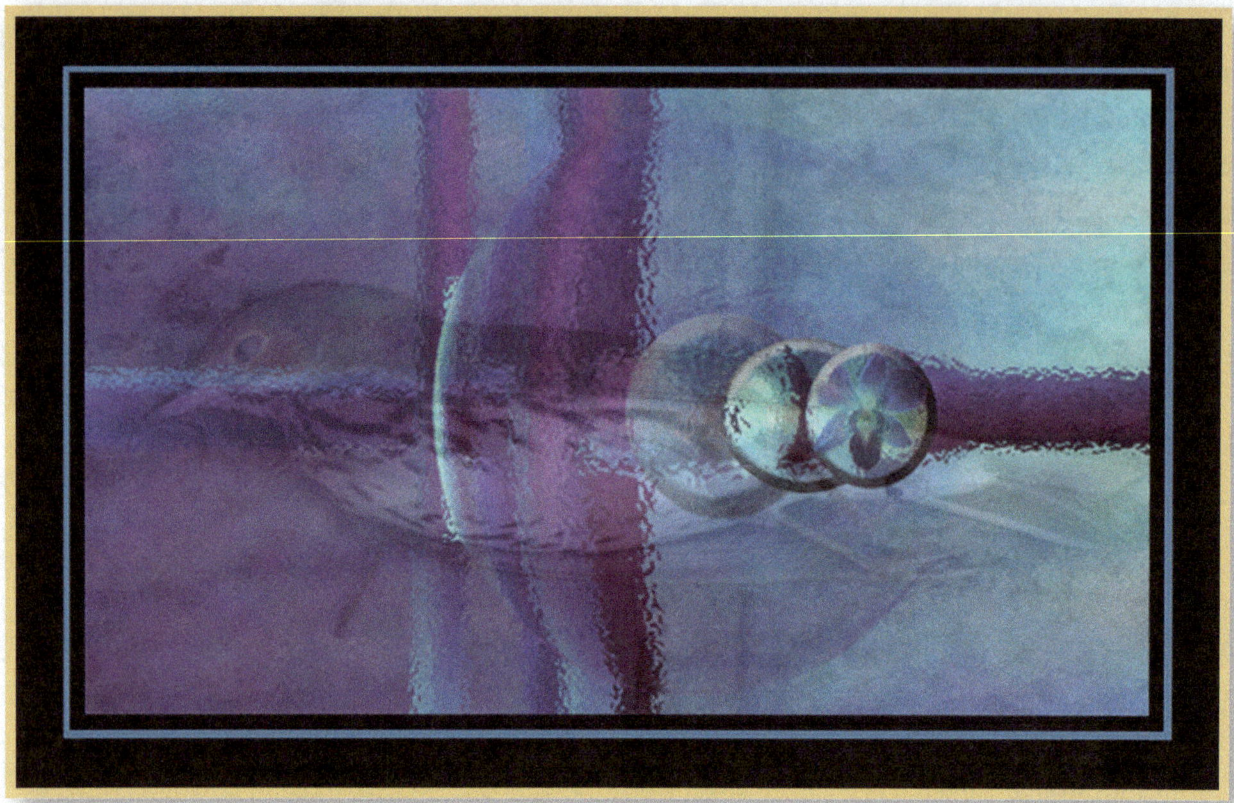

TITLE: **Transcending Death**
SUIT: **Council**
CREATOR: **Lee Prouten**

"I Am the sparrow who reminds you of Death. When it comes (even to the smallest creature), it offers opportunity to transcend one's earthly state."

the archetype directly in your physical body or experiencing it with another person. And there are transforming deaths that are not of the physical body but of dreams, relationships, jobs, or other endings.

When this card is drawn in a reading, its energy has something to do with moving on, leaving something behind, or some kind of change. The images that you choose for this card will reflect your deepest sense of this archetype, its benignity or its ferocity, its transitory nature or its finality.

Gathering Your Images

As you gather images for your Council suit, let your intuition do the browsing, and not your analyzing mind. Leaf through magazines or piles of torn-out images, letting your less conscious Soul reach for what is powerful, numinous, and mysterious for you. What calls to you may seem curious and strange to your logical mind. "Now why do I like, or fear, this image so much?" you may wonder. Don't try to figure it out, but go ahead and pick it up. Later cut the image out, find a new background and glue it on your card, thereby acknowledging its call to you. Create your card almost from a dream state. It does not have to be complex with many images, or even aesthetically beautiful. Simple can be powerful as you create cards for your Council, and indeed for all the cards of your deck. Later, when you are speaking from the card's image in a reading, or journaling from it, you will begin to see who this Neter is and be able to give it a name. It is also possible of course, that you will intuitively recognize who this Neter is from the first moment the image appears. It may grab you while screaming its name into your inner ear! Either way is fine for the creative process.

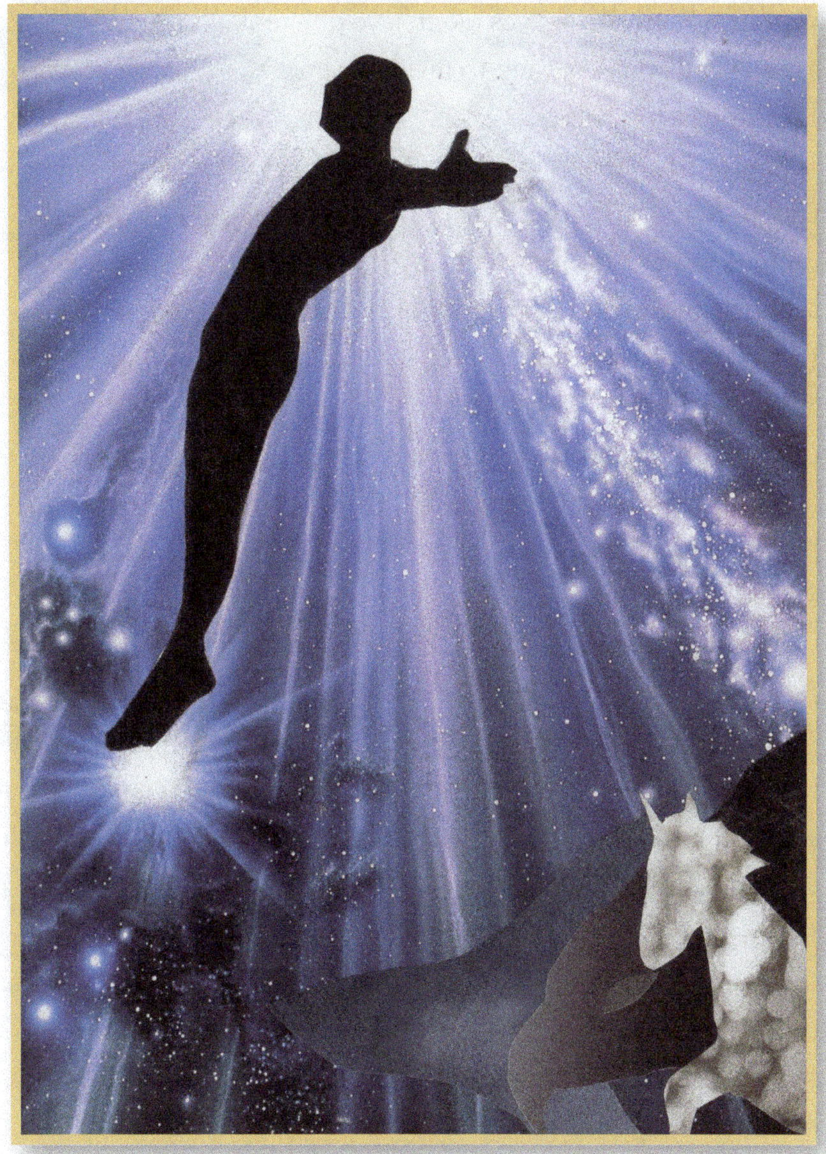

TITLE: **Death**
SUIT: **Council**
CREATOR: **Mariabruna Sirabella**

"*I Am the One Who* is diving up into the light."

Can You Have More Than One Card for One Archetype?

Let me emphasize again that this is a personal deck, and you won't make cards for every archetype you can name. Concentrate on cards for the big ones whose energy moves strongly in your life story, or for ones whose energy is there but seems asleep, and you want to arouse it in your soul.

An example of this last might be the archetype of *Gratitude*. The vital energy of *Gratitude* is transformative is all life stories, so, if it is sleeping, it would be well to awaken it with a card of its own. Its energy then could use your Committee member named *My Grateful Self* as its disciple and emissary.

Your Council suit may include two or more cards for big ones that energize and direct your life. These archetypes often have different aspects and you may want to make separate cards for each aspect. For example, one person for whom the *Pattern-Keeper* archetype is very prominent has three different images on three cards: *Dancing the Pattern*, *Cooking the Pattern*, and *Sorting the Pattern*. Each of these cards reflects an aspect of this one compelling archetype that grips and guides her soul. Another person has images for the *Feminine Creator* on one card and the *Masculine Creator* on another. There could be a *Fierce Warrior* card and a *Gentle Warrior* card. In my deck I have an *Old Fool* and a *Dancing Fool* and also a *Feminine Fool*. I cherish all three cards, and each interrupts me in a different way. When I draw the *Old Fool* it often has to do with the "surprises" of growing older. The *Dancing Fool* is more energetic and demands that I still participate in the dance and not sit on the sidelines and watch. Sometimes he is really annoying in his insistence. The *Feminine Fool* is gentler and has more to do with the surprises of nature and of emotions.

When your death card is drawn in a reading, it has something to do with moving on, some kind of change.

When you have several cards in your deck you can begin to do readings with them, individually and, hopefully, in small groups. Then the hidden messages of the cards will bubble up and amaze you. The Council Neters have a central energy that stays constant, like the *Creator* energy is always one of manifestation; their answers to your questions, however, will be different each time, and often exactly what you need to hear. It will be as if you are taking a kaleidoscope full of all the bits and pieces of your life and holding it up to the light. There, even as you look, the unique patterns are falling into place. You can see the changing beauty of your story.

Here are just the last few lines of a poem, one that it is definitely about bringing into consciousness the central archetypes of your story. It is by D.H. Lawrence and is titled "Song of a Man Who Has Come Through."

What is the knocking?
What is the knocking at the door in the night?
It is somebody wants to do us harm.
No, no, it is the three strange angels.
Admit them. Admit them.

CHAPTER 9

The Shadow Side of Neters

In preceding chapters I have often mentioned the Shadow side of our various Neters, and, in the section on definitions, I gave you a preliminary description. Now I will discuss this important subject in more detail. If we are aiming to become conscious individuals we must look unblinkingly at negativity when it creeps into our personal lives and into the fabric of the world. This is a problem that philosophers and theologians have pondered ever since thinking began. Whole philosophies have been constructed around the problem of evil, and why it exists and persists. SoulCollage® enters into this collection of ideas with a way of looking at negativity which is a synthesis of spiritual and psychological points of view.

TITLE: **My Restored Self**
SUIT: **Committee**
CREATOR: **Pam Renner**

"*I Am One Who* has endured destructive elements fueled by fear and rejection."

Every Form Has Shadow

First, *our spiritual understanding*: In SoulCollage® we say that *every form* that exists, invisible and visible, energetic and material, is manifested from one mysterious and formless Source and therefore is, because of its origin, *holy*. This includes archetypal forms of our Council suit, as well as all the Neters of the other three suits. Each one has its own unique form; some exist in the invisible middle realms of human and cos-

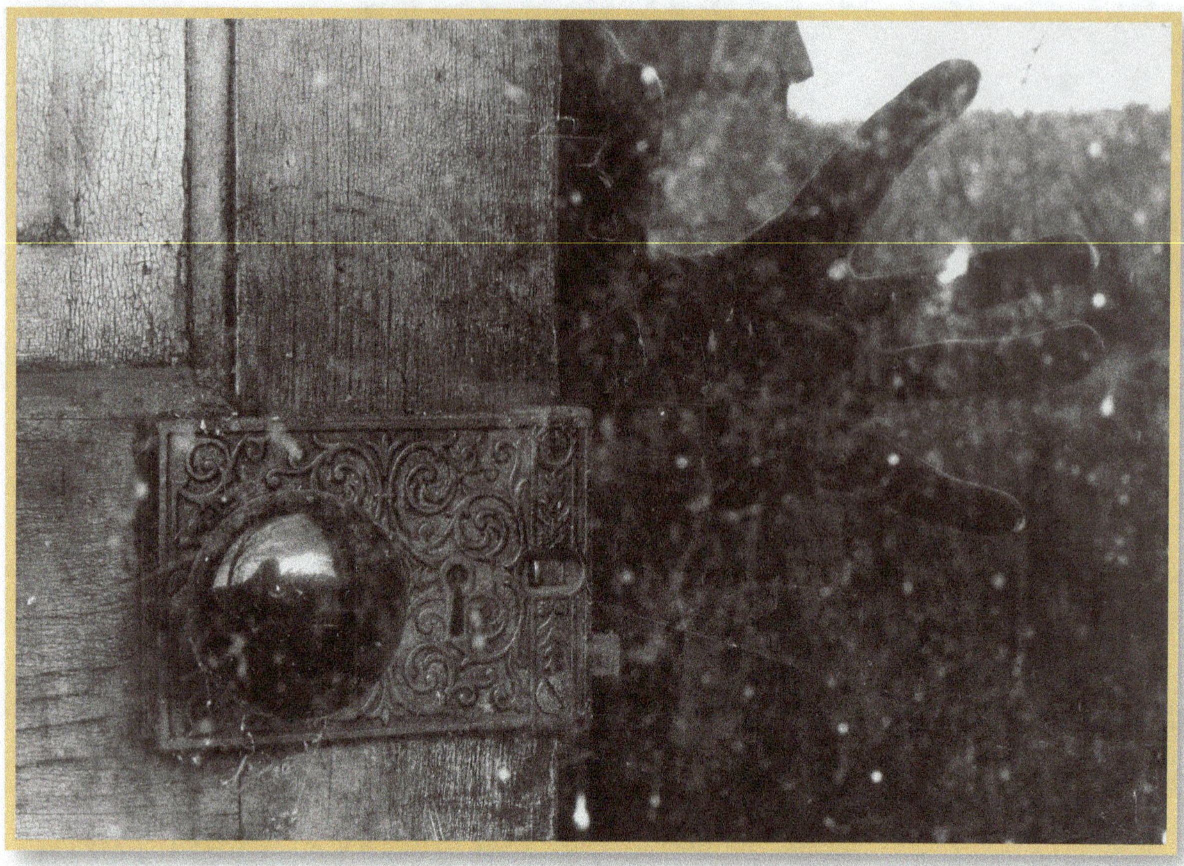

TITLE: **The Other Side**
SUIT: **Council**
CREATOR: **Laren Leonard**

"*I Am the One Who* haunts your heart and mind with the unanswerable question, 'Where did they go?'"

mic consciousness; the rest exist in the visible realms of matter. All these forms, these Neters, are interrelated because of their common origin from Source. At the same time, all of them, as long as they are in an individual form and thus partially separated from Source, *have the potential and the freedom to lose their balance.* Human beings seem to have more freedom than other forms in this matter of balance. This does not mean that humans are necessarily off balance, but that they can become that way, and when they are off balance it makes for sickness in individuals, communities, and throughout the planet. It produces degrees of negativity. The more the imbalance, the more the negativity.

This understanding is different from dualistic models of reality which draw a strong line between good and evil, seeing a cosmic war between them, with forms lining up on one side or the other. More in the tradition of mystics from every faith, SoulCollage® sees every form as a mix of positive and negative, and this mix constantly shifts as the density of imbalance changes. Good and bad, therefore, can be understood and worked with as a matter of losing or gaining balance. Central to this is the spiritual understanding that all forms issue from One Source, all are holy, and all forms have the potential of reaching a balance that will allow them to fulfill their essential imprinted design.

Shadow Is Out of Balance: Too Much or Too Little

For the *psychological point of view,* SoulCollage® turns to C. G. Jung and his followers, particularly James Hillman. Jung called the ill-health of forms their *Shadow*. He realized from his work with patients that out-of-balance energy in human psyches is also vital and passionate energy. It arises out of our primitive and instinctual nature. It is energy that resists the repression of civilized ways. This very often becomes exaggerated and self-centered energy, but it can also be strongly creative. It is energy that has "gold" in it, Jung said, because it is so filled with raw vitality. But it is also energy that can hurt the self and others when it expresses itself in unbalanced ways, especially in the terribly unbalanced ways of hate, greed, violence, and reactive fear. Most people work hard to forbid expression of Shadow energy in their external behaviors; we repress its urgings into the darkness of our personal unconscious. We "forget" it exists hidden there, and we refuse to look at it because it is so uncivilized and contrary to our ethical values. If it is pointed out, we will deny it. One way we unconsciously expel this repressed Shadow energy is to criticize that very fault in others. This is called "projection" in psychological lingo.

> *As long as we refuse to recognize Shadow in ourselves, we are in its power.*

So, to summarize this basic position, *SoulCollage® sees the Shadow as vital, primitive energy that is out of balance.* It can be exaggerated and out of control, or it can be absent when needed. Too much or too little. If this sounds like too mild a description of the "evil" you see in the world or in yourself, let me emphasize that the Shadow of every Neter can become very out of balance and very deadly. But much of its deadliness comes from its unacknowledged and unexamined nature. As long as we refuse to recognize Shadow in ourselves, we are in its power.

Our Responsibility in Working With Shadow

What then is our personal responsibility for working with the Shadow in ourselves?

1. First, our own Shadow needs to be recognized as being there potentially or actually within each of our Neters. We can work on this responsibility by naming Shadows and including images of them in our SoulCollage® deck. Their grip on our Souls begins to loosen the moment we let our consciousness shine on them; it loosens more as we dialogue with them.
2. Second, these Neters are to be investigated closely enough that they can be mined for the gold of their vitality. This is done by listening to their history and hearing what they deeply want when they act in shadowed ways. What are they afraid of? What are they trying to make happen? Can their powerful energy be put to other, better uses?
3. Third, they must also be held to account and brought back into balance for the good of the whole self and of others around us, our families and communities, and the world. Like a child out of control, they must be embraced, disciplined, and redirected.

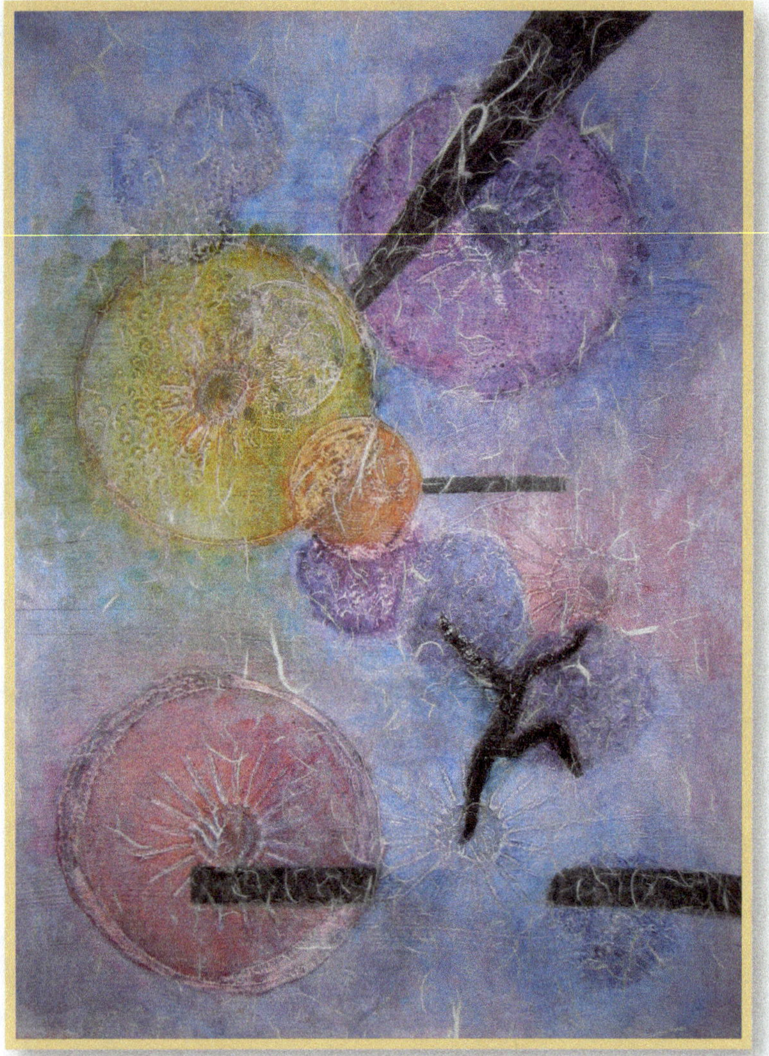

TITLE: **The Journey**
SUIT: **Committee**
CREATOR: **Carol McNamee**

"I Am One Who has broken free and embraced the journey."

This "both/and" way of dealing with Shadow is central to SoulCollage.® Even one personal Neter that I refuse to recognize and work with towards better balance can impact the balance of the whole of creation. We are that interrelated, that interwoven with each other.

To summarize then, we must pay attention to the Shadow sides of our Neters because they won't disappear by our ignoring them. They will simmer in their negative, off-balance energy, and find new ways to erupt and express themselves. Your Observer Committee Neter has a responsibility to take a flashlight and descend into the darkness of your less conscious self, and find the repressed and shadowed Neters living there. SoulCollage® is a tool.

Rumi's wonderful poem called "The Guest House" has these final lines:

The dark thought, the shame, the malice,
meet them at the door laughing
and invite them in.
Be grateful for whoever comes
because each has been sent
as a guide from beyond.

Making a Card for Your Protector Neter

After several years of doing Shadow exploration in workshops, we have found that having a *Protector* SoulCollage® card to serve as a supportive ally is valuable when you go on this recovery journey. It can be a Committee member that you would designate as the *Protecting Self* or a Council Neter like the *Warrior*. It could even be one of your Companion animals or a Community Neter that holds this protecting energy for you. We begin every one of my Shadow workshops by having new people choose a strong image to act as their *Protector*, and make a card with it. Those with several cards already in their decks may select one to serve in this capacity. We work with these Neters so their protecting energy is strongly felt and internalized; then, using the Observer, we begin the work of going into the unconscious. As people meet up with shadowed Neters, this Protector Neter serves as a filter so that strong, negative energies are less overwhelming. It is really quite amazing how this works. Images can serve as very powerful guides and allies in Shadow work, just as they do in the rest of SoulCollage® work.

Refraining From Tempering "Shadow" Cards

Some people have chosen to add some "light images" or "positive" energy to their Shadowed SoulCollage® cards, a little piece of protection right on the card itself, perhaps up in the corner. Let me suggest that you refrain from doing this, and let your *Protector* card be enough. It is best to let the shadowed Neter have its very own card in which to express its "negative" energy fully and without reproach. Don't dilute it even if it is very uncomfortable. Let me quote a SoulCollage® Facilitator, Robin Cooper-Stone of Virginia, who talks about this:

> *I know some people have been hesitant to make "dark" cards, feeling that making and using such a card somehow reinforces the "dark undesirable," and some feel compelled to include a "more positive" energy on their "shadow" cards. However, I've found that integration comes from accepting, listening to, working with, and finally incorporating these "shadow" aspects over time. In my experience, I've found that many cards I'd thought of as extremely negative have revealed unexpected wisdom over time, and in some cases, their meanings have changed — another gift of integration.*

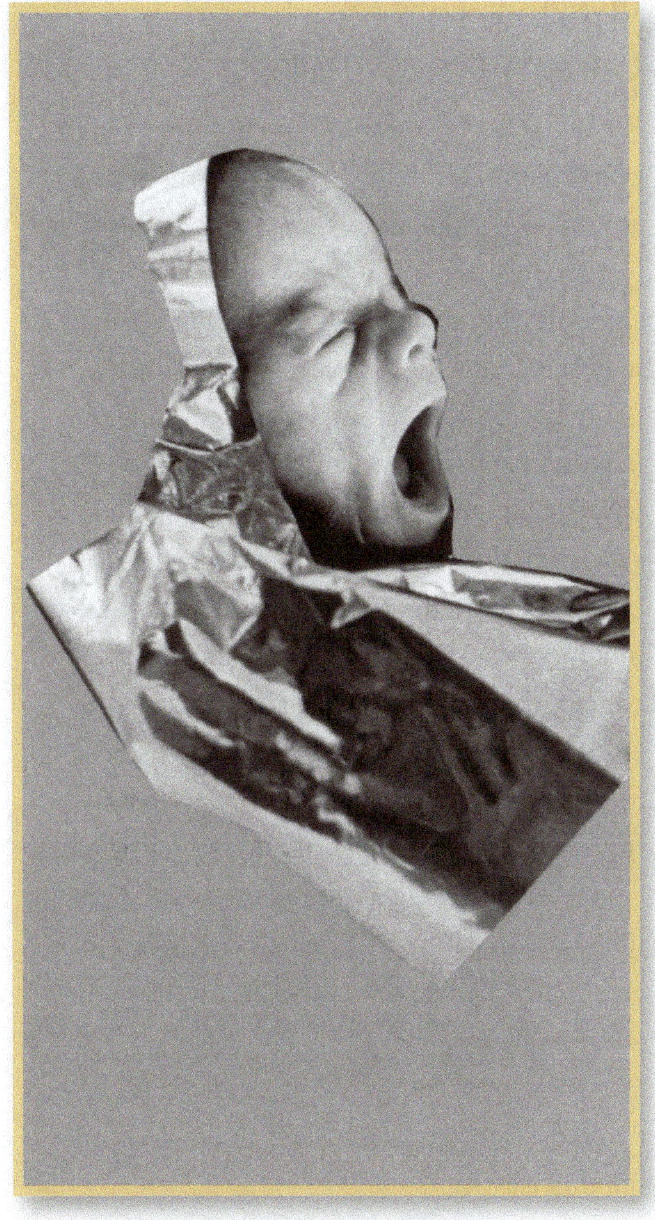

TITLE: **Screaming Baby Self**
SUIT: **Committee**
CREATOR: **Marti Winters**

"*I Am One Who* screams to be heard, to be noticed. I scream to let out my pain. I scream I AM!"

Shadow in Committee Neters

We meet our Shadow daily in the personality parts of our Committee. The mixture of good and not-so-good is fairly easy to spot in these Neters if we are willing to let our *Observer* shine its light on them. Our *Wounded Child* may sleep most of the time but then suddenly become exceedingly demanding. She may fuss so much she stops the action of the whole Committee. Our *Critic*, normally felt as a mean and negative jerk, can be shown how to use its energy to give useful nudges in a nicer way. We notice how our *Judge* becomes so arrogant about correcting someone else's opinions that the person won't listen to us anymore. We see our *Organizer* going from being wonderfully helpful, to acting so compulsively that she shuts down our spontaneity. We see the *Artist* who once loved to create now being self-critical and refusing to paint anymore.

One long-time SoulCollager, Alyson Kennedy, describes a bossy Neter in her Committee this way:

> *There is a shadow side to her and a very good side as well…this is the part of me that is able to assess things really quickly and to get rid of them if they are not going to do me any good…but she also sometimes makes snap judgments about things and has me toss away something maybe I should not have tossed away. Like friendships. Sometimes she's too quick. I have always had this changeable Neter around in my psyche.*

The Ego: A Collection of Essential Parts

Many Neters in our Committee suit belong to what has long been called the *ego*, a word with diverse definitions and connotations. Here is mine. *Ego is a collection of certain personality parts essential for a human's survival in the world.* It is not intrinsically bad or good. We cannot rid ourselves of it, nor should we try. When these Neters act in a balanced way they watch out for our well-being, physical and emotional. Very often, though, they go about their jobs in selfish and self-defeating ways, and therefore the word ego has taken on a negative meaning. But it is the Shadows of our ego Neters which are negative and not the ego in itself. Ego Committee Neters often become greedy and paranoid and wasteful and obsessed, signs of Shadow. These negative traits have to be recognized and worked with to bring them into better balance. We can do this work by having our *Observer* Neter step back and objectively observe without bringing the *Critic* along to judge and condemn. This way we become conscious of shadow activities among our Neters. We can dialogue with them and look for ways their needs can be satisfied without them being so obnoxious. We do not work to be rid of them any more than we would a naughty child. We accept and correct.

It is the Shadows of our ego Neters which are negative and not the ego in itself.

In SoulCollage® we imagine the ego as strong and controlling and as the "I-oriented"

Neters who sit at the head of the Committee table and run the show. Examples of these might be: *Competitor*, the *Judge*, the *Perfectionist*, the *Controller*, the *Critic*, the *Ambitious Self*, the *Rule Maker*, the *Planner*, the *Clock-Watcher*, the *Budget Keeper*, and so on. Every human has a similar ego grouping, and yet each person has a different mix. They will vary in energy, in size, and in the density of their Shadows. Some people will have a big *Controller*, others a much smaller one. Some people will have a huge *Competitor*, and some almost none. The descriptive names you choose for your Neters can be your own choice, and they will vary from deck to deck. They can even be proper names that are fun and which you will easily remember. My *Competitor* is named *Bert the Beat* because he looks tired and worn out from the hard game he has been trying to win for so long. He appears ready to quit the game...but not quite yet!

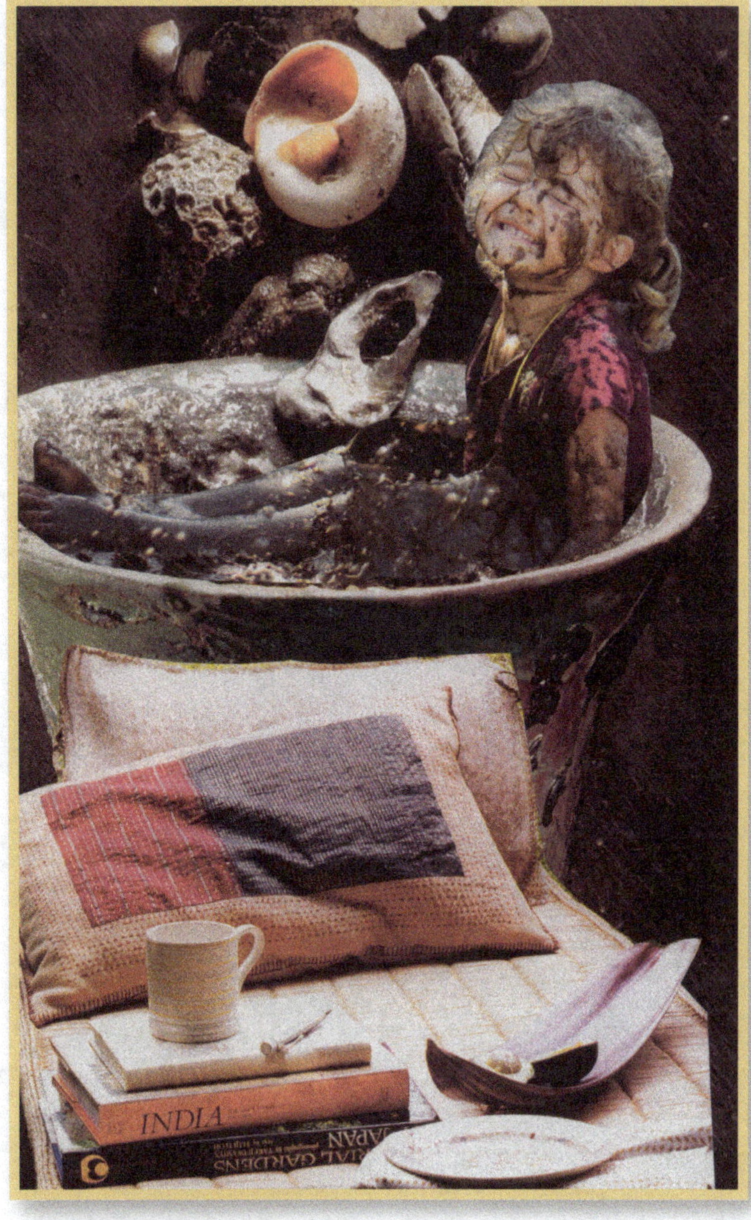

TITLE: **Balance**
SUIT: **Committee**
CREATOR: **Glenda Rice**

"*I Am One Who* reminds you to bring balance back into your life."

A large part of the SoulCollage® process for many of us is this growing consciousness of our ego Neters and the making of separate cards for them. Then we work to bring them back to some degree of balance so they will cooperate and share power, and especially so they will learn to look out for the needs of others as well as of the "I". Finding images and making cards for them, especially the ones that frequently lose their balance, will help you accomplish this. Just having its own card and a name seems to help a Neter relax into a more balanced position on your Committee.

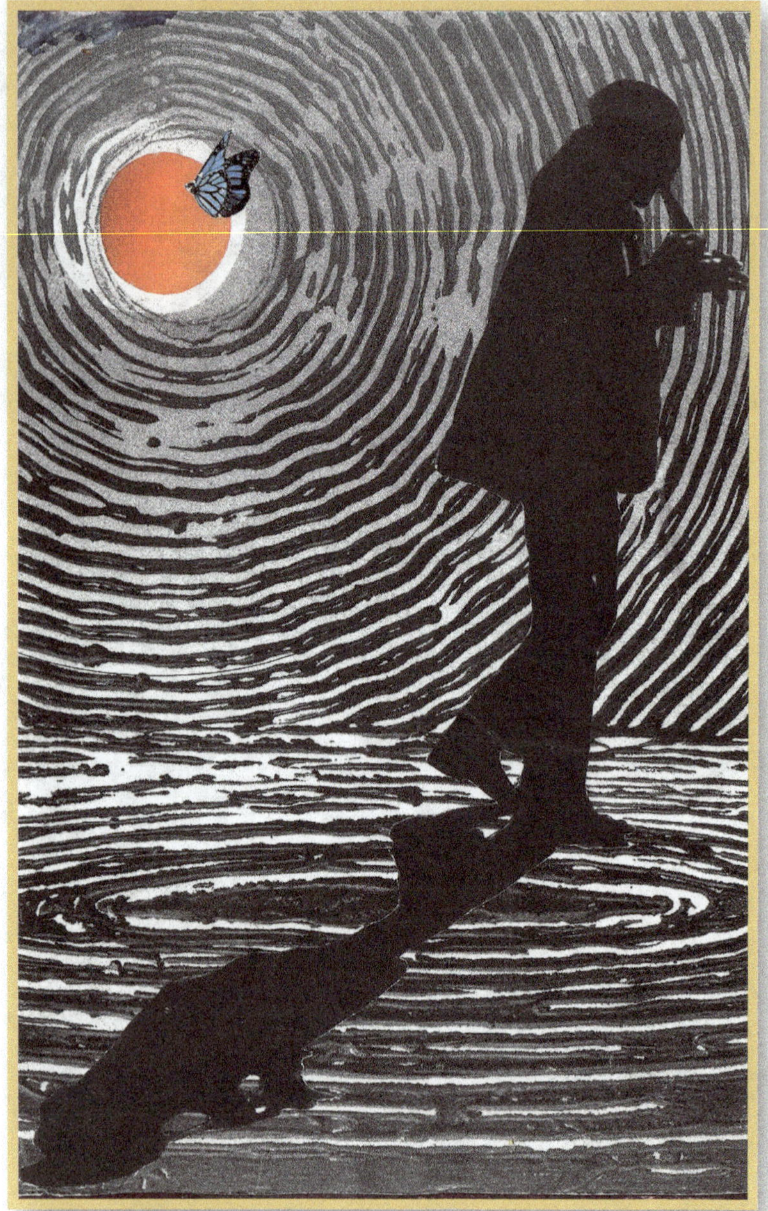

TITLE: **Creator**
SUIT: **Council**
CREATOR: **Dori King**

"*I Am the One Who* walks ahead of you guiding the way. *I Am the One Who* walks beside you giving you comfort. *I Am the One Who* walks behind you giving you strength."

SoulCollage® cards that you create for difficult ego Neters should have images that accurately depict their shadow energy. Don't be afraid to have a few cards in your deck that make you shudder when you draw them. On the other hand, and I want to emphasize this, *it is also important to have humorous images for some of these characters* so you smile rather than frown when you draw them. Often they can be helped back to a balanced way of acting just with a laugh and shrug.

A Few Cautions With Shadow Work

We all have hidden and unconscious inner parts, many that have been there since childhood. Doing this Shadow exploration with intuitive processes such as SoulCollage® will uncover some of these Neters, and the discovery can prove surprising and disturbing. That is one reason I recommend creating a *Protector* card to use while doing this part of SoulCollage® work.

You may discover some inner child parts that are wounded or angry or lonely, and have not been consciously remembered since they were relegated to your unconscious years ago. You may find a humiliated teenager or a raging victim, or one who is sure she is not okay. You may find a part that refuses to accept any blame for anything. Or one who takes on all the blame for everything. When you find such a part of yourself, if you feel able, go ahead and look for images to make a SoulCollage® card for this Neter. Most likely the images will find you. Make a card and then dare to share it with others and try speaking from it. This will help you in the healing and balancing of this part, and in integrating it into your more conscious Committee. Think about what other inner Neters you have in your deck that might listen to, nurture, and dialogue with this part. Place those cards around this Shadowed Neter as part of its healing.

People generally go only to an inner depth that they are able to handle. However, if you are suddenly overwhelmed with a forgotten memory, see a therapist and take your cards with you to help you work with what is coming up. If you are a SoulCollage® Facilitator facilitating groups and are not yourself a psychotherapist, do have ready a licensed referral. Find a therapist who will understand about the use of images in doing Shadow work and SoulCollage.®

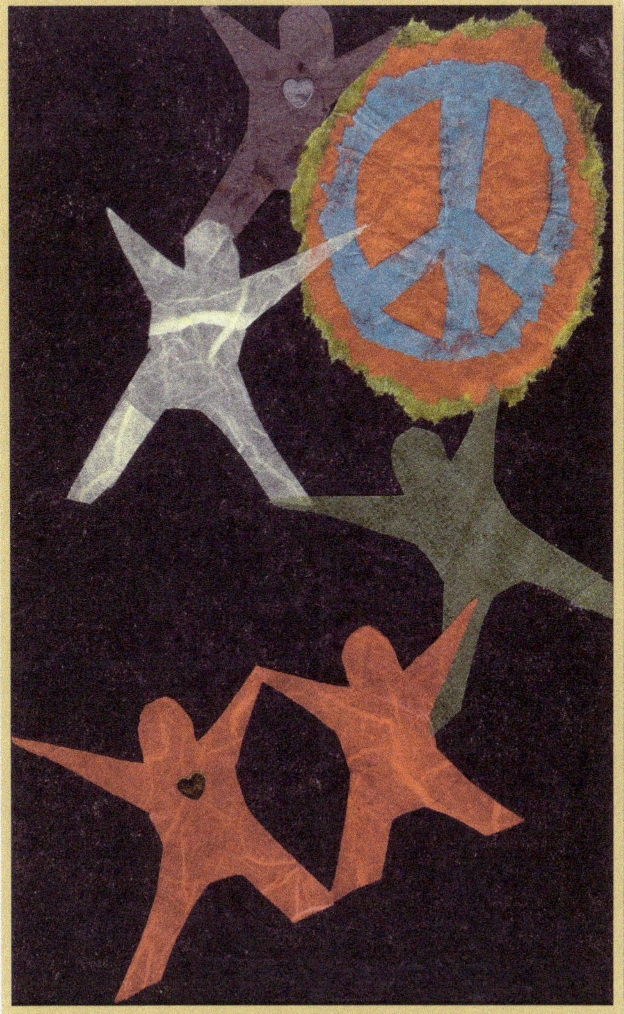

TITLE: **My Resister Self**
SUIT: **Committee**
CREATOR: **Nancy Weiss**

"*I Am One Who* calls my companions together, and together we fight, cry, sing, for peace."

The Shadow in "Positive" Neters

I want to remind you briefly that even the most "positive" Neters, like the *Nurturing Mother*, the *Happy Child*, and the *Observer* can sometimes lose balance and show a shadow side. Again the Shadow usually shows up in exaggeration or in absence. The *Nurturer* can become overbearing in her nurturing and stifle the one she cares for. The *Happy Child* may hide and not show up when her energy is most needed. The *Observer* can overdo its "stepping back" and make you too self-consciousness, so you are always watching yourself. As you create positive cards, let yourself imagine how this Neter might behave if it were out of balance. It is not necessary to put an image on your card to show this Shadow side, but just know that it could arise. The potential is there in every Neter in your deck.

Only the three Transpersonal cards, which are formless and silent, have no potential Shadow.

The Shadow in Community Cards

It is not hard to spot the Shadow in our Community Neters. We choose mostly sentient beings to be part of this suit because of their humor, their passion, their trustworthiness, their wisdom, their love, and other desirable qualities. Yet we also can see how these very attributes, when compulsive, rigid, ill-timed, or missing, can cast a Shadow. And sometimes even their best energy is not useful or healing or wise for us at that moment. Our "outer" Community Neters are not balanced perfectly all the time, just as our "inner" Committee Neters are not. Usually you won't put an image on a Community card that shows this person's Shadow side—not unless that Shadow energy is significant in your relationship—but know that the potential is there.

SoulCollage® sees the Shadow as vital, primitive energy that is out of balance — too much or too little.

The Shadow in Companion Neters

The seven Companions are invisible Neters that are closely aligned with our physical bodies and also our energetic and subtle bodies. For those of you who are kinesthetic and especially in tune with your body, these Neters will be lovely guides and helpers. With practice even those people, who seldom pay close attention to their bodies unless a problem arises, can learn to check in with these Neters, and take some direction towards better physical and emotional balance.

If you have chosen these animal guides intuitively, using the guided imagery visualization, they are likely to reflect energy imbalances just by the animal that came up and how it moves. Instead of rejecting odd or uncomfortable ones, try stepping into their energy and seeing what they can tell you about the balance and flow in this particular area of your body. Is the animal stuck or sleeping or caged or is it moving freely? Does it feel smooth and balanced when you imagine moving inside the animal, or does it feel shadowed somehow with too much or too little energy. This is one way you can discover the Shadow in the Companion Neters.

You may have physical discomfort, pain even, or fatigue and heaviness. Working with the animal "living" in that area of your body may be a way to visualize and assist healing. Beyond the physical imbalances are the more emotional needs located in the subtle body. Here are some of the needs associated with each chakra:

In the **first chakra** there is a need for security and safety.

In the **second chakra** there is a need for regeneration in sexuality, emotions, and creativity.

In the **third chakra** there is a need for a personal sense of mastery and centeredness.

In the **fourth chakra** there is a need to receive and give the *agape* type of love and compassion.

In the **fifth chakra** there is a need to communicate and receive information and wisdom.

In the **sixth chakra** there is a need to intuit and know, and to envision the larger picture.

Finally, in the **seventh chakra** there is a yearning towards Oneness and wholeness.

All of these can become shadowed. The animal in each chakra may be able to communicate to you even before your *Observer* notices an imbalance consciously. Do some work then with the animal of this energy center. This may help balance and heal the emotional need. Dialogue with the animal, enter into it to see what is distressing it and to find out what it needs for healing.

Your Companions cards may ask to be changed as a Neter animal changes, as its Shadow lessens, and as it moves more freely. You may want a couple of images of this same animalon one card, each one showing a different energy. Your Neter animal may even evolve into another, perhaps stronger, animal, and this is fine. Glue a new image partially over the first or make another card and put the old one aside in a separate box. If there is a recurrence of the old state, you can retrieve it.

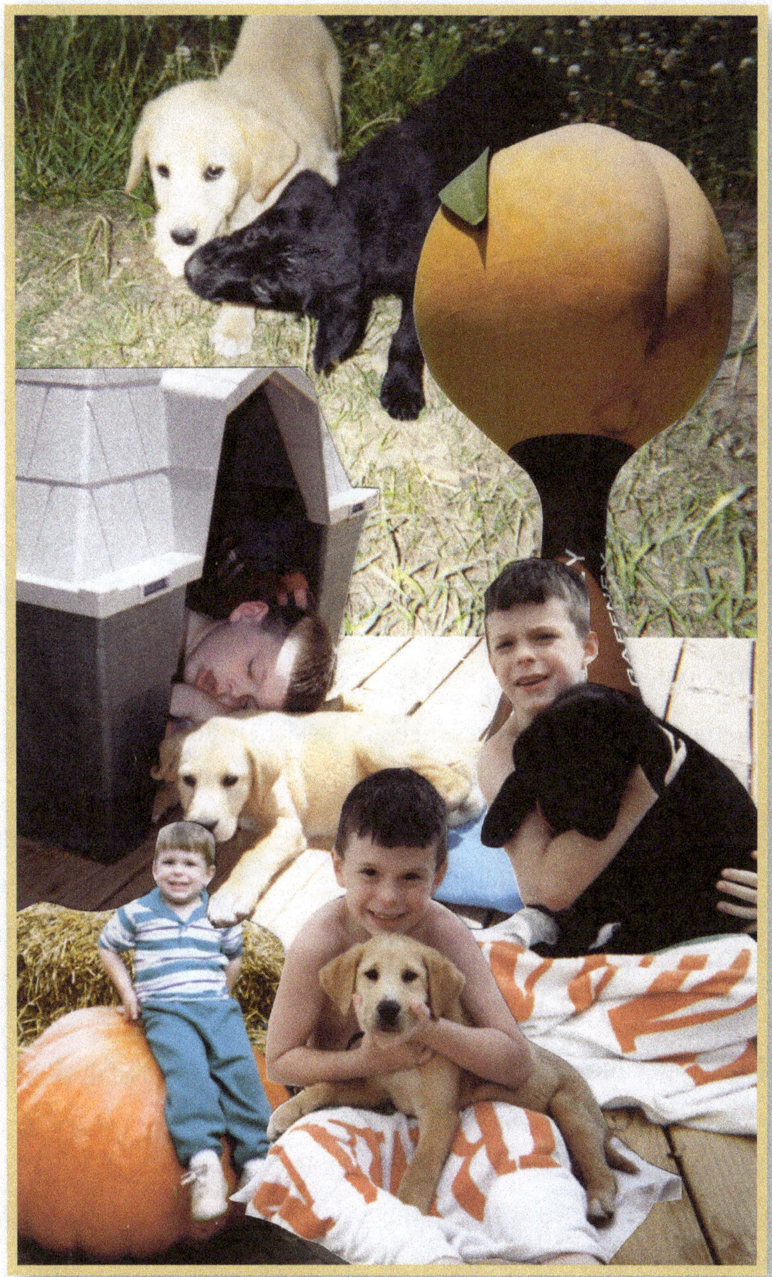

TITLE: **Holding Light and Shadow**
SUIT: **Committee**
CREATOR: **Mili Dillard**

"*I Am One Who* finds that lovingly holding the shadow as well as the light of my child allows me to more compassionately hold myself."

It's a good practice to check in daily with your seven Companion Neters, perhaps just by touching their energy centers in your body.

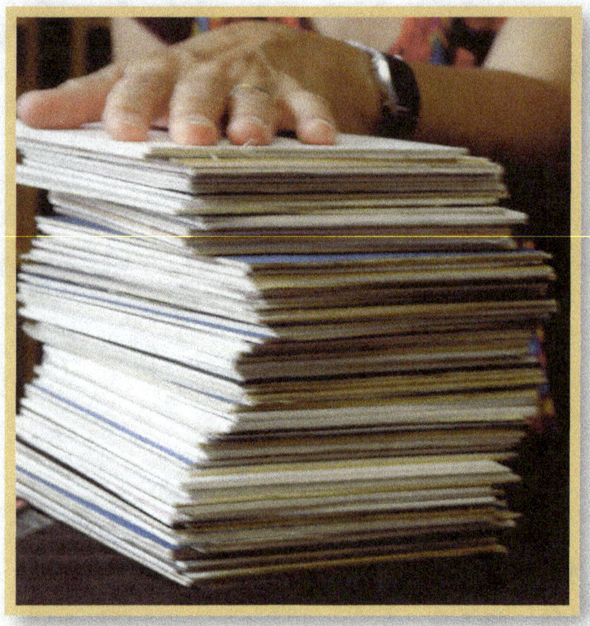

One SoulCollage® deck

Thank them for their presence and ask them to be awake and flowing during this day.

This takes only a minute, perhaps during a yoga practice or meditation.

The Shadow in the Council and in the World

Archetypes move externally throughout history, as well as internally in our individual Souls, and they can display Shadow energy in both realms. Sometimes archetypal Shadow energy is huge and overwhelming both to civilizations and to individuals. Hence we must learn to recognize whether Shadow is present in the Larger Story or just in our own personal story or both. We need to find ways of protecting ourselves, our communities, and our world. As we become more conscious we can help to balance this Shadow even when it is stronger and more overwhelming than our personal Shadows.

Many people have difficulty accepting the actual presence of archetypal forms in the world, and find it even harder to accept this mix of positive and negative energy in them. It's a view of the cosmos that assumes a middle realm of reality, one between our everyday material realm and the vast and formless Source that underlies all existence. This realm is also mysterious and invisible, but it is a realm of real energetic forms. We largely depend on imagination and intuition to access this middle realm, with the help of myths and stories of many cultures over eons. We of the twenty-first century have grown up in a culture where science, rational and materialistic philosophies, and fundamentalist religions have long ridiculed this middle realm, calling such belief superstitious, illogical, not provable, and even heretical. As a consequence, forms of dualism have grown up and underlie most Western thinking; good and evil forms are often seen as very separate. "Either/or" thinking prevails, and wars are fought about who is in— on the side of good—and who is out— on the side of evil. Evil is consistently projected out onto the "other", and exclusive ideologies that create hate and war around the planet have come to rule in many places.

The reintroduction of the imaginal "middle realm" of archetypal Neters, of gods and goddesses, or just vital energetic forms, will help change dualistic ways of thinking. It replaces either/or thinking with a more inclusive and, I would say, more spiritual view. It allows us to again recognize the presence of the many archetypal Neters who have acted in the world throughout history and who are still here with us now. We would do well to turn to both old and new myths to see the imaginative representations of these archetypes. The *Great Mother,* for example, has been known and celebrated for eons. We can imagine her bestowing her abundance, her beauty, her fertility, her constancy, and also watch her as her mood changes, her shadow rises, and she rages or withholds. Remember the Greek myth of *Demeter,* the *Mother Earth* goddess, who became so distraught over the abduction of her daughter *Persephone* by *Hades* that she mourned inconsolably and withheld her nurturance from the earth. Everything began to die. She paid no heed to anything except her loss until *Zeus* intervened to save the world. In modern times we see this same Shadow of the *Great Mother* as she withholds rain in places, and then sends hurricanes perhaps in anger because her ice is melting or her species are dying. Those who are especially gripped by this angry *Mother* archetype are conscious and busy with *Warrior* energy, trying to get the help of other powerful archetypes who may have the power to pacify her and rescue the planet. The *Great Father* perhaps or the *Pattern-Keeper* or the *Tribal Chief.* However these too have their Shadows. Wise and loving *Father* gods sometimes get obsessively jealous and become violent against innocent beings and other gods. *Father* or *King* archetypes have often become repressive especially of feminine archetypes, and patriarchal hierarchies grew up that still continue. Surely this is their Shadow showing. As we become conscious, we can recognize what is Shadow and help with the balancing.

As we become conscious, we can recognize what is Shadow and help with the balancing.

Balancing the Anima and Animus

I want to give you a quote from Emma Jung's book, *Anima and Animus*, one that illustrates this mix I am speaking about. She is discussing the presence of the Animus archetype, or masculine energy, as found within a woman's psyche. The animus is strong and logical, and of Spirit energy that can easily be overwhelming: But when women *succeed in maintaining themselves against the animus, instead of allowing themselves to be devoured by it, then it ceases to be only a danger and becomes a creative power. We women need this power, for, strange as it seems, only when this masculine entity becomes an integrated part of the soul and carries on its proper function there is it possible for a woman to be truly a woman in the higher sense, and, at the same time, also being herself, to fulfill her individual human destiny."*

This is a good example of finding the "gold" in a strong archetype, after it is brought into balance in the Soul.

The archetype of the *Hero* is another masculine archetype that has grabbed many, many humans over centuries. We see it in the popular stories of today as well as in myths of long ago. There is the valiant *Hero* or *Seeker* who leaves home and travels long distances and faces all kinds of trials, to find the "Grail". *Percival* and *Odysseus* and *Frodo* and even *Harry Potter.* But the *Hero* can be so caught up in his heroic quest that he is irresponsible to friends and to those he has left at home. Odysseus's pride caused his whole crew to die. *Penelope* and her

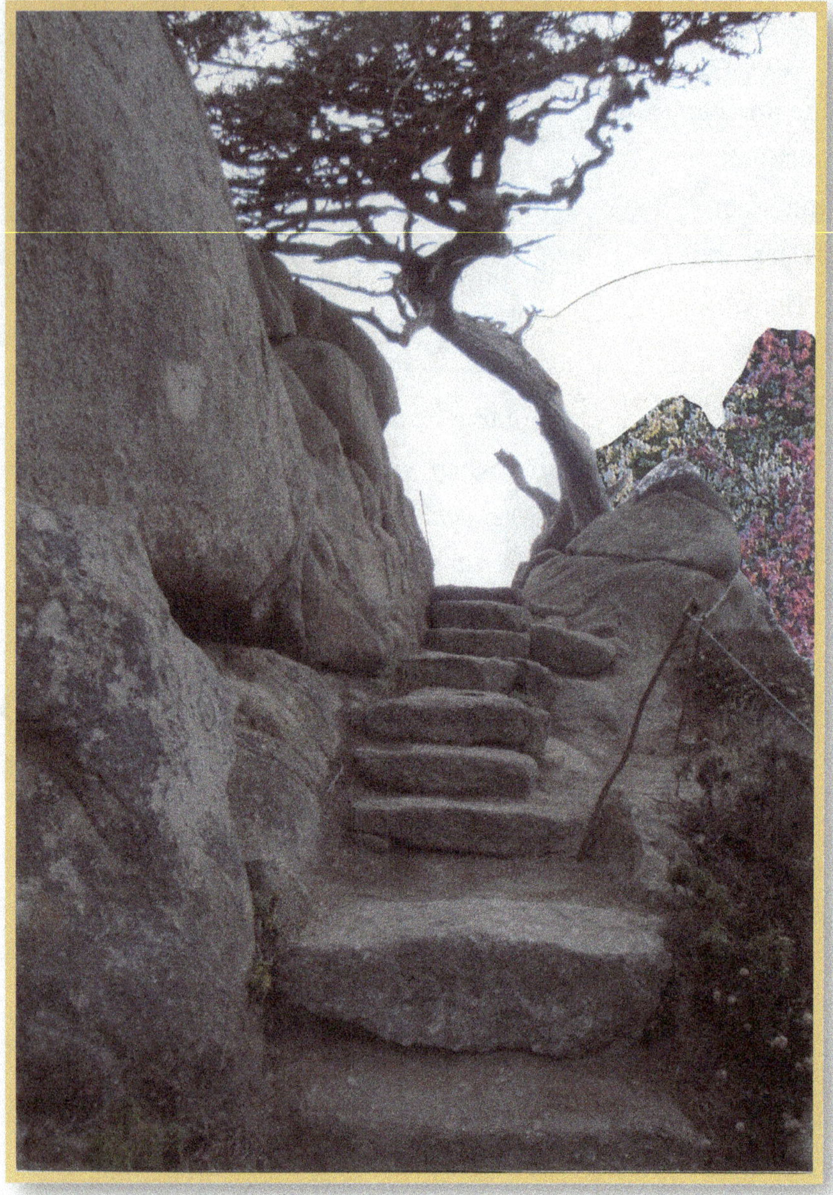

TITLE: **Determination**
SUIT: **Council**
CREATOR: **Miriam Goldberg**

"I Am Determination, fired by Hope and Certainty."

son waited for years for *Odysseus* to wake up to a balanced self and return home!

Another archetype, the *Warrior*, whose true job is to protect the children and the feminine of the tribe, often becomes overly zealous with a love of power, rationalizing and deceiving the human it inhabits, and using violence when more peaceful methods could work. Again the Shadow of excess and blindness and pride shows up in this mythic archetype.

Very often it is our personal Committee Neters who are caught up in the Shadow of the powerful Council Neters who grab and use us. Then it feels as if we are compelled to act in these shadowed ways, and we claim that somehow "we were just following orders". The *Provider Self* or even the *Shopper Self* may be overtaken with the shadow of the *Consumer* archetype along the continuum from poverty (Shadow of absence) to sustenance (Balance of "enough-ness") to greed (Shadow of too "muchness"). Greed is an enormous and devouring Shadow in our present world. Families and communities and nations are often caught as groups in this Shadow. And there are other shadowed archetypes alongside it. We may look out and recognize it, but usually we feel, as individuals, that we can do little to counteract such overwhelming imbalances.

However, the truth is that we can do significant work in the correction of archetypal

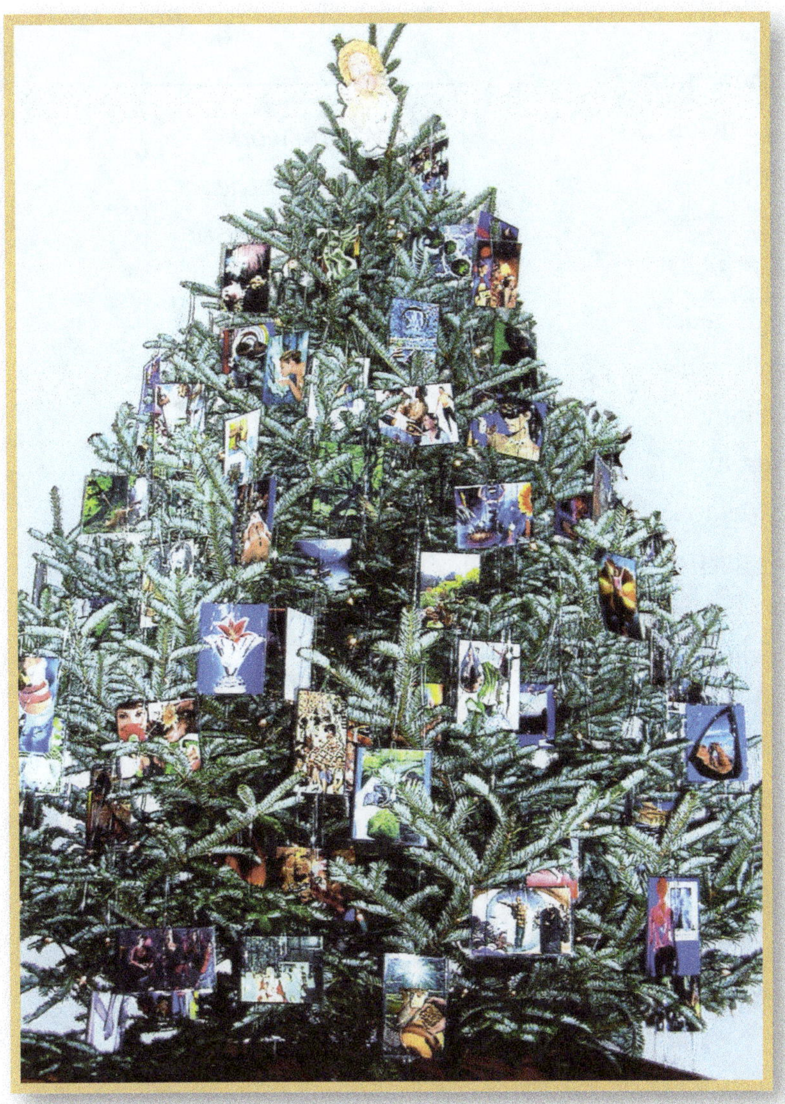

She hung her SoulCollage® cards on a live tree to give herself a positive experience to heal holiday traumas of the past.

opposing camps whether within our individual souls or within our communities.

Hold in your consciousness this thought: inside every Neter that comes from Source is a spark of the holy. Overlaying this spark, is a constant flow of Neter energies, and these energies shift and change constantly. They give us life and vitality, and they also lose balance and give us grief. These Shadow imbalances can act as prods to keep us evolving as human souls; they can keep us ever striving towards better balance. We are not children, still naked in Eden, innocent, and untempted. We are awake now, and we can recognize the Shadow as well as the Light in ourselves and in others. Our human job is to embrace the Shadow to find its vitality and to understand its needs and fears and anger. At the same time we must work with all our strength, and with the help of Neter allies both within and without, to correct the Shadow's selfishness, greed, and violence.

Shadows. First and foremost, we can step back and become conscious of them. We can identify Shadow within ourselves through work like SoulCollage® and other processes that look squarely at Shadow. Next we can join up in communities, and, depending on which Council Neters are strongest inside our Souls, work towards balancing some of this planet's Shadows. We can work to counter the Shadow of dualistic thinking that splits good and evil into

Here is a heartwarming story of a woman who had been badly abused in her past, especially during the holidays. Christmas had ceased to be a happy time for her. As a part of her healing she created, over time, many SoulCollage® cards, a lot of them showing the Shadow energy of her past woundings. When

Christmas was approaching one year she decided to have a live tree in her house again, and to use as her tree decorations just her SoulCollage® cards. Here are her words about this tree and its meaning:

> *It was an absolute thrill as my "super" SoulCollage® emerged. As each collage was added I only felt my heart open a little more! ....This tree stands tall and proud (taking literally half of my living room); it gently holds my collages, my story in its entirety. My collages leave me in awe every time I rush by the tree and then stop and pause. Every time, I see something new. I hold the past in a lighter way. I look at some collages and think they should upset me…some of the shadow cards. In reality, they don't at all. There have been cards that are shocking to me and should take my breath away. The reality is the shadow cards have truly been a relief because finally there is a way to express what has been locked inside of me for years.*

We can work to counter the Shadow of dualistic thinking that splits good and evil into opposing camps whether within our individual souls or within our communities.

CHAPTER 10

Creating Your Deck of SoulCollage® Cards

Let's turn now from the theoretical underpinnings of SoulCollage® to the creative and fun part of making these cards. Eventually, if you stay with the process, you'll make a large number of them, but for each person there's that very first card. I encourage you to read on here, and then step over into that moment of creation.

A card can be simple, with just a couple of images, or complex, with several images, and decks can contain both simple and complex cards. This will be your choice, and will depend on your style and creative bent and also on the images that attract you. Ninety-nine percent of SoulCollage® cards, and there have been thousands of them made, are *collages.*

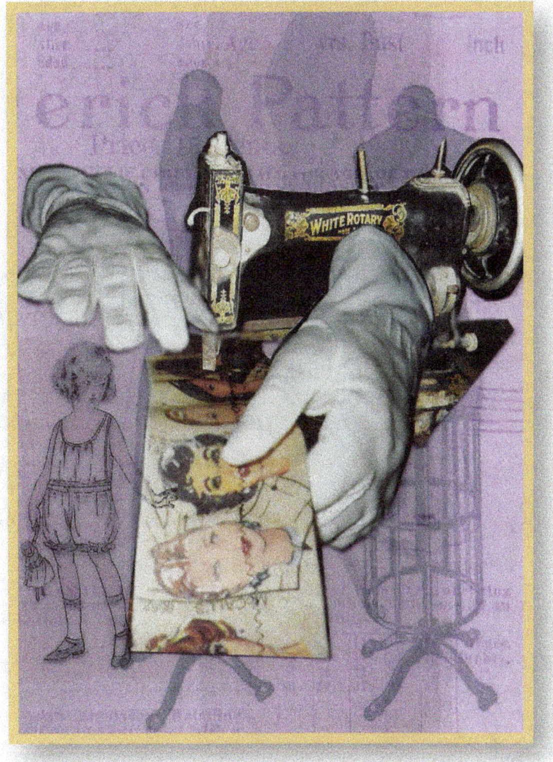

TITLE: **Child of Legalism**
SUIT: **Committee**
CREATOR: **Pam Renner**

"I Am One Who resists containment and conformity."

People choose powerful images from magazines, catalogues, greeting cards, and on-line stocks of images, which can be free or for sale. Then they work with them, carefully cutting them out and pasting them together on pre-cut cards. Collage is our medium of choice partly because it quiets fears you may have about not having talent to make "art". Everyone can choose an image, cut it out, and glue it down.

However, we consider collage far more than simply an accessible, inexpensive, and fairly quick tool. The images you select, ones that grab your attention in a compelling way, will continue to bring jolts of surprise and insight long after the card is made. One woman who is an instructor in a theological seminary says this about her use of collage:

> *Collage is the core way I demonstrate that the meaning of images can be transformed by context, and that we can make meaning and share meaning with others through these visual images. Even though I have been a professional artist for twenty years, making SoulCollage® cards came to me as a revelation of the power of images.*

Finding Images

The very first step towards card creation is to gather old magazines with interesting pictures. Ask friends, neighbors, doctors to give you their used copies. Watch the catalogues and brochures that cross your desk. Be ever on the alert for interesting images. Pay no attention to the words surrounding them.

Browse through pages and peruse the images almost in a trance state. Usually you are not looking for any definite thing. Try to keep your analytical mind quiet. Stay open and let images choose you. In this browsing state your less conscious Neters will be watching too, and they are the ones who may insist, "Tear out that one!" Or, "Select this one." Or, "Get that one you just passed over." Often you won't consciously know why an image is so compelling to you, but tear it out anyway. Usually there is an abundance of images so you can gather all you want. No need to skimp in this area. You can also gather lovely background pages, skies, and landscapes and interesting designs that you may eventually place under an image. But first and foremost you will gather images of beings, human, animal, young and old, male and female. There will be an expression, a movement, a story in the face or hands or body posture that speaks to you in some familiar and powerful way. Again, don't analyze just yet. This image-gathering is primarily right brain work; the left brain will have a turn to make comments later in the process.

The images that grab your attention in a compelling way will continue to bring jolts of surprise and insight long after the card is made.

Getting Started with SoulCollage®

As you sit down to create a SoulCollage® card you will need to have sharp scissors, some kind of good glue, and some precut cards. *These cards should be all the same size*, perhaps 5 inches by 8 inches as in prepackaged blank cards available on the SoulCollage® website. Smaller than 5 inches by 7 inches is too confining, and larger than 5 by 8 inches becomes unwieldy for a deck of cards that you will transport and lay out to work with later on. Most of us use mat board that can be bought in pre-cut packs (see above) or in large sheets you have to cut yourself at an art store. Cutting these cards neatly and to size is a tricky job but there may be a mat board cutter at your art supply store, or they may cut it up for you. It's nice to have the edges even and smooth and the cards exactly the same size. If you are working with a large population as

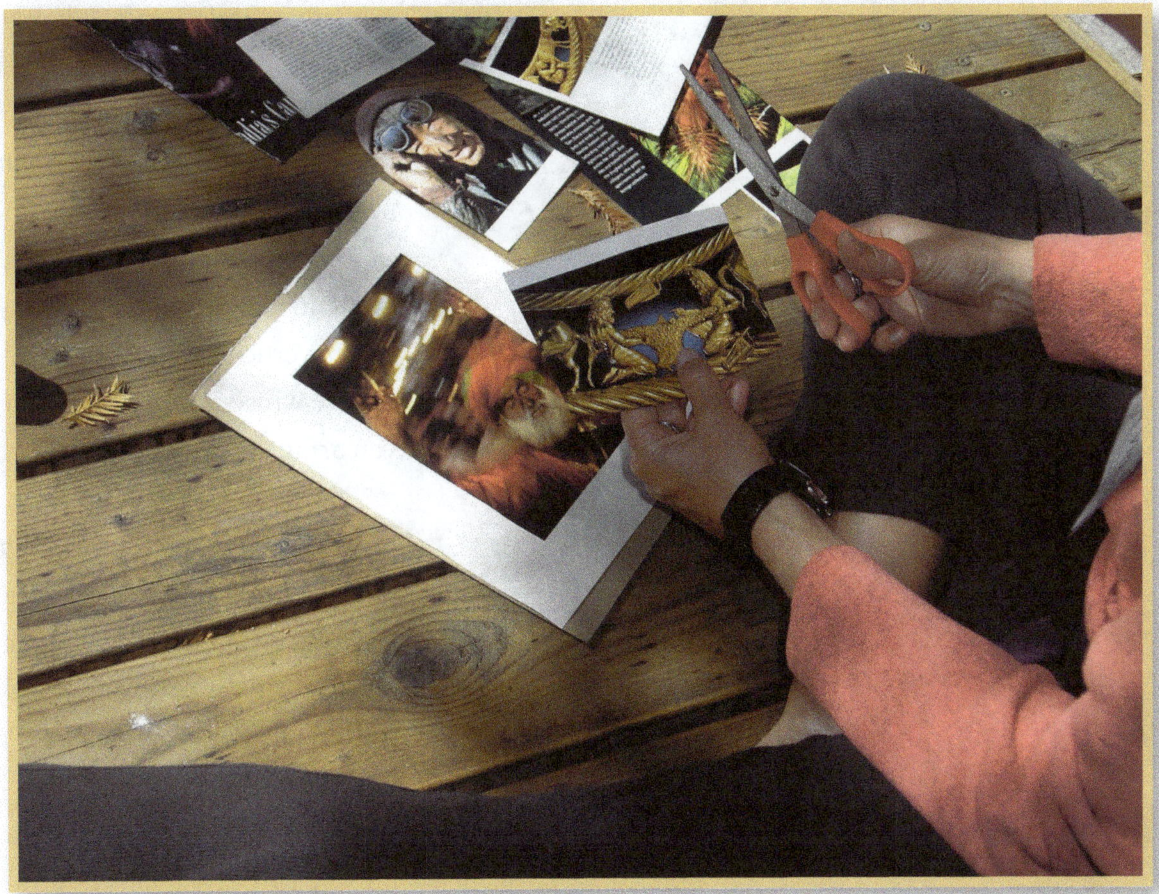

Making cards using a frame or viewfinder

in a school or hospital, you can also cut up file folders, or find tablets of thick water color paper in the right size. The packages of pre-cut cards make it very easy to get started without going to the effort of cutting out cards.

Another optional but useful tool is a *frame* or *viewfinder*. This is a piece of plain paper or cardboard, usually 8.5 by 11 inches. Carefully cut a piece out of the middle, one the exact size of your cards, so what you have left is a frame. Use this to organize your collage pieces before you glue them down. You can place it over an image that seems too large for your card and perhaps see how just one part of the image is enough to carry the energy you want; then cut the rest away. You will learn to use this frame in several ways, but it is not essential to have one.

When you have gathered these simple tools, lay out your images. Choose one to begin with that has the most compelling energy—a powerful, intriguing image that grabs you. Generally you will cut it out, away from its original background. This may take time as it is best to really cut carefully around the edges of the image. If some of the background is essential to your image, then cut part of that out as well, but not with straight lines as in a square shape. Cut with curving lines, including only what you really want. Jeri Bodemar, a

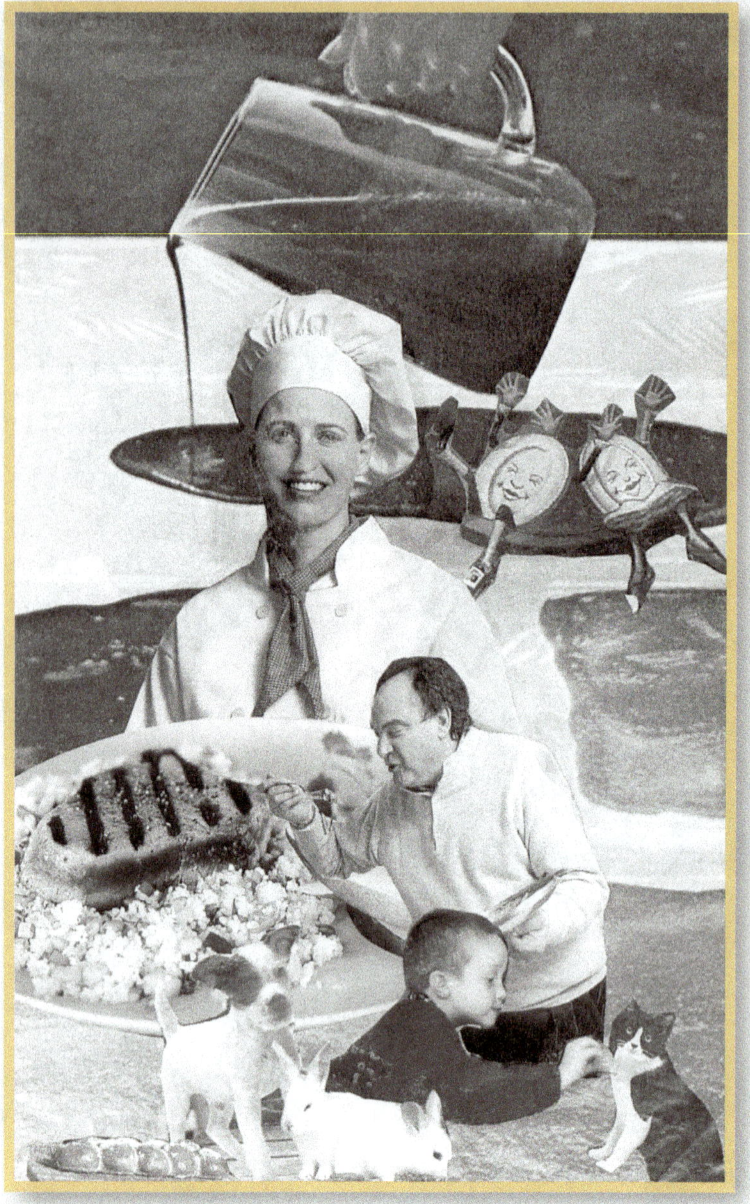

TITLE: **Best Cook**
SUIT: **Committee**
CREATOR: **Anonymous**

"I nurture my family with food that is good for health and good to taste. I even let them lick the beaters and steal from the kettle. They are happy!"

SoulCollage® Facilitator in California, says that when she is cutting out an image, she feels like she is blessing it.

Many have found that tearing an image out, when you want to include some of the background around it, gives a lovely feel. Some have created many of their cards with this tearing technique rather than with the sharpness of cutting.

Some of your cards will be best laid out horizontally and others vertically. Either is fine, so choose which way works best as you arrange your images.

Now you will want to decide on a new background on which to glue your image or images. Find something that sets them off and gives, by its context, a new and special meaning to the image. You may want to try several before you decide. No need to hurry to finish a card… let your fingers move pieces around within your frame or on a blank card. Let the image itself guide you. Perhaps you will want to include two or three images on the one background, *images that all seem to have a similar energy.*

If you are gluing on the color side of your mat board you could leave a tiny edge of that color showing as a frame around your collage. You also might decide to use the mat board color itself as part of the background.

There are times an image appears in a form that is perfect just as it is. You may not want to do anything except cut it to the size of your card and glue it down, no collaging needed.

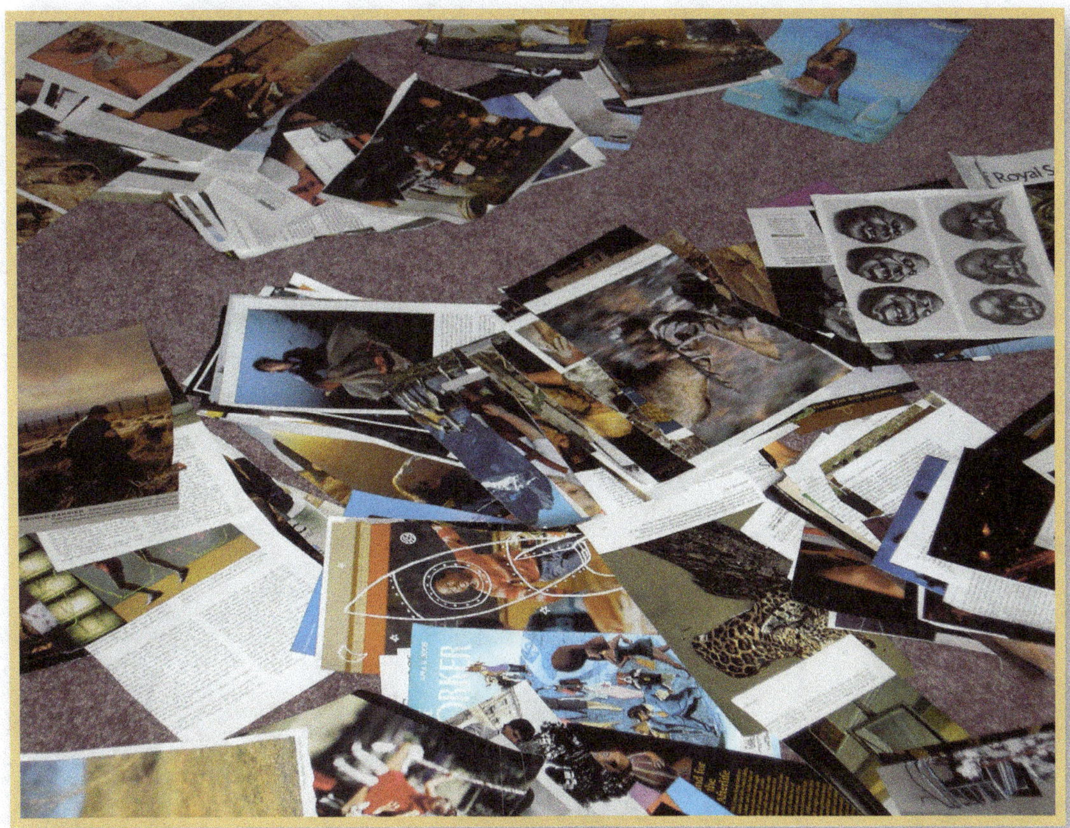

Finding images

This is perfectly okay since *you are not going to copy, sell, or trade these cards. They are for your personal use.* However, most of the time I'm sure you will find it more creative and exciting to collage images together on a new background. Then it becomes your personally created card symbolizing one Neter of your Soul.

One Energy Per Card

A further word about this principle of one energy. *Each card in a SoulCollage® deck is meant to have one primary energy.* Try to have one namable Neter as the inhabitant of each card so it has its own contained space! People beginning the process often put too many Neters on one card. It may be that they have not yet gotten the habit of stepping back in consciousness and seeing their many parts, all working together like the organs of one body, but still different in function, in health, and in attitude.

SoulCollage® is basically a process that increases consciousness about these complex inner workings of a Soul, so we encourage people to work on identifying their inner parts and making individual cards for them. This is done intuitively by placing images with a similar energy on one card.

If you have distinct inner child parts, each should have its own card. The *Wounded Child,* for example, will not be on a card with the *Curious Child* or with the *Happy Child,* even though you have all three on your Committee. Each of these has distinct energies, so they will need different images on different backgrounds on separate cards. There might be more than one image that you find for the same Neter, but they all point still to the same basic energy. Thus, when you draw a card in a reading, you will be able to name it and intuit what its energy would say to the question you are asking. There may be some cards, especially in the Community suit, where you include several images of several beings, as a group of people or a group of pets. This is fine, but even here there needs to be a specific energy that comes from this group. The group itself is considered one Neter and speaks as one.

Another modification to this rule would be if you are creating a card for a Committee member, and you want to include the Council archetype that is using this Neter, perhaps in the background. The *Warrior* may be standing behind your *Political Activist*, the *Creator* behind your *Artist Self*, and the *Great Mother* behind your *Nurturing Self*. Again the energy in these duo cards is the same, though it is magnified in the Council Neter. You could include these in the Council suit if the primary image is the archetype, or in the Committee suit if the primary image is the local story Neter.

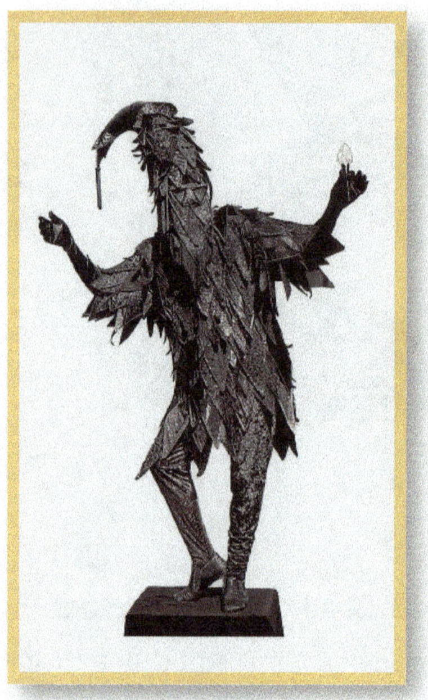

TITLE: **Jester Noir**
SUIT: **Council**
CREATOR: **Kira Jones**

"Ha ha! Come play with lights in my dark realm. *I Am the One Who* tricks and treats – know which is which?"

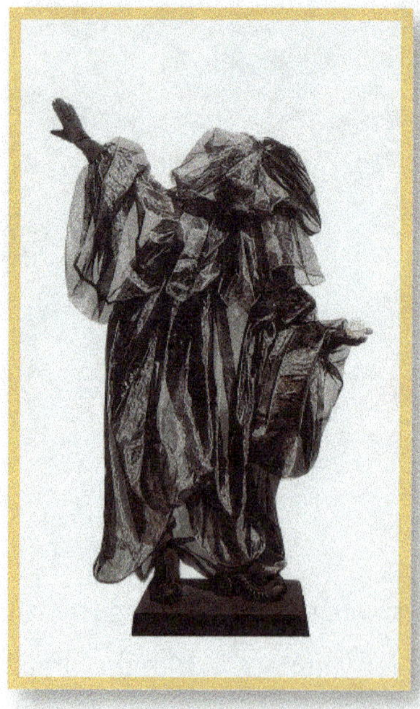

TITLE: **Smoke & Mirrors**
SUIT: **Council**
CREATOR: **Kira Jones**

"I Am not what I seem. I am beautiful and obscure, misleading and beguiling."

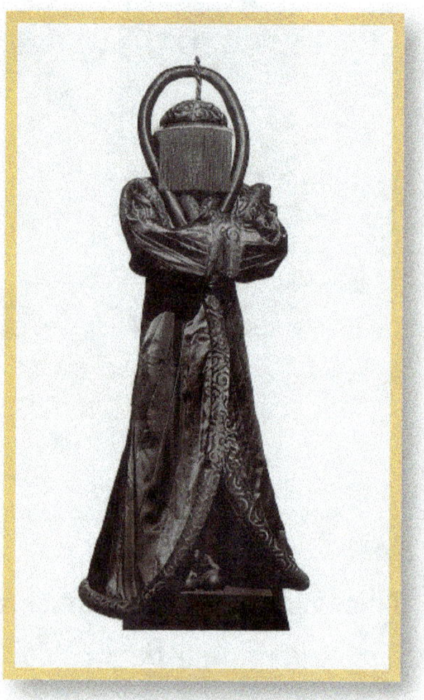

TITLE: **Manchurian**
SUIT: **Council**
CREATOR: **Kira Jones**

""I Am the Veiled Empress. Bow to me. You must obey me in all things without question."

Using Words as Part of a Collage

As a rule, don't! I know, SoulCollagers hate rules, and there are very few. You can break this one about words occasionally if you must. I have, myself, included the name of the Neter or a line of poetry on a few cards. The reason to avoid words on your collage is this: when you turn over a card to consult it, your eyes will go first to the words before they go to the image. The left brain immediately wakes up and grabs on to the words which are its domain, and it will try to take over the reading by analyzing the words for meaning. Images attract the attention of the right side of our brains, and when there are only images, this intuitive side stays in charge and will go deeper into the uncharted territory of the psyche. It is this side of our brain that can see the whole picture at once and surprise us with wise answers that seem to come from some deeper place. Enough said. Words are great, and we love them dearly, but let them come later.

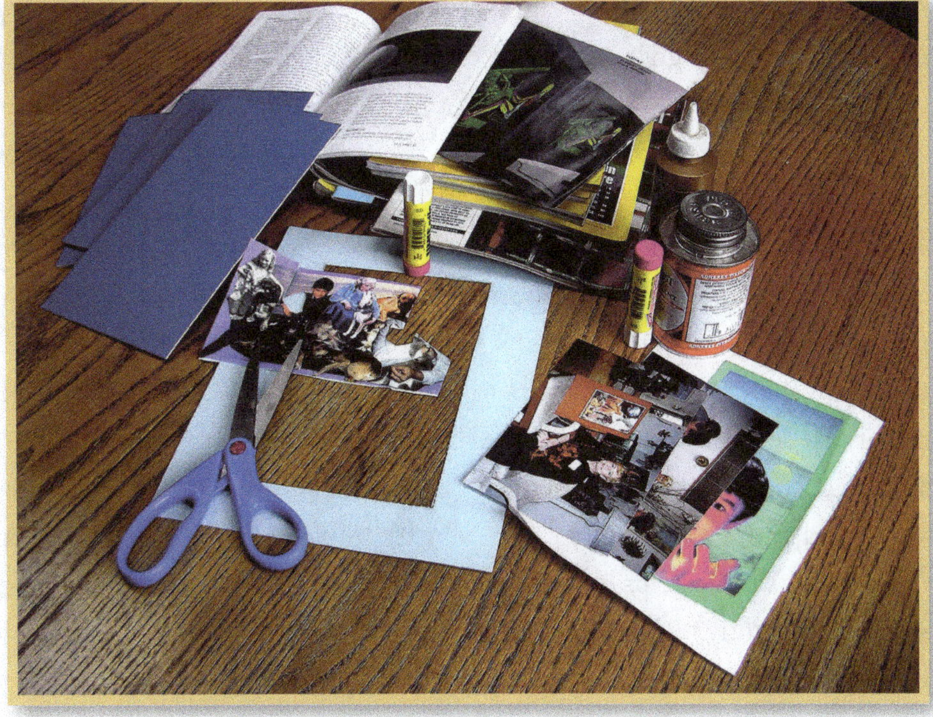

All you need is scissors, cards, glue, and images you will find everywhere.

Looking Intentionally for Images

In the same vein, the searching for images is initially and primarily a right-brain, intuitive process as I've described earlier. When we browse without intention, images seem to find us as much as we find them. This happens because our less conscious mind responds swiftly and naturally to visual images and carries more feeling than our logical mind.

Images seem to find us as much as we find them.

This said, there will be times *when we set out intentionally to find a certain image.* This is especially true for the suits of the Community and the Companions. You may go to your photo albums and select images of family and ancestors; you may take your camera and go out to take pictures of friends. When you have discovered an animal in one of the chakras, you will look for a picture of that animal displaying energy as it did in your visualization. If you are doing a thematic gathering and everyone is creating cards for a particular Neter or group of Neters, you will browse with both intention and openness. Always stay open to surprise. Very often, when you are intentionally searching for one thing, an image for a totally different Neter will grab your attention. Tear it out to work with later.

Glue!

Glue has been the subject of much debate among SoulCollagers over the years, and there's no consensus. In workshops we use archival glue sticks of the best quality. (It seems to be important with glue sticks that both surfaces are coated with the glue rather than just one. This helps images to stick permanently.) Rubber cement is excellent but it can be toxic in a closed room if several people are using it. "Yes" brand glue is a favorite of many. Spray glue is only good for large pieces such as backgrounds or for card backings, and it can be toxic also. Avoid cheap glues or pastes as they will not stick well and they will wrinkle. Be sure to put glue on most of the surface of the image, not simply around the edges. Bubbling can be a problem. Have another card whose edge you can use to press images flat immediately after gluing or keep a brayer in your box. You will find the glue and other tools that you prefer, so have them nearby and ready! Pieces will constantly come loose on your cards as you shuffle them and let others look at them, so have your glue stick handy for repairs.

Try your best to have your cards well crafted. You may be using them for years.

The artistic quality of a SoulCollage® card is not the primary focus in SoulCollage,® and yet try your best to have your cards well crafted. You may be using them for years and sharing them with others, so take time and some care.

There are ways of protecting cards with an acrylic matte varnish if you like that look and feel. But remember that no card can ever be considered totally finished. Our Neters are always changing and, hopefully, evolving. We have found that plastic sheaths "flap seal bags", available at www.clearbags.com in 5 1/8" X 8", are the exact size of the pre-packaged blank SoulCollage® cards available online. The people who use these sheaths like them also because, if they want to add images to a card in the future, they can easily take it out and work on it.

Technology

Some of you will choose to use certain software on your computer to work with your images, and this can offer many possibilities. I won't begin to describe them as you know them as well, or much better, than I do.

SoulCollage® does not advocate copying or infringing on the copyrighted work of others in any way. SoulCollage® cards are made for personal use, and we do encourage SoulCollagers only to copy and alter copyright free art or art for which they have purchased rights. Still it is wise to keep a file of your cards on your computer just for your personal use in case your deck is lost, damaged, or stolen. If this happens, you would be able to reconstruct your deck. This tragedy has happened, and, alas, with no back-ups! You can also share your cards online within a private platform such as World of SoulCollage®.

Covering the Backs of Cards

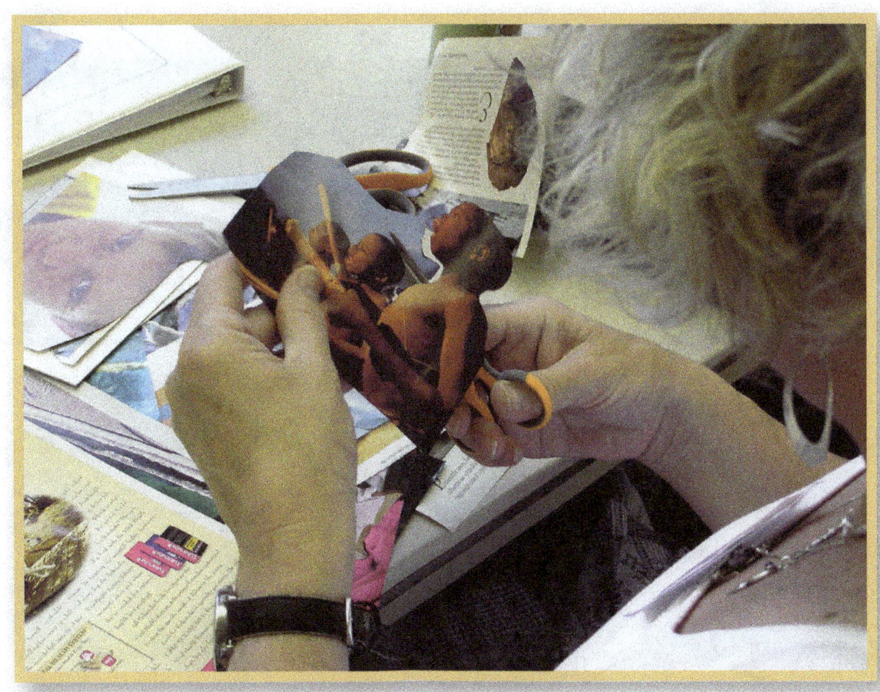

Carefully cutting out an image from its background

We cover the backs of our cards primarily to distinguish between suits when we are drawing cards in a reading. So, after you have "finished" a card, or at least feel complete with it for the moment, you may choose to cover the back with some lovely paper. Find wrapping papers with designs that are simple, without words, and don't have such a distinct design that you will learn to identify a certain card by the backing paper's pattern.

If you are working with the four suits in your deck and the Transpersonal cards, you will need to find five different wrapping papers that you like and that go well together. Each suit should have a special backing that will identify its cards. Be sure to purchase enough backing paper so you won't run out, especially for the Committee and Community and Council suits as those will have the most cards. Not so much paper is needed for the Transpersonal Cards and the Companions. Cut pieces of this paper out that will exactly cover the back of your card and glue it on well. Here, it is important to glue the entire surface and press it down with the edge of another card so it's smooth.

The purpose of this backing is two-fold; it makes your card more beautiful and finished, and it also helps in a SoulCollage® reading which I will describe in the next chapter. You will be able to "draw" cards from your various suits without knowing consciously what Neter you are choosing.

With some of your cards you will know what Neter it is as you create it, and therefore its suit. The Companion animals and the Community beings are examples. More difficult to distinguish may be the Committee Neters and the Council Neters. I talked about this difficulty earlier, so I won't go over it again. It may take time and several readings before you are ready to name a card and decide its suit. When you do, you can go ahead and back it with the proper backing.

There are many SoulCollagers who have made large decks of cards and never put backings on them. This is okay, of course, and doing it does take time. Some people have simply used different stickers on the card backs to distinguish the suits and this works fine too. Don't, however, write on the backs of your cards, because this makes them easy to identify and your conscious mind will resist drawing the more shadowed cards.

One final word about the suits. Some people choose not to distinguish between suits at all, and the images on these cards will be just as valuable and wise as ones distinguished by suits. They will still work well in readings. So, if suits seem too rigid or artificial or complicated for you, make cards and back them all the same except for the Transpersonal cards which do need to be easily separated out for readings.

The value of suits is that it stretches you to be more inclusive and diverse in your collection of Soul images. Suits help you imagine Neters, guides, allies, and challengers, in areas of your life where you might not dream of looking for them.

So now let's go on to discuss readings, which are at the very heart of the SoulCollage® process.

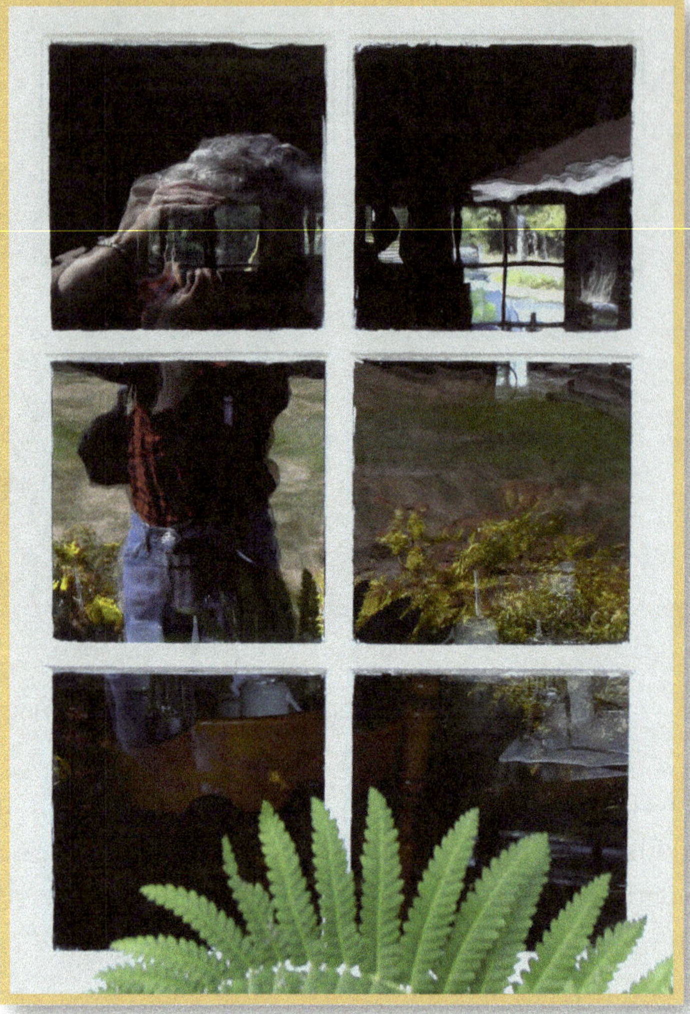

TITLE: **Image-Maker**
SUIT: **Committee**
CREATOR: **Laren Leonard**

"*I Am One Who* captures your imagination. You are drawn to me by the silent song of light in a language without words."

CHAPTER 11

The *I Am One Who...* Process

TAPPING INTO YOUR INNER WISDOM

I will begin this chapter with an email from Kathleen Abley, a SoulCollage® Facilitator from Ontario, Canada, reporting on a recent workshop:

> *A woman in my workshop this weekend told me that she was skeptical about all this "weird stuff" but had just come to keep a friend company. I was a little stumped at her bluntness and told her that I valued her honesty. During the workshop she got very uncomfortable yet managed to make two cards. When she spoke from the "*I Am One Who...*" her words were so simple and profound that we all had tears in our eyes. She told us all that she amazed herself because she had been certain that this process would not get through her "closed mind." I received an email from her this morning saying that SoulCollage® will be part of her journey.*

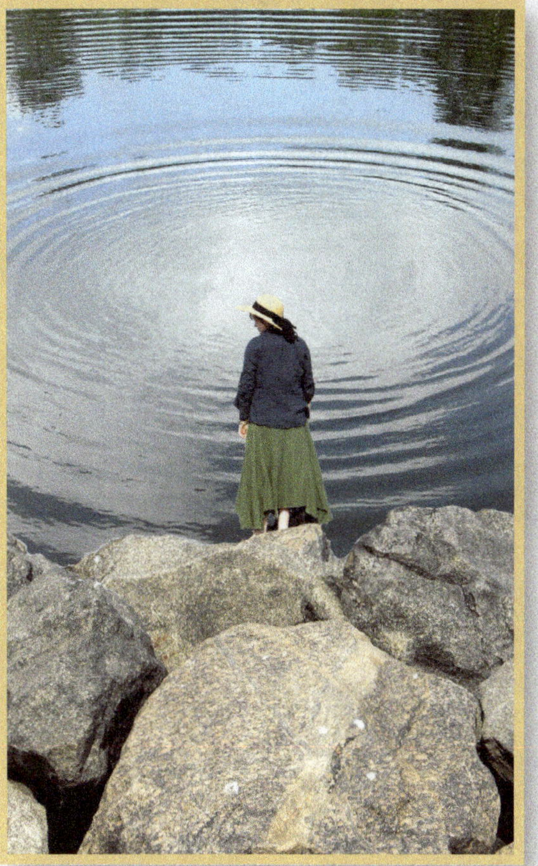

TITLE: **The Seeker**
SUIT: **Committee**
CREATOR: **Catherine Anderson**

"*I Am One Who* is forever seeking new ways of knowing."

In this chapter I will talk in some depth about what this woman discovered almost accidentally––how we can tap into our inner wisdom through images and intuition. Perhaps you will have the same astonishment she did when you delve into the mostly untapped wisdom of your Soul.

Who is usually the wisest teacher about one's life journey? Surely it must be our own Soul who alone knows our

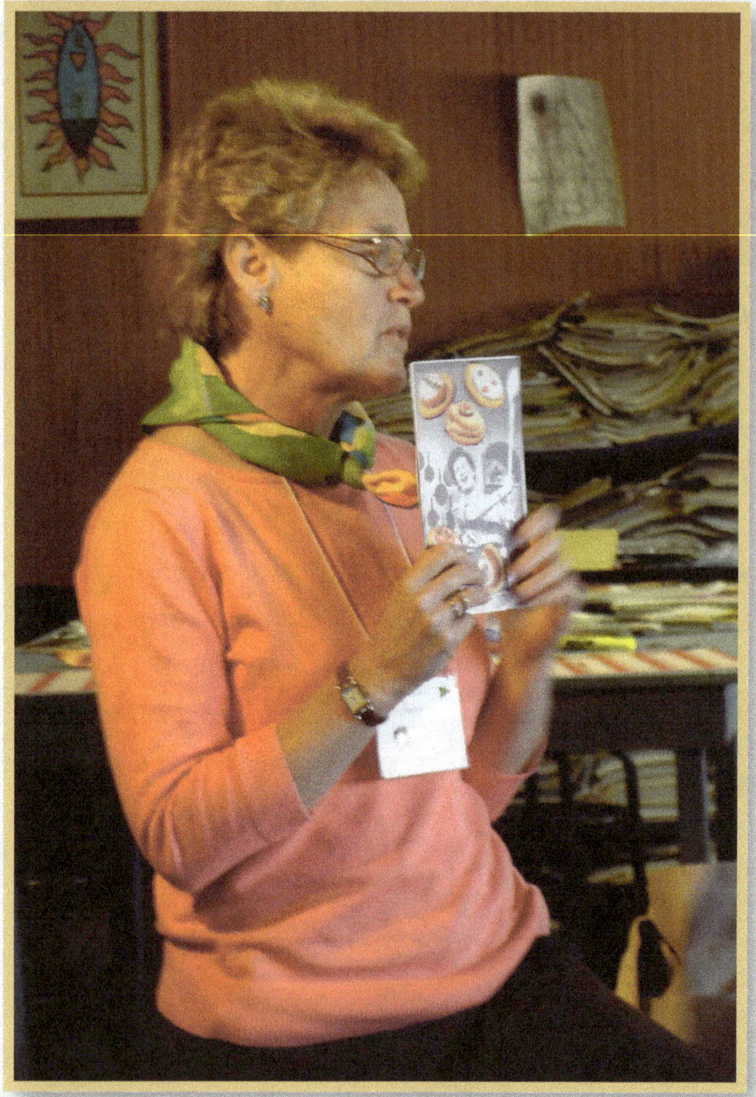

Audrey Chowdhury shows her card and talks from it using the *I Am One Who...* process

PHOTO BY JENISE ENGLISH 2009

SoulCollage® is a way of anchoring our wisdom through consulting our cards. In readings we allow our Neter images to speak aloud, using our imagination and intuition. An apt metaphor is to imagine these ideas and visions fermenting down in our depths, but with no voice. One woman wrote, "*For some unexplained reason, when an image begins to speak with the words* I Am One Who... *some of these ideas, emotions or visions wake up, put on special words as presentable "clothes" for an appearance, and come forth on your tongue. Imagination and intuition link together with the image, and bring about this bubbling up out of your less conscious Soul. Your words slip around the mind, around the Neters who would stop them because this is "just a silly game of imagination."*

personal coding, our history, our talents, our passions, and our dreams. The problem is that most of this deep wisdom surfaces in sudden ideas and thoughts, in dreams, and rememberings that often vanish as quickly as they come. At times they are pulled back down and repressed by Neters in our Committee who are skeptical of intuitive wisdom or who are afraid to listen to it. What we need is some sort of anchor to secure these thoughts when they arise, some way to "net" them.

The *I Am One Who...* Process

From the time you tear out your first image and wonder what it symbolizes, begin to use the *I Am One Who...* process to let the image speak to you. This is not the same as analyzing or interpreting the image, ways your logical mind will want to use. This is an intuitive way of listening to the self and is a well-respected form of empathic participation in the essence of something or someone. In this case it is participation in the essence of an image, and it will give life and surprising consciousness to what looks like just a photo. Another name for this is "role-playing". At first it may seem awkward or childish to speak aloud this way, but trust that there is "gold" in this process, and give it a try.

You can begin practicing the *I Am One Who…* or *I Am the One Who…* with an image you have just torn out, and later with images on the cards you create. It will be a primary tool in the readings you do with cards, and I'll describe how those are done in a moment.

First gaze deeply at your image. Is it a person? A child? Is it an animal? Perhaps a cat? Perhaps a tree? Step into the image and feel its energy, its mood, its intention. Imagine it has a history, and that it has a voice. Begin to speak, or write if you are journaling, using the words, *I Am One Who…* and go on from there, describing yourself as if you were the image, where you are, what you are doing, giving little personal descriptions:

> *I'm a little kid about ten. I seem to be poor and lost. I am scared and hungry.*
>
> *I'm a wild tiger in the jungle and I'm sleeping on this branch but I'm also awake and watching. I am powerful and no one bothers me because I am so fierce.*
>
> *I'm a tree in a forest. I am tall and beautiful and alive. I am well-grounded, for my roots grow deep and wide under the forest.*

Step into the image and feel its energy, its mood, its intention. Imagine it has a history, and that it has a voice. Begin to speak, or write if you are journaling, using the words, I Am One Who…

After you have covered the obvious in the image, allow your imagination to probe deeper into the subtle possibilities of what this being might want, need, fear, expect, or intend. Stay with the true voice of the image, with its energy, and don't add things you *wish* it would say. Keep using the *I Am One Who…* as a start to your sentences, as that will help you stay in the image. After a while you can drop those words and simply say, "I Am…" and go on.

Role-playing an image is more powerful than talking about an image or describing it objectively. Let me show you the difference. When talking about an image you might say: *"This looks a little bit like me as a kid when I was unhappy. He looks like he got scolded and is mad about it."* Saying this will get you something, but never the awareness jolt that becoming the image can give you. When you step into the image, you will say something like I Am One Who… *is really, really mad and sad. My Dad scolded me for something I didn't do, and I would sock him if I could. I can't do anything to get back. I get scolded all the time for stuff, and it's not fair.* Feel the difference. The second has emotion in it, and you will actually feel the emotion as you speak.

Practice the *I Am One Who…* process until you are not worried by the strangeness of it. The value of becoming the image and speaking from it is well worth the effort it takes to overcome any awkwardness you may feel. You can practice with any image even if you are not

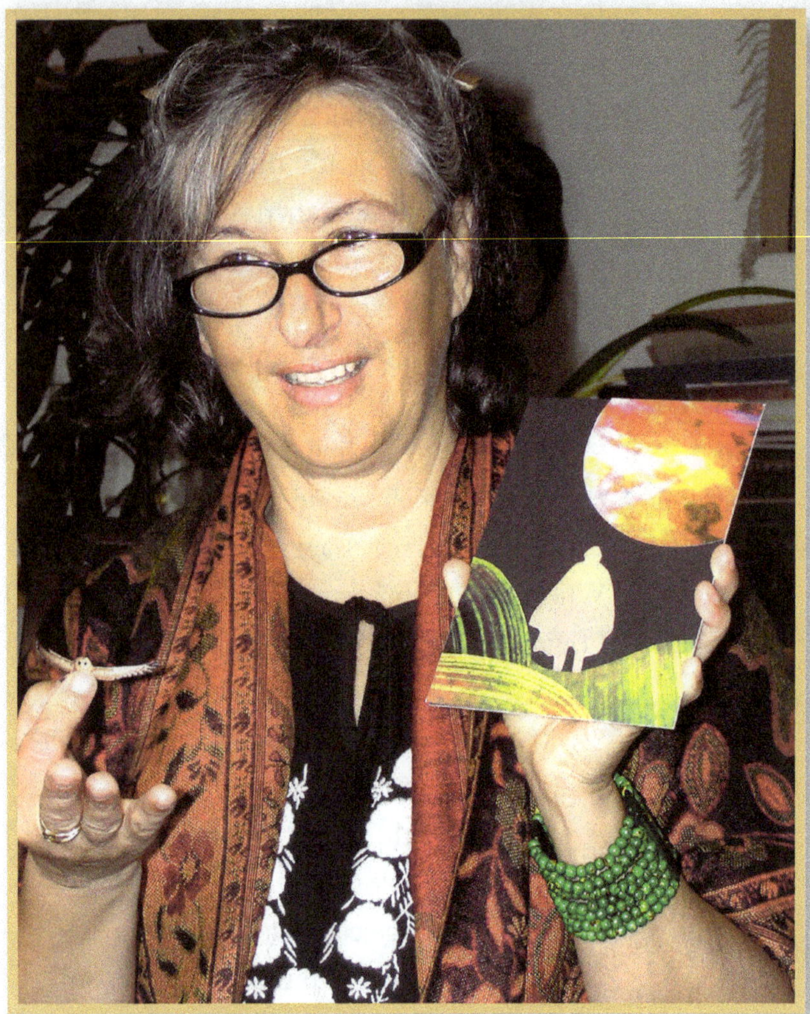

Mariabruna Sirabella holds up her card to speak from it using the *I Am One Who....* process.
PHOTO BY SEENA B. FROST

off the top of your head". This is why, in SoulCollage® work, we highly recommend doing some of this work in a supportive group. Perhaps a small, ongoing group. In most introductory workshops we have people begin right away choosing a few images that call to them, and then, sitting in a circle, introduce themselves using the *I Am One Who...* process with one of these found images. There is no discussion or questioning at this time, but just the simple speaking from the image, one person after the other. It's a different and powerful way of introducing a group to one another. Afterwards there can be a time for each person to write down in their journals what they remember saying. Or a scribe might be jotting the words down for each person.

These two activities: *finding a compelling image* and then *speaking aloud and without rehearsal from this image,* form the essence of the SoulCollage® process. Underneath many of the cards in this book you will be able to read a few of the *I Am One Who...* words that the creator of each card has recorded. Look at the images and then read some of these. This will give you a good idea of this practice.

sure if you will adopt it as a Neter and make a SoulCollage® card with it. Speaking from its energy will help you begin to sense the name of this Neter, and whether this is energy that is strong in your life. If not, put it down and find another that is more compelling.

If you are by yourself you can write your words in a journal. However, writing is more left-brain and is not as spontaneous as speaking the words aloud. The *Angry Child,* the *Judge,* or the *Heart Chakra* animal will speak up more freely if you are simply "speaking

The Importance of the Name

You will see also their names under the cards that appear in this book. I want to talk for a few paragraphs about the significance of a card's name. Naming a card is not a casual thing, just as naming a child is never done lightly. Time and thought need to go into it, since the name is meant to encapsulate the primary and essential energy of each Neter.

I'm going to quote some lines from the Jungian scholar, Helen M. Luke, and her book *Woman: Earth and Spirit.* This is a book I love and recommend to anyone wanting more of the Jungian underpinnings of the SoulCollage® process. She says:

> *The power of the Name is a great and holy theme in all religion and myth, in the whole history of consciousness.... With the name there comes to us the power of detachment and conscious choice....* [p. 75]
>
> *We know, then, that in approaching our own depths, we are searching for the right names for the unseen forces within us. This is very far from arriving at a mere intellectual definition. It is the search for the true symbolic image in which we recognize the essence of the thing, a word in which the indefinable is expressed beyond intellectual categories. In the process of searching we bring to bear all the powers of intellect, imagination, feeling, and instinct, and then perhaps the name will become known to us as if by accident, arising spontaneously from the depths, bringing a new, intuitive certainty, the word made flesh, the union of opposites.* [p. 76-77]

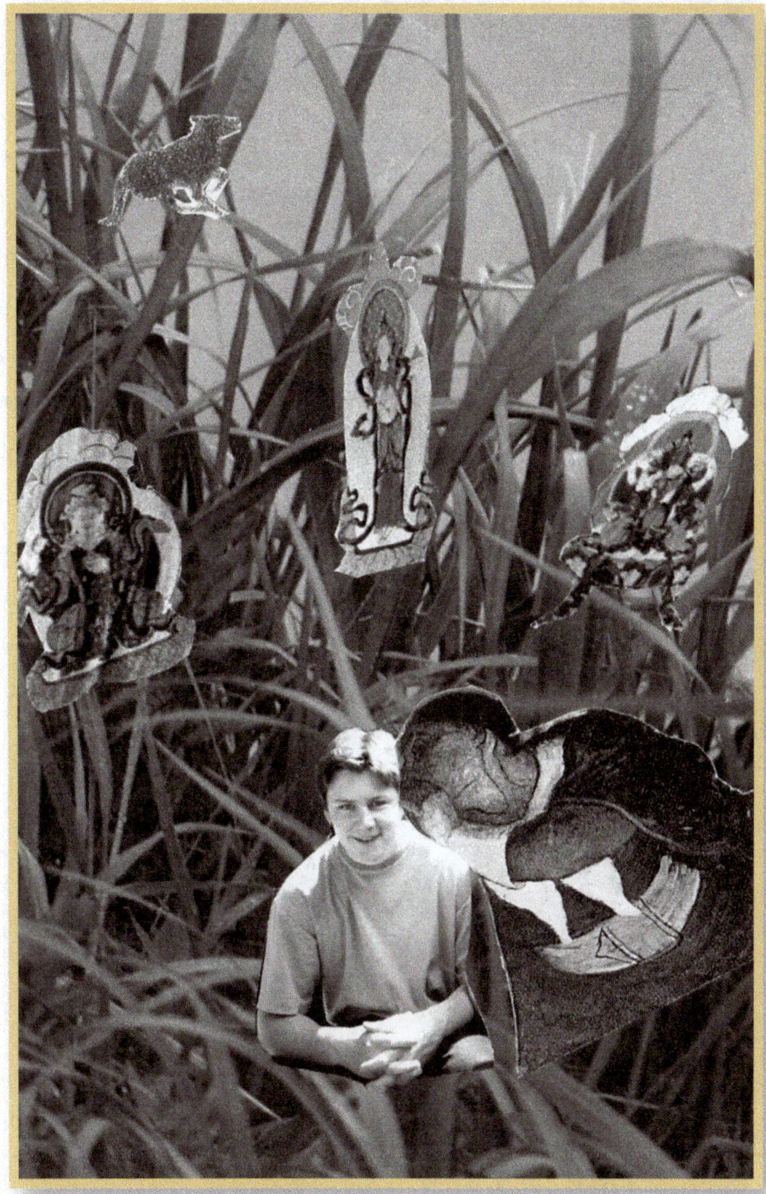

TITLE: **Dustin**
SUIT: **Community**
CREATOR: **Kelly Sims Dovas**

"*I Am One Who* says, 'Let go completely. Surrender all you hold dearest.'"

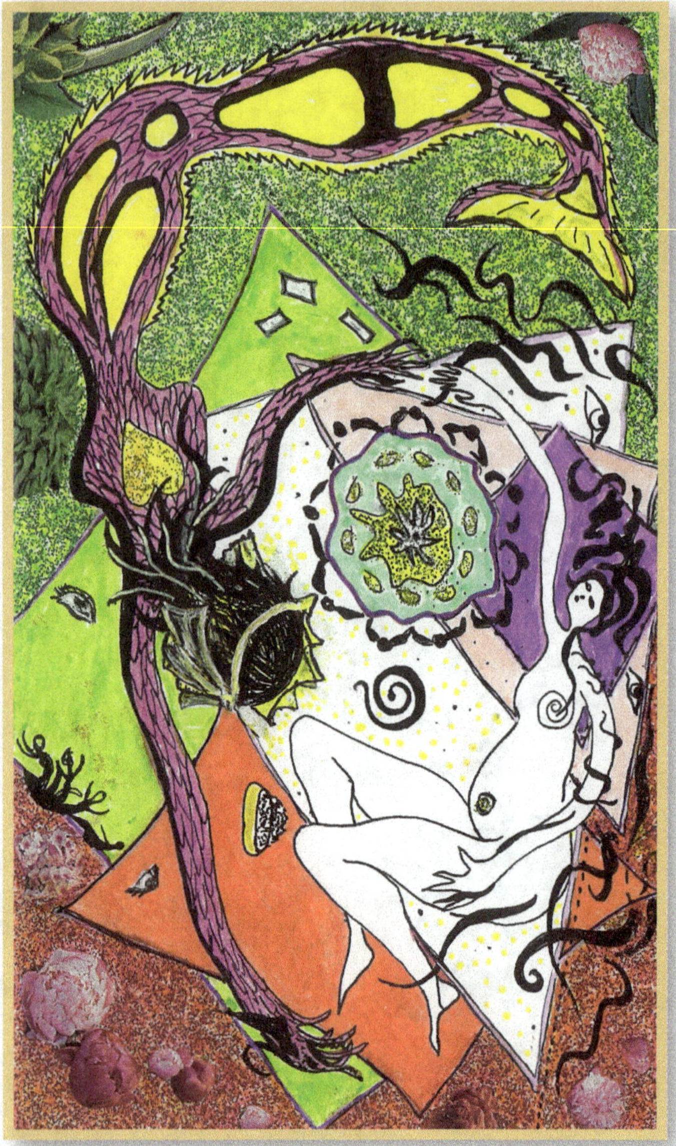

TITLE: **Circle**
SUIT: **Witness**
CREATOR: **Wendy Grace**

"*I Am the One Who* teaches you to go into the power of circle. Many have entered before you and many will after you. Enter my circle, enter my life. I Am transformative."

As she does throughout her books, Luke uses myths and fairy tales to illustrate her points; here she uses the ancient story of Rumpelstiltskin and the hero's desperate search for his true name. If you remember, the princess must learn his name to keep her first born child, and finally, after much effort, the name is given to her almost by accident.

All this is to emphasize the importance of finding, and often waiting to be "given", the true name of a card. It is mainly through speaking from the cards, using the *I Am One Who…* process that its name will arise. It will be a special word or set of words: the name of a mythic character, a noun, an adjective, a quality, a feeling … some *name* that truly encapsulates the primary energy of the Neter image on a card. Sometimes these names will come quickly as they do for many Committee cards and in most Community and Companion cards. But sometimes the name will take several readings to discover, especially in the more mysterious Council cards. Allow yourself to keep searching for it because knowing the name will help you become more conscious, more of a detached Observer of this Neter. From this *stepped-back place* you will be able to make choices about it, help balance it, and entertain it with appreciation.

Now I will go on to describe a more detailed way to consult your cards about your life questions. It is a way that is at once therapeutic, spiritual, and highly imaginative. It often leads to surprise and transformation.

> *SoulCollage® anchors our wisdom when we consult our cards using our imagination and intuition.*

CHAPTER 12

Consulting Your SoulCollage® Cards

READINGS WITH SOULCOLLAGE® CARDS

Your SoulCollage® deck may eventually contain a hundred or more cards. However, as soon as you have created a few you can begin to consult them about questions that matter to you. We call this intuitive process *"doing a reading,"* and basically it is dialoguing with your own inner guides or Neters. Very often the answers you receive from deep within your Soul are surprising, wise, and, once in a while, life changing.

Reading SoulCollage® cards is not the same as consulting divinatory cards such as the Tarot although the actual physical process is similar.

TITLE: **The Seeker**
SUIT: **Committee**
CREATOR: **Mili Dillard**

"*I Am One Who* searches via my constant question, 'Are You My Mother?'"

Briefly here are the basic steps in our process:

1. First you write down your personal question.
2. Then you *draw* from your deck a certain number of cards without looking at them, putting them face down in front of you.
3. Then, one at a time, you turn the cards over and ask each image your question.
4. Holding each card in turn, *step into the image,* and, starting with the *I Am One Who...* words, speak to your question from the energy and wisdom and perspective of this Neter.

This form of a reading is not something esoteric or occult. It is not about forecasting the future. The cards do not have meanings predetermined by any tradition or another person. Each card has a meaning that you will intuit for yourself, and every time an image is consulted, you will come up with your own internal answer. *In SoulCollage® no one reads the meaning of the cards for you; you are the reader of your own images, and speak to your own questions.* Even if you are loaned cards from someone else's deck until you have created enough of your own, even then you read from the images yourself, without any information about them from their creator. Synchronicities may and often do occur around the question and the cards that are drawn, but this is not a process that depends on any unusual or psychic powers. It is an intuitive dialogue with one of the Neters of your many-faceted Soul. Everyone has intuition and imagination and is able to do it for oneself.

In SoulCollage® no one reads the meaning of the cards for you; you are the reader of your own images, and speak to your own questions.

Creating Sacred Space

Doing a reading is a soul-tending activity, and you may want to create some sort of ritual space when you do it. This is true both for readings done by yourself, or when you are sitting in circle with a SoulCollage® group.

Arrange it so you won't be interrupted. You might select a lovely cloth on which to lay out your cards, using either a table or the floor. You might choose to light a candle in the center. Have all your cards stacked neatly in front of you, face down. Place your Transpersonal cards in the center, face up. These cards stay in the center throughout the reading as *silent* symbols of Source, of the Mystery that holds all individuated Neters as One.

Before you actually begin the reading you might pause for a moment of silence. You could seed this ritual moment with the words of a poem, a guided visualization, breathwork—all of which can help quiet your thinking mind. Work to still the chattering Committee Neters, the caretakers, list-makers, and especially critics and skeptics. With discipline and ceremonial preparation, these local story Neters can stay silent long enough for your deeper consciousness to be awakened by your images.

Finding Your Question

Perhaps you have come to this SoulCollage® reading with a question all ready in mind. Perhaps you have been thinking of what you want to ask during the time of silence. Perhaps you want to repeat a question you've asked before. All these methods are fine, but take time to find the question. Over many years of doing readings, we have discovered that the question asked is nearly as important as the answers given. First, the question needs to matter to you. It should not be frivolous, although it can seem light-hearted and even humorous. Let it have to do with your life journey in some way, with what you deeply want. Avoid phrasing the question in a "yes" or "no" form, because that limits what you may receive. You can be general and "big" in your question: "*What special*

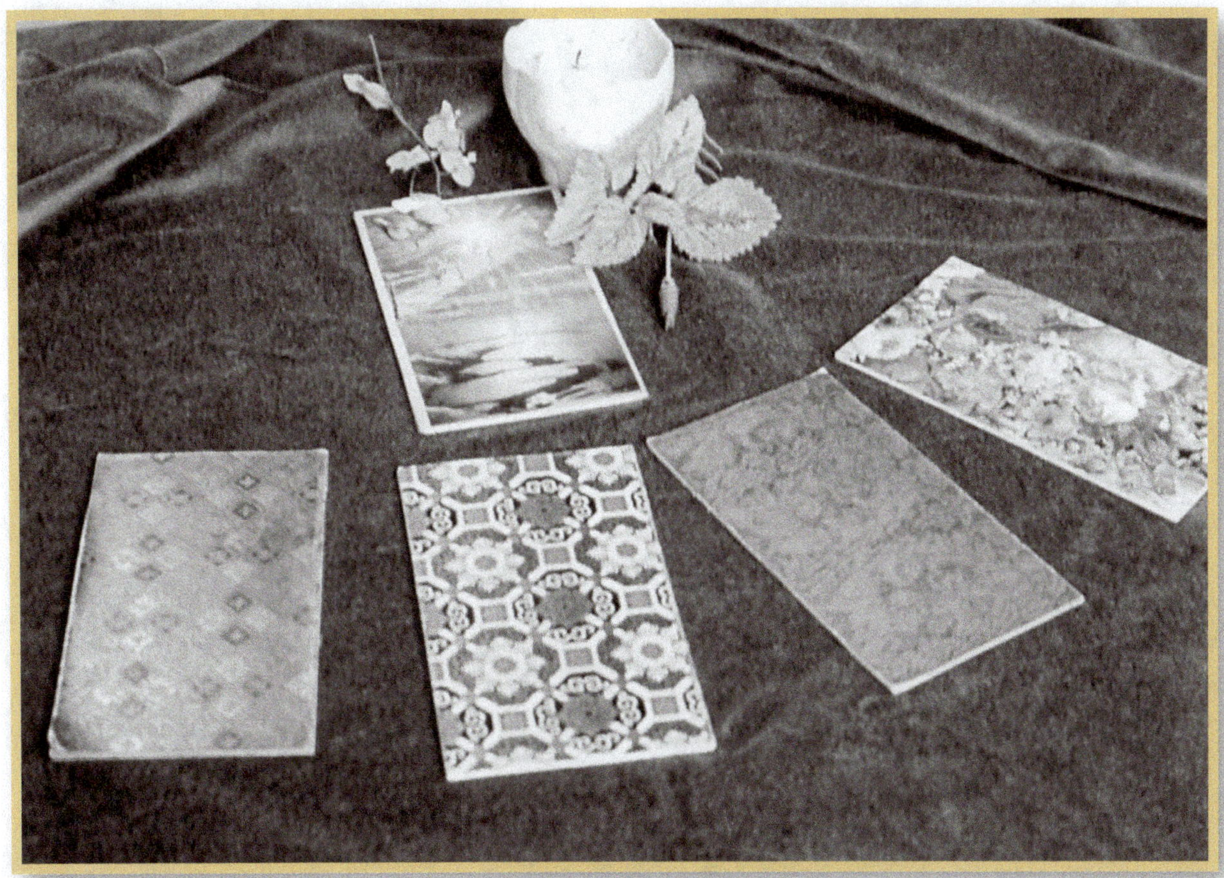

A four-card reading laid out face down, with the Source Card turned face up above

gift is mine to give to the planet right now?" Or it can be very specific, having to do with a current life problem: "*Who will help me control my inner Judge this week?*" Either way, keep the time frame of the question short and definite. These are not cosmic and forever answers you are asking for, but more immediate ones.

When you have decided on your question, write it down at the top of a blank page in your journal or on a tablet. Make it as short as possible, without extra explanations or directions. Don't dictate the answer you want by the wording of the question. Leave it open to various perspectives. For example, don't ask, "*How can I get my aging Mother to eat better and go to church functions like she used to?*" That already directs your Neters to the answer you want. Instead just ask, "*How can I best help my aging Mother?*" Simple and short and open-ended. If you are working in a group you will pass the page with your question to another person who will become your scribe for this reading; be sure to make it legible so they can read it back to you. Be sure there is enough room on the page for answers from all the cards in this reading, perhaps four.

If you are working alone, write the question as if you were going to pass it to someone. You will be the one to write the answers as you intuit them. You will be your own scribe.

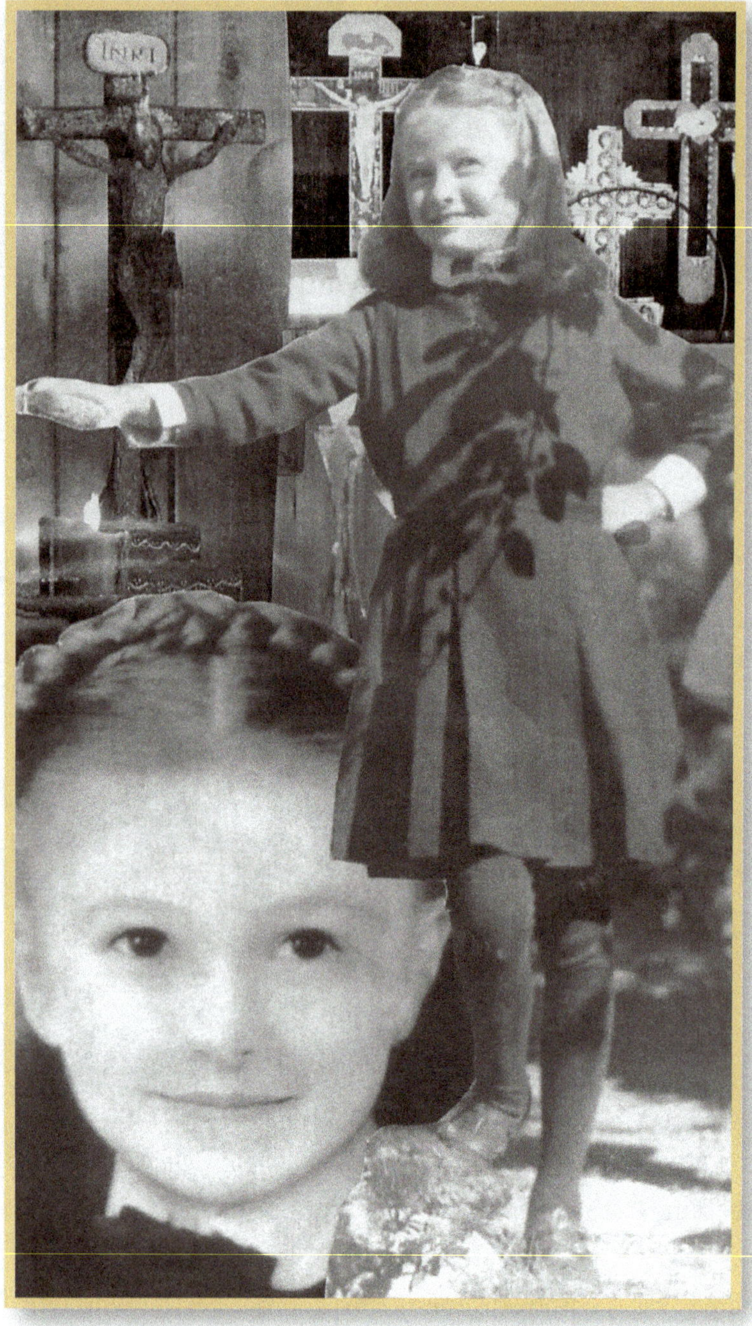

TITLE: **The Catholic Girl**

SUIT: **Committee**

CREATOR: **Gretchen Sentry**

"Nuns taught me shame. I learned stubborn resistance I also learned to light candles, and I still do that. I still treasure my trait of stubbornness."

Sample Questions for a Reading

Here are some sample questions to give you ideas and to help with wording. All of them can be answered by a Neter on a drawn card, one who begins with the words *I Am One Who…*

What Neters will help me find balance in my life in this next week?

Where are my playful Neters hiding?

Who will help with my anger energy?

What Neters have advice about my relationship with (name)?

What Neters want to go on this trip with me?

Which of my potentials shall I focus on now?

Who will help me deal with my jealousy?

What do I need to know about this pain in my neck?

What Neters have input about this decision?

Who will help me with my anxiety?

What Neters will help me inspire others?

What can you tell me about how I feel stuck?

Who wants to be with me this next month?

Who will support me in this caretaking task with (name)?

How can I deal with the negativity of my boss?

How can I have fun this week?

A good practice is also to shorten questions. Try just three or four words!

Who will help?
Who is obstructing?
Who wants to go?

Formulate your question so it truly has meaning for you. Date your page and write it down. It is perfectly all right to repeat a question if you do a lot of readings. If you can't come up with a question, one helpful idea is to draw a card from your deck. Look at it, become the image and imagine what question this Neter might ask.

Working with a Community Question

If you are working in an ongoing group, there are times, perhaps on a day your whole community is grieving or focused on a special event, when you choose a community question. This would be a question that everyone asks their cards. Work together on how to word it and then each person will write this same question on their sheet of paper.

What Neters will be with our friend, Mary, in her sadness?

Who in me can I offer to the world in this crisis?

What Neters want to join together to celebrate this holiday?

How can this group be most helpful to one another?

Proceed with the reading in the usual way, a way I will now describe.

Laying Out Your Cards for a Reading

With the Transpersonal cards in the center and your questions written, you are ready to draw the cards you will read today. Spread your cards out, *face down,* in front of you and draw, *one at a time*, the number of cards you want to consult. Do this, thinking of your question, letting your hand drift over the cards and feeling their energies. Let the cards almost choose themselves. If you have the cards backed by their suits, you can draw one from each suit. This will give you a wide range of Neter answers. If not, simply draw at random the number you have decided on for this reading. Four is the recommended number if you are giving yourself time enough for a full reading. This will take some time, perhaps three to five minutes per card. If you are in a group with several people and have a limited time, draw three or even two cards per person. Or choose four and finish the reading at home on your own if you run out of time.

Place these cards in a row right in front of you, still face down with *their identity still un-*

To Do a Reading

- Take time to pose a question that is important to you.
- Spread your cards face down.
- Draw the number of cards you want to consult. Leave them face down.
- Turn over each card in turn, using the *I Am One Who...* and speaking from the voice of the card in answer to your question.
- Journal after each card speaks.
- After all the cards speak, look at them together to see what they will say to you as a group.

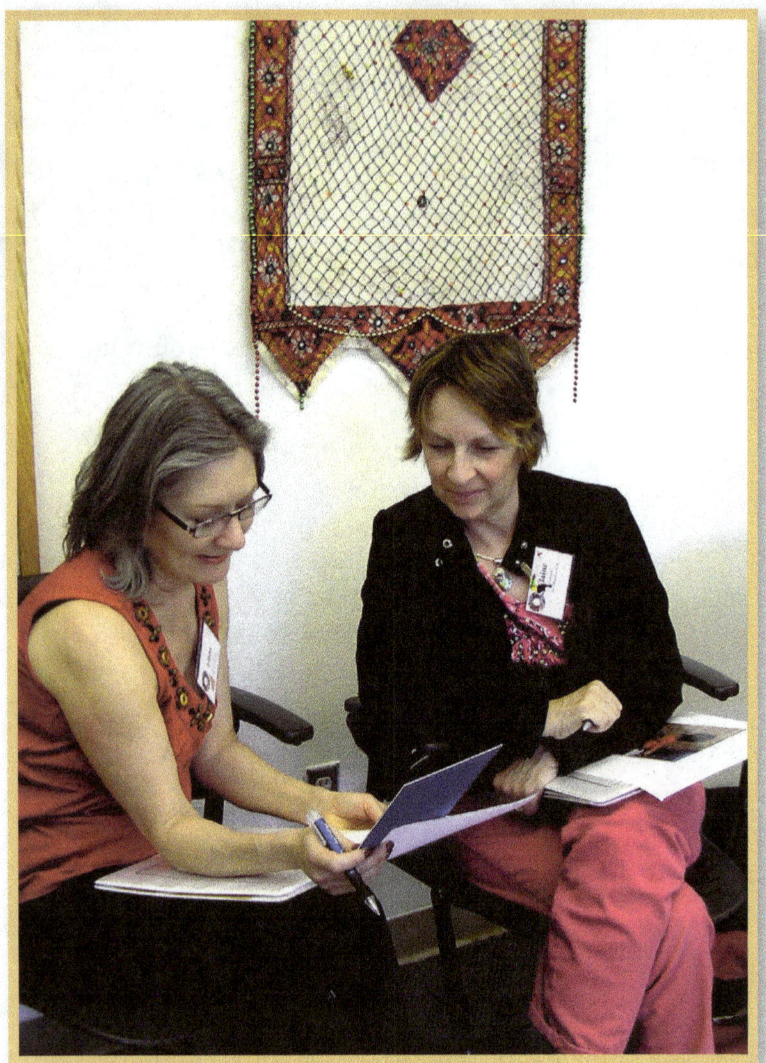

Left to right: Libby Schmanke and Elaine Richard share a reading.

known to you. Don't peek at them! Put your other cards aside so the space is as clear as possible.

Doing the Reading

Now you are ready to begin the reading. If you are alone you will read the question, then turn over the first card, see what it is, and begin to speak as the Neter of this card. You can write at the same time as you intuitively "speak" unless you are recording your voice. Name yourself… *I Am your* Curious Child Neter, or *I Am your friend* Jim, or *I Am your* Heart Chakra Bear, or *I Am the* Warrior *Neter of your Council.* If you don't know what the name or suit is yet, simply begin to describe yourself: *I Am the One Who… is still a mystery and I….* Then describe yourself generally for a few sentences, telling about the energy you feel in the image. *I have strong, fierce energy*, and *I am always on the move….* Or, *I am generally critical of whatever is going on inside my person….*

Next go to the question: *What I say to you about this question is….* and answer as fully as you can. Let the words just bubble up, uncensored. They may meander around some before coming to the point. Or they may answer very quickly. They may be poetic. Very likely they will be surprising. The most important thing is to *stay in the energy of the Neter* whose card has turned up. Don't edit or add words from some other part of you. Don't step out and comment or editorialize. Stay in the role you are imagining as fully as you can. Answer the question with the energy of this particular Neter. It may not be an answer you are expect-

Having witnesses to your reading encourages the Neters to reveal themselves.

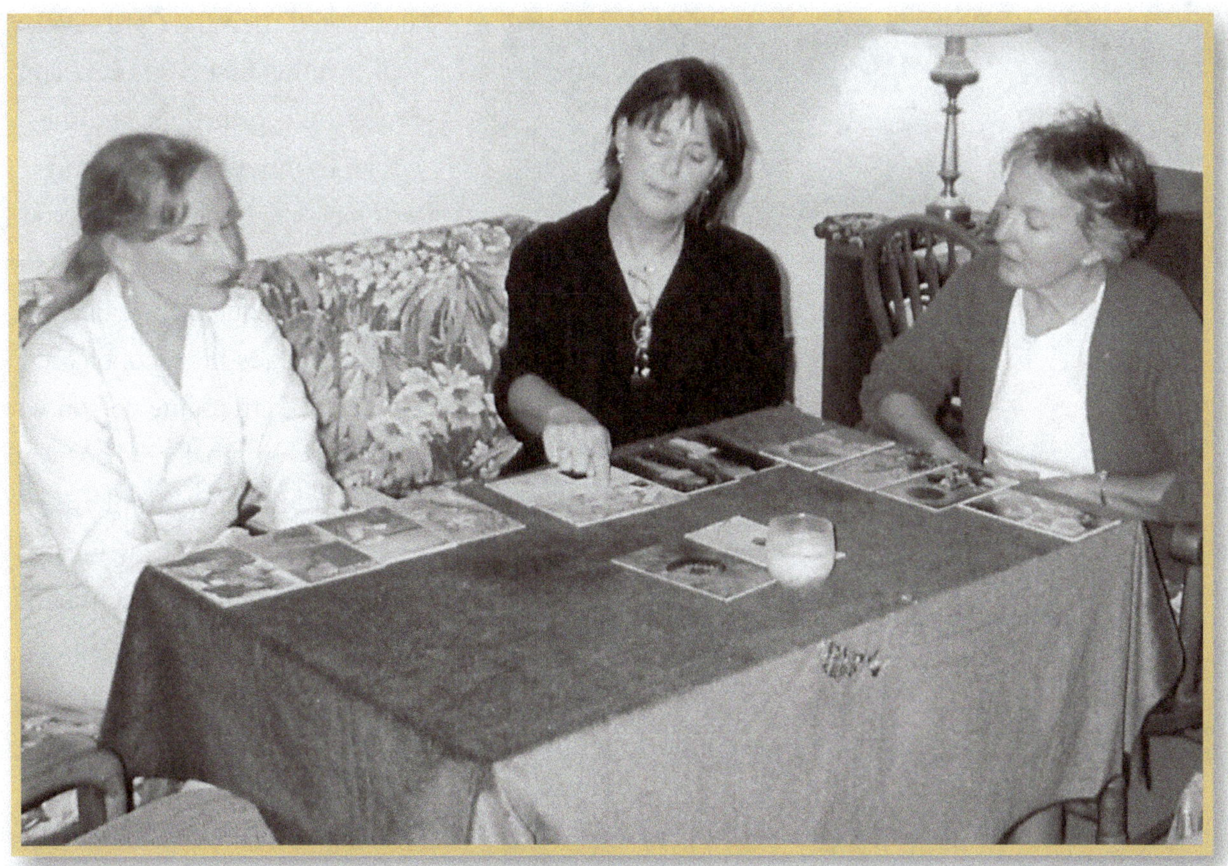

Left to right: Alyson Kennedy, Leta Delurgio, and Bobby Tucker consulting their cards

ing to hear. It might say that it doesn't know anything about this question. However, more than likely, it will have something to say that is surprising and relevant. Don't go on and on if an answer comes up in the first three or four sentences. On the other hand, sometimes you will feel an inner urge to stay in the image and probe deeper. If there is a Facilitator with you, she may ask you a question or encourage you to keep exploring.

Doing Readings in Groups

Doing readings in groups of supportive people is even more powerful than doing them alone. It is as though having witnesses encourages the Neters to reveal themselves. Four or five is enough people for one reading group, so, if you have more people, divide into more groups. If you have six people, divide into two groups of three. This will keep you from being rushed if you have just a couple of hours to spend with a reading. And two hours is probably enough time for a group to be sitting still and concentrating.

Each person prepares for the reading in the way described above, writing a question and drawing the cards to be consulted. One person will begin by turning over a first card after hearing their question read aloud by the person scribing for her. I will talk about the Scribe in a moment but let me first describe a format that works best for group readings.

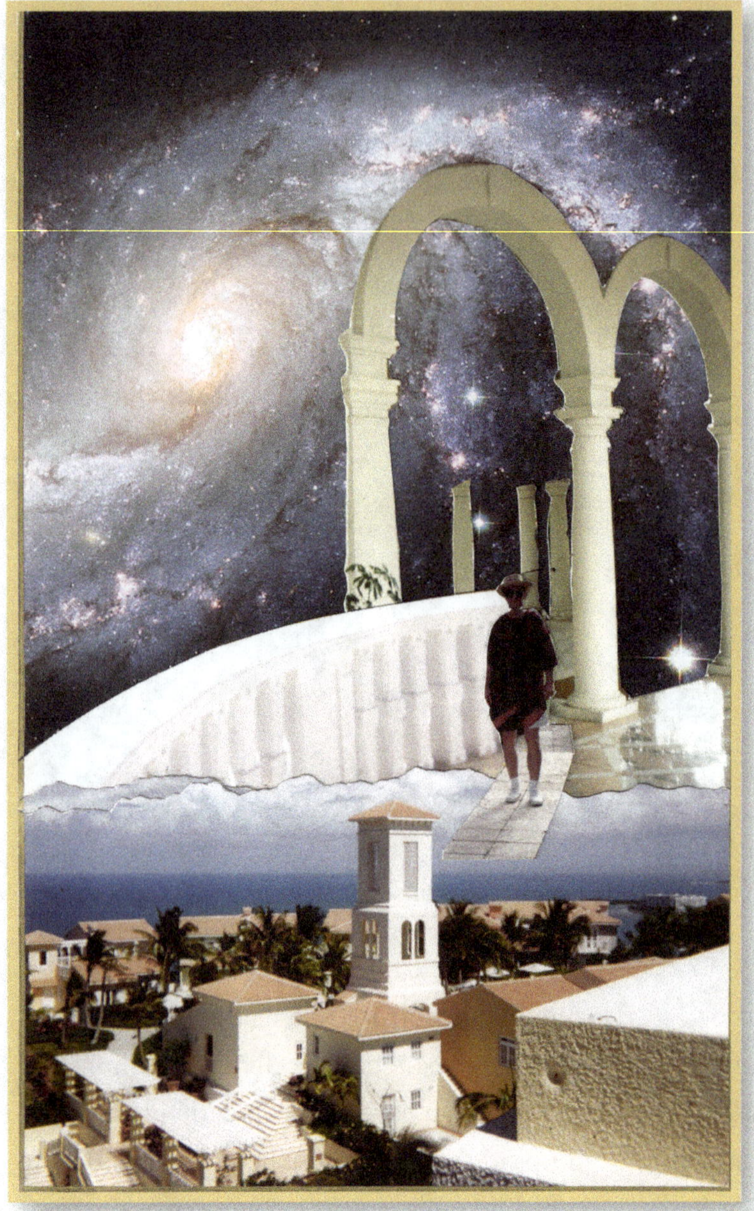

TITLE: **Stargate**
SUIT: **Committee**
CREATOR: **Johnny Dillard**

"*I Am One Who* manifests my own destiny, my own experiences, and my own reality."

After one person has read one card, move on to the next person who will take a turn as "Card Reader". This person gives his question to a different person to be his Scribe, listens as the "Scribe" reads the Card Reader's question aloud, and then the Card Reader will turn his first card over. This process is repeated around the circle. Eventually each person will have read one card and you will come back to the first person. He hears his question read again and then reads his second card. His scribe is the same person who scribed for him before. Thus you go around the circle until everyone has read all the drawn cards in front of them. We recommend this alternating way, instead of one person reading all their cards at one time. This keeps the interest high. Also, no one fears they won't have a chance to read. This method lets people sit with the words of one card before going right on to the next.

The Role of Scribe

To help readers stay in their intuitive mode, it is better if they are not writing at the same time they are speaking. This is why, in groups, you will assign a Scribe for each Card Reader, a person who reads the question aloud to the reader each time before they turn over a new card and then writes down the answers given by the image. Scribing is an art you will learn. It is not necessary to write every word. You can summarize and leave out repetitive words. You don't have to write *I Am One Who…* each time it is repeated but simply start with *I…* and write the words spoken from the im-

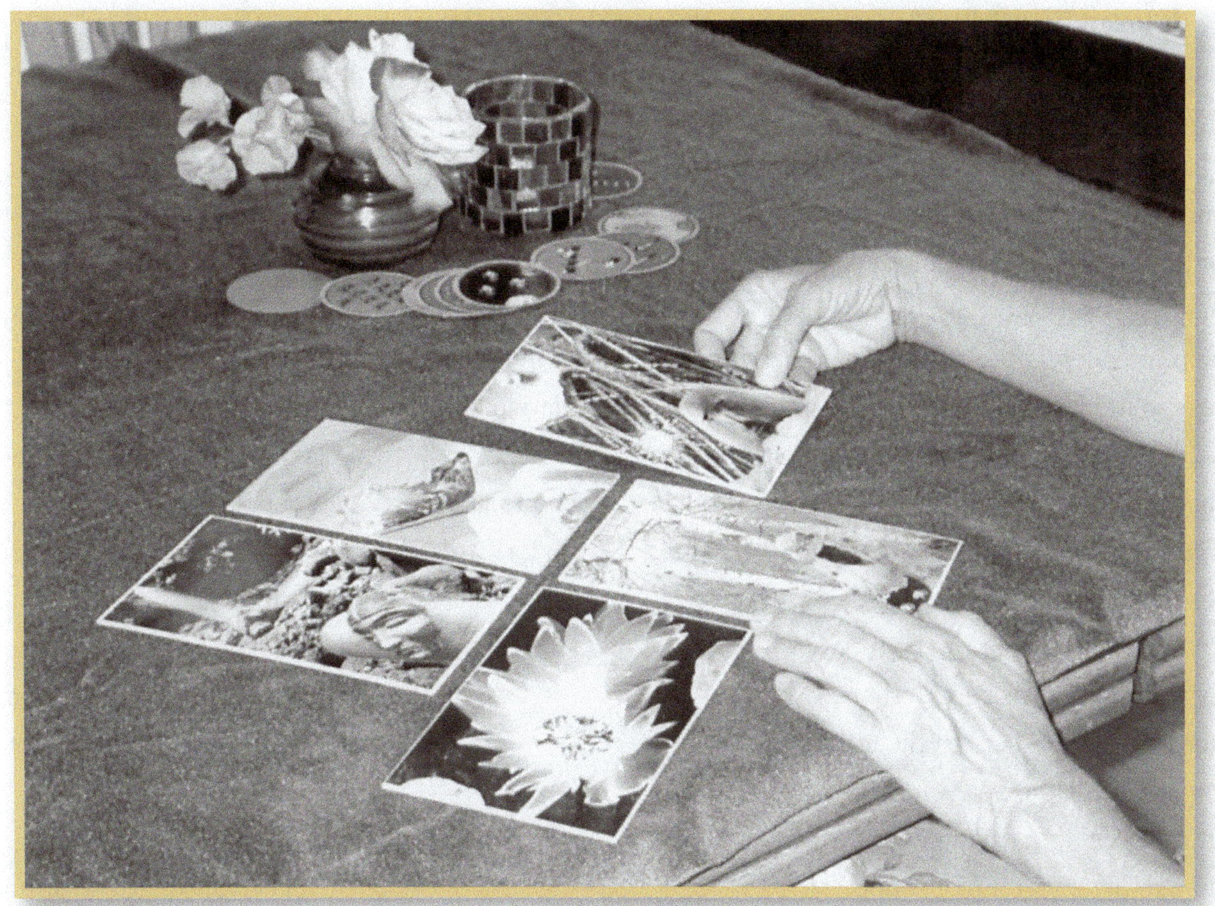

A four-card spread with the Source card. All cards are turned over by the end of the reading.

age. Don't include the asides and explanations that a reader may put in unless they are very relevant. You can also ask the reader to pause so a rush of words can be recorded. Or ask her to slow down. Write legibly so you and the reader can read it. The Scribe can write on a clean sheet of paper or directly onto a fresh page in the Card Reader's own journal, if the Card Reader prefers.

The Scribe Reads Back

An extremely powerful way to end a reading is for Scribes to read aloud, both to their Card Reader and to the whole group, the words they have written down.

In ongoing SoulCollage® groups, at the end of a session, each Scribe should read their answer page to the whole group and particularly to the card reader. Read first their Card Reader's question, then the name of the drawn cards, and then the words it spoke. If the Scribe is able to read the lines with expression it often sounds like a *wisdom poem*. For the Card Reader it is a revelation of what their intuition has just sent forth, and people love hearing their words read back to them. People can then take their page home, put it in their journal, and refer to it during the time between group meetings. Sometimes they work their words into finished poems and bring them back to share.

In many SoulCollage® reading groups there will be a SoulCollage® Facilitator who has been trained, who organizes the group, and is paid. This person won't be reading his own cards, and may choose to be the Scribe for everyone or have that function rotate. Also this Facilitator may ask some questions of each Card Reader to help him along or to prompt him back into first person mode. The rest of the group members hold the role of "Witness" and do not interrupt the reading with comments or with their own interpretations or experiences. After the entire reading is complete, and if everyone agrees, there can be time for the group to ask each other questions and reflect on the total experience. However, think of this process as a ritual more than a therapy group. It is not the idea to prod people into going deeper and deeper, or even to go into places that they seem to be avoiding. Witnesses will listen, show they are interested, and appreciate the images and the honesty.

We often select, without consciously choosing, cards that are of importance to our question.

The Cards Reveal Many Perspectives

Remember that in SoulCollage® readings you receive more than one answer. This is one of the many values of this process; *there are always several perspectives.* It is as if you are taking your question to an inner council of several wise beings. One or two answers may be especially outstanding and memorable. Others may seem less relevant or helpful, but later make sense in ways that surprise you.

Very often shadowed Neters turn up, ones who may be the cause of the problem presented in the question! He or she may tell you something you really don't want to hear. But it is well to listen to this Neter's answer because it often gives clues to the reason for the problem. For example, your *Scared Child* could show up in answer to your question about a new relationship. Interesting that she comes up, because she is the very part of your Committee who is stopping a new relationship from moving forward. She can now tell you why she is so afraid and what she needs to help her get over it. Some other Neter may be needed to get her through her fear. Possibly such a helper will show up in one of the other cards in the reading.

Every SoulCollage® reading is fresh and full of possibilities. It is the *"not-knowing"* element that makes it so interesting, not knowing what Neters are going to appear to answer a question. This is why we do not choose the cards to read, but let them be chosen for us by some hidden, synchronic knowing that resides in our unconscious and in the energy of our hands as we draw.

Synchronicity

Over and over again I have heard people comment, after a reading, *"These cards are so amazing!"* What they are talking about is synchronicity, a word C. G. Jung used to mean *"meaningful coincidences"*. The understanding here is that Soul is not limited to time and space the way conscious mind is limited. Our Neter energies are deeply interwoven, constantly overlapping, influencing each other mysteriously and continually. There is a correspondence between the intuitive mind of the questioner and the answering paradigm, in this case the SoulCollage® cards. Somehow we select, without consciously choosing, cards of importance to our question. This doesn't always happen, of course. And it happens more consistently when there is an important question asked, when there is openness to the process, and when there is a sense of expectation, rather than doubt or cynicism. It happens when imagination is respected and trusted. Furthermore, as Jung says, it happens most often when "an archetype is activated".

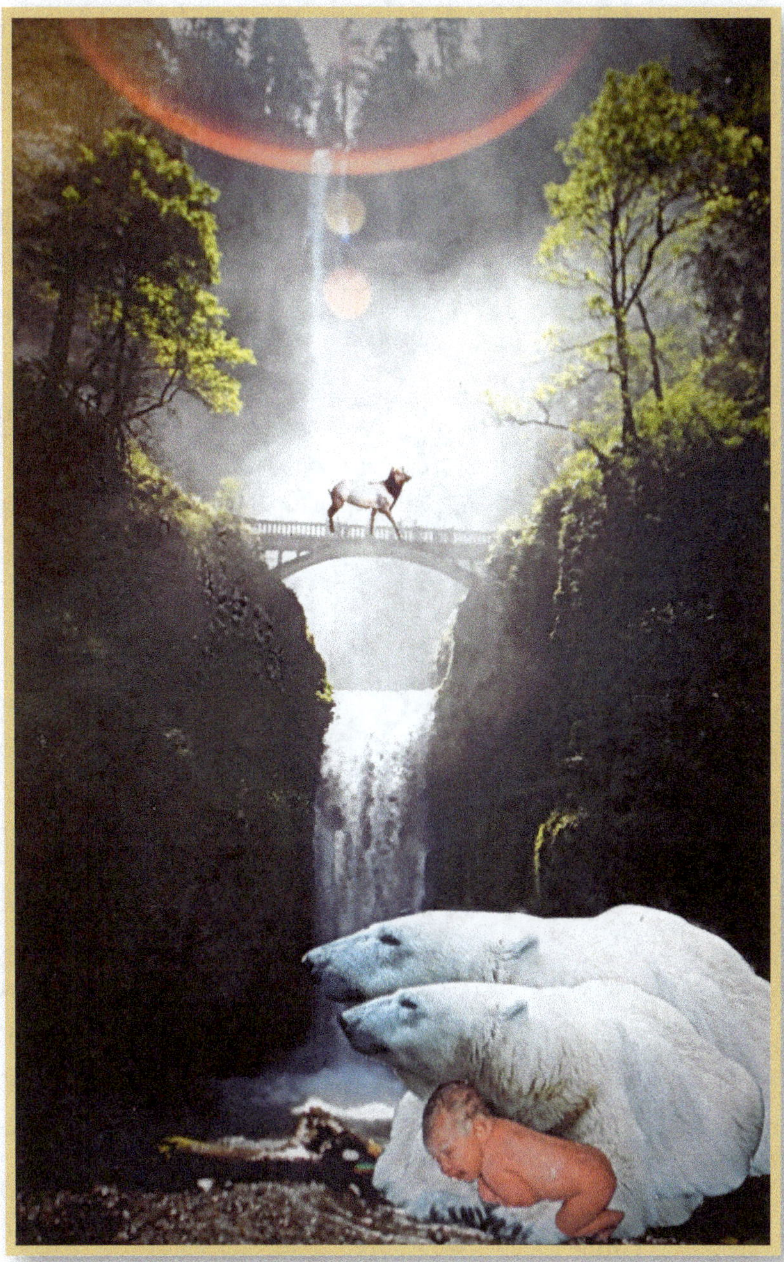

TITLE: **Guardian Angels**
SUIT: **Council**
CREATOR: **Colleen Benelli**

"We Are the Ones Who hold the babies when they come to Earth on the rainbow light."

Myths and Symbols

What I think Jung means, when he talks about the activation of archetypes, is that our personal unconscious is linked to the vast Cosmic Unconscious which contains the realms of the archetypes. It is as if our individual Soul is a tiny tributary of a great flowing river, and *when our personal story merges with, or is touched by, the universal Neters of this great river, we experience this as meaning, as joy, or as direction.*

These archetypal Neters have been manifesting into forms throughout history in countless myths and stories and traditional symbols. Our personal Soul, deep down, *knows* many of these myths even if we have never studied

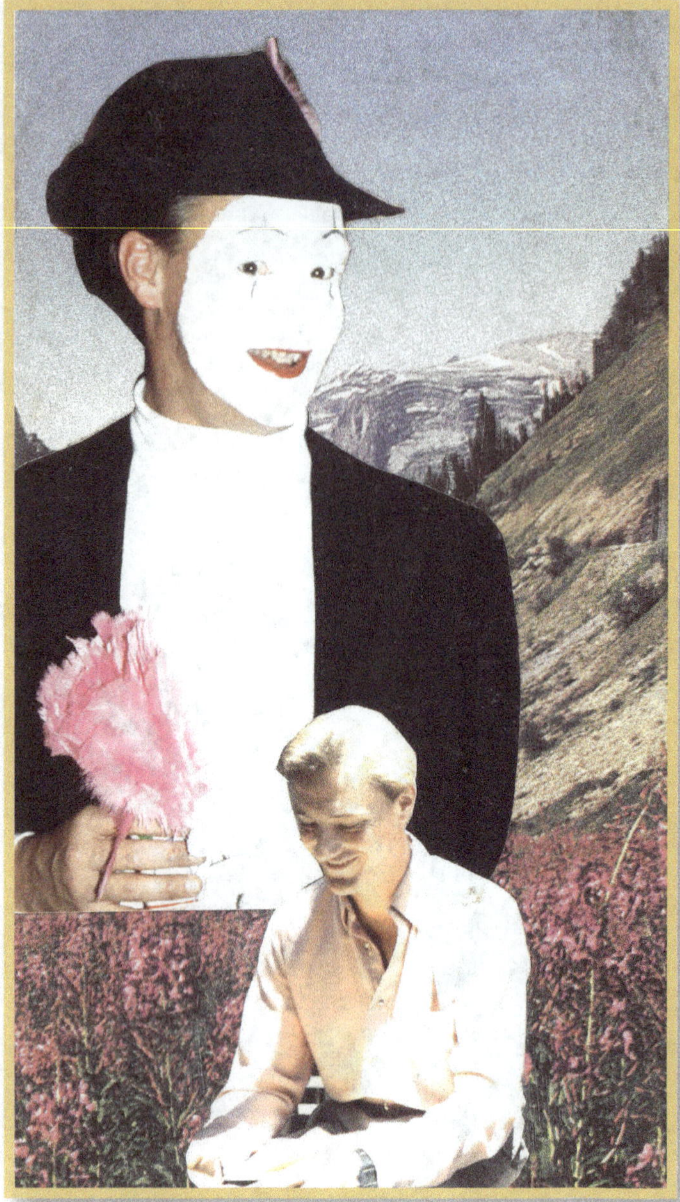

TITLE: **Paul**
SUIT: **Community**
CREATOR: **Meg Gorney**

"I Am your big brother, and I have a lightness of being to offer you and all my friends."

them. They are part of our spark of Source, our SoulEssence, our coding. Therefore, we are drawn to certain images, to divine figures in human forms that enact specific dramas; we are drawn to images of rocks, water, and certain colors— even certain shapes. Eventually each of our SoulCollage® decks will take on a sort of style or flavor that is distinctive. They reflect our own personal and unique Soul.

The images we choose, especially for the Neters of our Council suit, often have a quality that is mythic. You may choose many images of seekers, adventurers, lonely travelers; or you may choose images of women and children, of caretakers, of earth goddesses; or you may choose images of animals that are Neters throughout all your suits. Some of these cards may be associated with mythic figures, either by a name like *Percival* or *Ulysses* or by a more general name like *Hero*. You might have *Mary* or *Kwan Yin*, or simply *Compassion*. You might have *Hercules* or simply *Strength*, *Aphrodite* or simply *Lover*, *Shiva*, or simply, *Destroyer*. These Neters, usually ones in your Council, come into readings with wisdom that feels especially synchronic. By this I mean that their wise words in readings are particularly meaningful in helping you recognize how your own SoulEssence is manifesting into vital, external forms. They help you see yourself cast somehow in a mythic role, living in a story that has been told many times before. This is meaningful because of both its universality and its direction. Even if

Be willing to take on the persona of an archetype when you draw its card.

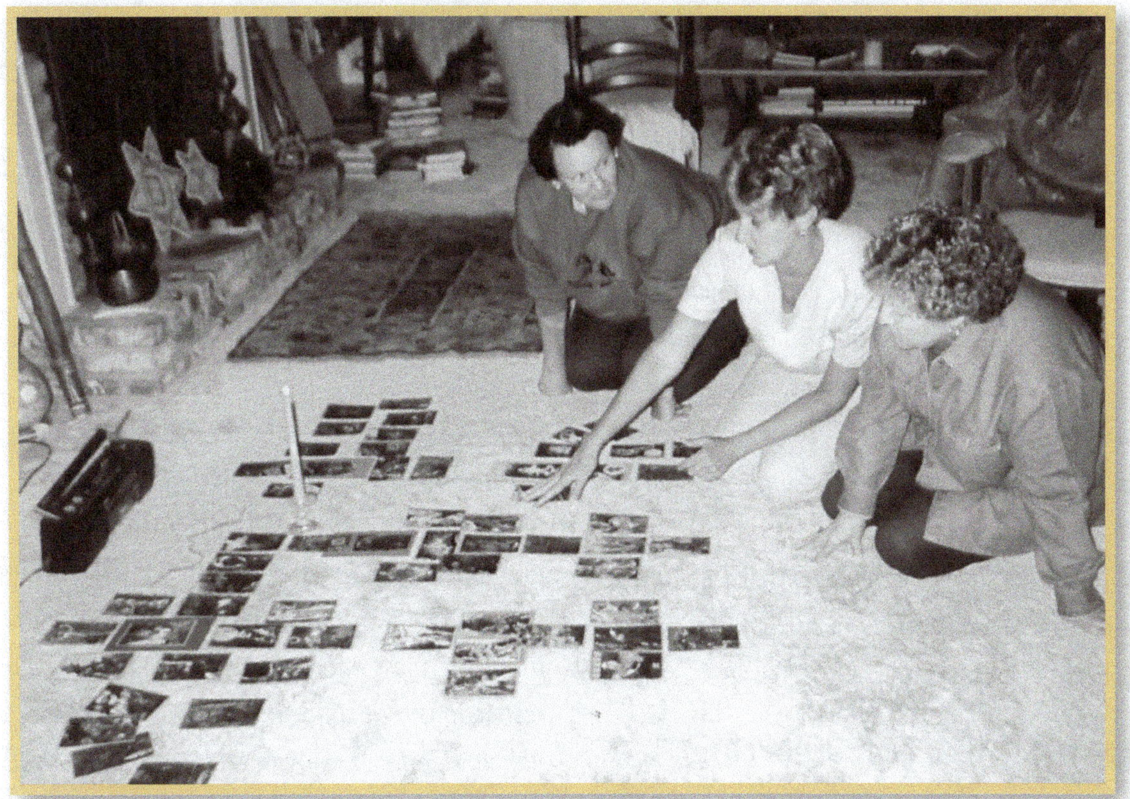

Laying out all my cards to see patterns, stories, themes of my life. Left to right: Mary Fenton, Jeri Bodemar, and Pam Gonsalves.

the journey is difficult and filled with pitfalls, it has purpose. Difficulties take on mythic meaning and make more sense in our lives because we now recognize ourselves as a part of an ongoing, yet eternal, Story.

Speaking From Council Neters

When you are speaking from the image of a Council Neter there will be largeness, even grandiosity, in its words and energy. These mythic Neters have been active for eons, and when they enter a life they always feel numinous and compelling, sometimes they even feel overwhelming. When they speak they will sound more external than your other Neters, and they may be commanding and wise, both at the same time. They may give you directions in no uncertain terms. They may speak of what they have done over the centuries, and what they want from you in the present and also in the future. Your Committee Neters who are grabbed by such an archetype will speak from a more interior place about their willingness to go along or their hesitation, hopes, and fears. Be willing to take on the persona of an archetype when you draw its card. You might even begin with the words *I Am the One Who…* when speaking from Council Cards, which could distinguish it from the *I Am One Who…* which may be enough for a card from the other suits where the Neters know themselves as just one of many. This might be one way to help you distinguish between Council and Committee Neters.

Two Readings as Examples

Reading #1

A four-card SoulCollage® reading done by Mariabruna Sirabella, a SoulCollage® Trainer from California.

This is a reading done using the least amount of words to formulate the question. The idea came from Seena's Lady Wisdom *who said one day: "Revise your questions and reduce them to three words". We tried. I found the revision of the question deepening and enlightening. It prompted me to cut through the 'story', search deeply within and get to the core of what was truly needed in that moment.* Here is an example.

QUESTION: "Who is obstructing?"

Card # 1—Pilgrim (Committee)

I Am One Who... *follows the intimations of another world and travels incessantly towards the Source. My steps are light and silent. My trails are of the Spirit and one day I will merge with its Mystery. In my shadow I isolate myself in spiritual arrogance. I think I can evolve alone. I expect mysterious spiritual riches to reveal themselves to me. In a strange way they set me apart, and I end up alone. As for your question, remember that even as Pilgrim I am part of a larger reality from which I receive nourishment. I can allow the osmosis and allow the exchange. I can drop the limiting stories, even the stories that sound positive. They often stop what may really happen.*

Card #2—Compassion (Council)

I Am the One Who... *embraces light and shadow with* Compassion. *I breathe the tears and the smiles of the world in even rhythm. My Shadow is sometimes excessive selflessness. In answer to your question I, your* Compassion, *am not in balance. Have more compassion for yourself to make it balance with the* Compassion *you show others. What sense of superiority makes you think your needs are less important than those of others? Who gives and who receives? There is only one of you, there are millions out there. Here is a mathematical mystery for you to decipher.*

Card # 3—I Am Freed (Committee)

I Am One Who... *liberates myself from the measuring stick of the self appointed judges. I free myself from binding clothes, from the lies of ordinary goodness, from the injunction to conform, from prettiness and propriety, from the rules and restrictions that suffocate my real self. I dance naked, and I sweat joy and aliveness. My Shadow is the figure in the background, the Maria Goretti syndrome. To answer your question: How many times do I need to remind you to free yourself from piety, from being the good girl, from being subdued, and all that s__t. To resolve what is obstructing, we need to dance more and reconnect with our body. Let's buy a fast red car.*

Card # 4—The Chthonic Horse (Companion, 3rd Chakra)

I Am One Who... *meets the world with clear unambiguous expectations. I look at fears straight in the eye and run voraciously in the wild. The four elements are my companions; they give me trust in my intuition, my abilities, my focus, and my courage. My Shadow is self-possession. To answer your question: Continue to love Light even when it is obstructed. Trust that the perennial cycle of coming and going will remove this obstacle and the first Light emerging from that obscurity will be precise and powerful like a laser beam. Feel in our body how my strong muscles vibrate in the run.*

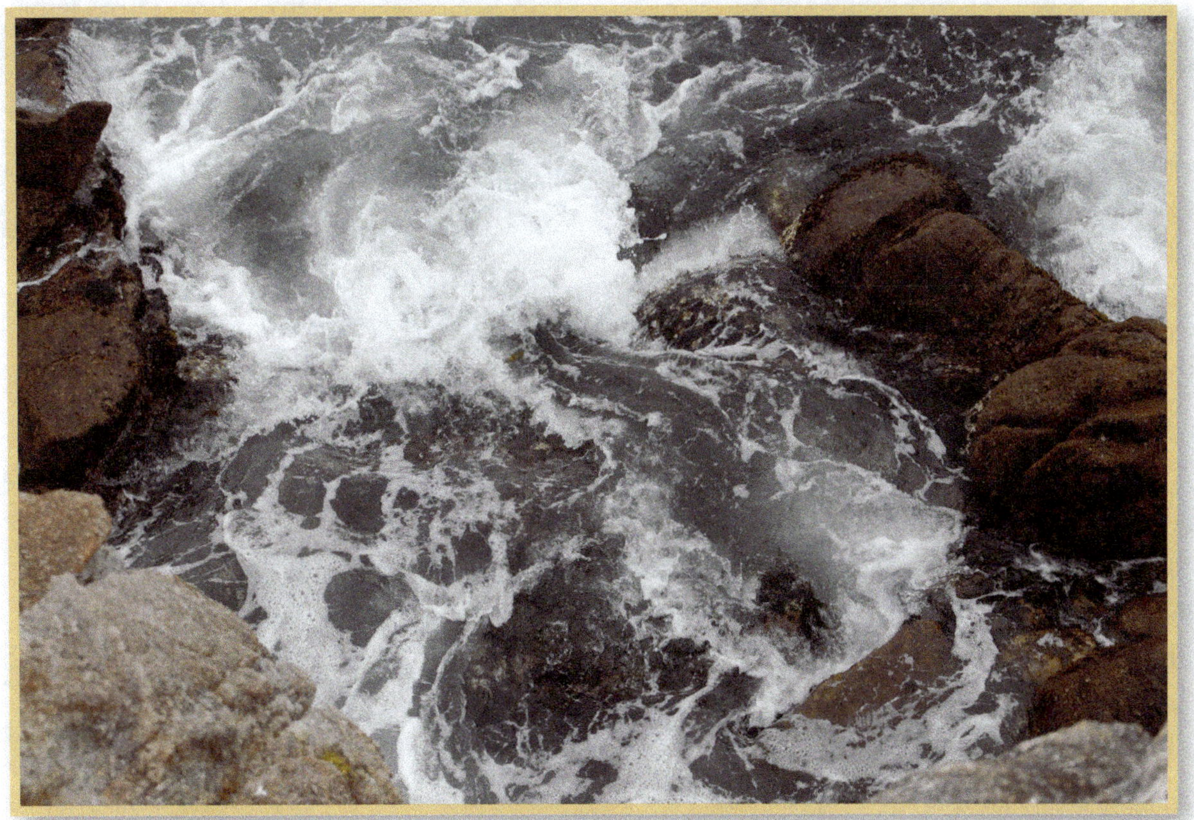

TITLE: **Ocean Designs**
SUIT: **Council**
CREATOR: **Miriam Goldberg**

Reading #2

A five-card SoulCollage® reading done by Miriam Goldberg, a SoulCollage® Facilitator from California.

QUESTION: How can I integrate creativity into my life?

Card # 1—Shiva (Council)

I Am… Shiva *of your Council. I am adorned with the forces of life. I shine love on you from the purity of the formless and remind you that form and formless are one. What I say to you about this question is: Dance and laugh with me! Stay unattached to all forms. Let your life force manifest the creativity while you and I delight in the creative play of radiance. I will always be with you.*

Card # 2—Fear of the Critic (Committee)

I Am… your Fear of Your Critic *Neter. I am terrified of your* Critic, *in all its vicious forms. I try to protect you from it, but I am imprisoned in my fear. What I say to you about this question is: Anytime you feel reluctance to express, place me and the* Critic *card side by side and see us as just one of many forces in your life. You must see us, you must face us directly, but you must not be trapped like I am. Freedom is your true nature. Stay free!*

Card # 3—Ocean Designs (Council)

I Am… *your* Ocean Designs *Neter. I offer an infinite abundance of designs with every wave, every breath, every pulse of the ocean. What I say to you about this question is: Look! See the magnificent swirling creativity in me, in life, everywhere. Feel the endless, ever-changing designs. Dance them. Draw them. Sing them. Breathe them. Come to me if you forget this abundant gift is yours always.*

Card # 4—Crystal Song Bowl (Community)

I Am... your Crystal Song Bowl *Neter. I catch the light and sing it into you. I bring the eternal to you, and you to both eternity and to this world. What I say to you about this question is: Play me. Let my tones lift and nourish your heart and your bones. Fill with me, relax into me, and rest in me. All doubt melts in my sound. Everything flows from the pure empty resonance I ring. Do not worry. Let it flow.*

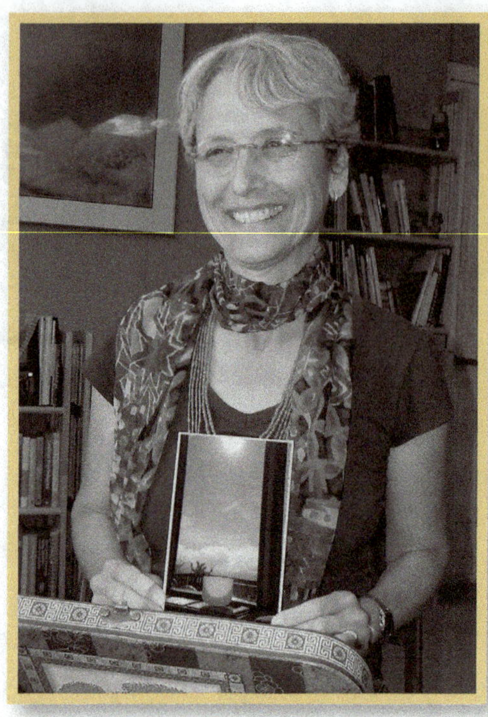

Miriam Goldberg holding her Crystal Song Bowl card

Card # 5—Creativity (Council)

I Am... *the* Creativity *Neter of your Council.* I Am... *the core creative fire of the earth and in everything in this world. What I say to you about this question is: You are my daughter. My riches are yours. Accept this truth, and all will manifest.*

CHAPTER 13

Surprise and Humor in SoulCollage®

I will spend this brief chapter emphasizing again the significance of *surprise* in SoulCollage,® and also in celebrating the Council member most linked to surprise, the archetypal *Fool*.

Plato said that the beginning of philosophy is surprise; I would say in the same vein that the beginning of *transformation* lies in surprise. This is because, despite the yearning of our Souls for change and growth, our Committee members generally work hard to maintain the *status quo* rather than risk journeying down unknown paths. To really begin to move and grow, we usually must be surprised, and this requires a nudge or a push from the *Fool*. He is the archetype of *Holy Interruption*. Hopefully, his push for us can come in the form of humor, of playfulness, and of synchronicities, rather than in more shadowed interruptions. The creative, right-brain activities of SoulCollage® are a perfect venue for a lighthearted entry by the *Fool*—if we can let ourselves relax and be surprised.

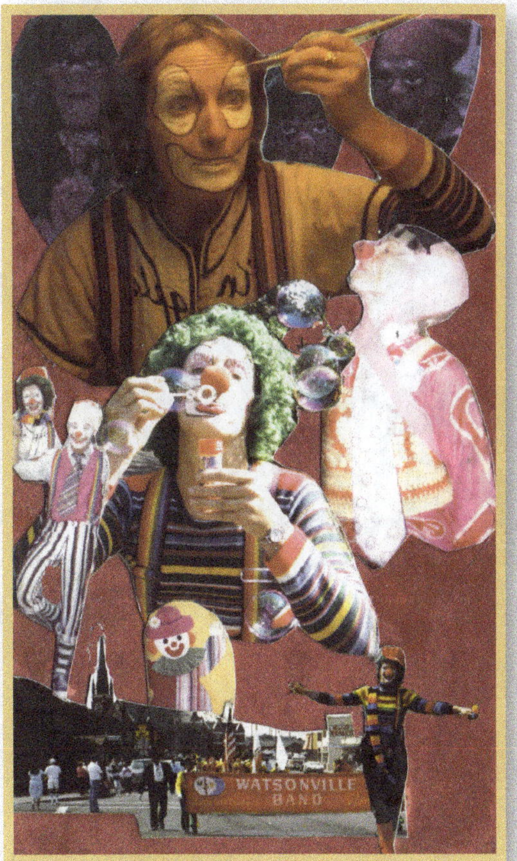

TITLE: **Wink (An Inner Clown)**
SUIT: **Committee**
CREATOR: **Seena B. Frost**

"*I Am One Who* loves to interrupt serious church services by dancing down the aisle."

I'll share with you here some relevant personal history. Twenty-five years ago I participated in an activity that, now that I look back on it, moved me down my path towards SoulCollage.® I was, for several years, a now and then clown! I attended some clown workshops and developed two quite different clown personalities. Both

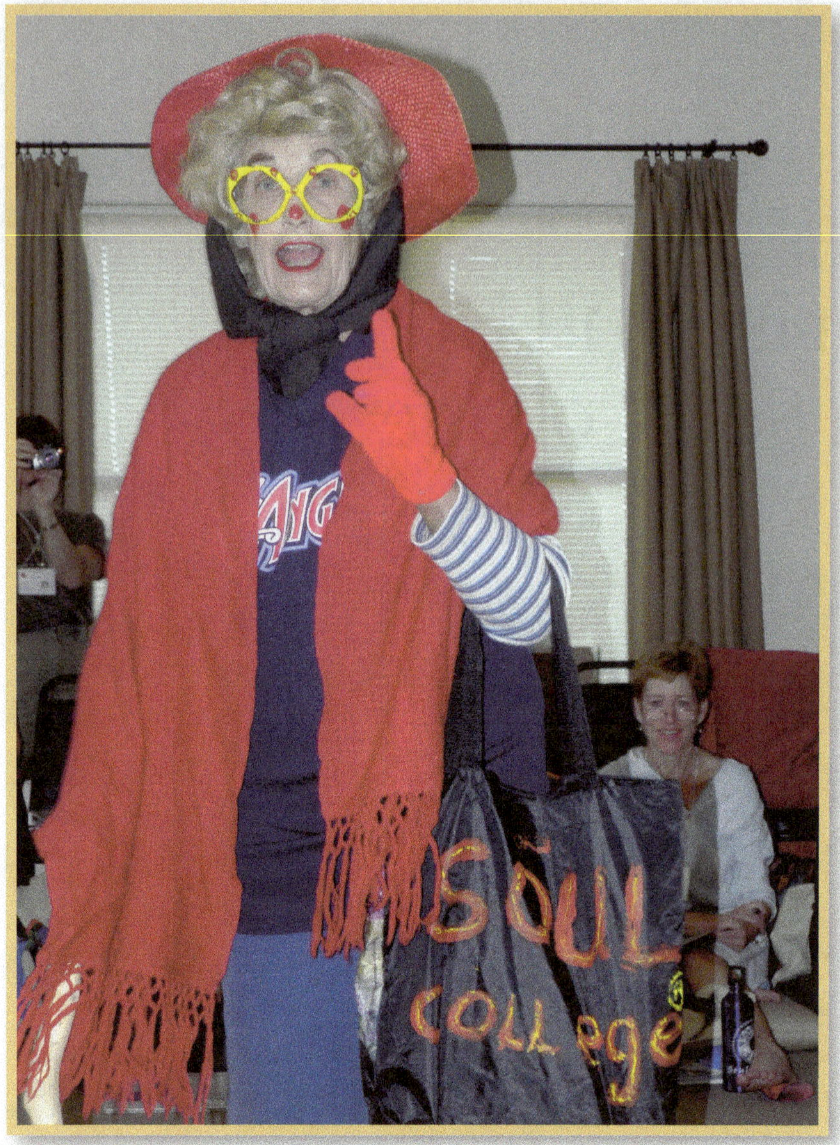

Ms. Anne Thrope (Seena Frost) at the 2009 SoulCollage® Facilitators' Conference in Tupac, AZ

PHOTO BY JIM SCHOFIELD

The surprise element in SoulCollage® lets us look at ourselves with new eyes, and laugh at ourselves with healing laughter.

were *interrupters* who delighted in surprising people. These two characters surprised me first of all because they were inner opposites of my serious, introverted, unsurprising external personality. The first was an old lady clown named *Ms. Anne Thrope*. She always carried a suitcase full of brochures, and she was eternally on her way to attend another and another and still another workshop. Most were *Jungian* workshops, mispronounced by Ms. Anne with a hard "J".

She would burst into various agency gatherings (I was then the director of a Family Service agency) and surprise the group with nonstop chatter about how she had to find the perfect workshop to help her get her life together. She made fun of what we therapists took so seriously in our work. People laughed at her and loved her. Less obviously, but truly, they were laughing at and loving themselves.

My second clown *persona* was *Wink*. He was a church clown and had gathered a whole troupe of Presbyterian clowns, teenagers on up to a woman in her late seventies. The troupe was named the Merry Meddlers, and we surprised more than one congregation by interrupting services, taking the offering, dancing up and down the aisles, and joyfully greeting people in the pews. Sometimes we acted out the Scripture lessons with words and pantomime. This unexpected arrival of the Merry Meddlers would suddenly transform the energy of a worship service. Inevitably *Inner Judges* would appear on some faces, but the *Inner Child* in most people burst forth in smiles and waves, and a sense of joy and closeness happened spontaneously. Those were memorable services, talked about for months and years. These same Merry Meddlers also danced down Main Street as part of Fourth of July parades. We waved our banner and surprised people on the curbs with smiles and handshakes and handfuls of candy kisses.

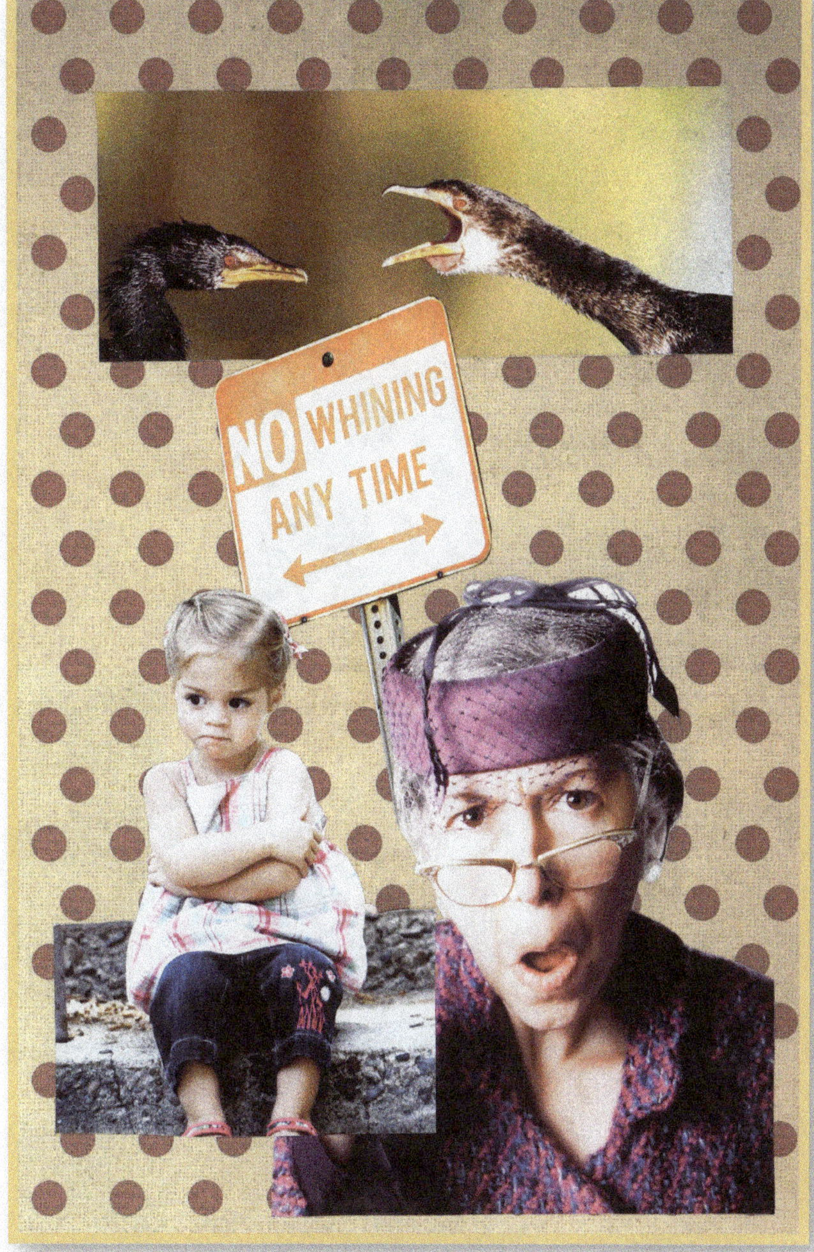

TITLE: **The Whiner**
SUIT: **Committee**
CREATOR: **Dori King**

"*I Am One Who* occasionally likes to whine. I feel this is a pretty good way to vent, to get feelings to the surface. I do know that whining has its place and then, I read the sign. Phooey!"

I mention these clowns because they were for me an entry to *"the laughter at the heart of things"*, or to that real sense of humor that laughs at the lack of proportion within one's self as well as in others. The first clown, Ms. Anne, came as a fool to interrupt the overly serious mentality of psychotherapists as we labor with our patients; Wink came as a fool to interrupt the equally serious and humorless worship in most religious services. Both were saying something like: "Why are you taking yourselves so seriously? Get over it! Come to the party."

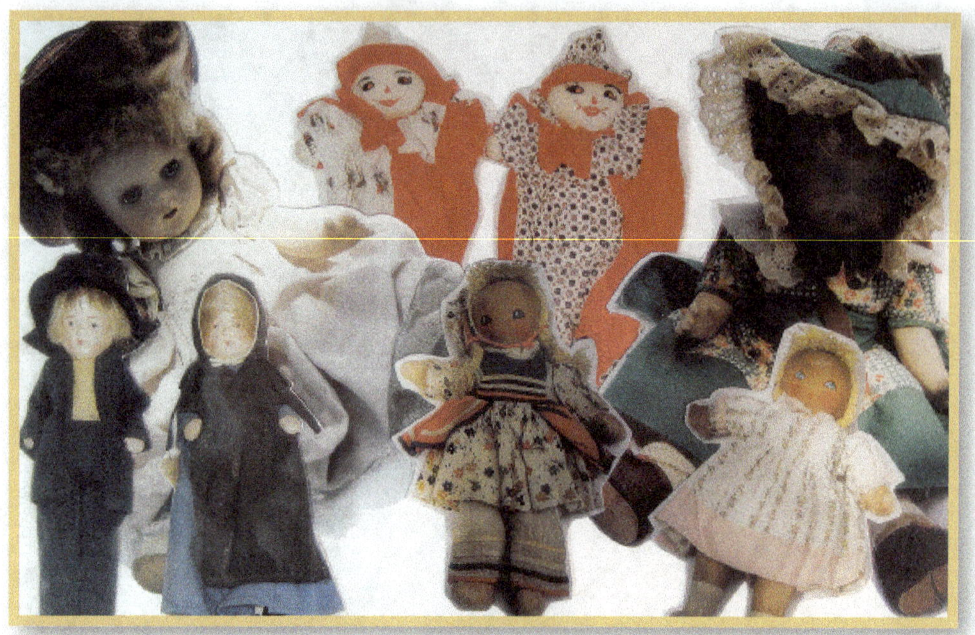

TITLE: **My Doll Collection**
SUIT: **Community**
CREATOR: **Kira Jones**
"We Are the quiet Ones who are always there for you. We will hug you, listen to you, dress up for you, play with you, watch you, simply be for you."

ways, or lazily being absent when needed. The question is, how do we alert a Soul, any Soul, to this inner reality? If a Soul's ego, (in other words, some ruling Committee members), is armored and afraid, it will not want to recognize that there is any lack of proportion, at least not in *its* domain. Such

Helen M. Luke, the Jungian scholar, has an essay called "The Laughter at the Heart of Things", found in a collection of her essays published under that same name. She writes:

> *We all laugh at the foibles of those around us, but those with a sense of humor do not laugh at a person; there is simply a feeling of delight in the ridiculous wherever it is manifest, and such laughter does not condemn the other or oneself but simply enjoys the sudden recognition of the loss of proportion in all our human conflicts and contradictions. It is a healing not a destructive thing––a delight in life, in its comedies and tragedies, its seriousness and absurdities…*" (p. 111)

This "*sudden* recognition" might also be written as the "*surprising* recognition" of lack of proportion. And lack of proportion is another name for what we call Shadow in SoulCollage.® Our Neters may be acting out in exaggerated

Neters may point fingers and laugh at others' disproportion, but this will not be *heart laughter* as Luke describes it in her essay. It will be brittle and barbed and even mean-spirited. So the question arises: is there any way to surprise ego defenses and provide foolish nudges to help Soul energy flow more freely? Perhaps on the wings of a hearty laugh? Where is *Ms. Anne* when we need her? Where is *Wink*?

What follows are several hints for making the *Fool's* entry more likely in your own SoulCollage® work, and how to bring it in when you share the SoulCollage® process with others.

1. Have a multitude of images available. Collect them from every sort of magazine, greeting card, photo album, newspaper. Images that have the power to surprise your intuition and your unconscious are *very unpredictable*. And they are different for everyone.

Be sure to collect odd and humorous images as well as serious and beautiful ones. Browse through the image sources in a sort of trance, without criticizing or interpreting.

2. Stay as playful as you can.

Let browsing for images be like a treasure hunt, with plenty of images, enough for you to have all you could possibly want. Just gather them as if you were a child gathering Easter eggs in your basket.

3. Continue this playful spirit while you create your cards.

The more you feel free to combine images in unpredictable ways, the more magical your card-making can be. The *Fool* may hand you an image that does not seem to make logical sense at all, and you will trust his guidance and reach for the scissors and glue. Later you will read the images and discover some reasons you may have been drawn to these particular images.

4. Speak from the images.

The most surprising part of the SoulCollage® experience is *speaking from the images*. Once you have been present at a reading and witnessed the surprise and amazement people experience when they turn over an image, step into it, and let their unconscious bubble up in unexpected and poetic words, then you will know what I am talking about. The words seem to ride free on their imaginations. Not always, of course. And there are degrees to such surprise. Sometimes tears come and sometimes laughter. Sometimes there is an "Aha" that helps the Soul grow a notch; sometimes the words simply describe a state of Soul that had been unseen and uncelebrated.

The most surprising part of the SoulCollage® experience is speaking from the images.

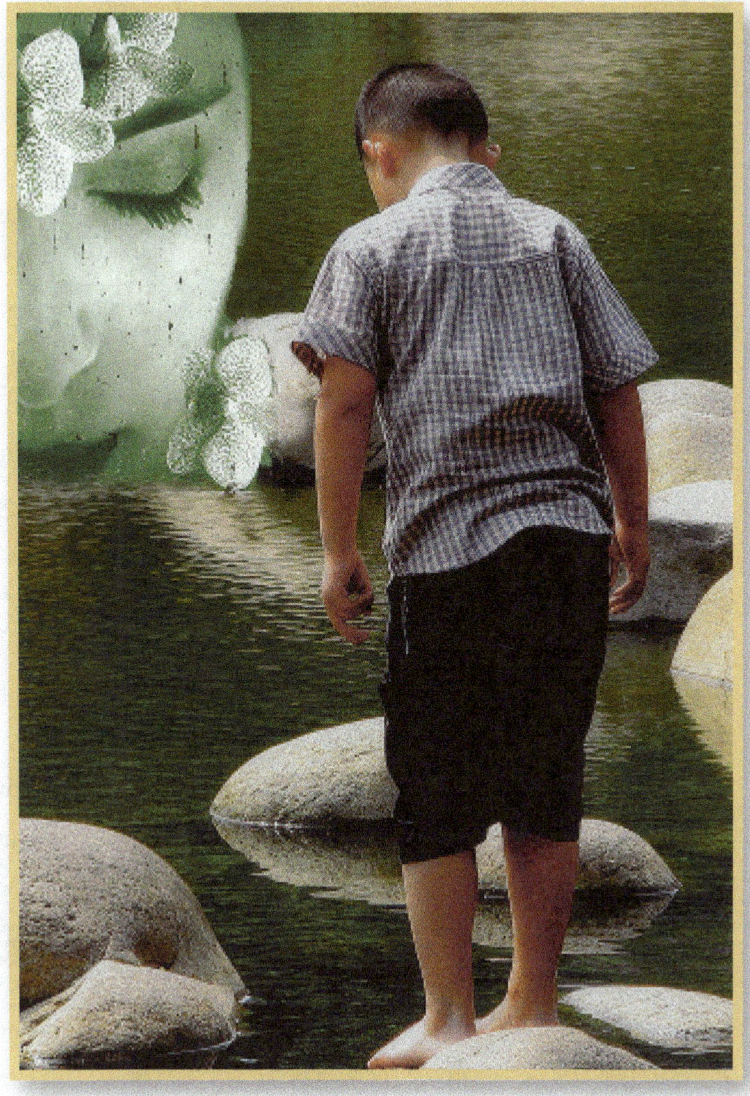

TITLE: **Confidence**
SUIT: **Council**
CREATOR: **Pam Renner**

"*I Am One Who* goes forward without hesitation."

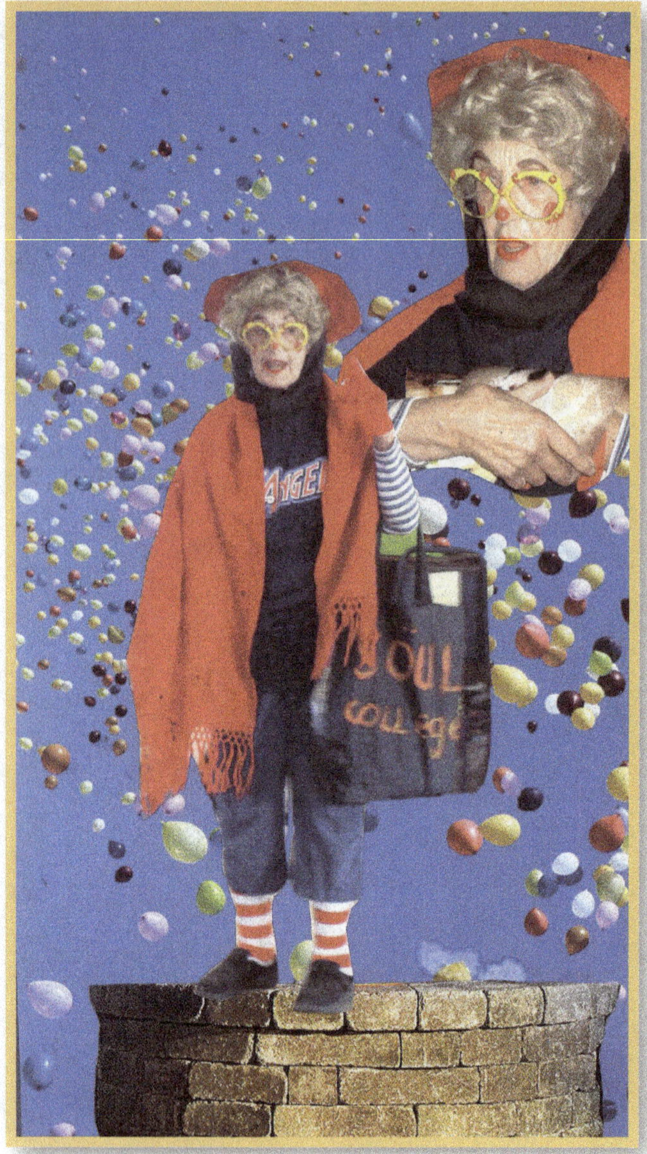

TITLE: **Ms. Anne Thrope**
SUIT: **Committee**
CREATOR: **Seena B. Frost**

"I Am the Neter within you who loves the Fool! He and I together bring surprise and laughter to SoulCollage® meetings, sometimes appearing in the shape of Ms. Anne."

5. Draw cards without knowing which ones you are drawing.

For the surprise ingredient to have its full effect, it is important that *a card be drawn from your deck and laid face down* until the very moment you turn it over to read. (See Readings in Chapter 12.) In order to maintain this surprise, don't write on the backs of cards or distinguish between them except by gluing on a backing which defines their suits. Choose suit backings that can't easily be distinguished by the spies of your ego (the logical mind) who might refuse to choose a certain card. The images on all your cards, over years, will continue to surprise you with directives, insights, and new healing wisdom if they are consulted in this way.

I truly believe that it is the *surprise ingredient* in SoulCollage® that enables us to look at ourselves with new eyes and to laugh with a kind of healing laughter. Then, when we take our cards into community and show how we can laugh at ourselves, others will laugh with us, and be able to see their own disproportions. Be sure to make an occasional silly card, especially for the disproportions in your Committee Neters.

> *The beginning of transformation lies in surprise. Cherish your interruptions!*

Here is a card for one of my inner clowns, Ms. Anne Thrope.

CHAPTER 14

Journaling With SoulCollage®

CREATE A JOURNAL FOR YOUR SOULCOLLAGE® CARDS

Many of you, I imagine, are people who love to journal. Your cards will be a continual source of inspiration and subject matter for any sort of journal that you keep. However, if you plan to work deeply with SoulCollage,® and if you expect to make many cards, let me suggest creating a journal dedicated just to this work. I recommend that it be a loose-leaf binder notebook so you can add more hole-punched pages when you want. At the beginning of this notebook could be a section where each card has its own introductory page, a general page about this one Neter. These could be indexed by the four suits if you are using the suits as a form of organization. I will give you a couple of examples of such initial pages in just a moment, but in short the primary information included on them would be the *name* of the card, the *suit* it is in, and a general description of the image, including the *primary energy* as you begin to experience it. After this description let the Neter answer these questions in its voice, and record the answers.

Who are you and what do you have to give me?
What do you want from me?
How will I remember?

At the end you can add on a relevant quote that matches this Neter's energy if one comes to your attention at some point.

TITLE: **Kwan Yin**
SUIT: **Council**
CREATOR: **Jeri Bodemar**

"*I Am the One Who* is dedicated to the enlightenment of every single person, to the enlightment of humanity as a whole."

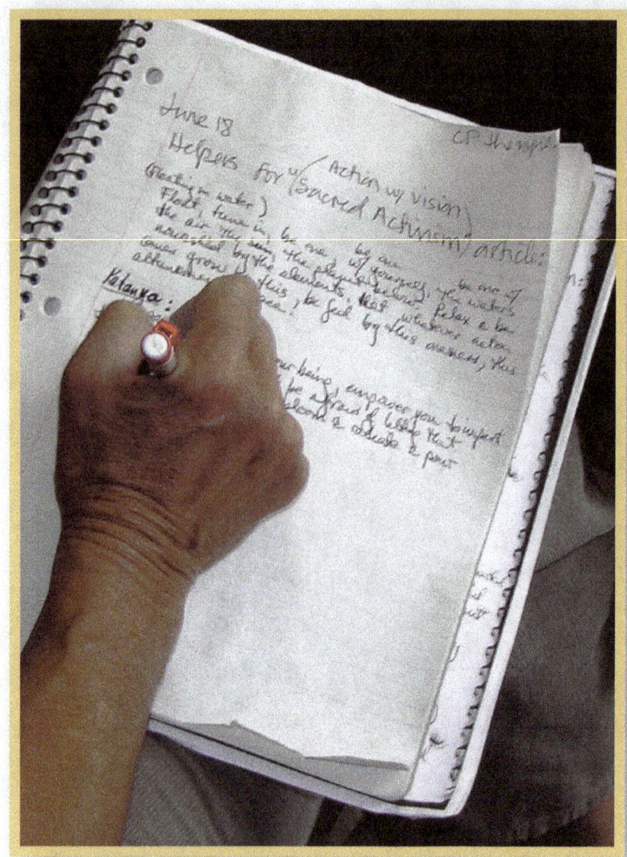

You can dialogue with your cards in many ways, one of which is journaling.

Do this kind of a page for each SoulCollage® card. It will help you find the heart of each Neter's wisdom and energy for you. Remember though that it may bring its energy to you in different words over the years, speaking new ideas every time you draw it in a reading. You are not freezing it in a single definition on this journal page, but only letting it introduce itself to you.

After you have answered these questions you might also write a few sentences to indicate the shadow potential for this card. How does the Neter behave when it is out of balance? If the card has a Neter that is shadowed in its primary energy, like your *Critic* or your *Perfectionist* or your *Rebel*.... then write, in this slot, how the Neter might act if its Shadow were not so deep and if it were moving into balance. How could this very same Neter serve you then? Find its gold.

Over time you may want to add or change this initial page as you receive more information. That's one reason to have it in a loose-leaf form.

In the remaining part of this same loose leaf SoulCollage® journal would be many pages for the readings you will do either by yourself or with a group. Always be prepared with enough lined, punched paper to add more of these pages as you need them. Date them, and be sure to keep this book and your cards safe. All together they will become very precious. Someday you may want to share them with grandchildren, and pass them down as a legacy that reveals your story, and your hopes and fears, from a heart level.

Examples of SoulCollage® Journal Entries

Example 1: Seena Frost offers a Community card as one example:

Name of Card: *Ninety-Nine* (Community)
Description: This Community Neter is *Louise Worthington*, laughing, looking upwards. Her face and arthritic hands show her age which is nearly ninety-nine years. There is a sense of the Crone archetype in her image. The background is a garden of flowers for Louise loved her garden.
Core Energy of the Card: Cherish your interruptions! Greet them laughing and invite them in. Be flexible.

Question: Who are you and what do you have to give me?
Answer: *I Am One Who* is a very old woman, and I am also your friend. I loved this life despite my losses and ailments. *I Am One Who* is active and interested in the issues of this world even now. As I told you once when you asked, the secret of my long life is that I have always tried to cherish my interruptions. I know that's hard for you, but remember it. I give you this direction as my gift.
Question: What do you want from me?
Answer: *I Am One Who* wants you to enter your old age with gusto, and live it fully and long. Don't be eager to cross over too soon. Learn from the adventure of aging, even its hardships. *I Am One Who* wants you to see what surprises old age will bring to you if you cherish your interruptions and stay fully involved in life.
Question: How will I remember?
Answer: Lovely white hair like mine will remind you. As yours grows whiter you will cherish it, and wrinkles too. They are beautiful.
Shadow of this Neter: There are times when interruptions will not serve you and you will need to protect yourself from them. Then my advice will not serve you and you must ignore it.

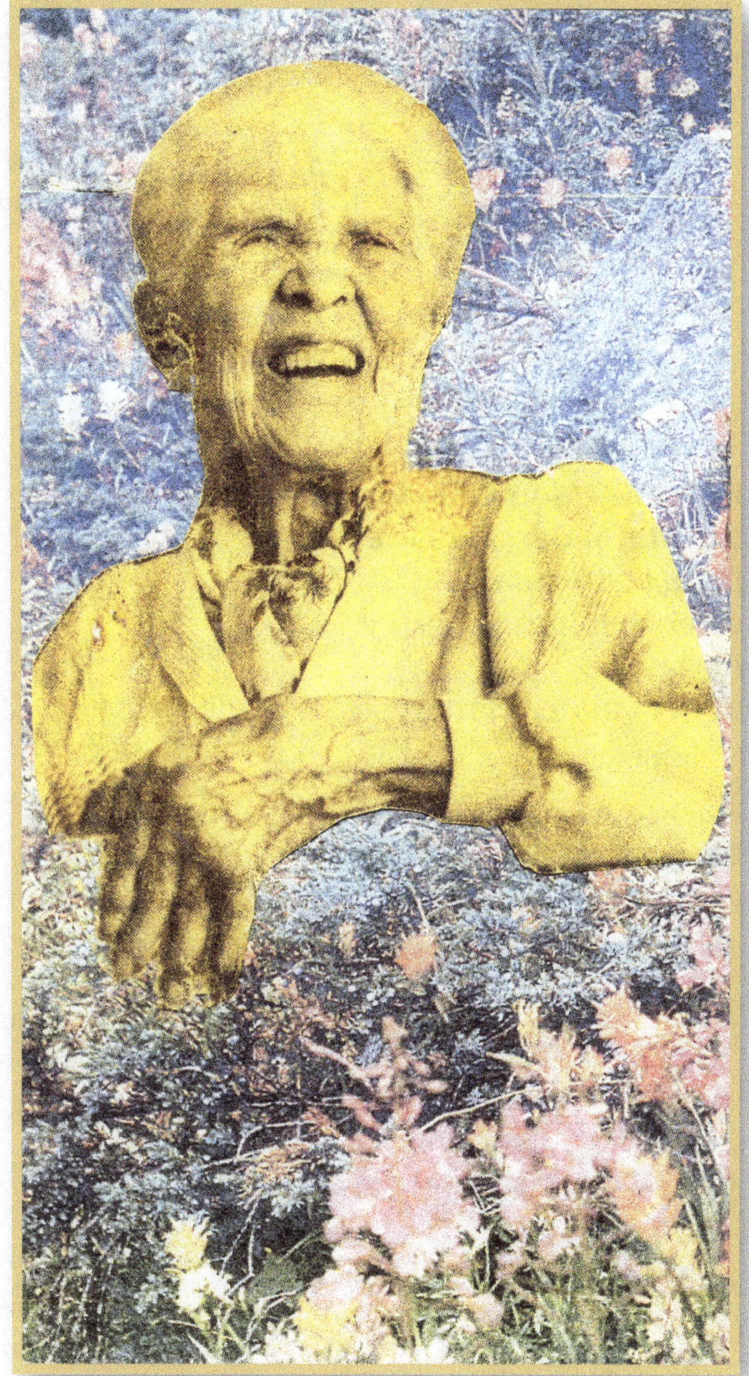

TITLE: **Louise Worthington**
SUIT: **Community**
CREATOR: **Seena B. Frost**

"Cherish your interruptions!"

Quote:

My soul is as young as the day it was created,
Yes, and much younger!
In fact, I am younger today than I was
Yesterday,
And if I am not younger tomorrow
Than I am today,
I would be ashamed of myself.
— from *Meditations of Meister Eckhart*

Example 2: SoulCollage® Facilitator, Jeri Bodemar, from California, offers her journal entry for one of her Council cards:

Name of Card: *Kwan Yin* (Council)

Description: This Council Neter is *Kwan Yin*, the Chinese Goddess of Compassion, who is represented in many other cultures as well. She is surrounded by a sky of light-infused clouds and garden leaves, a burning candle, and a symbol of "As above, so below."

Core Energy of the Card: Remember the power and existence of compassion in the world and in your personal life.

Question: Who are you and what do you have to give me?

Answer: *I Am One Who* is dedicated to the enlightenment of every single person, to the enlightenment of humanity as a whole. I continue ceaselessly to return to this life, this planet, until humanity reaches a new consciousness, a place of compassion, unity, and peace. I carry that consciousness within and project that dream and possibility to all those around me. Compassion is my focus and my purpose; in that I am steadfast.

Question: What do you want from me?

Answer: *I Am One Who* reminds you of the power of compassion and reassures you of its existence. I want you to rest in this remembrance and to know the power of your compassion for others AND for yourself.

Question: How will I remember?

Answer: Every time you see my statue in your garden, or anywhere, you can pause and feel the power of your compassionate heart—and of all other compassionate hearts.

Shadow of this Neter: *Compassion* means *to suffer with* and sometimes one may suffer too much for the apparent lack of compassion in this world, and end up feeling despair. Or, one may have too little compassion for oneself, or a particular group.

Quote:

Compassion is the radicalism of our time.
— H.H. the Dalai Lama

Someday you may want to share your cards and journal with grandchildren and pass them down as a legacy that reveals your story from a heart level.

CHAPTER 15

Individual Work With SoulCollage® Cards

MAKE TIME TO CREATE CARDS

Very often your first card was created in a workshop setting. You attended to investigate what this process called SoulCollage® is all about, and found yourself sitting at a table collaging an image on to a card. There were others around you doing the same thing, but for that moment you felt alone and engrossed in your own creative process.

If you were captured by the beauty, surprise, and possibility of creating these personal cards, then you may want to find time at home to add many more cards to your deck. Get into the habit of always looking for images. Search through catalogues and magazines that cross your desk. Then, one day, you'll decide it's time to sit down with all these random images and create cards. The creative juices will start flowing and you may work until the wee hours without noticing how late it is. These creative card-making periods often happen in spurts. Between them you continue to collect images wherever you can find them.

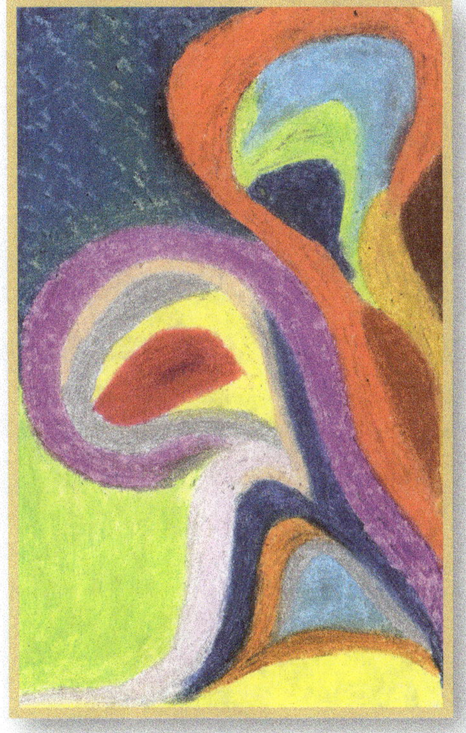

TITLE: **Great Mother Goddess**
SUIT: **Council**
CREATOR: **Buffy Marie Collison**

"I Am the One Who is a steady force in your life."

Many people, and this may include you, find it hard to set aside time for this personal work. It will help to have your images, some cards, and the glue handy, perhaps on a book shelf, easily available, beckoning to you all the time. If you can link up with another person who also wants to make cards, this will help you assign the time. Or you can make an agreement with someone to regularly meet for lunch specifically to share the cards you've been making at home.

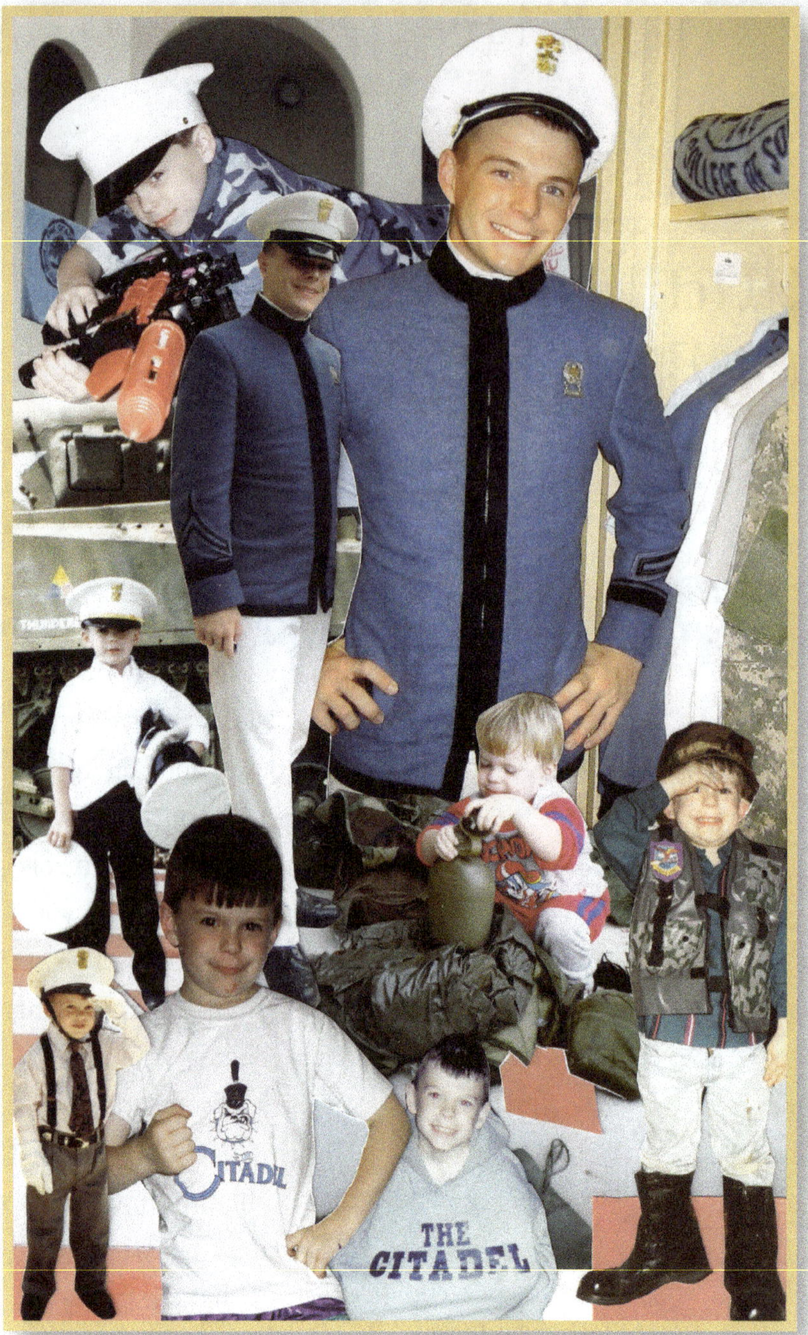

TITLE: **Buddy III**
SUIT: **Community**
CREATOR: **Mili Dillard**

"*I Am One Who* is fully my unique self AND a proud lineage bearer of traditions."

Draw Cards Daily

Have your cards close at hand in your home, not closed up in a box and tucked away. Perhaps a little altar space can be placed in a corner of the room where you create or where you meditate. Have all your cards stacked there, face down, except the Transpersonal cards. Leave those cards on top and face up. Draw one or two cards from your SoulCollage® deck each morning and see these images as your Neters-of-the-Day. This is a practice I've been doing for twenty years, and I strongly recommend it. Put these two cards somewhere you can see them during the day; then return them to the deck the next morning when you draw two more. It takes only a few moments. I always draw one Community card and the other from one of the other three suits. (I distinguish the suits by the backings on each card.) If the Community Neter is a person who is present in my life, I will send him or her some special energy. I may even email or phone them to let them know their card came up and that they are being remembered. I also record the names in my daily journal, so I can look back and see who has come up and when, and if there are synchronicities occurring.

Making SoulCollage® Cards for Dreams

Dreams can be a great source of personal images as they are closely related to your Neters. If you work at remembering your dreams you may want to incorporate some of the most powerful dream images into your SoulCollage® deck. Especially include those beings that reoccur and who act as archetypal forms that challenge, interrupt, or direct you. It is seldom easy to find an image that exactly matches a dream image. However, certain random images you have picked out and stored away may show a similar energy to your dream characters. Check through your file of images for ones to be on dream cards.

If you work with dreams in therapy or in a dream group, share the cards you create around a special dream. Choose other Neters that are in your deck to dialogue with a dream Neter, and this may uncover its significance. You might try finishing an unfinished dream with the intuitive help of a Council Neter that you select from your deck and bring in for a consultation. You can even have a full Council meeting to discuss the meaning of a dream image. There are many ways to investigate dreams using your cards, and you will discover ways that work well for you.

If you want to add pieces of your own art work, this is perfectly fine with any of your cards. Include bits of your paintings or sketches or photographs as they fit into the collage you are creating.

The suits help stretch us to acknowledge parts that are on our edges or in our depths.

Do You Create Additional Suits?

Some people who have made several cards for dreams have created a separate suit for dream Neters. This brings up the whole question of the four suits described earlier, and about adding to them or subtracting from them. Let me talk a little about that here.

The suits are simply a device to help you organize the parts of your many-faceted Soul, and to help you mentally expand the limits around who might be included as part of your Soul. The suits help you remember to include Neters you might not have thought of, but ones who present you with important "gifts." A number of people have chosen to ignore the suits all together and create their cards without such designations. These cards are just as powerful and they work just as well in readings. Some people don't include the Companions suit; some overlook their Community Neters. Some only make Council cards. Again, these decks are perfectly fine; however they will miss some Neters who, if included, might give them new and surprising perspectives. Our Souls are widely diverse in their many parts. We are complicated beings! The suits help stretch us to acknowledge parts that are on our edges or in our depths.

As to adding suits, this too is okay, but it will complicate your deck, perhaps more than necessary. Dream Neters usually fit into one of the suits, either the Council, if the figure is archetypal, or the Committee, if the figure is a

As much as possible, I recommend this in regard to all sorts of other Neters: special holy places where you have been, or love to visit, can go in the Community suit; the Muses can go in the Council suit, and so forth. When you are drawing your cards in a reading it is better not to have small categories of Neters beyond the four basic suits which are identifiable by their backings.

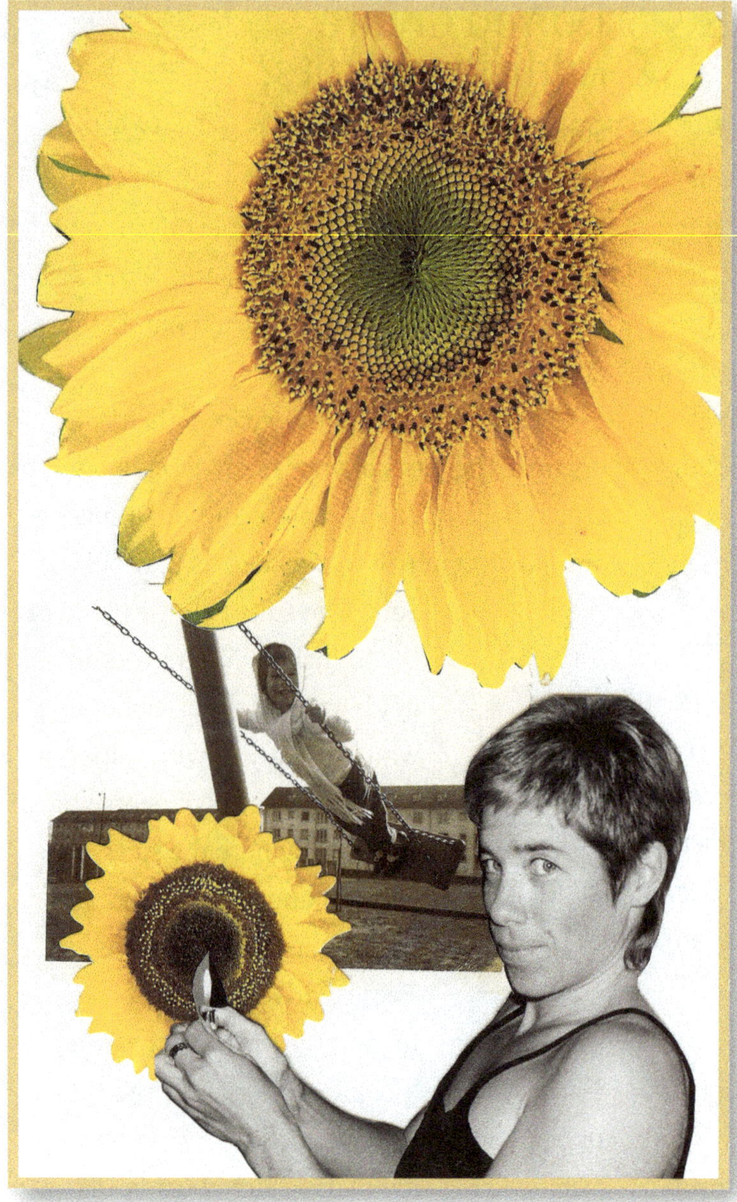

TITLE: **Light**
SUIT: **Council / Committee**
CREATOR: **Kira Jones**

"I Am your light and will never, ever go out. I Am eternal. I Am omnipresent. I Am the sunflower and the flame of playfulness and joy and mischief."

local story part of you. There may be an animal who visits often in dreams who may be one of your Companions. So it's my general recommendation to put dream images into one of the four suits unless you are working continually with many dreams.

Prayer and Meditation

Those of you with a spiritual or religious practice may want to find ways to integrate SoulCollage® cards into it. One Facilitator introduces people to the process as SoulCollage® Prayer cards. The creating of the cards, the journaling with them, the meditating on them and the readings, *all are considered prayer* and all are done in a prayerful way. Much of the work is done in silence. If you wish to, consider the whole SoulCollage® process as a way to dialogue with the Divine. Your intuition allows you to deepen into perspectives that seem to come from another realm, and they do. You are engaged in *"Soul conversation" which is the language of the heart*, and all spiritual persuasions recognize and use this language.

For those of you who meditate, you could place the Transpersonal cards in front of

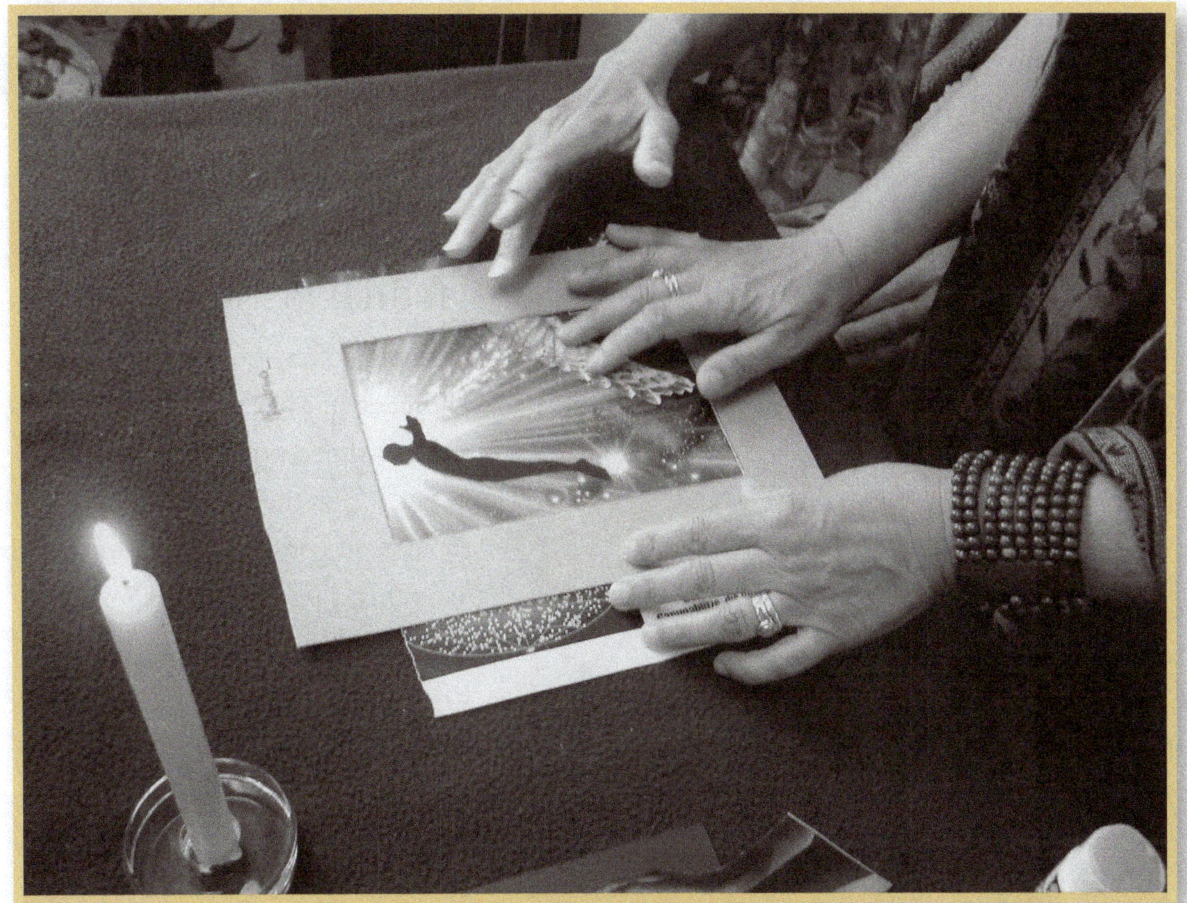

Making SoulCollage® cards is meditative

you as you sit in silence. Perhaps you can focus on one of them as you might a mantra, and let it carry you into spaciousness without thoughts or words.

Some of your cards will symbolically reflect archetypes that are significant in the particular faith that you follow; they may embody the stories and beliefs that guide you. You will love to draw these cards in readings and as part of your daily ritual. You can use your imagination to dialogue with them about your life. This way SoulCollage® will become integrated into your particular spiritual practice, and, if it proves significant and feels appropriate, you may decide to share your cards and your dialogues with your religious community.

Making a Card for the Inner Healer

There are a number of current writers who teach about using intuitive skills in one's own self-healing. Carolyn Myss in her *Energy Anatomy* (book and audio) teaches of various ways we can call on our *Inner Healer*, a Council member, to assist us in our own health care. I recommend that everyone create a card for this archetype, using whatever image or images of a Divine Healer feel most powerful. Make this card even if you seem to have little need for such a Healer just now. At some deep level of psyche we all need healing, and having the image present in

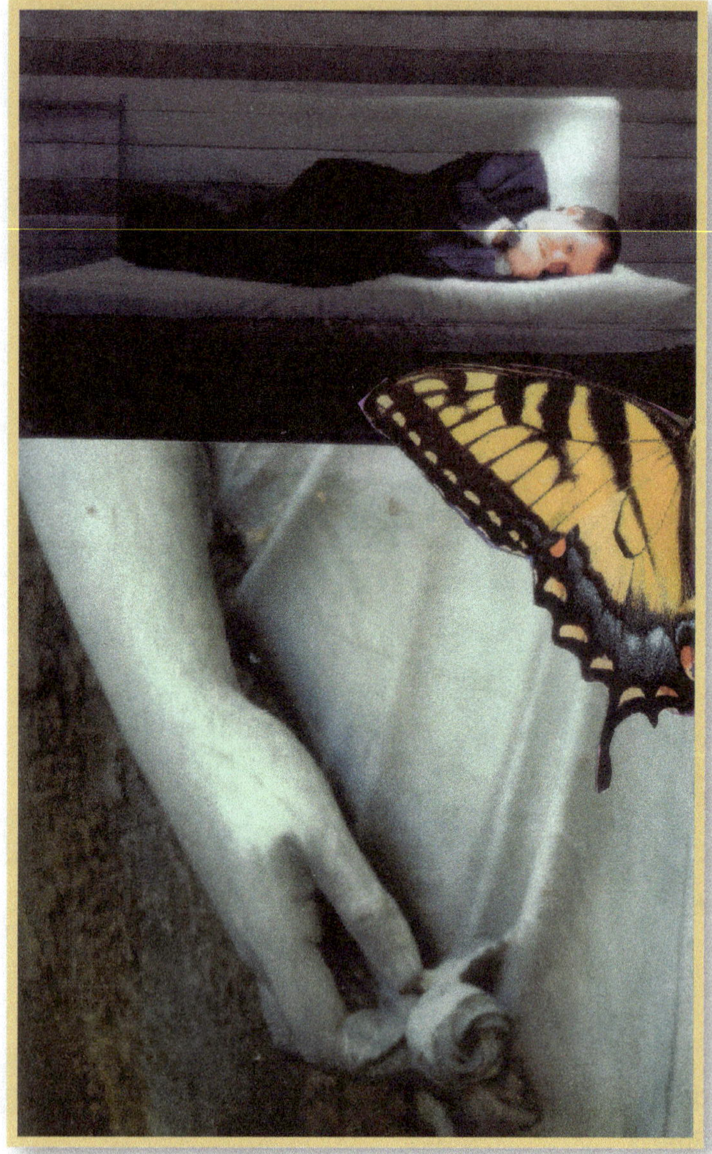

TITLE: **Consumption**
SUIT: **Committee**
CREATOR: **Roberta Rook**

"I Am One Who has known the paralysis of grief."

your deck will bring you into a greater state of consciousness about your own health.

As you work intuitively with your cards, consulting them and bringing in the *Divine Healer* and other archetypes to dialogue with suffering parts, you may discover clues to self-care. These may be in the form of specific directions to change your pace, your relationships, your work habits or situation—all possible changes for finding better physical, mental, emotional, and spiritual health.

Working with Health Issues

A woman once showed her homeopathic doctor her SoulCollage® cards; she exclaimed how much more she learned from these cards than from all the patient had ever told her in words. Wouldn't it be wonderful if every health provider would take time to learn about our Souls before deciding how to treat our illnesses?

Since this is not likely to happen, we can help ourselves by using our Neters to explore what is happening in our bodies, the places we may be stuck or out of balance. We can learn to call on the energy of certain Neters in our deck to lead us back towards a healthy balance. Then we can inform our doctors more precisely, even as we work energetically with our own healing. One SoulCollage® Facilitator, Win Griffen from California wrote this to me in an email:

I have just now been diagnosed with another breast cancer tumor. This is the third time out! The first was in 1993, then 2003 and now, December 2007. I can now count all my ribs on both sides! It is cool to reclaim my little girl chest!

I had made a Cancer card, a Rage card and a Death card earlier in the year with, of course, my Source card behind each image. This weekend I made another Cancer card, another Rage card and another Death card. Then at a workshop I made a Victory card. They are very powerful and healing for me. I no longer feel rage. I feel gratitude for the cancer as my teacher. My life is so much more balanced now.

Win is not unique in the SoulCollage® community. Many are making cards of their particular illnesses, speaking from them, and finding insight from the messages they receive.

I'll share a second example, one from Cynthia who lives in Georgia and who suffers from Multiple Sclerosis. She found the SoulCollage® process and began making her deck of cards totally on her own. Here is a quote from one amazing email that she sent me:

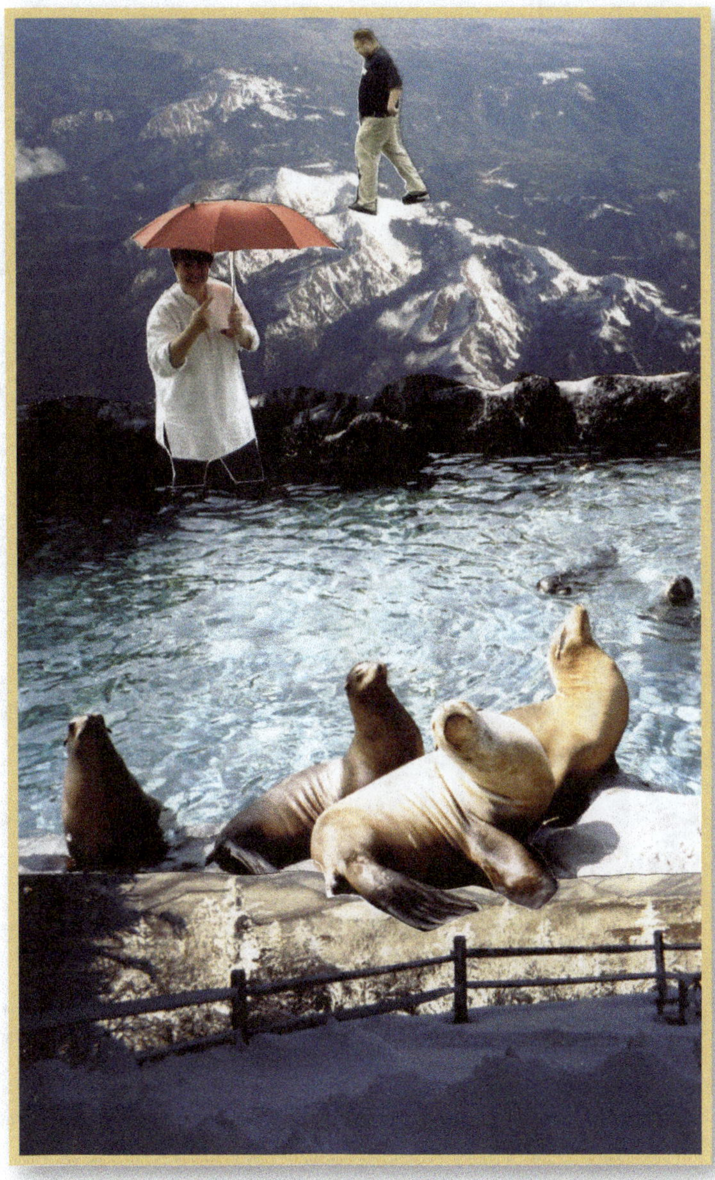

TITLE: **Wading Pool**
SUIT: **Committee**
CREATOR: **Johnny Dillard**

"*I Am One Who* is finding that my confidence and competence are expanding with each step I take in pursuit of my quest to navigate and experience the full depth and breadth of my emotional waters."

> *We can learn to call on the energy of certain Neters in our deck to lead us back towards a healthy balance.*

With MS you feel like pieces of you are falling off or chipping away like nail polish. It is like a continuous grieving of your soul that was the hardest part for me to deal with. SoulCollage® has helped me to focus my frustrations and document my joys in a healthy endearing outlet. I consider myself very positive and yet over the past several years I have had some pretty downer days. I am so blessed to have so much good in my life, and I am very grateful that your work helped change the MS stumbling block into a stepping stone. . . .I have a desire to reach out to others who truly need a

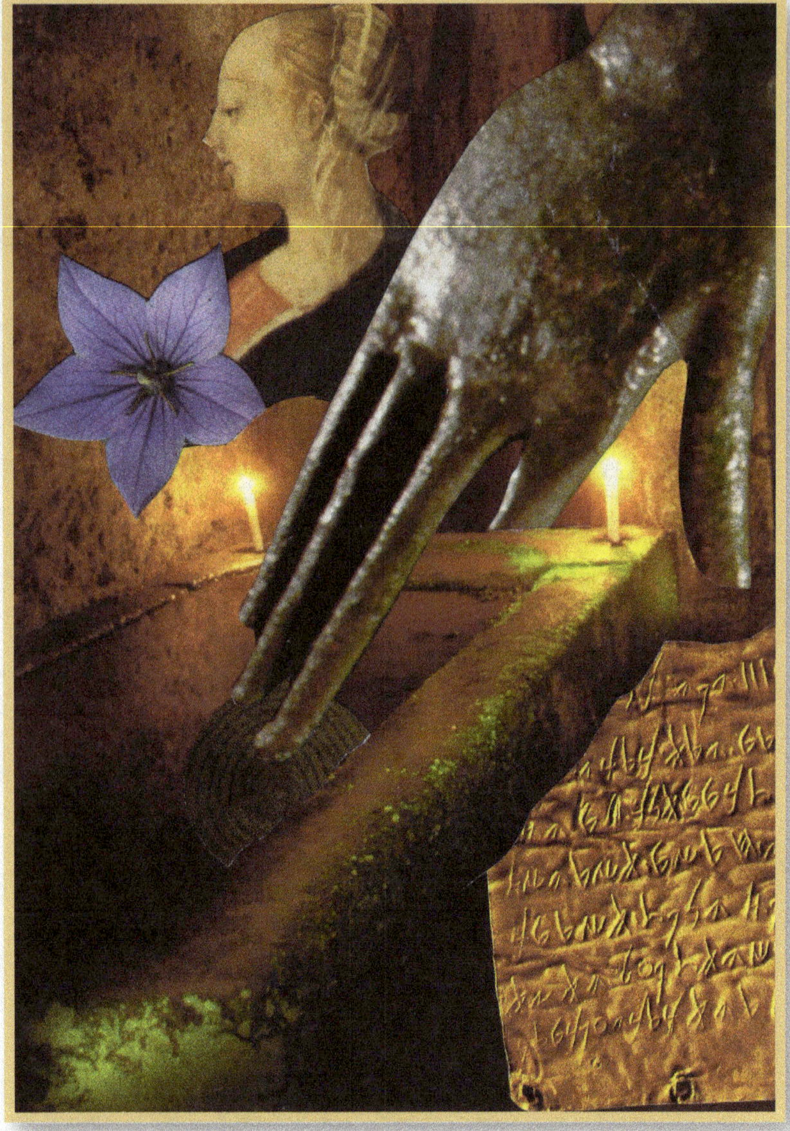

TITLE: **Healer's Fountain**
SUIT: **Committee**
CREATOR: **Mariabruna Sirabella**

"*I Am One Who* humbly reaches for the Fountain of Time to invite healing in my time. I am there invited to touch the waters of all beginnings and to gather information in its ripples."

> *source of hope. Not just MS people but other ill people who need to remember a better time and place. I just wanted you to know that you have inspired me to reach out from a place I truly felt had died. I started to forget who I am and felt like my life was fading away.*

You can imagine what a joy it is for me to receive an email like this one, and I thank Cynthia for taking the trouble to send it. I hope she will go on and share the process with others who are ill, because her example will be an inspiration to them while they have the joy of creating their cards.

Each of the four suits may include Neters that can help with our mental, physical, and emotional health—or sabotage it. The energetic suit of the Companions is especially useful because you can engage these Neters to scan and report on blockages in various energy centers of the body. You can focus on a hurting area using a light trance, and then imagine the animal in that general area bringing their special energy to balance and heal. Perhaps you will notice that a Companions Neter is losing energy, is hurt, perhaps even looks lifeless. Then bring your *Inner Healer* strongly into your imagery, and visualize this Neter restoring health and life to the Companion animal. Repeating this visualization several times a day, relaxing and focusing on it, may well promote a shift towards balance and better energy flow.

Also make Committee cards for the parts of yourself that are suffering. These might be the *Blind Self* (either physical or emotional), the *Limping Self*, the *Asthmatic Self* (suffocation on a physical or emotional level), the *Tumor in the Breast*, the *Depressed Self*. And so on. These Committee members have a story to tell, a history; they have their special needs and complaints to speak about. They want to be recognized and given their own "container image" on a card. Don't ignore them because you have read in some current literature to focus just on the positive. This works just so far. We also need to seek out, recognize, and embrace our hurting and hard-to-deal-with Neters.

It's helpful, when you make cards for these demanding and hurting parts, to consciously remember that they are not the whole of your Committee even though, at present, they may want all of your attention. Your other Neters are still there, the healthy and happy ones, available to dance in your Soul.

If you are in treatment with a clinician, take your cards to an appointment and read from the images.

SoulCollage® as a Tool in Psychotherapy

C. G. Jung loved alchemy, and the psychotherapeutic process that he developed and practiced with individual clients was truly a form of inner alchemy. The principle was this: together clinician and patient separate out the patient's personality parts, examine and understand them, and then *help them integrate back together into a new, more whole, personality.* The "inferior metal" is transformed into "gold" in this new form. But it doesn't happen without the hard work of the separating and examining.

SoulCollage,® with its emphasis on the Many and the One, is an excellent tool to use in your own psychotherapy work or as a therapy tool if you are a clinician. Here are words from a clinician and SoulCollage® Trainer, Mariabruna Sirabella. She is talking about the *integration and transformation* that can occur when a client achieves a sense of wholeness:

> *SoulCollage® intrinsically invites this rich process to unfold, but when it is intended and "tended" consciously in a therapeutic setting, its potential is greatly amplified. While this is not the place to examine in detail why this is so, I want to recall that C. G. Jung has repeatedly said that image defines the essence of psyche. It is therefore through what Jung called active imagination that we can dive in the circular, timeless realm of our inner world, and organically swim in its deep waters to release what binds us. SoulCollage® is a remarkable vehicle and cauldron for active imagination. Its practice yields enriching shifts, not only by activating what is possible (new postures, perceptions, beliefs and thought processes) and by strengthening what is already there, but also by releasing traumatic pattern responses and transforming Shadow material. In weaving image and "right-brain" language, SoulCollage® invites new categories of meaning and opens new worlds of creativity to explore.*

If you are in treatment with a clinician, take your cards to an appointment and read from the images. Experiment and see if this could be a valuable tool for the separating and integrating of your psyche.

Working with Addictions

Some Facilitators who are also clinicians are introducing SoulCollage® to clients suffering from addictive behaviors, and they are having good results. This is a report of such work from Suzie Wolfer, a clinician in Oregon and also a SoulCollage® Trainer.

> *Most clients struggling with chemical dependency suffer from mistaken identity. They confuse the thoughts of their body's* Addicted Self *with the* Authentic Healthy Self. *The genetic pattern that makes drug and alcohol use a supercharged dopamine high gradually eclipses the real self. The day by day process is so subtle that most people never realize the ruse....*
>
> *SoulCollage® comes to the rescue by externalizing the voice that votes for drug and alcohol use, and all the behaviors that support it. And even better, with skilled use, SoulCollage® can also help each client find and strengthen the Healthy Self.*
>
> *Most clients vaguely realize that their drinking or drug use creates some problems, but often minimize the impact it is having in their lives. However, when clients make a card for* The Con Man *or* The Saleswoman *or the* Con Artist *they begin to see who and what is doing the thinking for them, without the stigma and judgment attached.*
>
> *With help, clients take back their role as CEO at the head of their personal "corporation." The very act of making and reading cards develops healthy, observing ego skills. They become powerful observers, rather than bystanders in their own lives. And they recognize that they have a troublesome, permanent board member, such as the* Con Man *or* The Depressed One *and learn to manage these characters. The client learns to identify the* Con Artist's *"advice," notice where it will eventually lead, and then take appropriate action as "Chair of the Board."*

SoulCollage® can provide a safe and creative way for nonverbal folks to share themselves.

> *SoulCollage® has unique power to launch clients out of their "gravity well" of logical thought, and put them back in the driver's seat again. Imagery has staying power. Long after the words are forgotten, images remain and continue working.*
>
> *Shelly, an attractive, intelligent 33-year-old woman in early recovery from alcohol problems had a wake-up call from her doctor who warned her of liver problems. She made a card for her* Con Artist *and interviewed her:*
>
> > *"I Am the One Who says relax, have a good time. Just one won't hurt. Who would know? Only idiots can't handle their liquor, and you're no idiot. Take the road with me. You think it goes nowhere, but with me, we'll discover new horizons, new friends, new experiences wherever we are. Just relax."*

Shelly discovered that her Con Artist *would encourage her to "just look at" all the bottles of wine at the store, to "test her strength" not realizing it was the slippery slope of a hypnotic induction to anaesthetize her to early warning signs of relapse.*

SoulCollage® is a Tool for Nonverbal People

The SoulCollage® process is a great tool for nonverbal folk to begin speaking about themselves. One therapist who works with young people in a clinical setting has a sixteen-year-old girl who refuses to speak aloud to her. The girl, however, eagerly creates powerful and revealing cards and then writes extensively from them, often in poetry. Through SoulCollage® she has found a safe and creative way to share herself.

Another SoulCollage® Facilitator, Kathleen Abley from Ontario, Canada, works in a group home setting. She wrote this about the experience of one person she works with:

Anne has cerebral palsy, which makes it difficult for her to speak. It takes time and patience to understand her, and when she is upset or in distress, communicating can take up a lot of her energy. In a SoulCollage® workshop Anne collaged a card called Hiding. *It is a picture of a person deep within a cave. It is dark except for the glow of a lamp on a miner's hard hat. When caregivers see her card and read the* I Am One Who… *statement, they can give*

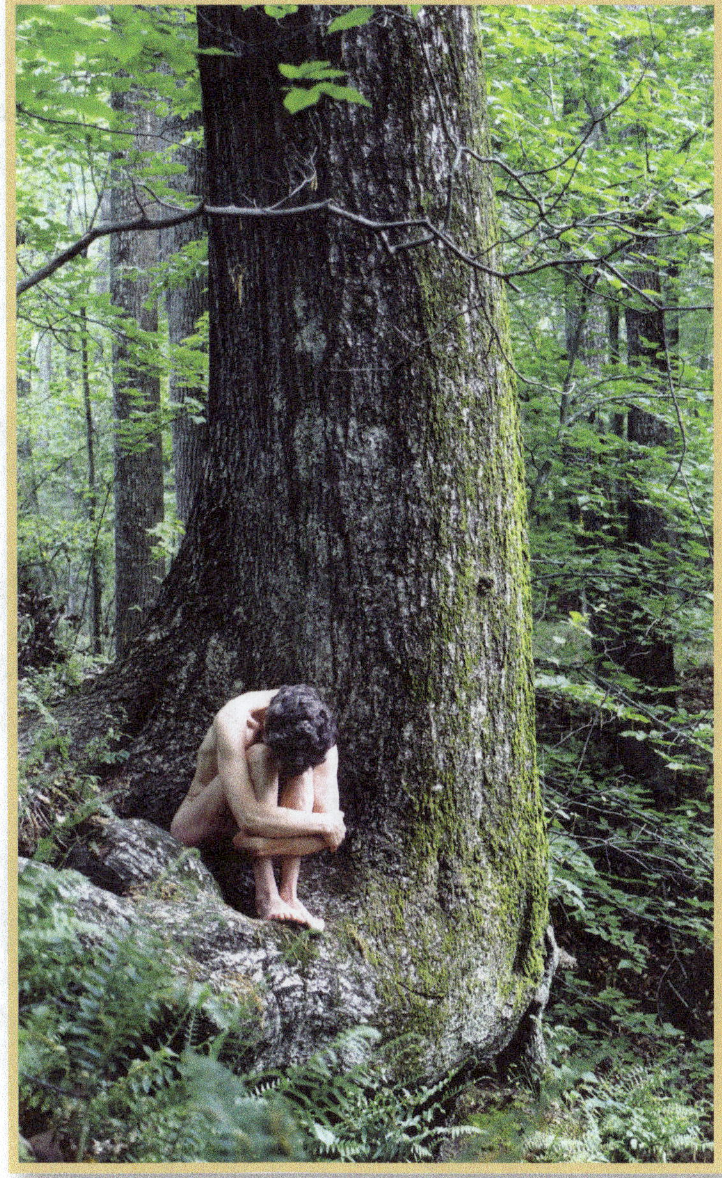

TITLE: **Sanctuary**

SUIT: **Council / Committee**

CREATOR: **Laren Leonard**

Council: "*I Am the One Who* holds your nakedness in the lap of my roots. My refuge is a safe and sacred place reserved for protection from hunting or molestation."

Committee: "*I Am One Who* feels naked and afraid. I come here to this Sanctuary for protection."

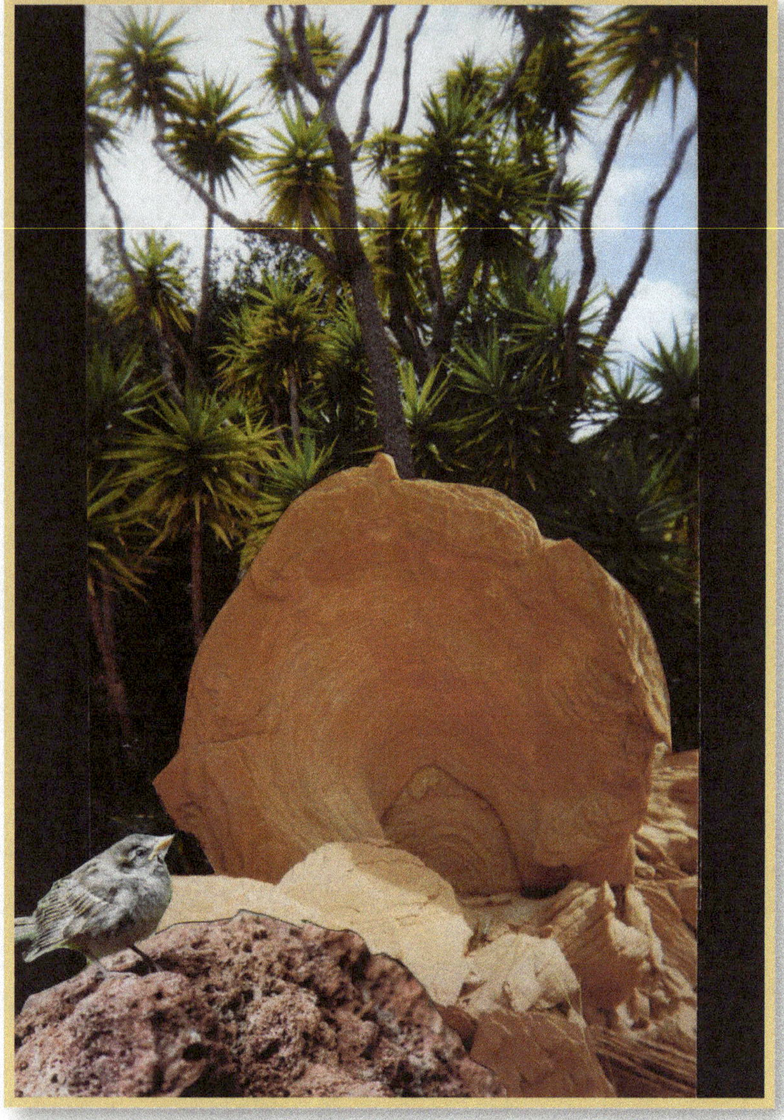

TITLE: **My Place in the World**

SUIT: **Committee**

CREATOR: **Mariabruna Sirabella**

"*I Am One Who* has learned that no matter how small, gray and apparently inconsequential I may appear, there is, for me a place in the world."

Anne the time that she needs and support her in a way that respects what she wants. This card has given Anne a way to communicate that is satisfying and effective. After using the images to evoke thoughts and feelings and to journal, Anne discovered a face in the rock, a face watching her. She was no longer alone.

People who think they have nothing to say about themselves, who are shy, stutter, or can't find words, will often create cards and then write or speak from them in ways they hadn't thought they could. When one steps out of the old limits of the ego Neters, into a new and unfamiliar image, one may suddenly speak with a new freedom. Perhaps it is the right brain that can now speak clearly about feelings, something the left brain could not do at all. Many therapists use collage as one of their tools for working with clients. The difference with SoulCollage® is that here the collage is small, on a durable card that can be carried around and kept as a reminder and an anchor. It can be used as Anne uses hers, again and again, as a quick way to communicate.

Poetry

Karin Lubin is a SoulCollage® Facilitator, Life Coach, and educator from California. She has found SoulCollage® useful in a high school classroom setting, and sometimes will scribe for teens when they are speaking intuitively from their images. After one young man had finished speaking, he listened while his words were read back to him and then exclaimed: "I didn't know

I was a poet!" What an incredible realization. This is a moment of consciousness many people never reach, and this boy found it with intuitive and imaginative speaking. The gift of hearing it read back opened a new window in his awareness of who he was and who he could become.

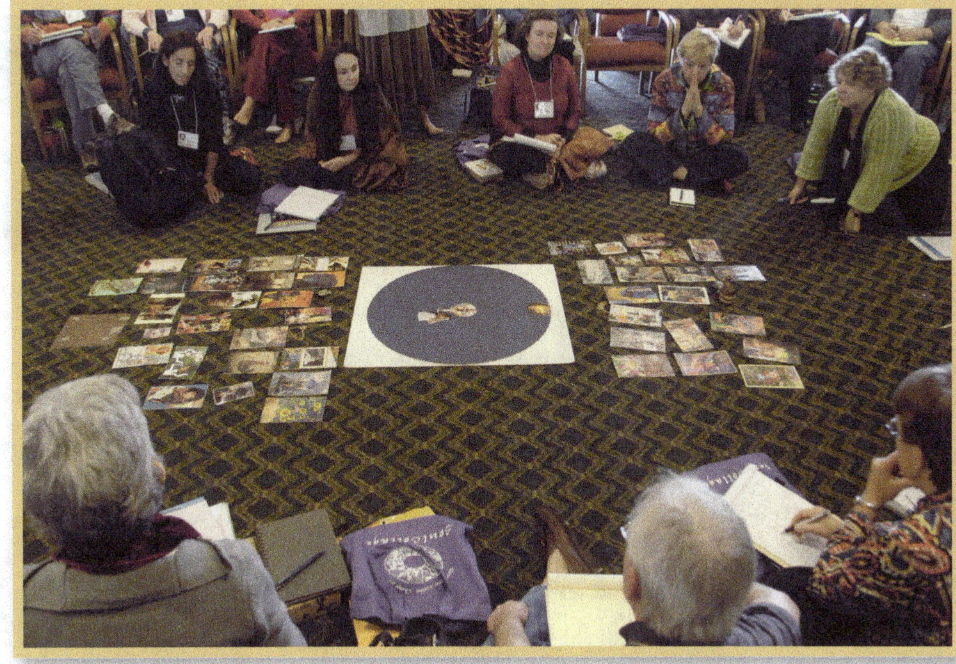

A group process with SoulCollage® cards

PHOTO BY CATHERINE ANDERSON (2008)

When you are working alone at home with your cards, you won't have a scribe unless you use the option of a tape recorder. But it is also possible to write down your own words as you think of them, and this is an excellent practice. Write without editing and don't allow your *Inner Critic* to derail you. You will find that the words you write, when you are speaking intuitively from an image, will often be poetic. You may want to take time later to put the words into the form of a poem.

Finding Themes and Patterns in Clusters of Cards

As your deck grows you may decide to lay all your cards out at one time, to see yourself evolving and your pieces of Soul fitting together in themes and patterns. You might want to do this on your birthday, for example, or on New Year's Day. There are several ways you could organize such a lay-out. Here is one possibility:

Place the Transpersonal cards in the center to symbolize your Oneness with Divine Mystery. Place some of your most powerful Council cards around them in a circle; then lay down rays coming from these archetypes. Let the energy of your other Neters determine which ray they belong in.

For example, coming out from your *Creator* card might be first a Companion card from the second chakra or from the fifth chakra. Next in the ray might be a series of Community cards for the teachers that have inspired and supported your creativity. Next would come Committee Neters who love to create like your *Artist* self, or *Musician* self, or *Designer* self, or *Writer* self.

You would then make similar rays out from the other Council cards. The *Great Mother*

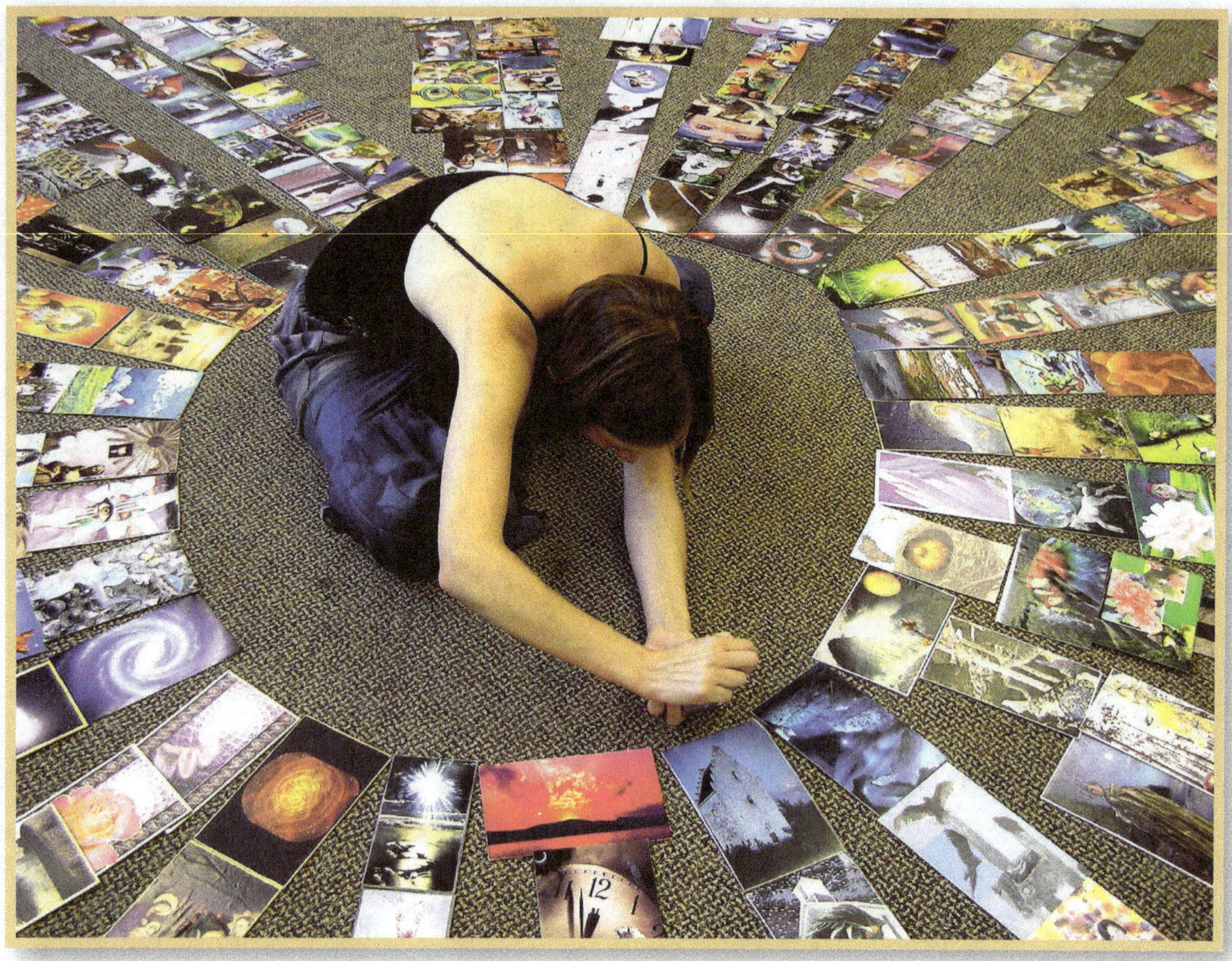

Gratitude for the Collage of Soul.

might be joined to the Companion animal of the *Heart*, then the cards for the nurturers in your Community, such as your historical *Mother*, or *Grandmother*, or *Mother Teresa*. Finally, lay down the Committee cards for your inner *Nurturer*, your *Parenting Self*, your *Caretaker* self, or your *Good Cook* self. Notice the patterns, and how certain cards belong together. Notice the repeating symbols and themes that seem to underline something about your unique *SoulEssence*. If you are doing this process with a friend or partner you could take turns doing these layouts, and together see and admire the patterns, themes and connections that are revealed.

Singing Over the Bones

I mentioned in my Introduction the story of La Loba, told in Clarissa Pinkola Estes' book, *Women That Run with the Wolves*. This story introduced me to a powerful and beloved member of my Council, one that I named *Singer Over the Bones* because of this telling of her story. This archetype has been my primary source of inspiration for the whole SoulCollage® process.

Imelda Maguire, a SoulCollage® Facilitator from Ireland, was also grabbed by this archetype, and she sent this marvelous de-

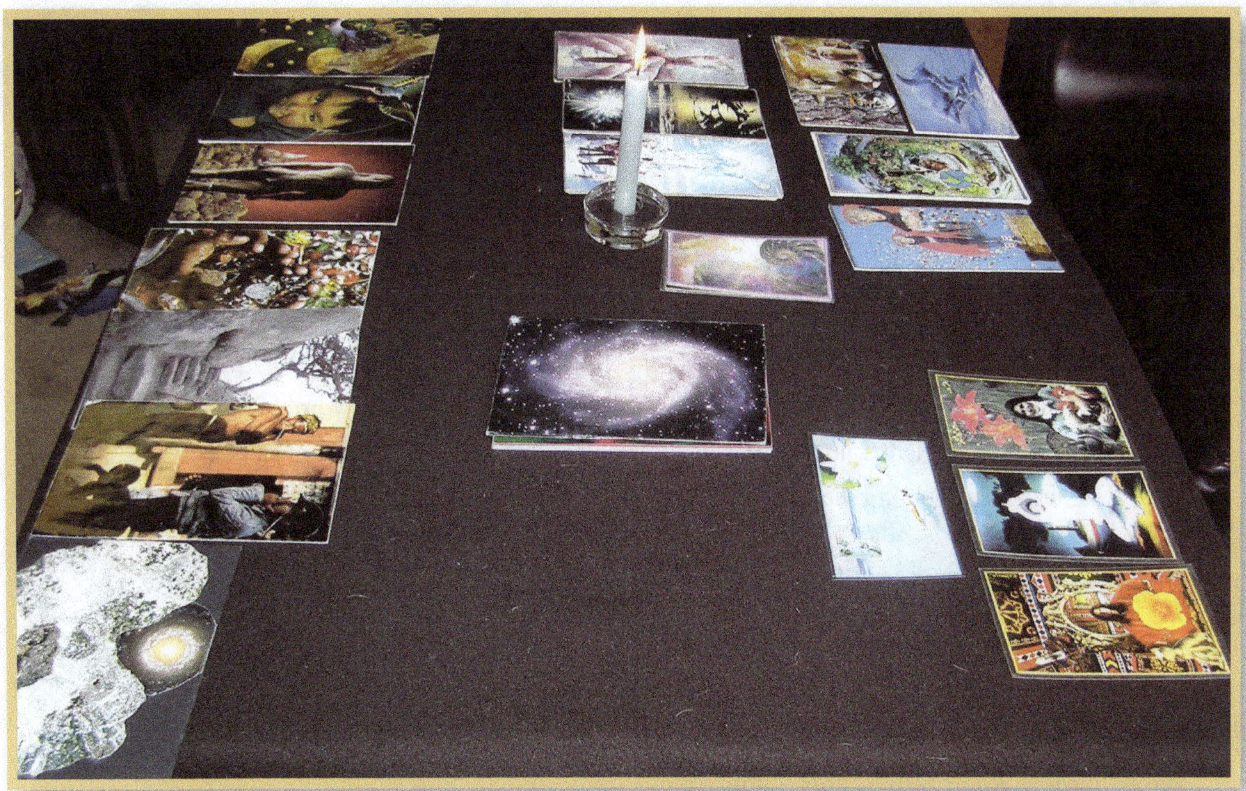

scription of laying out all her cards and then "singing" over them.

> *I moved about my living-room floor, laying down cards intuitively until they were all arrayed in a "sunburst" radiating out from a central grouping of my* Source, SoulEssence, La Loba *cards, and a new card I was calling* Going into the Dark Places, *but which I now call* The Hero's Journey. *When the last card had been placed on the floor, I sat back and contemplated the picture arrayed before me. The bones were gathered … and there was life in them. There IS life in them. Some cards, like ligaments and tendons, support other cards. Some fall together in natural groupings, like ribs or vertebrae. I found my journal and wrote:*
>
> > *And the time came, when the woman saw how each piece holds another piece in its place. And there was no "wrong," no "late," no "slow" in her path. The time it took to gather the pieces was the time it took.*
> >
> > *When she was ready to sing life into her bones, she was ready, because she had learned to sing, breathe, and weep. She was ready to go down into the dark places and emerge again, because she had been able to see her own heart, because she had become ready to take away her mask, because she had taken the time to witness, because she had known the death of love, the loss of love, because she had learned to love… .*
> >
> > *And so she came to the place of life, and she saw that her doubts and her pain were sisters to her joy and her dance. She saw that the gifts of the uni-*

verse come in prayer, in fun, in ancient wisdom, in the guardianship of an angel, in sisterhood. She saw that she was held in the palm of God's hand. She saw that she was held by the love of many, by the gifts of musicians and artists; she saw that the Children's Fire is protected by the fire-carrier and the mystical child. She saw that all time is Now. There is this present moment. She saw that she has been blessed. And she was grateful. And she wept.

When I had spent a long, long time sitting with my cards, the music that had been gently playing in the background turned to something very rhythmic and I just had to get up and dance. So I danced my cards. I danced La Loba, *I danced the bones together, and sang them, and it was good.*

Perhaps you can tell that Imelda is also a poet!

> *"The woman saw how each piece holds another piece in its place. And there was no "wrong," no "late," no "slow" in her path." ~I.M.*

CHAPTER 16

SoulCollage® in Groups

COMMUNITY DEEPENS THE EXPERIENCE

Your first experience of SoulCollage® may have been in a group, perhaps an introductory group presented by a trained SoulCollage® Facilitator. There you will have created your first cards, and shared those cards with others using the *I Am One Who...* exercise. Or you may have discovered the process at a conference of some sort where you chose an image that was powerful for you, and made a card with it. However, after these beginning experiences, you most likely went home with the SoulCollage® book and a few blank cards, and found yourself on your own to continue the process.

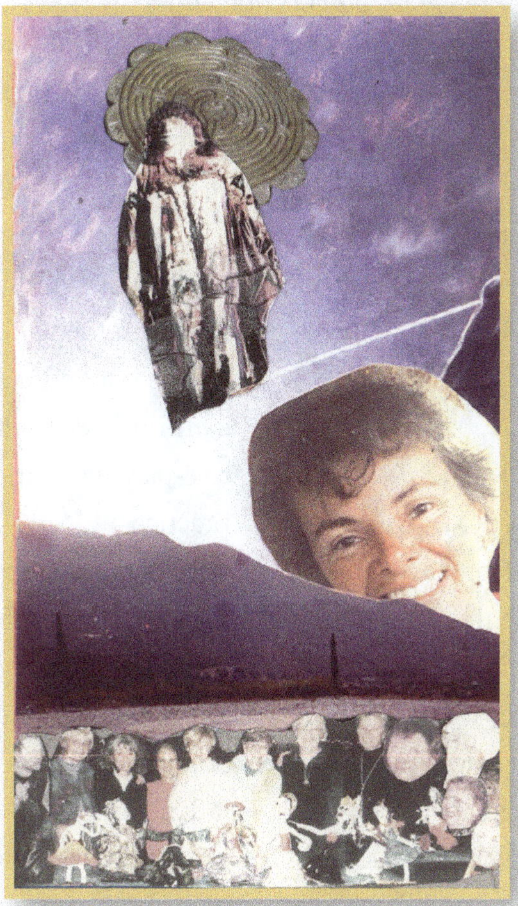

TITLE: **Robin Van Doren**
SUIT: **Community**
CREATOR: **Seena B. Frost**

"We Are all Ones who live and create on the edges of possibility."

Over years of SoulCollage® work we have found that people who join together in some sort of SoulCollage® group are more likely to continue both creating and exploring their cards. SoulCollage® cards just seem to *ask to be shared* with others! The process of laying them out and speaking from them means more if you have other SoulCollagers present to witness, appreciate, and scribe for you. Also, a group will help you find courage to explore your images more deeply.

So, find or organize a group of perhaps two to eight people who will commit to meeting regularly. It will keep your strong initial interest alive. For those of you who don't know others who are interested, there are often workshops on the internet where people are "meeting" to share and read their cards. *Editor's Note:* Check at World of SoulCollage® (soulcollage.org) for listings of workshops.

In this chapter we will look at ways people have integrated their personal SoulCollage® practices into various kinds of groups. These may be groups that already exist such as church groups, support groups, creative arts groups, or groups of friends. If SoulCollage® becomes important to you, and you want to share SoulCollage® with others, it is important to complete the SoulCollage® Facilitator Training. *Editor's Note:* See Chapter 19.

SoulCollage® cards just seem to ask to be shared with others in community!

Typical Formats for Ongoing Groups

Let's begin by supposing that you have gathered a few people together to share this interesting process you've discovered called SoulCollage.® Don't begin your time together with lengthy explanations. What intrigues people is the hands-on, creative experience. Immediately, even as people arrive, have them silently choose a couple of images from a pile that you have torn out ahead of time—a big pile of diverse images of people of all ages, with many kinds of facial and body expressions. Don't cut the images out of their backgrounds or sort them into topics. Just have torn-out pages lying loosely on tables or on the floor.

If people didn't chose images as they first came in, then, when you are ready to start, allow them five minutes to find images that grab them in some way; no need to give a lot of explanation; just say "*let the image be compelling and powerful to you.*"

Sitting in a circle, everyone introduces themselves, even if they know each other. In their introductions ask them to say their names first, and then speak directly from one image using the *I Am One Who...* process. (See Chapter 11.) You will want to demonstrate. Then go around the circle with each person in turn doing this, without stopping to make comments or ask questions. Nudge them a bit to stay in the voice of the image if they begin to step out and talk about the image. If they can't do it, don't insist. Some people find this role-playing a little difficult and will need to practice.

This initial experience clearly demonstrates the central three elements of SoulCollage®: *images, imagination, and intuition.* After doing this round of introductions [as a trained SoulCollage® Facilitator] you may choose to talk about the process and share. People can go directly into making cards with the images they chose. Any or all, in any order, is fine. But again, too much talk is not needed. This is a right-brain process especially at the beginning, and words tend to engage the left brain too early, so reserve the theory and explanations to sprinkle in along the way as people are ready for them.

Now let's go on to imagine an ongoing group where everyone knows the process and has been making cards for a while. Occasionally such a SoulCollage® group will decide to meet for several hours in one day, allowing substantial time for members to individually browse in piles of magazines, choose images, and *create cards.* After that perhaps you will share a pot-luck lunch, and, after that, gather to *speak from your new cards* using the *I Am One Who...* process. Finally, a good, long period of time should be dedicated to *doing a reading together.* If you have six or more people, you would split into groups of three or four for the readings so each person has time enough to draw and read three or four cards. Some closing circle of sharing would end your SoulCollage® day.

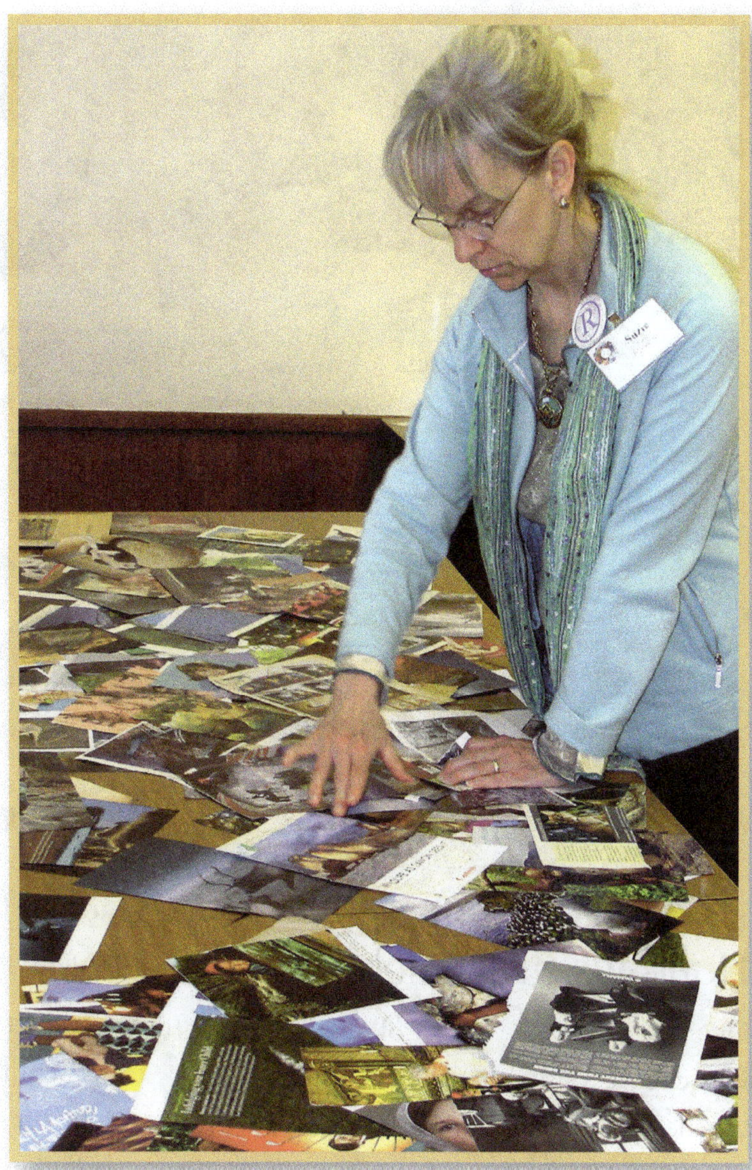

Suzie Wolfer looks for images.

Another format for a regular SoulCollage® group is to meet for two to three hours, once a week or once or twice a month. During this time people can *share and speak from new cards* created at home, and then *check in* about the last reading the group did together and what synchronicities people have noticed since then.

In the second half of such a meeting, everyone would ask a new question and *do another reading together.* Someone in the group scribes the words spoken from a card while the Card Reader reads. Someone will need to be in charge of setting up the table and space so there is a feeling of ritual, and so outside disturbances are minimized. It will also be important for everyone in the group to have carefully studied the way we do SoulCollage® readings, and understand the roles of being a Card Reader, Witness, Scribe, and Facilitator. (See Chapter 12 on "Consulting Your SoulCollage® Cards".) The SoulCollage® Facilitator Training (See Chapter 19) goes into greater depth about the experiences that can occur during readings.

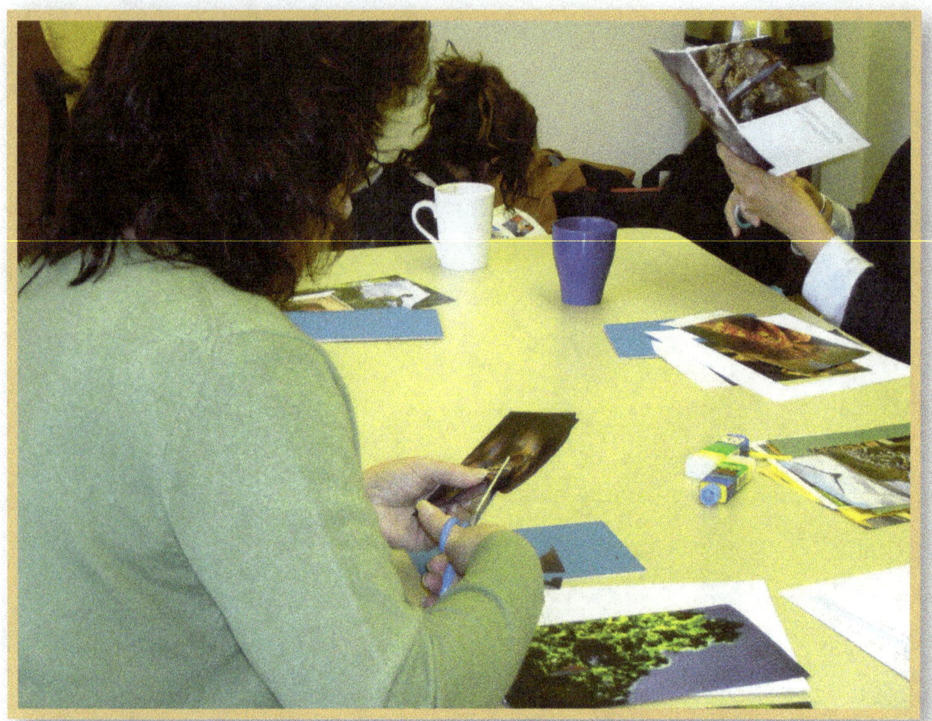

A group at work making SoulCollage® cards

PHOTO BY KYLEA TAYLOR

Thematic Gatherings, Holidays, and Celebrations

One way to vary the format of ongoing groups is to choose a suit or a theme to work with for the meeting(s). Around Thanksgiving it's fun to create a *Gratefulness* card for their deck. This might be a Committee card for *My Grateful Self*, one of the Neters I recommend everyone include, or it could be a Council card for *Gratefulness* as an archetype.

Christmas or Solstice

Before Christmas there is the theme of *The Divine Child* archetype or the arrival of the *Lightbearer*. Another possibility would be to take a day to create cards for your positive and negative Neters who rise up during this holiday. The *Generous Self* or the *Happy Child* or the *Good Cook* might be there; or, more shadowed, the *Over-Spender*, *Scrooge*, the *Addict, Overwhelmed Mom* and so forth. Each person would explore the Neters that are personally theirs. Other holidays can suggest other themes.

Birthdays

Birthdays can be honored by having the special person put out all their cards on the floor, and everyone acts as witness to the patterns revealed as the cards are arranged and moved around. The fêted person uses his or her intuition to help identify themes.

Community Suit and Ancestors

Sometimes a Facilitator chooses one of the four suits and has a group focus on the Neters belonging there. A SoulCollage® Trainer, Noelle Remington, reported how her group in Seattle, Washington spent months on the Community suit. Part of this time they worked with each person's ancestors and the lineage coming down through them to the present. All reported that this concentration was most rewarding. (See Noelle Remington's report on these workshops at the end of Chapter 6.)

Companions

Facilitators sometimes focus on the suit of the Companions and do visualizations for each of the seven chakras at successive meetings. Music and movement after the visualizations help you experience the energies of these Neters. Then create the cards.

Celebrating Humor

Focusing on creating cards that are humorous, especially Committee cards, is another excellent idea. Hopefully such a day would be a day of laughter and fun, and also help people take our annoying Neters more lightly.

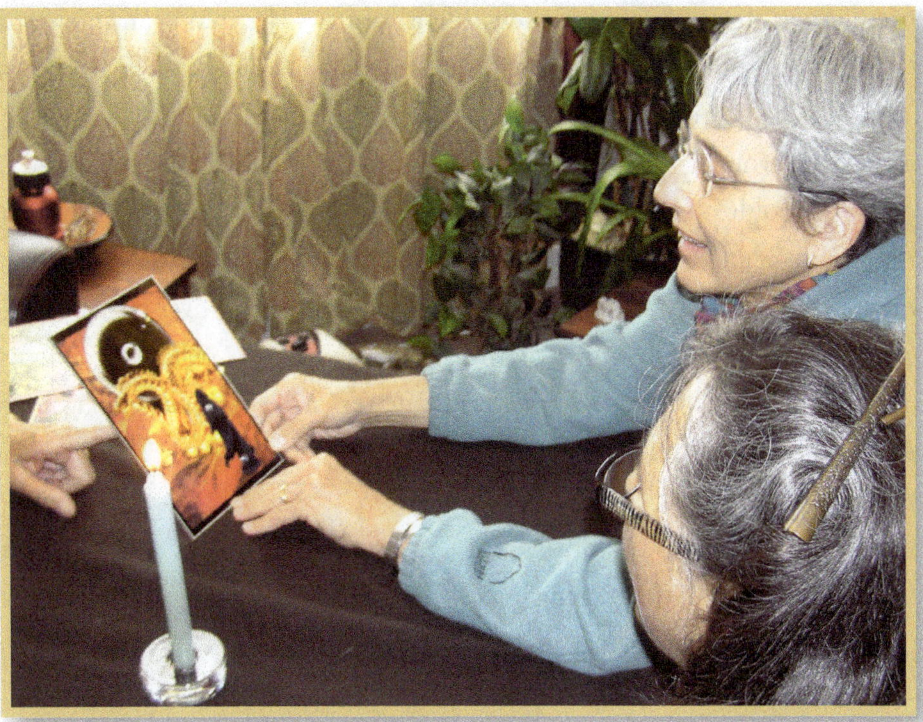

Miriam Goldberg (top) and Mariabruna Sirabella (front) consider a card.

Therapy Groups

SoulCollage® adapts extremely well to both individual and group therapy by Facilitators who are licensed practitioners. In fact, before we designed a structure that relies more on the *Inner Healer* than an external Facilitator, the original purpose of this method, when I designed it in the early 1990s, was to serve as a tool in my psychotherapy practice. I used card-making and card-reading with certain individual clients and even more with small therapy groups. It was in these groups, some of which have met regularly for years, that we experimented and shaped the process that is described in this book.

Today there are many psychotherapists, art therapists and life coaches who are also trained SoulCollage® Facilitators and who are integrating SoulCollage® into their practices. As Sue Gelber, a SoulCollage® Facilitator from northern California, says so beautifully:

> *SoulCollage® is a fun and friendly way to collage ourselves back to wholeness.... The meaning of each card is personal and evolves over time, providing access to parts of Self and personality long-forgotten or even abandoned at times, manifesting otherwise unnamable facets of who we are, or even who we are becoming.*

The suits of the Committee and the Community may be the most obvious choices to work with in therapy and in coaching. These are what we call the suits on the *horizontal line*, or *"local story"* suits. They have Neters in them from the evolving personalities of individuals and from their supporting communities. Separating the personality into parts, identifying these parts, and then role-playing them (Committee Suit) are all well-established practices in many therapy models. Identifying the support system (Community Suit) around a client is also very much a part of therapy and social work.

What SoulCollage® adds to talk-therapy is the visual element of images, the intuitive element of speaking from an image, and the tactile element of actually creating something that can be held in the hand and kept as an anchor. Art therapists, of course, do this already in many ways. This kind of imaginative work brings the right brain into the healing process, to give balance to the cognitive left brain that provides explanations and interpretations and solves problems.

Many psychotherapists, art therapists, and life coaches integrate SoulCollage® into their practices.

If a therapist uses a Jungian modality or is a spiritual counselor, then the suit of the Council will be important. In the Council suit are the archetypal forms that exist on a vertical line within the Soul, linking each individual's local story to the Larger Story. When a client identifies certain invisible, universal energies operating within the self, he or she is more able to recognize deep patterns and ongoing passions. It helps the client find meaning beyond the immediate moment. When mental suffering and confusion begin to make sense through myth and metaphor, this experience can be tremendously healing.

There are SoulCollage® Facilitators, who are also clinicians using the process in clinics and hospitals with mental health patients who are severely ill. Sometimes it works well; sometimes it may not be appropriate. However it often is an integrating tool. A SoulCollage® Facilitator from Virginia, Robin Cooper-Stone, talks about her own healing journey and how SoulCollage® helped:

> *[As I created] SoulCollage® cards that "spoke," the trauma began to lose its hold over my life. I believe that we cannot heal what we cannot visualize. The very act of finding images brings trauma into the realm of the Soul. There the trauma can be confronted, worked with, and accommodated so that eventually it loses its terrifying, god-like power. This is part of integration; trauma gradually becomes merely one of many life events instead of the central event that controls the way we live afterwards.*

This is a beautiful statement of the way images can help the Many become integrated into the one self, while still remaining distinct as memories and events. These don't go away, but, by being identified and then "contained," each within the frame of one card, they lose their "god-like power". Robin Cooper-Stone continues telling of her experience using SoulCollage®:

> *I advocate making cards to represent trauma and aspects of trauma. I've seen SoulCollage® cards depicting traumas ranging from various forms of childhood victimization to life-threatening illnesses and divorce. I've also seen cards depicting traumatic symptoms and disorders like Post-Traumatic Stress Disorder, as well as the tools for dealing with them:* Containment, Centering, Grounding, *and* Mindfulness, *to name a few.*

Using SoulCollage® Within Religious and Spiritual Groups

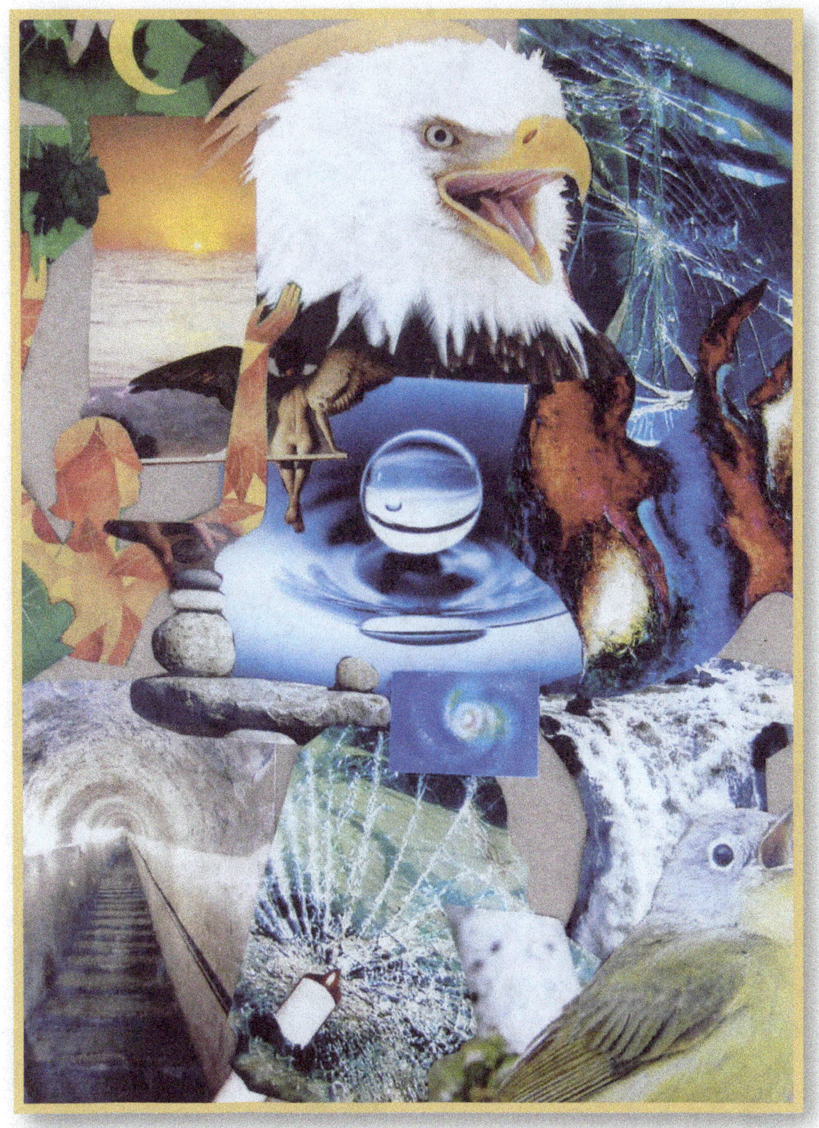

TITLE: **Eagle / SoulCollage® Prayer Card**
CREATOR: **Marjorie Hoyer-Smith**

"*I Am the One Who* protects you on your spiritual journey. I carry your prayers and bring you strength, courage, and wisdom. *I Am the One Who* sees the overall pattern of heaven and earth, the interwoven connection between truths of the material and spiritual world. I offer dignity and grace, power and fierceness as you proceed into the height, depth, and breadth of your sacred walk."

Although SoulCollage® was first used in group therapy, we have found over the years that it is a deeply spiritual practice when done reverently and with that intent. One Facilitator/therapist says "It is a Sacred portal to the Mystery we call God. Healing becomes graced with beauty and ease."

Dialoguing with powerful and mysterious images may, at first glance, seem irreligious and unsafe to some believers, but neither is true. There are safe ways that SoulCollage® can be adapted to fit almost any religious group which is not opposed to image and art. Sometimes, just changing the language a bit will be enough to reassure people that this is not an occult practice, but a natural, intuitive process which can deepen experiences of Spirit and fellowship. SoulCollage® work can lead towards truly joyful experiences of God within our Souls, so I hope you read on and see if any worrisome questions are answered.

One Facilitator, Marjorie Hoyer-Smith, is also a Presbyterian minister in California. She has adapted SoulCollage® into a continual experience of prayer and calls the cards *SoulCollage® Prayer Cards*. Marjorie does not usually distinguish the four suits, but simply has people find images, create cards, journal with them privately and then read from them in a group setting. Here is her description:

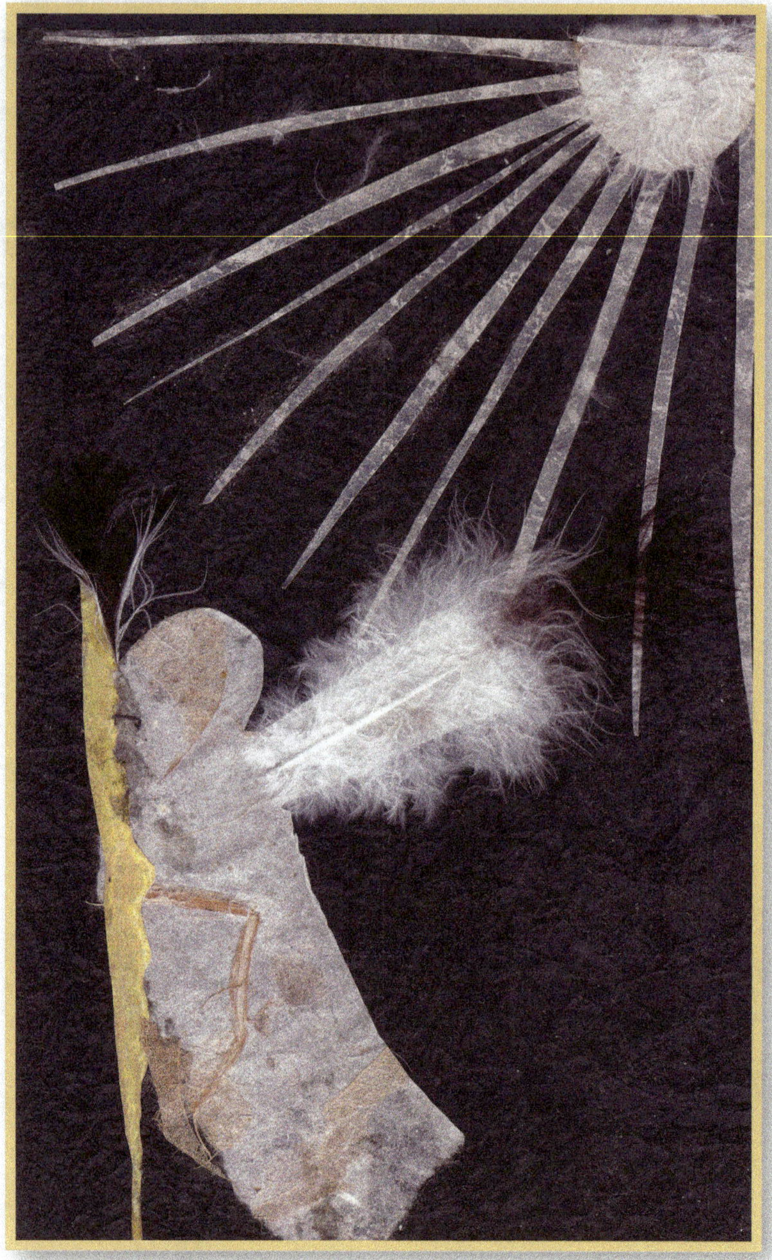

TITLE: **Source**
Transpersonal Card
CREATOR: **Nancy Weiss**

From a SoulCollage® Prayer Card point of view, selecting images, making cards, journaling, contemplating, sharing, is all prayer. For example, images are selected and cards made in contemplative silence; "reading" becomes meditative prayer along with journaling; the "interpretive dimension" is the deep place in the human psyche/soul/body where dreams and wisdom come from, the place beneath our conscious knowing where the Mystery of God meets us in our interior self...; contemplative prayer is entry into further depths (in God); sharing with another becomes both "Holy Listening and Holy Witnessing" to another's life story.

So, with this minister/Facilitator, the whole process, from start to finish, is prayer. Much is done in silence; some in holy conversation. Grounding SoulCollage® in prayer invites persons of faith to step into a safe place, a sacred space, to explore known and unknown parts of themselves—places in themselves that they might not face under other circumstances. Prayer beckons people to enter the Mystery, confident of God's presence.

Creating a deck of faith-oriented or Spirit-oriented cards could easily become a focus for an ongoing group in a church, temple or synagogue. Cards representing ancient individuals from scripture and story could go in the Community suit along with your own ancestors, family, and friends. You would choose characters who truly grab you by their deeds, their courage, or their words. In the Judeo-Christian traditions, these might be *Ruth* or *Esther*; *Mary Magdalene* or *Mary the Mother*; some may want to include *Moses* or *David* or *Isaiah* or *Peter* or *John*. Find images to represent these people in religious magazines or choose images to create a more contemporary version of who they might have been. When you draw one of these cards in a reading you will feel the strong energy of that historical person, and will be able to intuit answers this Neter might give.

Your suit of Council cards could include cards where images symbolize the attributes of the one God you worship, the ones you experience most deeply. Perhaps you will have a SoulCollage® card for the *Creator* aspect, and one for *God as Father* and/or *God as Mother.* Some will want cards that depict the *Teacher God* or the *Law Giver.* Some may have cards for the *Buddha*, *Kwan Yin*, or for various gods of the Hindu pantheon. The list could go on and on. These become your Council Neters along with other archetypes such as *Grief* and *Death*, *Gratefulness* and *Transformation*. These images will eventually come to live inside your Soul and speak to you without need even for the card to be in your hand. They will guide, nurture, and inspire you.

SoulCollage® can be valuable to those who are grieving.

Using SoulCollage® in Grief Work

Pam Gonsalves was in my original women's group, back in the early nineties. She came faithfully to the meetings of her "Neter Group," even after she was diagnosed with pancreatic cancer. For three years she attended and worked with her cards with respect to her coming death. In the course of that time she created a new, hopeful card for *Death,* replacing a grimmer one she had made before her illness. Pam used several of her cards to help her speak with her pastor and friends about her illness; it was easier to show them the images and talk through them about her feelings. After her memorial service we displayed all her cards as people gathered. The sense of her presence was palpable, especially for those of us who had been hearing her read from these cards for years.

Since Pam's death we have found again and again how valuable SoulCollage® can be to people involved in the grieving process. This is true for the people dying and also for the people gathered around the dying such as family, friends, and caretakers. Often there is much time spent sitting, waiting, and hanging out—sometimes alone, and sometimes together. This can be a time to look for images, to cut and paste, and to create cards. They can be made with old photos as well as found images that honor events of the past; they can symbolize emotions that are difficult to share, and some will also be visionary cards of healing and hope.

There are now many SoulCollage® Facilitators who are hospice workers, both staff workers and volunteers. Many of these have been trained as SoulCollage® Facilitators because of one woman, Roberta Rook. She is the Bereavement Coordinator for Hospice of the Chesapeake, in Maryland, and is a SoulCollage® Trainer. This is what she says:

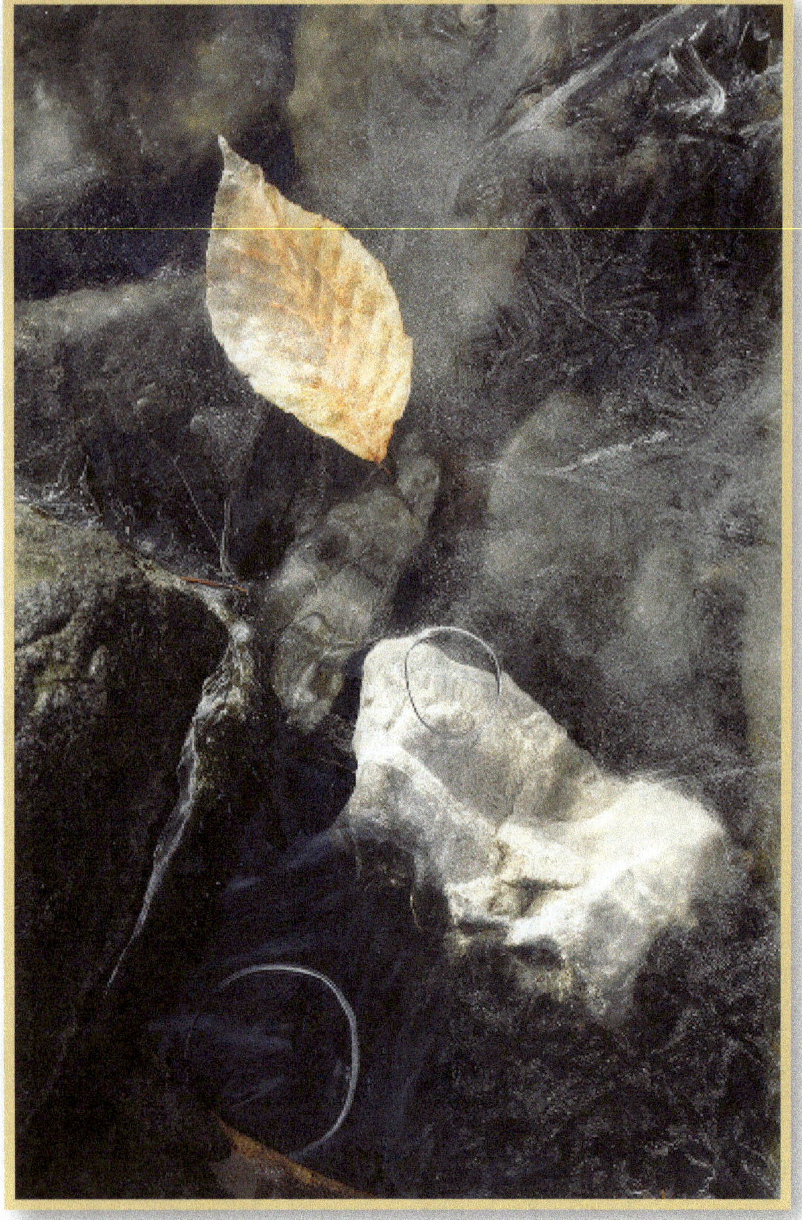

TITLE: **Winter Ice River**
SUIT: **Council**
CREATOR: **Laren Leonard**

"*I Am the One Who* brings stillness to life. I let there be rest of breath, capturing air bubbles beneath my surface."

The potential uses of SoulCollage® for hospice and bereavement work are myriad. For dying hospice patients and their families, the collages can serve as powerful tools for life review and communication in the face of loss and death. For those attempting to cope at the end of life, SoulCollage® Council cards can provide focal imagery for spiritual reflection and solace. Finally, creating collages can help the bereaved in the journey to healing through the illustration of themes and topics, such as grief feelings, commemoration of and relationship with lost loved ones, future directions and possibilities, and the restoration of hope. Cards with prominent "dark" or "shadow" imagery can be balanced by the grounding All of Source, or by cards reflecting the potentiality of healing and growth. A group leader doing SoulCollage® work with a hospice focus has the opportunity to facilitate expression and communication around life's most important issues—honoring those who have died, accommodation to profound change, and meaning-making in the face of ultimate challenge.

Another SoulCollage® Facilitator, Laren Leonard from Maryland, personally benefited from SoulCollage® work, and later took the SoulCollage® Facilitator Training. She was willing to share her difficult story, as well as a card she created to help her through her grief.

> *After two sudden traumatic deaths in my immediate family, I went to Hospice for help, where [a counselor] allowed me to have my own process. After months of talking I realized that I lacked the strength and courage to be deeply vulnerable to such catastrophic loss. The Sumerian myth of* Innana, *and her journey to the underworld, offered an archetypal figure who surrendered her psychological and emotional defenses. In this story, I found courage in metaphor as a hand-hold throughout my own descent into the darkness of death, loss, and grief.*

I want to restate Laren's words, because these eight words speak volumes about how SoulCollage® cards work in the psyche: *I found courage in metaphor as a hand-hold.* The images, which often are metaphors for ancient myths, give a "hand-hold" as they suggest a meaningful Larger Story that mirrors our personal *local story.* The ancient Sumerian myth of *Innana,* Queen of Heaven, and her descent to the underworld through seven gates of loss is a myth of great power for anyone experiencing on-going loss. The myth appears to end in Inanna's death, but after three days her death is followed by her resurrection to life and full power. Thus it becomes a metaphor for hope. See Laren's card, *Winter Ice River.*

Roberta Rook goes on to talk about how SoulCollage® is a help for hospice workers as well as their clients:

> *For the staff who serve these families, creation of SoulCollage® cards can help provide release from the emotional and physical intensity of hospice work, provide a process for reflecting on emotional balance in their lives, and offer a means for revisiting the deep spiritual passion that so frequently is an underpinning of working with the dying and bereaved.*

Jean Weiss, a SoulCollage® Facilitator from California, reports another experience sharing SoulCollage® with hospice caregivers, a group which has a diverse ethnic make-up.

> *It was extraordinarily colorful mayhem! My exhortations to "sacred silence" during the collage-making time were met with compassionate oblivion (lower voices for five minutes or so, and then eager chatting and laughter among women whose enthusiasm was not to be contained). For our final round, after all collages were shared and everyone clapped for everyone, we offered each other holiday and New Year's blessings in our native tongues. These languages were: Japanese, Cantonese, Vietnamese, Tagalog, Spanish, Serbo-Croatian, Polish, three African languages, English, Mandarin, and Tongan. I was awed.*

Work-Related Groups

Several other Facilitators have taken SoulCollage® into their work-places. They've found that even a session or two works well to create more community and more empathy between people. If current scientific research is correct, we will all do better in our stressful jobs if our busy left brains are balanced with more right-brain activity. This will help us think more globally and creatively, which may well be essential in the working world of this new century. I refer you to Daniel Pink's quite readable book, *A Whole New Mind,* for more about this shift and its workplace requirements.

One SoulCollage® Facilitator, Radiah Harper from New York City, tells about how she uses SoulCollage® in her work-place.

> *I work at a museum, and I facilitated a workshop for education interns there. Using a theme to focus them, the interns got right to cutting and pasting, and came up with language for describing their cards that was reflective, surprising, and moving. These young professionals voiced fears about their own teaching and working with audiences, and gratitude for the opportunity to express their personal side within a work context. They noted that the process was meditative (not some old art project!) and felt like ritual....*
>
> *It was a thrilling experience for me and has bonded all of us in a way that might not have been achieved in their ten-month stay at the museum. My hope is that these interns will remember their own feelings when they interact with the children visiting the museum.*

Many are using SoulCollage® in hospice work, both with people dying and also with the people gathered around them—family, friends, and caretakers.

Another example of a work-related venue comes from SoulCollage® Facilitator, Gabrielle Townsend from Oregon. She reports using SoulCollage® with a group of fifteen staff members in a Humane Society facility. She had people choose images from a pile she had prepared, just as they came into the room. Here are her words:

> *The staff was incredibly burned out by time / energy / reorganizational issues. I briefly introduced SoulCollage,® had them do the* I Am One Who... *exercise with their images, and then invited them to make a card that symbolizes the gift they bring to the organization. They were so moved, and the images now hang in the building to remind them of their worth and value. They were excited to invite the Executive Director into the room to show her their creations.*

These kinds of experiences may be just one-time exposures to the SoulCollage® process, but they are valuable nonetheless. Some people may decide to investigate further, get the book, and continue the process.

Creating a Group Collage

For those of you who are doing your SoulCollage® in a group as well as individually at home, I'm going to suggest an additional process that is powerful and fun, and which emphasizes the community element. This is best undertaken when the people, such as Facilitators, in the group have been making individual cards for a while, done readings together, and recognize themselves as a true community.

The process is simple: have a blank mat board on which every person in the group will place an image representing herself or himself. Marjorie Hoyer-Smith, the pastor/Facilitator I mentioned earlier, often does this kind of group collage towards the end of a gathering or church conference. This is an example where a group of twelve people have been working for a time by themselves, journaling and meditating, and then they gather back together bringing one image of themselves for a communal collage. I'll let you read Marjorie's words as she described it.

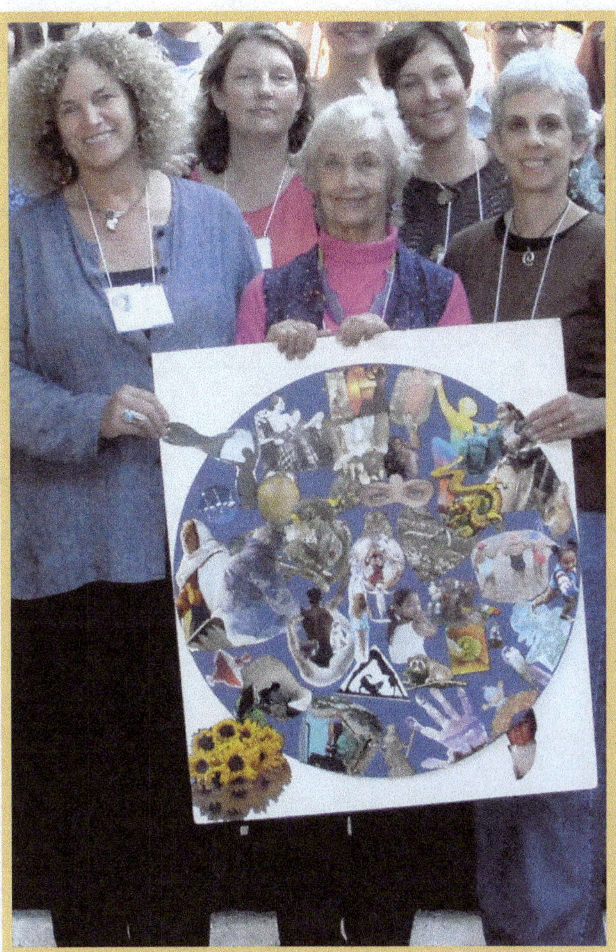
A community collage made at the 2008 SoulCollage® Facilitators' Conference

PHOTO BY CATHERINE ANDERSON (2008)

Upon return they were to select an image that attracted them, and cut and glue it onto a large communal SoulCollage® mat board. I gave instructions before they left and spoke about tending the images as sacred, because each image would represent a part of an individual sacred story. Once an image was placed on the larger SoulCollage® it was important to realize there was going to be a certain process of releasing or "letting go"; also, the image not only reveals personal story, but becomes part of the community's story.

I spoke to the card making process itself, that when making an individual SoulCollage® card, images tend to overlap; parts are exposed while other parts are covered. To make the communal card, the invitation was to look at what had already been placed, tend to the intuitive and creative sense of the placement of the images, know that there can be overlap but to do so with awareness and sensitivity, knowing you will be covering a part of another's expression. Become spatially aware, story-aware, color-aware, etc, with the knowledge that a communal SoulCollage® is an expression of the whole. When finished they returned to their seats.... I facilitated a brief group sharing about what it was like to select the image, to glue it to the larger card, etc. Then we had a time of communal gazing, and I went around the room and held the card in front of groups of people for a period of time so they could get another look at the whole.... Then I asked what more they could see.... The reflections and responses became a deep, communal sharing of the whole...lots of insights, reflections on personal/communal story, the week's theme, and laughter!

This is a wonderful process to highlight the paradox of the One and the Many that underlies all of SoulCollage.®

I decided to follow Marjorie's example and facilitate a group collage myself. We did this at the second annual conference of SoulCollage® Facilitators where fifty Facilitators from many states met for a weekend at Asilomar in California. In the midst of all the panels, talks, card making, and net-working, people found time to choose one image to represent themselves, and over time each glued her image on to a large, round mat board. On the previous page is a picture of some of the group assembled at the end, communal collage completed.

Men and SoulCollage®

You've no doubt noticed by now that the vast majority of cards in this book have been submitted by women, and the vast majority of quotes from Facilitators are also from women. If you are a man and you've read this far you may be wondering if this process is really meant for you! Well, we surely hope so. We expect that over time we will become a community that is more balanced in numbers of men and women.

Men who try SoulCollage® are usually surprised at the fun they have being creative.

I have been asking men the question about why men do not seem as eager to try SoulCollage®, and the first answer I get is that men like action. They want to be moving and competing and excelling; or sitting and watching while others do that. Most men are not attracted initially to cutting and pasting images on to cards. Such an activity seems too feminine, a lighthearted, whimsical way to spend time, and not worth their time and attention.

Women on the other hand are natural collagers; they collage things all the time. They arrange and rearrange furniture, clothes, food ingredients, and whatever else is around to refurbish, recycle, and renew. They are drawn to SoulCollage® because it feels familiar to this intuitive nature. Men who venture to attend are usually surprised at the fun they have being creative and also at the depth of their experience as they consult their cards. Often they become converts and continue on. The problem is that men seldom come to try it unless they have already done a lot of spiritual and therapeutic work and can foresee the possibilities.

I asked some of the men who are presently SoulCollage® Facilitators to help me understand why men seldom enroll in workshops. I will share pieces of their answers. Daniel Cook, a SoulCollage® Facilitator from California, states simply that "Men are not as drawn to going deep inside or understanding relationships even with themselves...." Daniel also poses the possibility that men see the process as "perhaps dwelling too much on one's parts which could be seen as being too much like therapy." Stanley Kim, a SoulCollage® Facilitator also from California, agrees that using more spiritual concepts, rather than therapeutic ones, may reassure some men. He suggests positioning SoulCollage® as an illustrative process of a *journey* that is spiritual, rather than emotional, as a way to help men be comfortable in this process.

However, another male SoulCollage® Facilitator from California, Richard Chance, appreciates this therapeutic part of SoulCollage.® He says:

> *It is this part of me that immediately saw the power of Soul Collage... it gave me a physical, outer method of expressing the many "I's" within me.... identities I know I have, but seldom consciously relate to in an orderly, practical way. So I see this work as an opportunity to find names for, and a deeper understanding of, my own identities, those of my community, and those of the Archetypal identities that "step into my life" through the cards.*

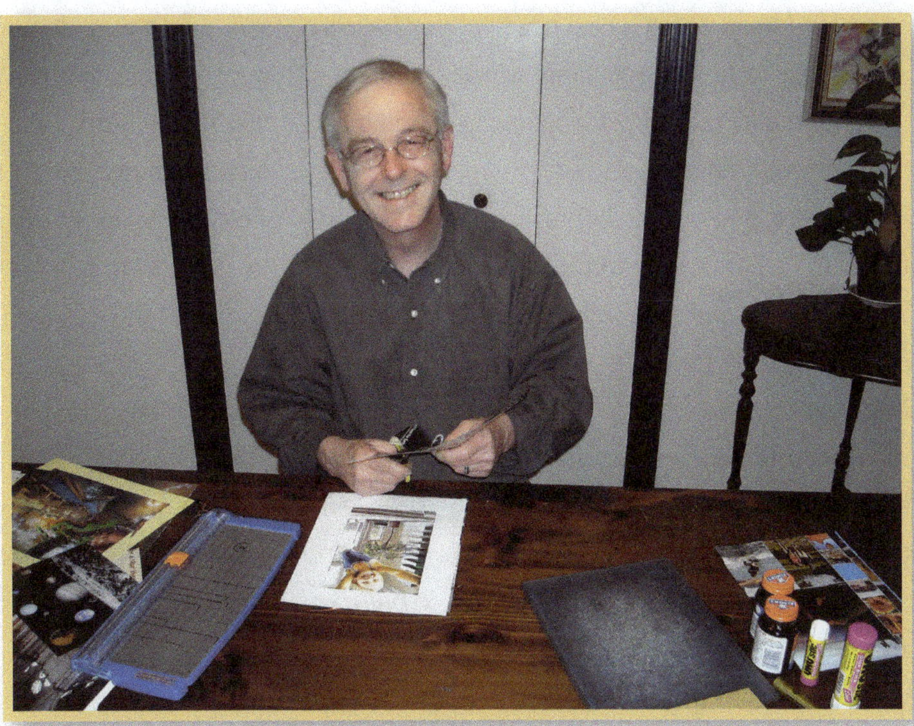

Johnny Dillard, SoulCollage® Facilitator, making a card

PHOTO BY MILI DILLARD

All this would seem to imply that some men are interested in working with the more intuitive or "anima" parts of themselves, and others not so much. Or perhaps, many more than we realize are ready but have not yet been actively invited to try it. On one thing, however, every man I consulted agreed: men want other men around them for support. They are hesitant to begin this work if there is only a woman leader and if most of the participants are women. Facilitator Stanley Kim reflects: *If there are no other supportive men, the shame of being vulnerable in front of women can be crushing.*

Those Facilitators who work together as a man and woman team attract more men to workshops. Randy Crutcher and his wife Karin Lubin have formed just such a Facilitator team. They are located in California and work internationally. Randy says:

> *Men in general are slower around self-disclosure. Given the individual therapist or leader and context, that can change and men can be incredibly forthcoming. Having strong and sensitive male role models makes all the difference in attracting men to an activity.*

Daniel Cook, whom I quoted earlier, hopes to do work with groups of men:

> *I would like to eventually do a workshop just for men in my men's organization, the Mankind Project, that focuses on what interests us in the men's work we all do: the four primary male archetypes—Warrior, Lover, Magician, King. It remains to be seen whether I could get any men to show up or if they did,* [if they would] *go on to build decks [of cards],*

but I think it would be a powerful supplement to the work we do. Another way is to present it at more men's workshops and gatherings or Jungian conferences.

These are just some beginning answers to the question of how to build a greater balance between men and women in the present SoulCollage® community, and I hope my words will encourage more men to become Facilitators and take this process out into our predominantly left-brain world. As the dawning paradigm takes shape one essential ingredient will be the growth of the intuitive and imaginative part of Soul, the so-called "feminine" or right-brain side of the equation. It is not a part that men lack, but it is more instinctive for women to use it easily, at least in our modern culture. Men need to be encouraged to find this anima within and develop it, just as women need to be encouraged to find their animus. Our future as a world may depend on finding this balance in every individual. We might even consider beginning SoulCollage® with boys and young men at an age when the anima is more accessible for development.

Our future as a world may depend on finding this balance of anima and animus in every individual.

I'll end this chapter with a delightful story told by Randy Crutcher about a workshop he and Karin led in Mexico.

In our recent SoulCollage® series in Mexico, a nine-year-old and a sixteen-year-old Mexican boy [both] *jumped right into the process. In the sharing circle where newly made cards were displayed, the nine-year-old was so excited he wanted to know who had made each card. The older boy shared his* I Am One Who… *which was translated for other adult participants into English. It was a very moving statement that genuinely reflected his love and connection with everyone and everything.*

CHAPTER 17

SoulCollage® with Children

CHILDREN LOVE SOULCOLLAGE®

As you might guess most children love to make SoulCollage® cards. They seem to quickly understand about their inner parts, and will eagerly make cards for a *Sad Self*, an *Angry Self*, a *Scared Self*, a *Rebellious* or *Stubborn Self*, a *Curious Self*, and on and on. With the help of images, they can start to identify difficult parts of themselves, and talk about uncomfortable feelings and behaviors. They can see themselves as being like a kaleidoscope with many parts constantly changing and still making a beautiful whole. They can learn to watch themselves with curiosity, and so begin on the road to consciousness!

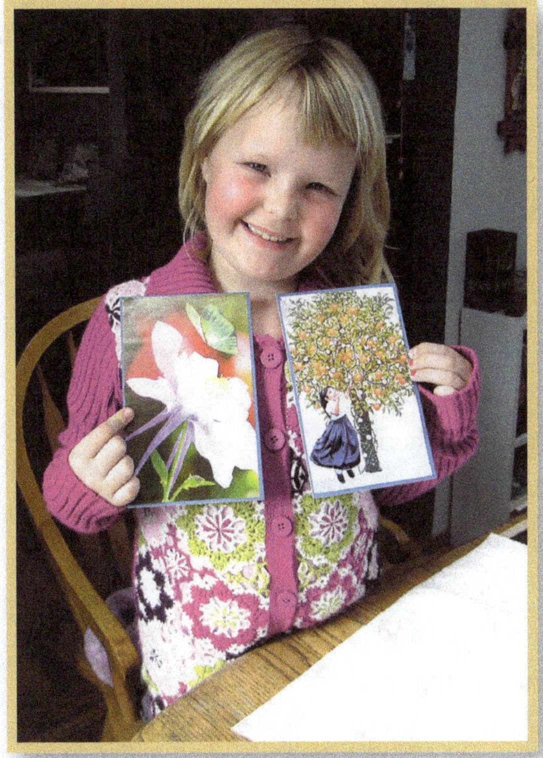

TITLE: **Carrie Frost, age 7**

Seena's granddaughter shows her SoulCollage® cards

You will need to find magazines with images that have children in them. Animal images will also have expressions and postures children recognize as like themselves. When children select images and paste them on to new backgrounds, the resulting collage becomes vivid and alive in their imaginations.

This is right-brain sort of work, and it's only later, in schools that so emphasize left-brain thinking, that children begin to repress their intuitive and creative abilities. For older children who may be more self-conscious with the process, it can be a valuable way to honor their imaginative, intuitive right brain. This process is similar to sand tray or puppet work because of its visual and playful nature. One lovely advantage of SoulCollage® is that children can take these small cards home with them, collect them over time, and cherish them. They may use them to identify

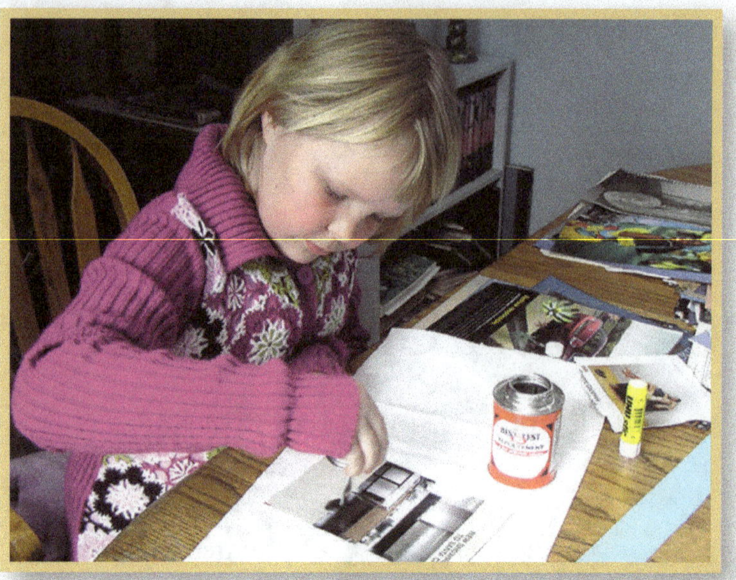

Carrie Frost makes a SoulCollage® card.

SoulCollage® in a School Setting

I will give you some examples of children's work with SoulCollage,® told by SoulCollage® Facilitators. Karin Lubin passed along the lovely story I told earlier about the teenage boy who discovered he was a poet. She described others of her students as well. This is a program in a high school designed to support kids who have had difficulty in other schools; here they are learning to be peer mediators. Karin says:

> *Most of these kids have intense family situations, like abuse, drugs, no home, may be already parents themselves. One student shared that she could use the cards to begin working with other students who were not ready to talk. They could begin by using images as a way to enter into a more relaxed state and then begin a conversation. One student thought the cards were a great way to express emotions and thought she might work on that, so that when her mother was asking her what was going on, she could start with a SoulCollage® card that expressed her feelings and, at some point, begin talking rather than getting depressed or screaming.*

Introducing SoulCollage® at Family Occasions

Sometimes there will be a family occasion where children can be involved in making cards. This is a story told by a SoulCollage® Facilitator, Sue Gelber from California, about such a party. Here the children are working on a

a feeling as it arises, bringing a card out of their room and letting it explain what is going on in their feeling world. Often children want to take their cards to school to share and other children become fascinated. Perhaps, one day, children will be doing SoulCollage® cards in school, and that would be a great boost to their right brains.

Children of adults doing SoulCollage® are usually very curious about what their parents are doing with pictures and scissors and glue. When Mom or Dad get out magazines and begin making little picture cards, children want to do it too. Set them up with their own cards to work on, perhaps a lot of cards made just from file folders or heavy index cards, and a safe, non-toxic glue stick. You can give them suggestions or not, whichever fits the child. One woman's twelve-year-old daughter began making Community cards for friends and family on birthdays and special occasions. This was her project, and she loved doing it. She was not interested in the other suits at all.

surprise for their grandfather whose birthday the family is celebrating.

> *I moved the girls and supplies outside and we SoulCollaged "in secret" at a picnic table. They loved it! The eight-year-old finished first and was helping the younger girls. My dad just thought we were doing an art project... but he later said he wondered. I suggested they choose photos that reminded them about Grandpa, what they thought was special. I also taught them to do the* I Am One Who…, *and to my surprise they were enthusiastic, willing, and able to readily name what they felt.*
>
> *Later, in the day, when everyone gathered for Grandpa's party, this is what happened. The SoulCollage® cards were "gifts" each girl could individually give.... Some took the spotlight and recited their* I Am One Who…*'s to Grandpa, and one was too shy and asked me to do it. The meaning on my Dad's face spoke volumes. It was the best party, and the whole energy shifted from our usual don't-know-how-to-connect, am-here-out-of-obligation negativity, to what I can best describe as "presence" and a one-day family awakening.*

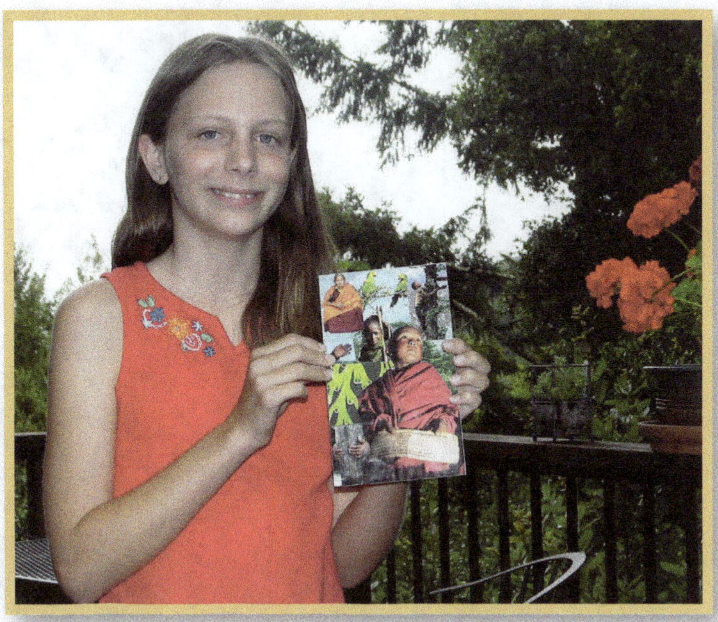

Victoria Bongard, age 12, reads from a card she made at age 10:

"*I Am One Who* pushes myself to work harder, who is afraid of heights but climbs higher, who needs support to reach the top, who sees the glass half full, who wants to know, who says the sky is the limit."

Children Have Even Done Readings

A SoulCollage® Facilitator living in Florida, Marie Cecilia Stevenson, is originally from Chile. She returns to her home country on occasion to teach SoulCollage,® and often will translate pieces of it into Spanish. She told us this amazing story about a child who was at one of her adult SoulCollage® workshops on our Facilitators' online group. At my request she agreed that it could appear in this new SoulCollage® book. It will give you an idea of the interesting stories I receive almost daily from the many Facilitators now sharing SoulCollage® throughout the world.

> *At our first session one of the women brought along her just turned seven-year-old daughter. I wasn't very happy about it since children can be disturbing sometimes, but we soon forgot about her, since she was behaving so well, reading on a chair. But I know she had her eyes on what we were doing at the table. By the third session her interest had scaled*

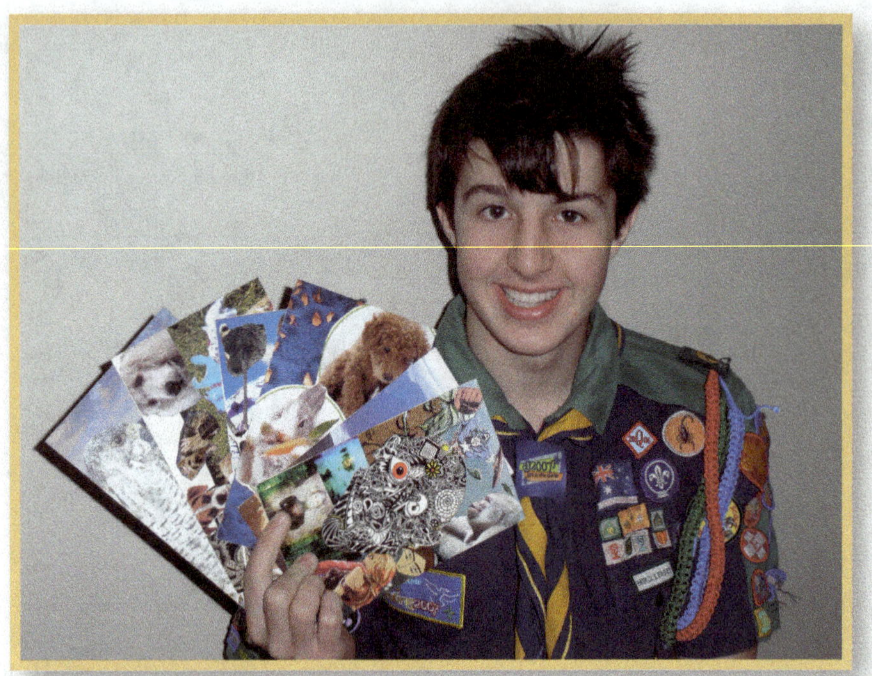

Kai Mann-Robertson, aged 16, got his Craft Badge from Boy Scouts at age 11 with his SoulCollage® cards.

PHOTO BY KAREN MANN (2010)

so high that, since we were a small group, I offered her the possibility to make cards. She jumped in with enthusiasm. She made two wonderful cards that day and the following session she shared, as everybody did, the I Am One Who.... *Our jaws dropped at her statements, they were so deep.*

That little girl grasped the whole process as a wise soul. At the fourth and last session, we had a reading, and I thought that wasn't for little Mia to participate in, but from the beginning she was the most enthusiastic about it. When her turn came to pose a question, she hesitated but the mother assured her that it was a safe place and she could ask whatever she wanted. She asked how the cards could help her because sometimes she felt frustrated in life situations. She drew a Happy Child *card and a* Fairy/Witch *card. What she came out with in her* I Am One Who... *words for each card was very powerful for her and for us all. We felt in the presence of a wise and ancient soul. Children are so pure and still so much in contact with their true essence that they are able to go very deep with the intuitive process. After the workshop, the mother emailed me thanking me for allowing Mia to participate; she had seen a big change in her daughter. Before, she had problems expressing her feelings and that after that last session she was able to better be in contact with and express her feelings. I am really happy with this experience because it showed me how much children this age can benefit from the SoulCollage® process. I feel very blessed to have witnessed the opening of a door to the Soul for these participants. I am in awe of the process.*

SoulCollage® as a Craft for the Scouts

Karen Mann, a SoulCollage® Trainer in Australia, sent me this story about her son, Kai.

My son who is 11 and a keen SoulCollage® artist took his SoulCollage® stuff to his Scout Group the other day. He showed his cards and explained about the process to the pack in order to get accredited for his Craft Badge.

He was very pleased to be able to show an autographed copy of the book and photos of his mum with the "famous author" as part of his presentation. He did, of course, get his craft badge!

Karen continued at the end of this story with a note to me: "I hope you're okay with SoulCollage® being called a "craft", Seena; the Scouts don't have a badge for Intuitive Processes or Personal Growth (yet)." And, of course, I am okay with whatever language works to have people enter into the process of creativity and exploration.

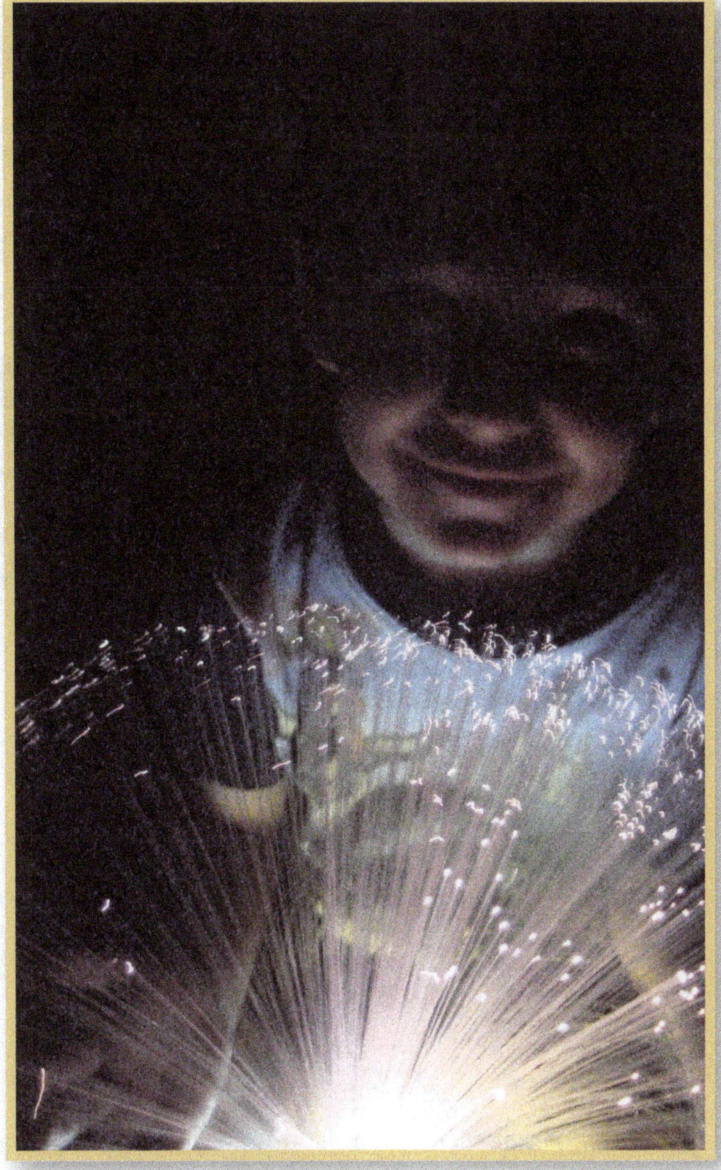

TITLE: **My Magic Boy**
SUIT: **Community**
CREATOR: **Kira Jones**

"I Am pure magic! I have the cosmos bursting at my fingertips. I love you forever!"

Doing SoulCollage® With Dying Children

A SoulCollage® Facilitator and Art Therapist from California, Hannah Klaus Hunter, works with children on the pediatric floor of a hospital, and SoulCollage® is one of the tools she uses. Here are her words:

The making of the cards is a tangible means for children to express their feelings.... The archetypal nature of SoulCollage® allows children to speak about states of being that they may not consciously be aware of, and the cards allow us, the people who work with them, to track the child's progress on their journey. The cards also become a legacy, a tangible gift, left for the living.

One of my most poignant cases involved an 11-year-old girl named Anya. She had been struggling with cancer for the entire time that I knew her, a period of three years. She was losing the battle and she knew it, although she didn't speak about it. Each week, she made the effort to come to art group even though she could barely use her

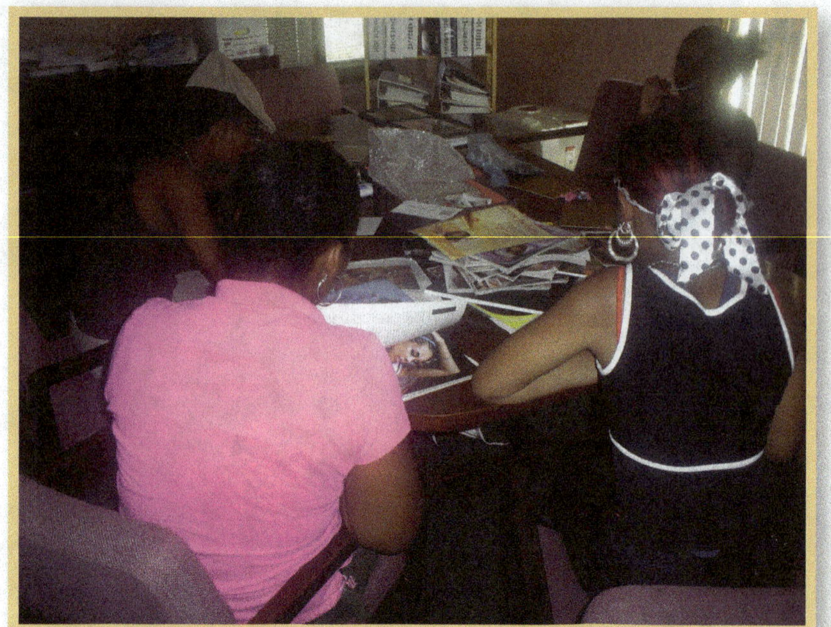

A non-threatening way for at-risk teens to share feelings and learn about themselves and their potential for creative expression

PHOTO BY MARILYNNE GARRISON

hands and stayed propped in the wheel chair. When I introduced SoulCollage® to the children, she began to create cards that featured images of birds flying, arching their way off the cards and into the sky. Asking in a quiet whisper for "one more card", she made one card after another. When she was done, I looked at the cards spread out on the table and saw her coming journey laid out plainly in the exquisitely transcendent images she had chosen.

These are some experiences that SoulCollage® Facilitators have had with children. They show the many possibilities well, and I'm sure there are more examples that have not yet come to my attention. I hope you will introduce your children or grandchildren or students or clients to the fun of cutting and pasting collage cards, and then encourage them to imagine what the image wants to say.

Using SoulCollage® with At-Risk Teens

Marilynne Garrison is a SoulCollage® Facilitator and a licensed Marriage and Family Therapist. She works as a Child Welfare Administrator with the Los Angeles County Department of Children and Family Service. She has spent countless hours advocating for and volunteering her time working with "at-risk" children and youth. She wrote in the SoulCollage® Neter Letter in February 2008 about her volunteer work with a group of at-risk teenage girls:

I was inspired to contact a particular program out of my strong desire to mentor "at-risk" youth. This non-profit's mission is to change the lives of high-risk and at-risk youth through creative arts mentoring, resources, and opportunities. As a result, each Tuesday evening you would find me at a group home in South Los Angeles, volunteering my time coaching a group of five restless, teenage girls. Challenged with lives of abuse and neglect, these older girls have been legally removed from their homes, and placed in the foster care system. Their life circumstances are emotionally charged, often resulting in painful and unexpressed feelings. Having worked in the Child Welfare system for the last nineteen years, I know the turmoil and difficulties youth face when separated from their family. Feelings of abandonment, fear, and loss are not uncommon. Through the process of SoulCollage® I offered these girls a non-threatening means to share their feelings, sort out their confusion, and learn about important aspects of themselves.

Frequently teens will rebel at the very thought of traditional therapeutic intervention. However, as a licensed therapist, and trained SoulCollage® Facilitator, I have introduced them to a way of introspection that centers less on talk and more on their intuitive ability to recognize images that mirror their internal world.

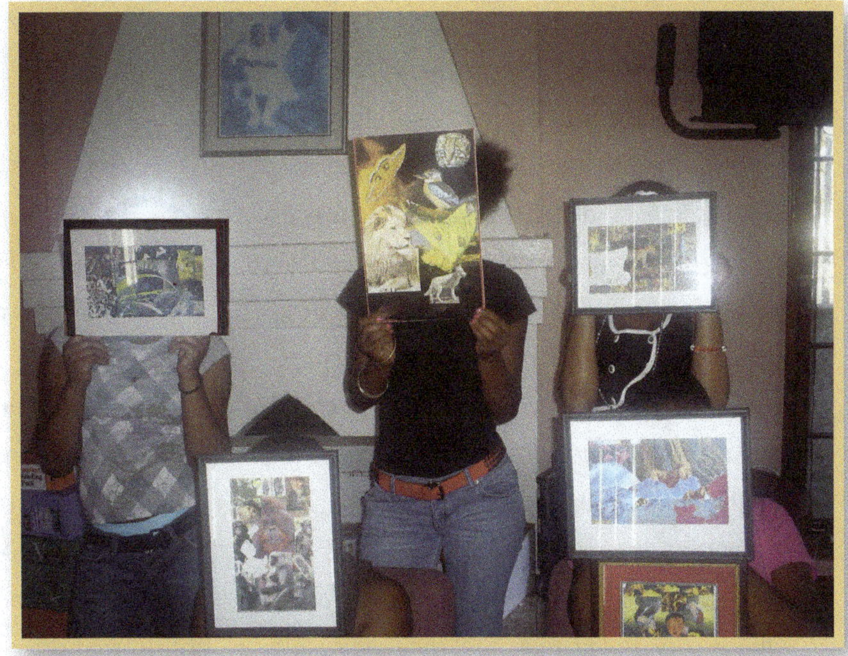

These collages of an "Animal Most Like Myself" were exhibited by teens at the 16th Annual Animagination Conference.

PHOTO BY MARILYNNE GARRISON

Initially the girls were skeptical and guarded, indicative of issues of trust and misgivings. To ease their doubt, I openly shared my genuine motivation and desire for their emotional and healthy well being. Gradually, they opened, offering glimpses of themselves through humor, dialogue, and disclosures.

The focus of the weekly workshop was to create SoulCollage® cards. They added these cards to their personalized decks. The materials required were minimal: scissors, glue sticks, mat boards, and magazines. Each week they were instructed to leisurely look through publications for images that they were drawn to. After carefully cutting their images, they created a collage. Most often they were asked to fashion a card that reflected an aspect of their personality, for instance: "the Shy One", "the Brave One", or the "Scared One." These "personality" cards went into their "Committee Suit."

Other times the girls were asked to create cards about significant people in their lives, people who are important to them. These people may be living or dead, known or unknown. These cards went into their "Community Suit." These cards represent those who guide, inspire, support, and love them. Through the creation of these "Committee" and "Community" cards, the girls explored aspects of themselves and their relationships with others.

The process has proven to be both therapeutic and insightful. What sometimes could not be said aloud became visibly apparent as images were glued upon their cards. We allowed time for sharing, a critical element of our work together, in which each girl presented her creation, a part of herself that she shared with the world of our SoulCollage® community. This time of sharing was honored and respected. Sometimes the sharing was inspiring, sometimes heartbreaking, and always was revealing. What resulted was a beautiful and creative piece of art depicting a part of them that they were eager to know better. As a leader, I facilitated their process, and as a group, they supported each other. Through our experience together, we bonded. They learned to accept and appreciate their variety and beauty and to know that they are each a collage of splendid woven threads.

Recently the teens were encouraged to submit their art to the 16th annual Animagination Festival, sponsored by Youth Opportunity United. The event was held at 20th Century Fox Studio and provided a day of learning and artistic exploration. Industry professionals from all of the major animation studios, computer graphics companies, and related fields spent the day explaining what they do, sharing their career paths, and providing foster youth with the promise of an exciting and rewarding career in the visual arts through hard work and creativity. This year's theme was "Animals." Each of my teens chose an animal most like them and created a collage. The resulting menagerie included a lion, jaguar, monkey, butterfly, and leopard. At the event, their art was prominently put on display in the student gallery. It was thrilling for them to view their creations. By their report, this event boosted their level of artistic confidence and provided a feeling of accomplishment and pride. I, too, celebrated their success.

This group continues to be a rewarding mentoring experience. It is in the giving that I receive. The hours that I spend provide me with a personal satisfaction in knowing that these girls are aspiring to recognize their true nature and potential. Their excitement and willingness to continue week after week is heartening. And their courage to face their fears and broaden their perspectives is a testament to the resilience of their spirit.

It is so heartening to hear of Marilynne's work and to know that many credentialed SoulCollage® Facilitators are working with children and teens to give them an experience of self-esteem, confidence in their unique creativity, and to help them express what is inside them, the feelings and experiences which otherwise might be quite difficult to share.

Editor's Note: Young children will be willing to pretend to speak from these images, and unconsciously they will embed their own feelings into their words. In order to protect children and offer them the safest environment for creative and emotional expression, the SoulCollage® organization advises clinicians and teachers who are trained to work with children to follow the guidelines provided by their professions and institutions for obtaining parental consent. Other persons should work with collage and emotional expression only with their own children.

CHAPTER 18

Other Imaginative Uses of SoulCollage®

MANY CONTEXTS, MANY APPLICATIONS

Since the first SoulCollage® book was published, I have received innumerable emails from people describing ways they use their cards. Many people are journaling from them and writing poems and stories suggested by the images. Many have adopted daily practices where they draw and consult a couple of cards. Many are creating cards for occasions like the birthday party I described earlier. Rituals for special days as the solstice, weddings, and graduations have been developed in which people use their cards in loving and thoughtful ways. I'll pass along to you, in this chapter, a few more interesting adaptations of the SoulCollage® process. Let them stimulate your own ideas! See how the cards can contribute to creative work that you already are doing.

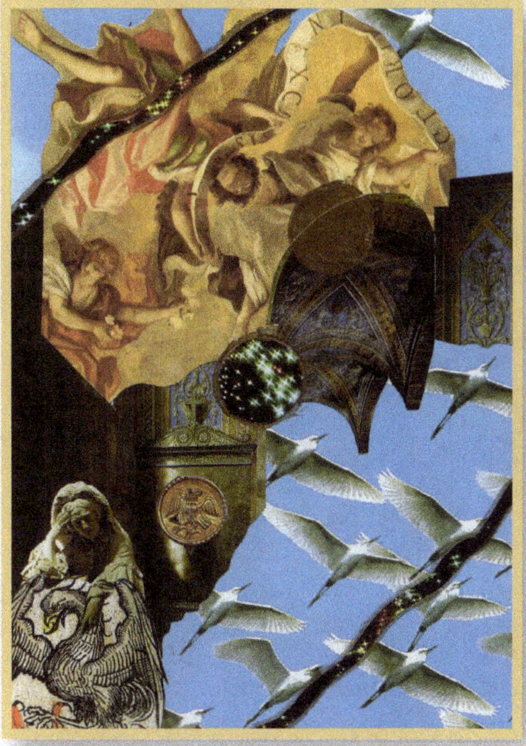

TITLE: **Music of the Spheres**
SUIT: **Council**
CREATOR: **Mariabruna Sirabella**

"*I Am the One Who* is chaos to all but to those who hear me in the flapping of wings, the rumble of thunder, the dripping of rain."

Visioning Cards and Astrology

I have been asked whether it's acceptable to make cards that *envision* one's evolving Soul, along with cards that reflect the Soul *as it is now*. And, of course, it is all right. There are very few rules in SoulCollage®! Making some envisioning cards, especially in the Committee suit, would be a great project. However, it will be most useful for you if you envision Neters already part of your Soul. Vision them as they would be in an awake, balanced,

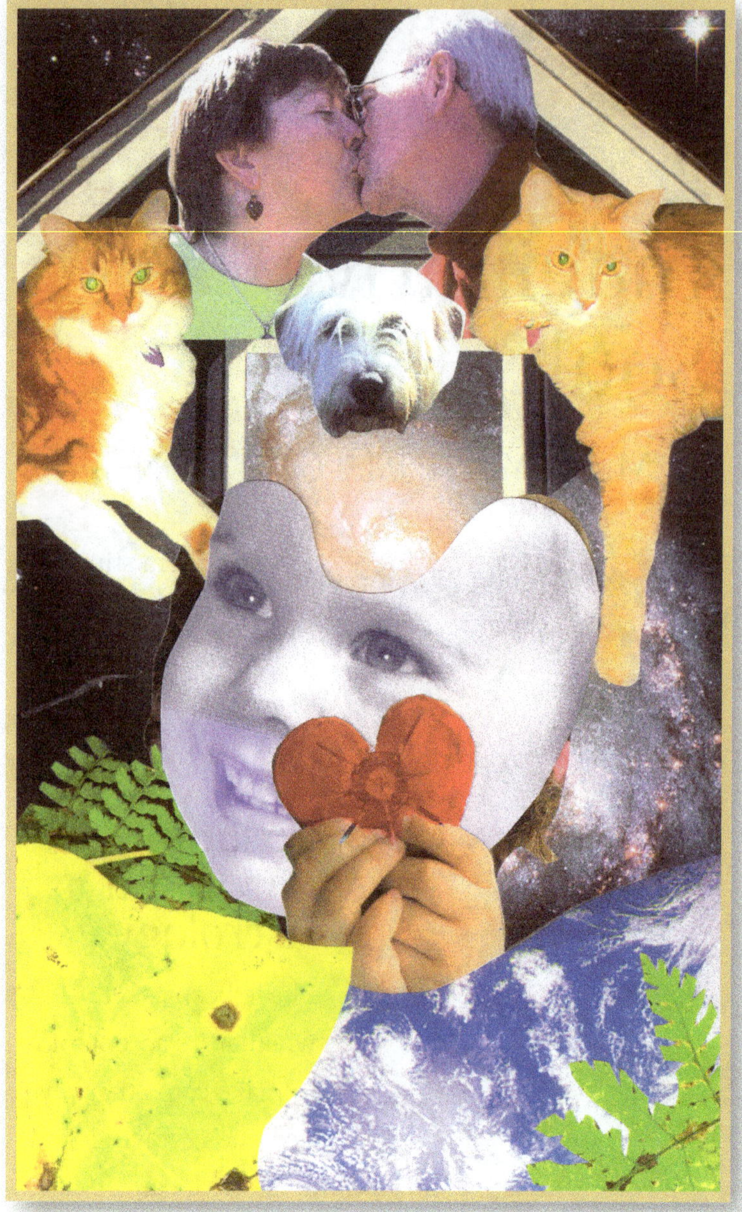

TITLE: **4th House – Home & Foundation Self**
SUIT: **Committee**
CREATOR: **Mili Dillard**

"*I Am One Who* smiles, 'Welcome home!' I join my family to create our home as a sanctuary of love and compassion to nurture the bodies and souls of each who enters."

and energized state. This instead of trying to envision Neters who are not really coded in your SoulEssence. Gradually, in this work, you will begin to know who is truly a part of your authentic self and whose energy would not be a good fit, attractive as it might be.

Mili Dillard, a SoulCollage® Trainer from North Carolina, created a process that integrates SoulCollage® and astrology and visioning cards. She calls it "The Maker's Gift Collage Visioning." Here are Mili's words:

Early last year, when I was looking for a way to personally do some visioning and planning, but didn't want to fall into my old trap of doing it in an exclusively left-brain, linear way, I came up with the notion of using the astrology wheel's house system as a way to comprehensively segment my life into "roles" for the purpose of doing some visioning and planning through collage.

I realized that a neat and manageable "eat the elephant one bite at a time" way to work with this visioning process would be to create a SoulCollage® card for each house––each card to portray in images my vision for my best self in that department of life. I've really enjoyed making these cards and am sharing the process with some ongoing groups who are doing one card per month at present. Each month we focus on one house or department of life to create an individualized collage expression for our personal vision for ourselves relative to that house.

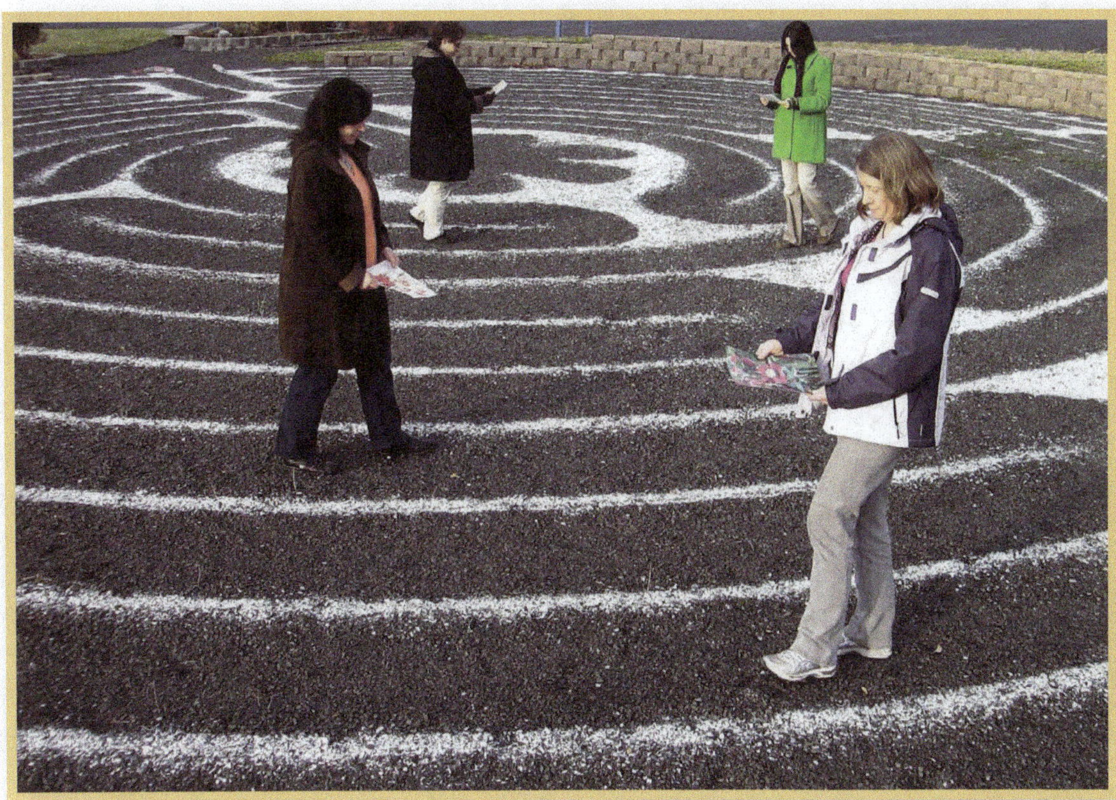

The Trinity Community Labyrinth in Pullman, Washington

As an example of one of the twelve houses in an astrology chart, I selected Mili's card for the fourth house which is the house of *Home and Foundation*. Her card is shown on the previous page with the *I Am One Who…* words.

Walking the Labyrinth

SoulCollage® can be linked creatively with many other processes. Here is an example of its use in conjunction with a labyrinth workshop. Susan Marra, a SoulCollage® Facilitator from Washington state, describes how she and a labyrinth facilitator worked together to make this event happen.

> *I co-facilitated a SoulCollage®/ Labyrinth workshop on the Council Suit. Robin Fuerst (a certified labyrinth Facilitator and SoulCollage® student) led an introduction to archetypes and presented information on labyrinth walking. I introduced the Council Suit of the SoulCollage® deck, had each participant find some images, and then walk the labyrinth holding their images. Upon completing their walk, the participants made SoulCollage® cards using these images. The resulting cards and readings had a power and depth that was truly enchanting, due in part to the added energy of the labyrinth!*

Movement Work and Body Dialogue

Some Facilitators have found creative ways to link SoulCollage® work with body awareness and body work. Every card in a SoulCollage® deck can be used in this way, not only the especially body-oriented cards of the Companions.

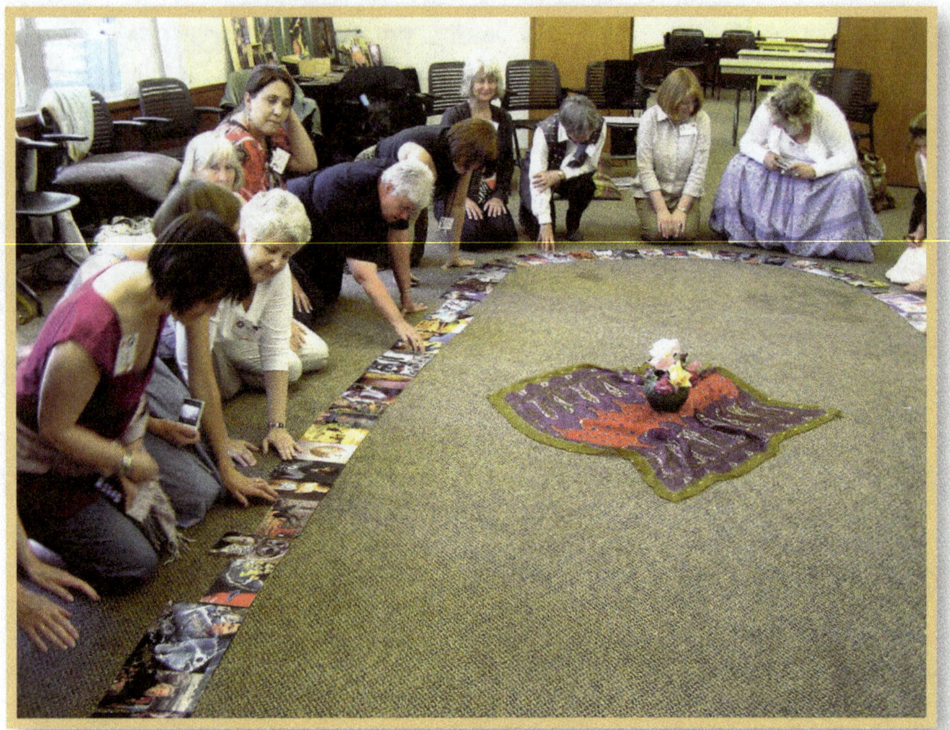

Group in circle of their newly-made cards

PHOTO BY KELLY LEVECK (2010)

Miriam Goldberg, a SoulCollage® Facilitator from California, describes dialoging between one's body and an image on a card.

> *The body has its own way of attuning to a card. Even when we are completely surprised by a card's images, we often feel the special "Ah!" or "Oh!" release in our bodies when the images fall into place. This spontaneous communion can be used to explore a card's gifts. We can start by asking ourselves, "When I sit with this card, where in my body do I feel a response, a sensation, warmth, energy, tension, 'butterflies'?" And then, as I let myself be with this feeling, I speak to the Neter: "Would you address that sensation? Share your wisdom about it?" Or I can ask the Neter "Where in my body do you bring your gifts? Your vitality?" And follow that exploration with "How would you like me to use these?" Another question might be, "If I allow this vitality, this gift, to flow in my body, how will it nourish me and my life?" After this kind of "body dialogue," if I will take a moment to just sit and behold the card, often it will actually "look" different. Then in the silence, I can feel myself receive a special blessing.*

If you are a person with a keen awareness of your body and its sensations, you will want to copy down these questions and experiment with dialoguing between your body and your Neters. And if you are not naturally so attuned, copy them anyway and practice.

> *Experiment with dialoguing between your body and your SoulCollage® Neters.*

Storytelling from the Cards

Once, on a SoulCollage® retreat, we tried an impromptu storytelling session that was great fun. Everyone placed their cards, except Community cards, in front of us, face down, for this process. One person began by drawing cards from her deck until one came up who could act as the hero or heroine of a story. She showed and named it: my *Scared Child* Neter. *Speaking from this image,* this person began a story with just a few sentences, creating as she spoke: "Once upon a time I peeked out of my hiding place, and called out to see if anyone was nearby who might protect me if I came out to play. It was quiet and I wondered if anyone heard me until..." At this point the first speaker paused and the next person drew a card from his deck, showed and named it, and then continued the story, staying at first in the person of the initial, heroine image as she met the second image, "...until I saw this beautiful deer standing there." Then he switched characters and integrated his new Neter imaginatively into the plot. It was a fourth chakra deer. "I am here, little girl, and I am gentle and loving, and I won't hurt you. Will you go on a walk with me and see who else is around in this forest? I will lead the way...." As this speaker paused, the next person drew a card and continued the story. In this way the story was woven by as many Neters as it took to tell the story and finally bring it to an end. Sometimes a time limit can be set, or a set number of turns decided on ahead of time.

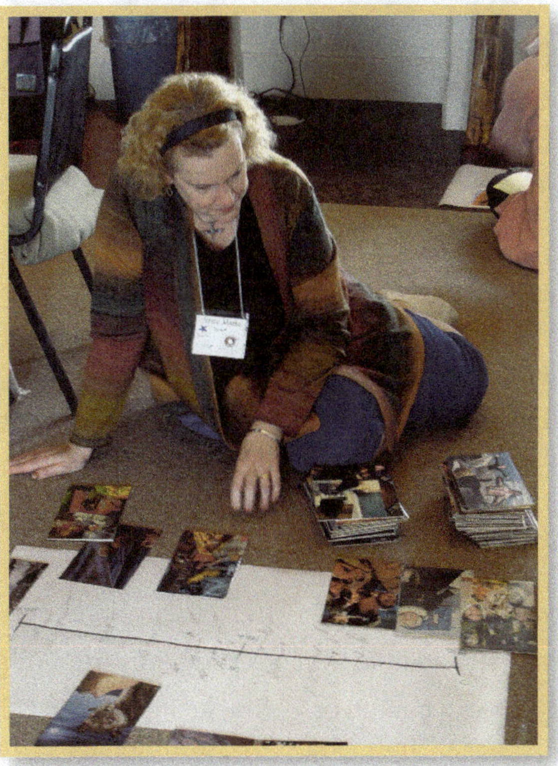

Anne Marie Bennett reading cards at the 2009 SoulCollage® Facilitators' Conference

PHOTO BY JENISE ENGLISH

These intuitive stories are often mythic in nature and always great fun. Sometimes they are quite absurd and sometimes quite beautiful. They can have a tragic turn and then recover and move on. You can do this process with a group as we did, and also by yourself. Choose a hero or heroine card and then spin the story, drawing one card at a time. It is much like a dream, except you are more conscious and have some control. At the same time the invisible spirits of the universe have the option of bringing the mysterious and unexpected into the present moment.

SoulCollage® Exhibits

On several occasions groups of SoulCollagers have mounted a SoulCollage® exhibit in order to introduce new people to the process, and also, of course, to share their cards. Some of these have been general exhibits where examples of all the suits and the Transpersonal cards are displayed; some have been mounted around a theme. One exhibit was devoted to the *Waterbearer* archetype. More than twenty people who had cards for this Council Neter contributed a card, and also an *I Am One Who...* to place at the bottom of the

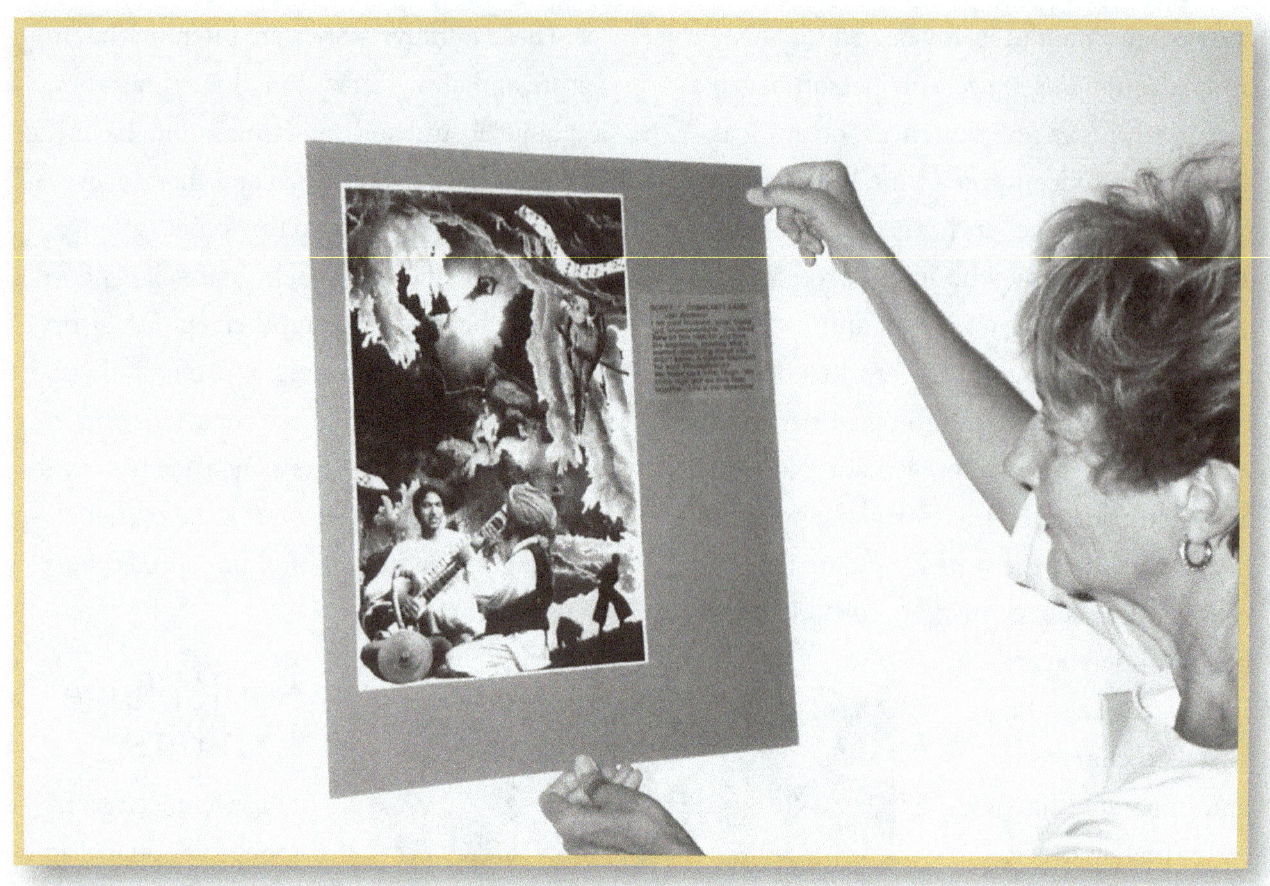

Jeri Bodemar with matted card "Scott" at a SoulCollage® Exhibition

mat. I wrote an article about this exhibit. Another exhibit centered on the theme of *Gratefulness.*

To mount an event like this you will need to find a space that would welcome this display, and also where they are safe. Since they are not for sale, the exhibit may not be one that commercial galleries will want to hang, but perhaps it would be welcome in a restaurant, an office building, along an inside mall, or in a church or temple meeting room or foyer.

Exhibits can be mounted quite simply. Mount chosen cards carefully on pieces of colored mat board. Print up the words including the name and the suit, and glue them below the picture. Of course, you can do something more professional with the framing, but this simplicity works quite well.

Also have a few mat boards with the actual size of the cards shown, perhaps displayed as if they were laid out for a reading.

We ask that at least five people be involved in such an exhibit, and that the pictures are not near any art that is for sale. To honor the artists and photographers that originally took the photos used in your collages we always make it very clear that *SoulCollage® cards are for personal use and not for sale.* To further avoid confusion we call such a showing a "SoulCollage® Exhibit" and not an "Art Show". "The Principles of SoulCollage®" and the "SoulCollage® Guidelines" (available at soulcollage.org) will be helpful in choosing which cards to hang and how to approach the organization of the exhibit.

Be sure to have hand-outs describing the SoulCollage® process available for people passing through the exhibit. This should include literature which shows the soulcollage.org website and the World of SoulCollage® community at soulcollage.org so that people who are interested can find their way to this work.

You will be surprised and pleased by the response that such an exhibit receives. If children's cards are involved, it will be very thrilling for them.

A Personal Retreat: A Gift of Wholeness

Mariabruna Sirabella, a SoulCollage® Trainer I have quoted in earlier chapters, describes how she does a personal retreat with her own SoulCollage® cards. Here are her words:

> *Intuitive stories told with the cards are often mythic in nature and always great fun. The mysterious and unexpected may come into the present moment.*

Whenever possible I set aside enough time to be alone and step into a personal retreat with my deck. I prefer to be in the safety of a monastery, retreat center or isolated cabin away from distractions. The intention is to deepen the relationship with my cards through full immersion in their presence and energy, and receive their gifts with more awareness. It works best to have, at minimum, one full day, although I highly recommend spending at least one night to share the dream time with them.

I create a simple sacred space by my bedside with the three Transpersonal Cards, and I place every other card along the perimeter of the room or in a large circle that encompasses my bed. I turn the space into an alchemical vessel where I will live and sleep surrounded by my Neters for a set amount of chronological time. I make sure my practical needs are properly taken care of and then enter ritual time, the time that matures the seeds. I use my familiar spiritual practices to attune and open myself, and to alert my senses and my mind to wisdom and transformation. I do yoga asanas, drum, meditate, and dance to the rhythm of my own breath and sounds. One card will grab my attention, and I will dialogue, move, and journal with it. Two cards may call for reflection on their opposing qualities1. I ask them questions. Others just want to be contemplated. I feel them. I let this experience flower in my consciousness. I allow. I write. Sometimes I make a new card. I listen to the images' resonance in my body. I listen to the silence, and I walk in nature. I breathe images in, I breathe images out. I stay present to the moment. Things happen. This energetic exchange between my full attention and their presence weaves a new tapestry within. The expanded consciousness lets these "mirrors of the self" organize in a new constellation. I come out of that time/space a more integrated whole; my soul seats more deeply in my body. New seeds are planted: time and opportunity will bring them to fruition.

[1] Sirabella, M. (2008). *Embracing Conflict/Transforming Change* (Audio). Hanford Mead Publishers, Inc.

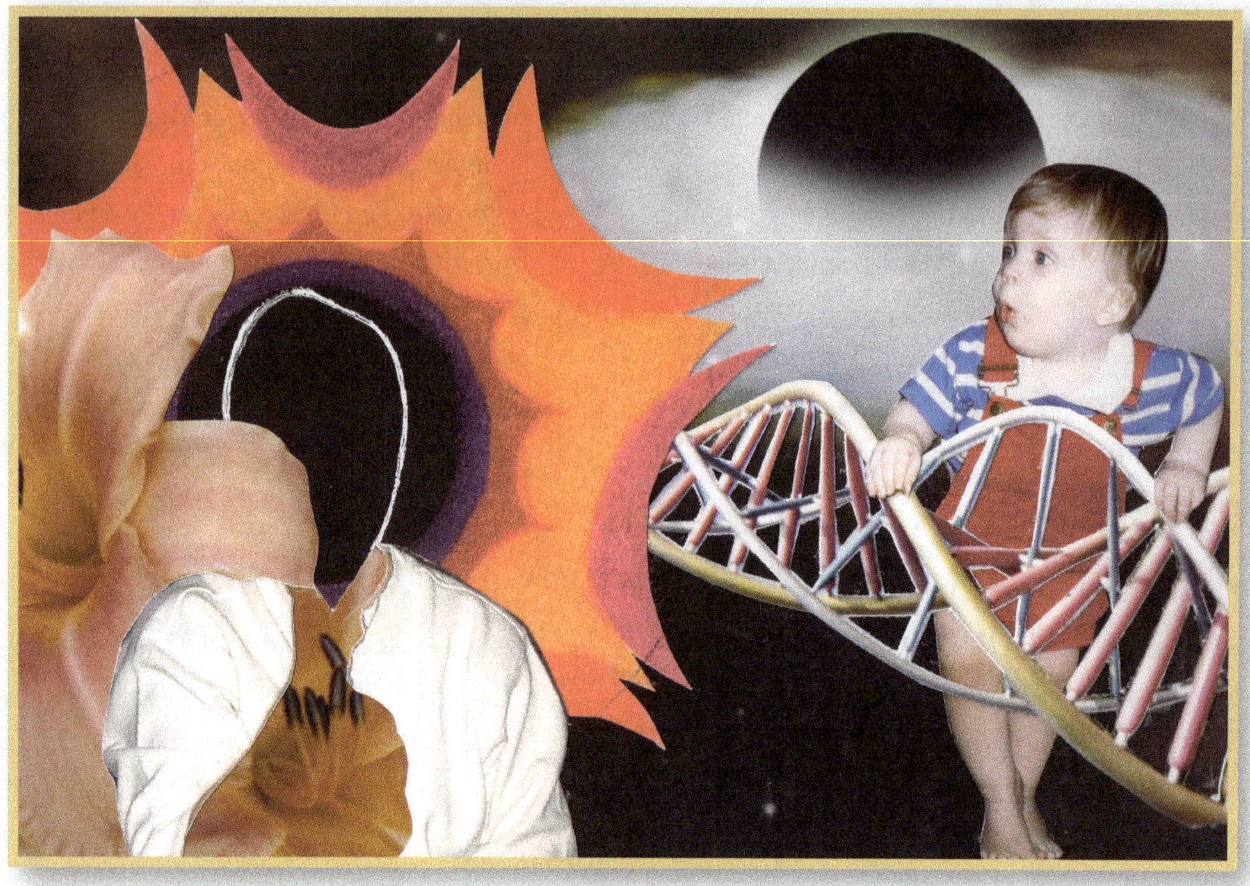

TITLE:	**Cosmic Connection**	"*I Am One Who* views the faces of Mother and experiences my cosmic connection...I Am One with the All."
SUIT:	**Committee**	
CREATOR:	**Mili Dillard**	

CHAPTER 19

Becoming a SoulCollage® Facilitator

INDRA'S NET

Very early in this book I talked about the ancient Egyptian word Neter, and how this single word pointed both to the Oneness of Source, and also the many living forms that eternally flow in and out from Source. In SoulCollage® we have adopted this archaic word *Neter* to mean, for us, all the many, many guides and allies and challengers of our Souls.

One metaphor for the Infinite that first appeared in second century Mahayana Buddhism was also a net. In that tradition it was called the *Net of Indra* and it depicts one vast, infinite Net as a symbol for all created universes. This net has no beginning and no end. Embedded within this net are an infinite number of many-faceted jewels—jewels that reflect constantly and forever every other jewel in the Net.

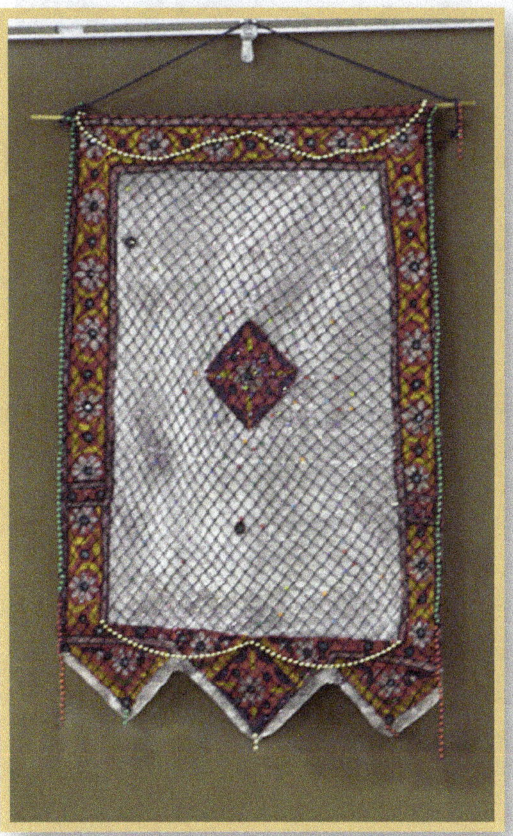

Seena crafted this version of Indra's Net to symbolize the One and the Many. Each jewel in Indra's Net reflects all others infinitely.

This image of Indra's Net has become a special symbol for Community in SoulCollage®. We experience this Net of Indra with ourselves as the jewels reflecting endlessly within it. From this place we know each person is an integral thread in the Larger Story. We even have a physical replica of Indra's Net to hang on the wall at some of my Trainings. Over the years some newly trained Facilitators have taken a moment to glue their personal "jewel" on to the netting of this icon, so now we have many, many jewels glittering there. And we expect many more will be added.

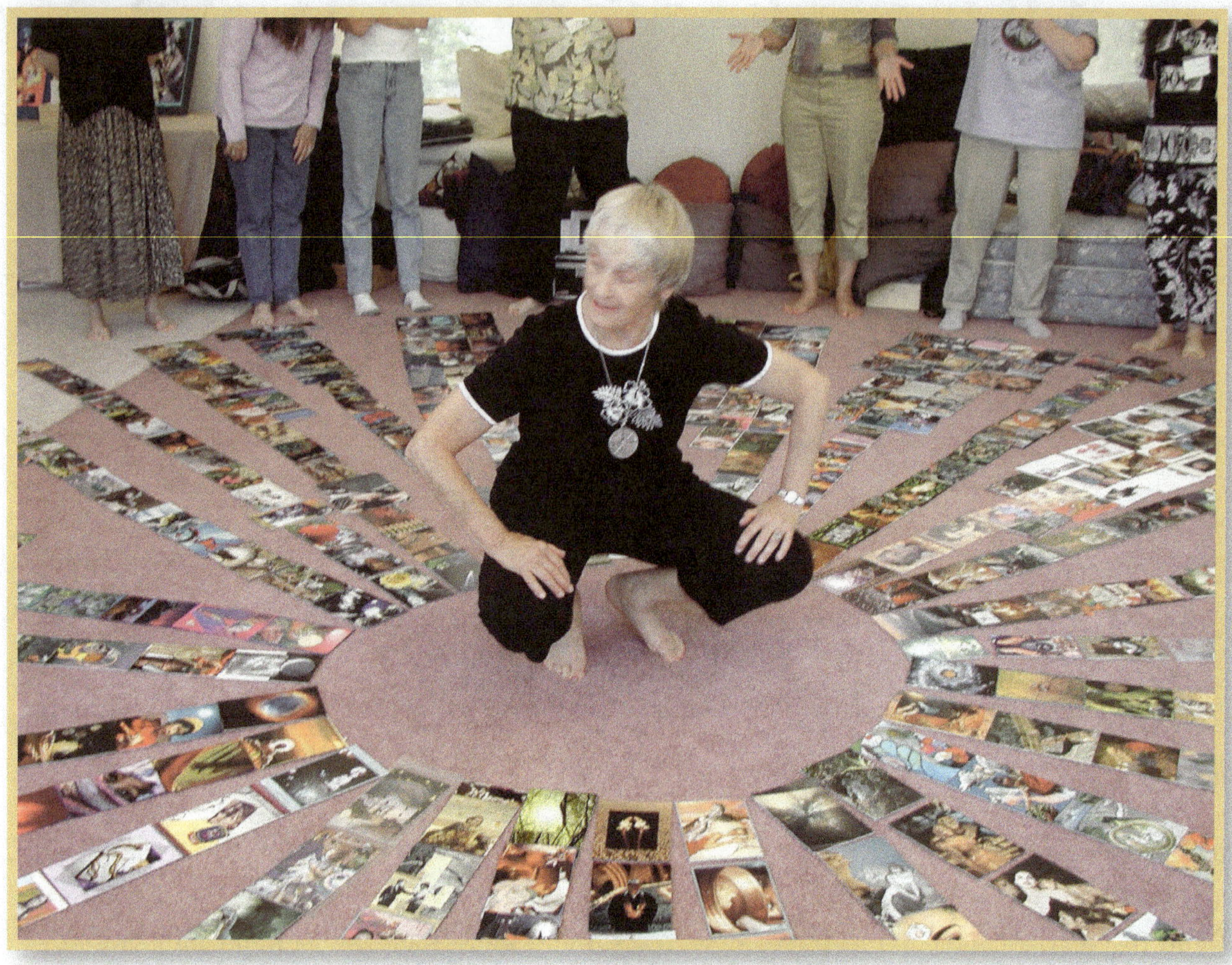

Seena Frost in the midst of a ceremonial circle of SoulCollage® cards

PHOTO BY CATHERINE ANDERSON (2005)

Sharing SoulCollage® Before You Have Taken the Training

There could come a point when you who are reading this book decide to join the growing community of SoulCollage® Facilitators which now reaches around the world. You may want to introduce SoulCollage® to friends, groups you are currently part of, your work place, or clients if you are a clinician. Of course you can do this sharing without completing a SoulCollage® Facilitator Training, but, if you do that, we ask that you name your workshop something other than "SoulCollage®..." and that you don't don't facilitate workshops with this method or call yourself a "SoulCollage® Facilitator" until you have taken the Training and received your certificate of completion. Thousands of people have taken this Training and found it valuable personally and professionally. We invite you to join the international community of trained SoulCollage® Facilitators if you are interested in sharing this useful, trademarked method.

The Benefits of the SoulCollage® Facilitator Community

If you do decide to join this community there are some definite "perks"! It will give you the freedom to advertise with the trademarked name of SoulCollage® and to call yourself a SoulCollage® Facilitator and be listed as such on the website soulcollage.org. You will have access to our monthly newsletter, and the privilege of advertising events on our website. There are discounts on materials, and invitations to conferences. Most importantly, there is a world-wide community with whom to share resources and experiences, and from whom you can get support and answers to questions you might have as you go about sharing SoulCollage®.

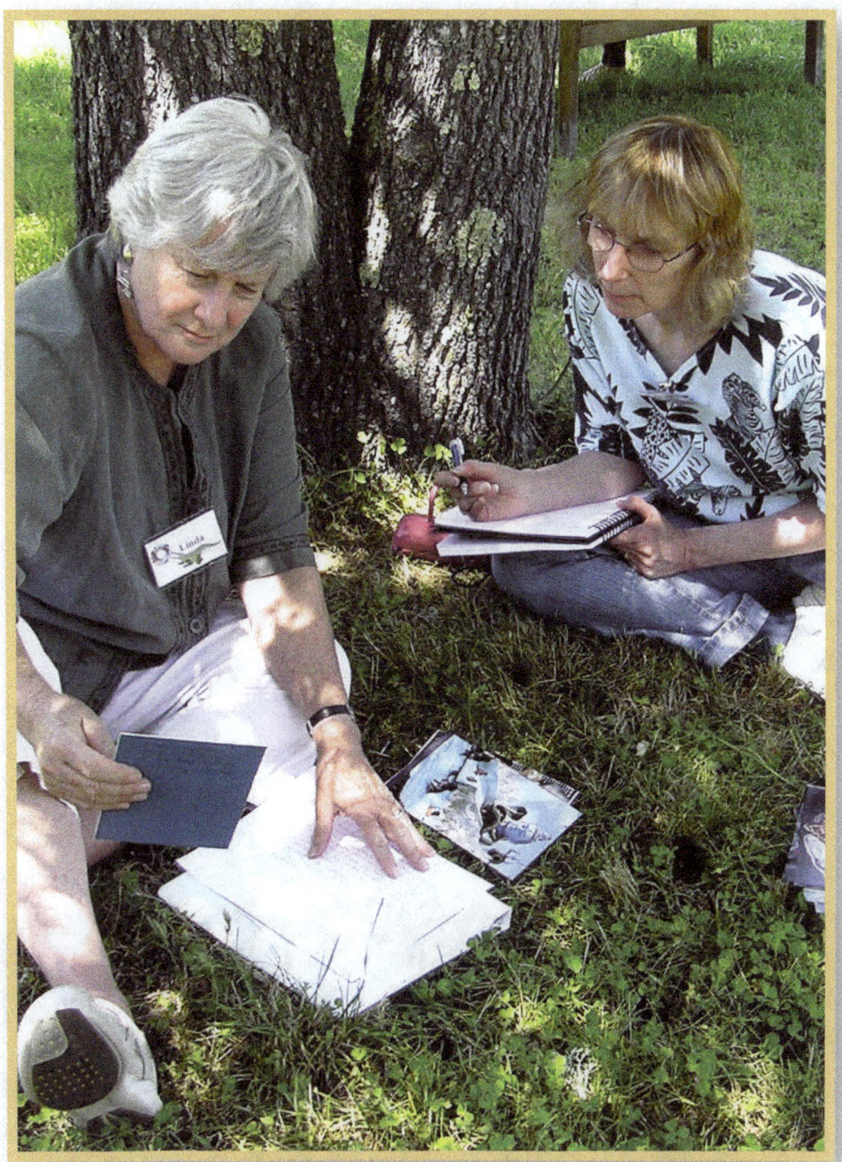

Left to right: Marla English and Rae Hight share about their cards at a SoulCollage® Training.

PHOTO BY SEENA B. FROST

Requirements for the SoulCollage® Facilitator Training

The basic SoulCollage® Facilitator Training is not a large time commitment, and if you are an adult, you are welcome to take the Training if you are enthusiastic and serious about passing SoulCollage® on to other people. The basic Training consists of didactic information you need to know and experiential training. There are only a few prerequisites of experience with SoulCollage® that you need to complete before you attend. These are listed at soulcollage.org. You can also find current listings of trainings in person, online, and in multiple languages.

There is a world-wide SoulCollage® community with whom to share resources and experiences, and from whom you can get support and answers to questions.

soulcollage.org

SoulCollage® Facilitators gather for their 2008 Conference at Asilomar in Monterey, California.

PHOTO BY CATHERINE ANDERSON

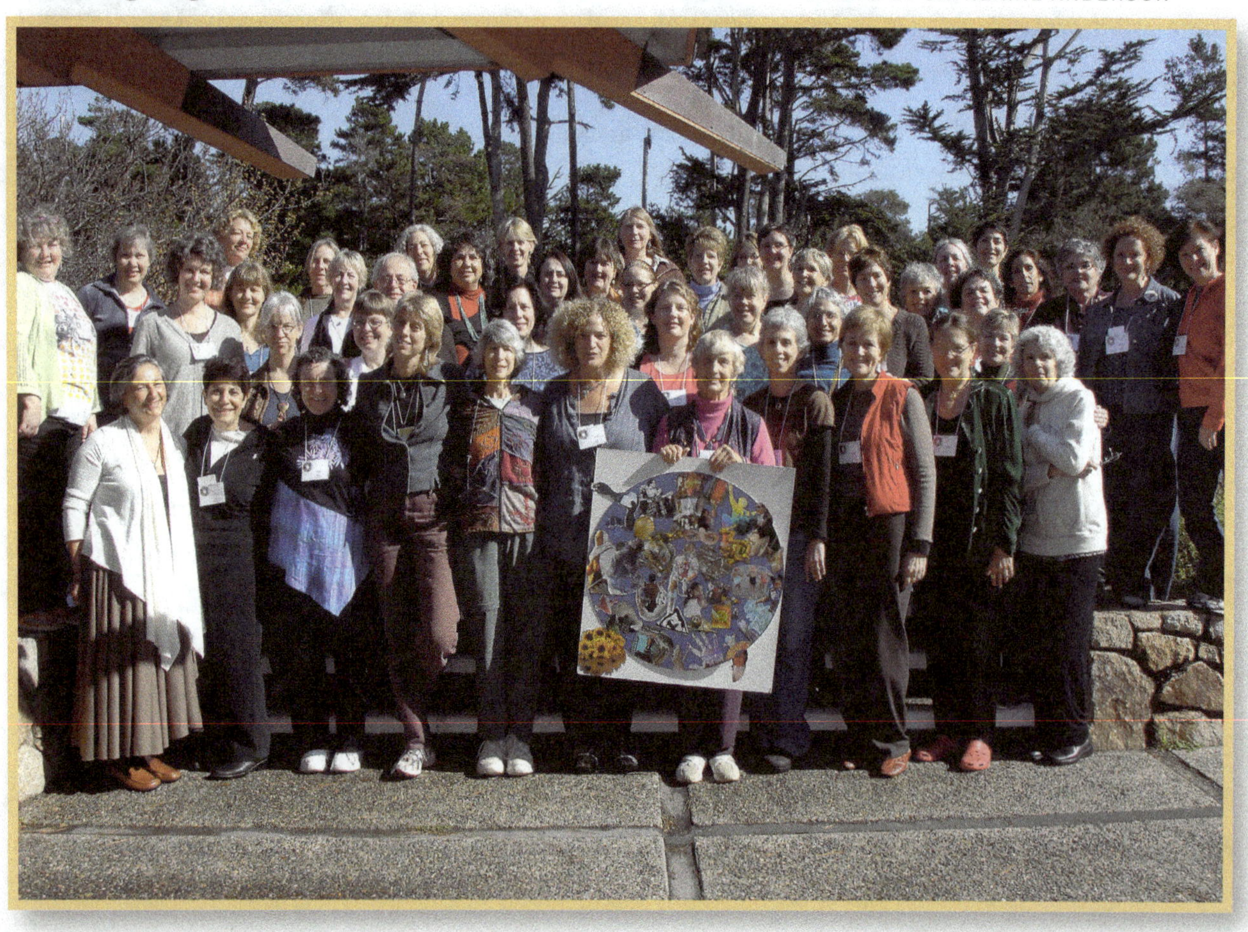

CHAPTER 20

Together We Are Evolving!

The first SoulCollage® book was printed in 2001, and at its conclusion I wrote these words: "How each of us nurtures, heals, and explores Soul will have impact on the vast cultural changes beginning to manifest. If we become more Soul-Conscious, we will become more powerful and effective as *Lightbearers*, as *Warriors*, as *Wise Women* and *Wise Men* of the 2000s."

Now it is nine years later, and I am writing the final words of this second book. The Larger Story has evolved since then. There are even more rumblings about a paradigm shift happening in the world than in 2000. Many healers and teachers and even astrologers are talking about it.

This local story has evolved as well. In mid-2010 SoulCollage® had 850 trained Facilitators in a total of 13 countries. By the time you are holding this book that number will certainly be larger. You can find statistics regularly updated at soulcollage.org.

I like to think that SoulCollage® has become one of the "imaginal cells" working within this still cocooned "old caterpillar" of a society to help it transform into the new "butterfly" of a society that many are envisioning. We are joining together with

TITLE: **As Above, So Below**
SUIT: **Council**
CREATOR: **Nancy Weiss**

"*I Am the One Who* holds the world in my hands, holding the connection between heaven and earth."

other communities of awakened human beings, and adding our special gifts of images, intuition, and imagination. We are working towards the balance of left- and right-brain hemispheres, and the balance of masculine and feminine energies. We are working to end the dualisms that separate people into good and evil camps by teaching that all beings are unique and at the same time holy, each being blessed with a spark of Source.

I invite you to join the community of SoulCollage® and be part of this paradigm shift, using the special tools described in this book.

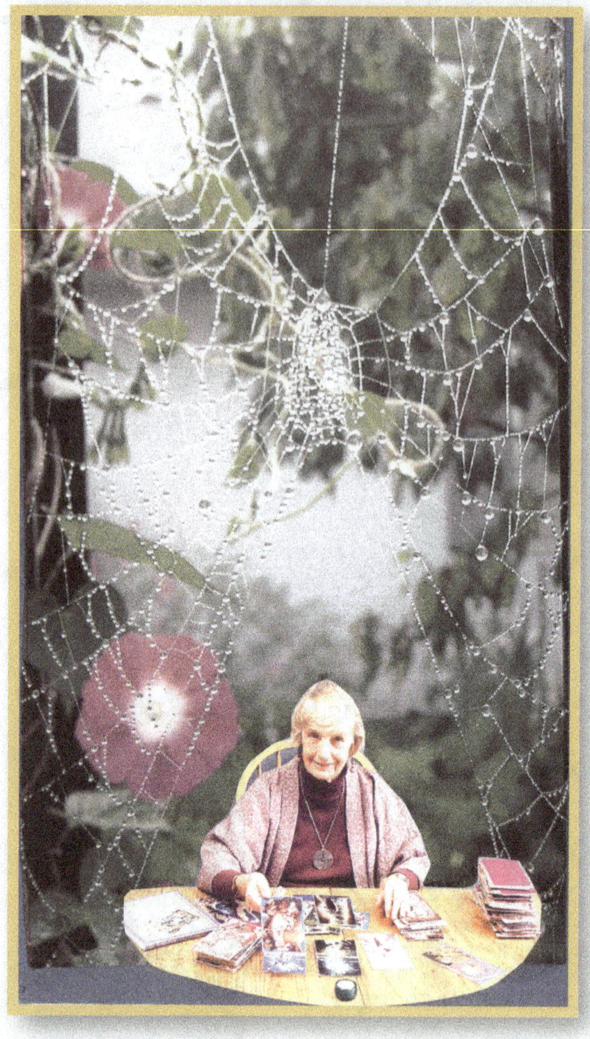

TITLE: **My Creative Spinner**
SUIT: **Committee**
CREATOR: **Seena B. Frost**

"*I Am One Who* spins webs of images to hold and heal my Soul. Whenever a bridge is needed between my Neters I create these cards. It is like spinning webs out of my dark depths."

> *"How each of us nurtures, heals, and explores Soul will have impact on the vast cultural changes beginning to manifest. If we become more Soul-Conscious, we will become more powerful and effective as* Lightbearers, *as* Warriors, *as* Wise Women *and* Wise Men *of the 21st century."*

Resources

World of SoulCollage®: The Official SoulCollage® Community

The official, global community is World of SoulCollage® (WOSC) where there are many free resources, information, and newsletters; personal or professional memberships; announcements of SoulCollage® workshops; and SoulCollage® Facilitator Trainings. Additionally, there are Villages of Interest for Facilitators who are applying the SoulCollage® method in various languages, geographical regions, or in specialized areas, such as therapy, grief, dreams, labyrinth, etc. Visit **soulcollage.org**

SoulCollage® App

A powerful SoulCollage® App is available for iOS devices (Apple iPhone, iPad, and Mac). It is very handy, anywhere you go with your devices, for drawing cards randomly, doing readings, and sharing your cards. It also insures you have a copy of your original cards and records of your readings and card notes. It is available in the Apple App store.

SoulCollage® Facilitator Trainings

When you have made some cards, done some readings, and feel that you would like to share SoulCollage® with others, you can find current listings of SoulCollage® Facilitator Trainings throughout the world and online at World of SoulCollage®. No degree or other previous experience is necessary to take the training. Only your own enthusiastic personal experience with SoulCollage® and an understanding of SoulCollage® basics. Only those who have completed the SoulCollage® Facilitator Training may facilitate this method with others and call themselves SoulCollage® Facilitators. Visit **soulcollage.org.**

Books Recommended by Seena

Bolen, J.S. (1985). *Goddesses in every woman. Gods in every man.* New York, NY: Harper and Row.

Campbell, J. (1970). *The hero with a thousand faces.* Cleveland, OH: World Publishing.

Cirlot, J.E. (1971, 1991). *A dictionary of symbols.* New York, NY: Dorset Press.

De Lubicz, R.A. Schwaller. (1982). *Nature word.* West Stockbridge, MA: The Lindisfarne Press.

Downing, C. (1988, 1996). *The goddess: Mythological images of the feminine.* New York, NY: Crossroad.

Fox, M. (2008). *The hidden spirituality of men.* Novato, CA: New World Library

Fox. M. (2002). *Creativity.* New York, NY: Tarcher/Penguin.

Gallegos, E. S. (1990). *The personal totem pole: Animal Imagery, the Chakras, and Psychotherapy.* Santa Fe, NM: Moon Bear Press.

Grof, S. (2000). *Psychology of the future.* Albany, NY: State University of New York Press

Harner, M. (1980, 1990). *The way of the shaman.* San Francisco, CA: HarperSanFrancisco.

Hillman, J. (1997). *The soul's code.* New York, NY: Warner Books.

Hillman, J. (1989). *The blue fire.* New York, NY: Harper & Row.

Hillman, J. (1980). *Facing the gods.* Dallas, TX: Spring Publications, Inc.

Houston, J. (2000). *Jump time.* Los Angeles, CA: Jeremy P. Tarcher.

Houston, J. (1997). *A mythic life: Learning to live our greater story.* San Francisco, CA: HarperSanFrancisco.

Judith, A. (1987). *Wheels of life.* St. Paul, MN: Llewellyn.

Judith, A. and Vega, S. (1993.) *The sevenfold journey: Reclaiming mind, body and spirit through the chakras.* Freedom, CA: Crossing Press.

Jung, E. (1985). *Animus and anima.* Dallas, TX: Spring Publications.

Matthews, B. Ed., (1986.) *The herder dictionary of symbols.* Willamette, IL: Chiron.

Metzner, R. (1998.) *The unfolding self: Varieties of transformative experience.* Origin Press.

Murdock, M. (1990). *The heroine's journey.* Boston, MA & London: Shambhala.

Pink, D. (2006). *A whole new mind: Why right-brainers will rule the future.* New York, NY: Riverhead Trade.

Pinkola-Estes, C. (1992). *Women who run with the wolves.* New York & Toronto: Ballantine.

Progoff, I. (1975, 1992). *At a journal Workshop.* Los Angeles, CA: Jeremy Tarcher.

Richo, D. (1999). *Shadow dance.* Boston, MA: Shambala.

Sams, J. and Carson, D. (1988). *Medicine Cards.* Santa Fe, NM: Bear and Company.

Watkins, J. and Watkins, H. (1997). *Ego States: Theory and Therapy.* New York, NY: Norton.

Wolkstein, D. (1991). *The First Love Stories.* New York, NY: Harper Collins.

About the Author

Seena B. Frost, M. Div., M.A. studied theology at Yale Divinity School, married, raised four children, and then received a Master's degree in psychology from Santa Clara University. She became a California licensed Marriage and Family Therapist. Special trainings with Jean Houston and Robin Van Doren inspired the combining of three of her life passions: spirituality, psychotherapy, and creativity. The SoulCollage® process and book have issued from this magical mix. Seena founded a world-wide, rapidly growing, intuitive collage movement called SoulCollage®, a collage method incorporating images, imagination, and intuition.

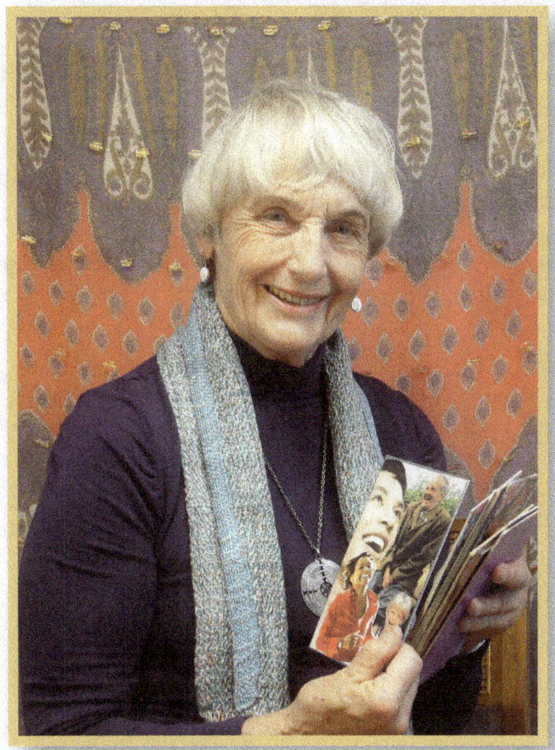

Seena B. Frost (1932–2016)

PHOTO BY BARBARA SUSAN BOOTH

Seena Frost is the author of the *SoulCollage® Evolving* book, eight audio home study courses, and *Journal of a Steadfast Fence*.

Index

SoulCollage® card titles are capitalized and the SoulCollage® Neters listed are italicized

Other books from Hanford Mead Publishers

Translations of SoulCollage® Evolving

Dutch, French, German, Italian, Mandarin, and Portuguese

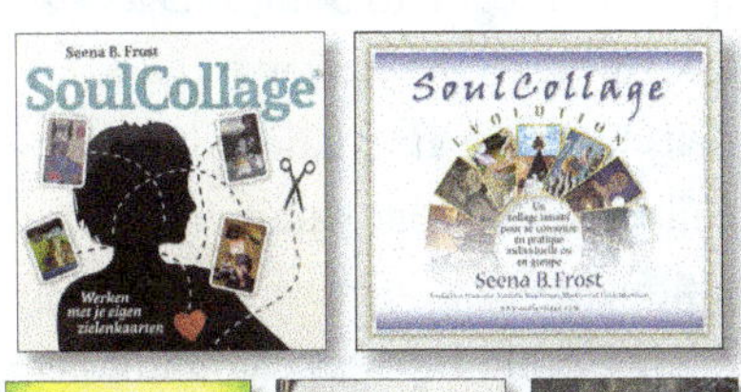

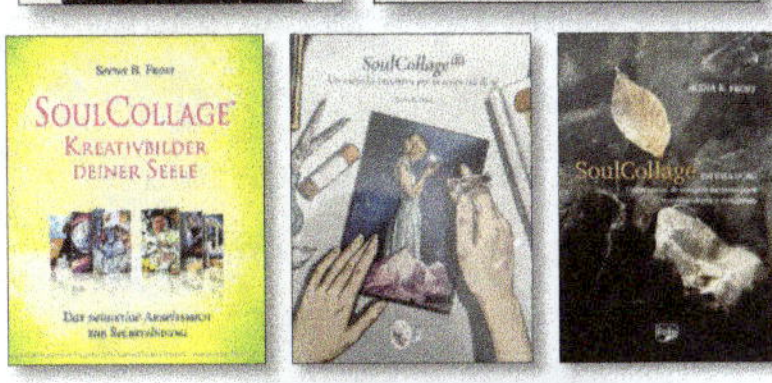

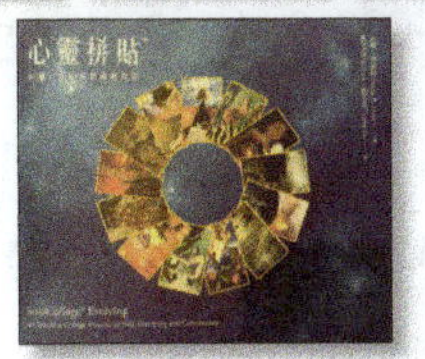

More from Seena B. Frost

Items listed are available at Hanford-Mead.com and/or Amazon.com

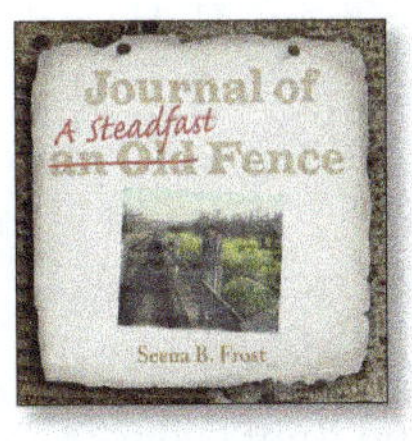

Journal of a Steadfast Fence

Seena B. Frost

This poetry/photo book was written by Seena Frost when she was 77. It is about spirituality and aging. Seena, the founder of a worldwide, rapidly growing, intuitive collage movement called SoulCollage®, took a morning walk beside a century-old redwood fence every morning for almost 20 years. She began to feel a relationship with different parts of the fence. She started naming them and talking with them and then journaling about her conversations. The poetry speaks in turn with the different voices of this fence about the experience of aging. Each poem is illustrated with the author's photo of that part of the fence which is speaking. ISBN: 978-1-59275-0191; 8 ½ x 8 1/2; 60 pp; softcover.

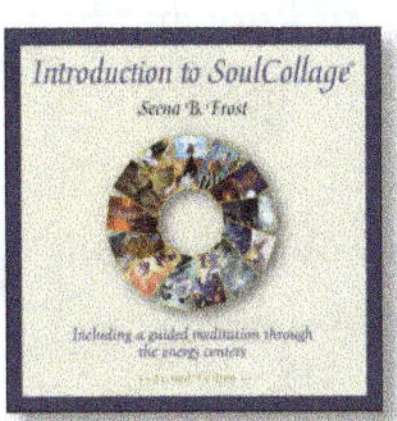

Introduction to SoulCollage®

Seena F. Frost

The Founder of SoulCollage® talks about this deeply satisfying art that anyone can do. With intuition and images we create personal tarot-like cards. Frost encourages us on this audio to use our own sense of inner direction and gives practical information that helps us use SoulCollage® to connect more to self, others, and Spirit. Frost also leads a guided relaxation through the chakras to identify animal images—allies for the Companions Suit of your SoulCollage® Deck. This audio is also available as a digital download from iTunes. ISBN# 1-59275-004-4 Audio download.

~ Your SoulCollage® Cards ~

An Audio Series by Seena B. Frost

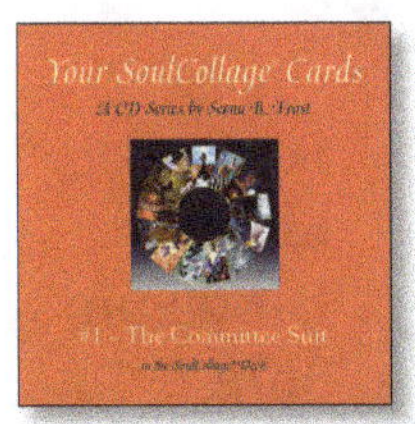

Audio #1

The Committee Suit

The Committee Suit is the psychological suit in the SoulCollage® Deck. Each card embodies a part of yourself, or a role you play in life. The Founder of SoulCollage,® Seena Frost, describes some of the common Committee cards (e.g., Happy Child, Lonely Child, Family Cook, Animal Lover, Angry Self, etc.) and how these cards are useful in honoring and balancing our many parts. Audio download.

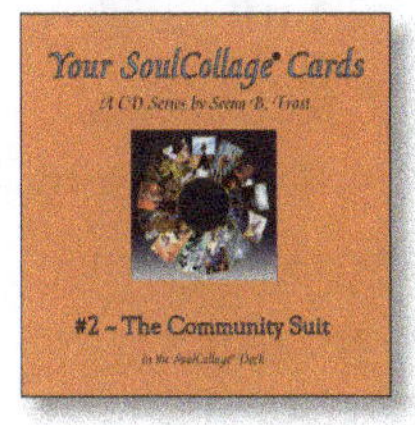

Audio # 2

The Community Suit

The Community Suit is comprised of cards representing sentient beings who have been important to you as allies, guides, or challengers. These beings may be living or dead, friends and loved ones, pets, those who are famous and hold important energy for you, or your ancestors, and even places and spaces that hold special energy for you. The Founder of SoulCollage®, Seena Frost, talks about the value of the Community Suit and gives ideas on how to work with it. Audio download.

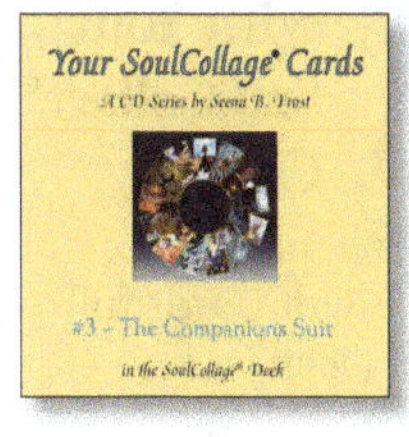

Audio # 3

The Companions Suit

The Companions Suit of the SoulCollage® deck contains cards representing our natural and primitive energies, ones that help us in various areas of life. The founder of SoulCollage,® Seena Frost, describes the ancient systems of yoga chakras and other traditional energy systems, and shows how making SoulCollage®

CONTINUES >

cards to represent our unique energies can give us guidance for both awareness of our bodily energies and for balancing our more subtle energy systems. Seena tells stories showing how people have worked with the cards of their Companions Suit. Audio download.

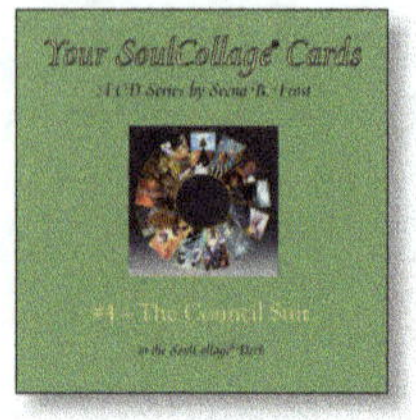

Audio #4

The Council Suit

The Council Suit consists of archetypes, the patterns and themes that populate our LargerStory. Council cards call to us and help us find and balance our larger purpose in life. The founder of SoulCollage,® Seena Frost, provides many examples of archetypes, provides guidance about the frequent confusion in identifying a card as a Committee card or a Council card, and begins to talk about the shadow inherent in every archetype (or Council Neter.) Audio download.

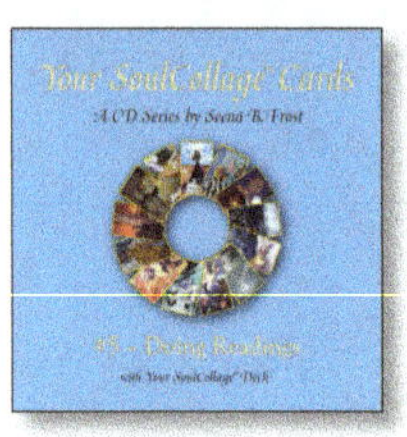

Audio #5

Doing Readings with Your SoulCollage® Cards

Track One: The Transpersonal Cards: The Three Silent Cards in Your SoulCollage® Deck

These cards do not exist as beings in form. They include the Source card, the Witness card and the SoulEssence card. The founder of SoulCollage®, Seena Frost, talks about the One and the Many as different ways the Soul exists. The Transpersonal cards represent the One and all the other cards represent the Many.

Plus...

Track Two: Doing Readings with Your SoulCollage® Deck

An essential part of the SoulCollage® process is the joy of tapping into our own intuition to answer life's questions. The images that have chosen us, the ones we have glued down onto cards to become guides, allies, and challengers in our deck are able to advise us by helping us access a deep place of knowing in ourselves. People who use SoulCollage® in personal readings using the signature "*I Am One Who...*" SoulCollage® process, are surprised at the depth of the answers they speak while talking as the card they have drawn. Audio download.

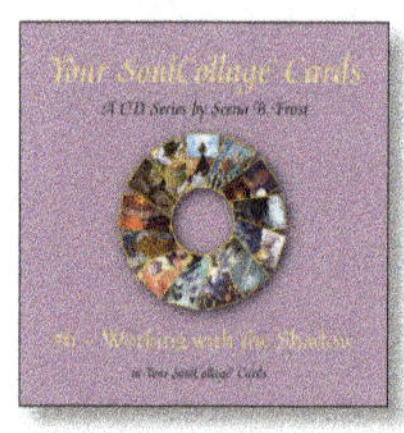

Audio #6

Working with the Shadow in SoulCollage®

The Shadow (a term from Jungian psychology) does not, as many people think, mean the opposite of something (like good vs. bad). An energy or part of us is shadowed, rather, if it expressing itself excessively or not enough. The founder of SoulCollage,® Seena Frost, gives many examples from cards of SoulCollage® suits and describes how to work to balance shadowed Committee, Community, Companions, and Council suits cards. Audio download.

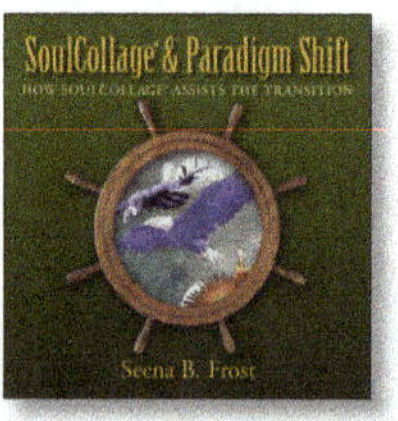

SoulCollage® & Paradigm Shift

How SoulCollage® Assists the Transition

Founder of SoulCollage® Seena B. Frost's last audio course contains her thoughts on the contribution of SoulCollage® to making a big collective human shift—a paradigm shift. It describes how elements that are integral to SoulCollage® also apply to the new world era that many see emerging from the collapse of the old paradigm: the uniqueness and relatedness of all beings, building of safe community, honoring of diverse perspectives, cultivating of imagination and intuition, and mystical and direct relationship to Spirit. ISBN: 978-1-59275-032-0. Audio download.

More SoulCollage® Books

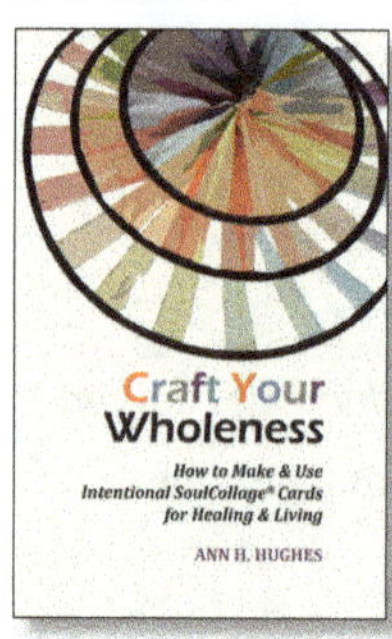

Craft Your Wholeness

How to Make & Use Intentional SoulCollage® Cards for Healing and Living

Ann H. Hughes

Discover how to catch, with grace, whatever Life throws your way and turn it into personal treasure. Make intentional SoulCollage® cards that can support you in healing your past, getting your life unstuck, learning to flow with change and exploring who you are and who you are becoming. It's fun and satisfying to enter the creativity zone, intuit how to express things you don't yet even have words for yet. You'll create collaged cards that grow into a deck you can consult to guide you on your healing journey, your life's journey. This one small book can be just the ally you need to inspire, encourage, and support you in the direction your heart wants to go. ISBN: 978-1-59275-0382

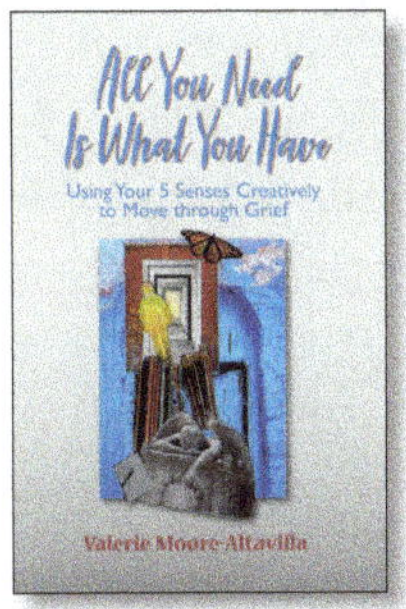

All You Need Is What You Have

Using Your 5 Senses To Move Through Grief

Valerie Moore-Altavilla

The universal experience of grief brings challenging feelings that may include fear, anxiety, confusion, sadness, and others—sometimes many feelings at once. We want to know how to cope and feel better. We want to know there is hope and help out there. There is so much uncertainty and change globally right now. We have experienced more illness, more death, the losses of work, travel, social connection, and many changes of circumstance. There is just more current grief in modern life, and many of us also have old griefs resurfacing, sometimes quite intensely.

The author writes to encourage you. As she will tell you, Valerie has been there with death and other losses. She became an art therapist because art expression helped her with her own profound passages through grief. She assures you that anyone can do the exercises she has shared in this book. Indeed, as the title says, "All You Need Is What You Have…" You already have your memories, your feelings, your intuition, and your senses. You can probably find somewhere around your home a selection of crayons, pencils, paper, magazines, scissors, and glue. You have what you need to be the expert of your story.

As if she were sitting down with you at your kitchen table, Valerie explains and illustrates these simple exercises and makes clear that the goal is the expression of your important feelings, not artistic perfection. These exercises utilize the five senses (vision, hearing, touch, taste, smell). The way forward is to spend some time checking in with your body. Your body is where you can find and be with the memories and nonverbal feelings that are always so central to deep grief.

Start with this short, simple book's encouragement. Find your own way forward to express your feelings. Move intuitively, at your own pace, gently and fully through your deepest grieving.

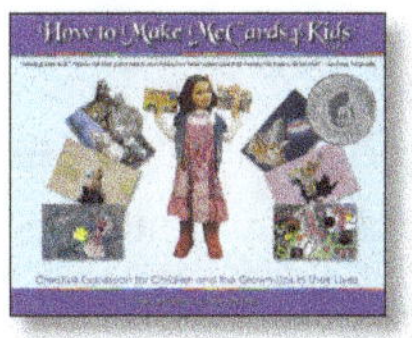

How to Make MeCards-4Kids™

Creative Expressive for Children and the Grownups in their Lives

Nancy Weiss and Jane Raphael

This book was written as a collaboration between a Los Angeles teacher and a Family Therapist. They adapted the SoulCollage® process to young children who made collaged cards to express themselves about their thoughts, feelings, and beliefs. In this book, these children show you their cards and their poems and tell you what making them meant to them. There are full instructions in the book for parents and teachers about how to provide the materials and the support to children to make MeCards4Kids. ISBN: 978-1-59275-037-5

More SoulCollage® Audios

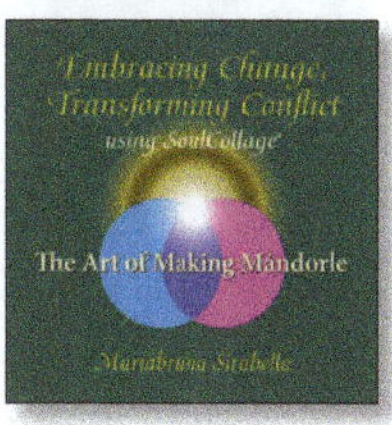

Embracing Change, Transforming Conflict Using SoulCollage®

The Art of Making Mándorle

Mariabruna Sirabella

Mariabruna, long-time student of Seena's and SoulCollage® Trainer, offers three guided journeys to to use with our SoulCollage® cards. These journeys are based on her long practice of yoga, shamanism, and psychotherapy. The journeys invite us to the practice of befriending change and of transforming conflict into harmonious relationship. ISBN: 978-1592750177. Audio download.

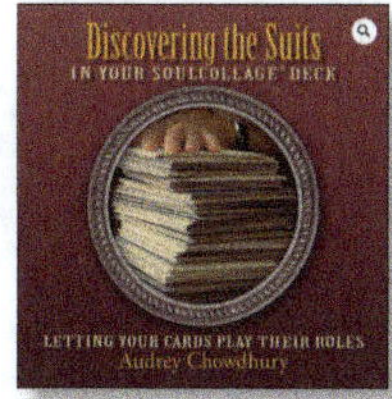

Discovering the Suits

Letting Your Cards Play Their Roles

Audrey Chowdhury

Art therapist Audrey Chowdhury helps you and your workshop participants or clients find insights and self-understanding within the structure of the SoulCollage® suits. The suits are the colors and forms giving clues for how to assemble the jigsaw puzzle of you. ISBN: 978-1-59275-034-4. Audio download.

Tracks

1. Introduction to the Suits
2. Why Work with the Suits in Your Own Deck?
3. Putting Together the Jigsaw Puzzle of You
4. Giving Your Cards the Attention They Want

CONTINUES >

5. Asking the Suits for Guidance
6. Shadow and Balance in the Suits
7. Which Suit? Finding the Right Home for a Card
8. Playing with Your Cards
9. How to Tell if a Card is a Transpersonal Card

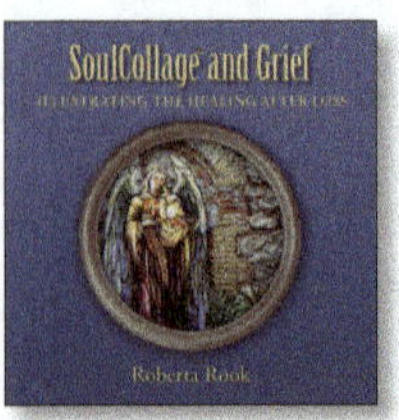

SoulCollage® & Grief

Illustrating the Healing After Loss

Robert Rook

Roberta Rook, LCPC, an experienced hospice coordinator and bereavement counselor, shares how she has used the expressive power of SoulCollage® in groups and with individuals in their journeys through grieving, and how the structure of SoulCollage® dovetails with the bereavement theory she uses in her work. Roberta assumes in her talk that the listener will have a basic understanding of SoulCollage®. ISBN: 978-1-59275-034-4. Audio download.

Tracks

1. The Power of Grief to Transform a Life
2. SoulCollage® Cards & the Questions of Grief
3. Facilitating Grieving in Groups with SoulCollage®
4. Deep Individual Bereavement Work: A Story

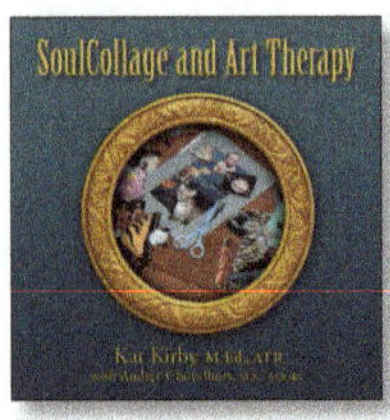

SoulCollage® & Art Therapy

Kat Kirby with Audrey Chowdhury

Kat Kirby, M.Ed., ATR, with Audrey Chowdhury, M.S., ATR-BC, have provided this audio introduction to SoulCollage® for art therapists, describing the basic structure and principles developed by Seena B. Frost and described in her book, SoulCollage® Evolving. They share stories of working with this powerful transformative process and tell how SoulCollage® has been used for decision-making, grief work, addiction recovery, eating disorders, stress and anxiety, relationship issues, "shadow" work, community-building; and with adolescents, the disabled, the elderly, and men. ISBN: 978-1-59275-0290. Audio download.

Tracks

1. Introduction
2. The Four Suits
3. Readings
4. The Shadow
5. SoulCollage® in Action – Stories
6. SoulCollage® and Community
7. SoulCollage® with Adolescents
8. SoulCollage® with the Disabled and Elderly
9. SoulCollage® and Relationship Issues
10. SoulCollage® with Eating Disorders and Addictions
11. SoulCollage® and Decision-Making
12. SoulCollage® with Grief Work
13. SoulCollage® with Stress and Anxiety
14. SoulCollage® with Men
15. Your SoulCollage®® and Art Therapy Journey

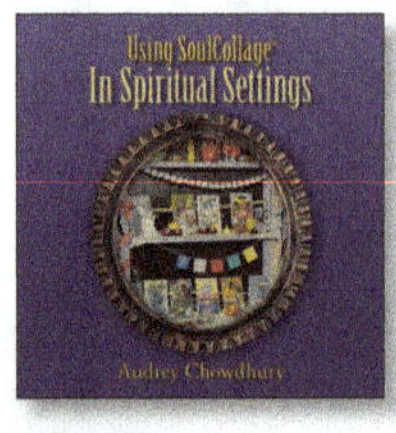

Using SoulCollage® in Spiritual Settings

Audrey Chowdhury

Art therapist Audrey Chowdhury finds SoulCollage® a highly effective practice, enthusiastically adopted by those seeking and those offering spiritual guidance. She offers a spectrum of compelling stories which illustrate diverse ways of using SoulCollage® in spiritual settings. She emphasizes the value of the SoulCollage® structure in spiritual work.

Tracks

1. Key Aspects of SoulCollage® for Spiritual work
2. Receiving Spiritual Guidance with SoulCollage® Cards
3. SoulCollage® & Prayer

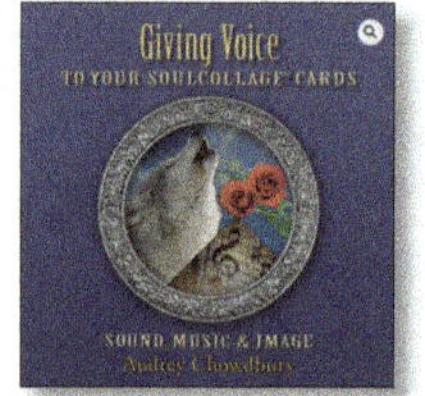

Giving Voice to Your SoulCollage® Cards

Sound, Music & Image

Audrey Chowdhury

Images want to speak, move, and make sound and music. By listening to their full range of expression, Art Therapist Audrey Chowdhury demonstrates how vocalizing can enrich your personal SoulCollage® practice and offer fun and insight to your workshop participants.

Tracks

1. Introduction to Sound and SoulCollage®
2. Conducting Your Inner Orchestra
3. Vocalizing a Card's Energy
4. Creating Harmonies Among Our Cards
5. We Sing to Them; They Sing to Us
6. The Music We Hear in Our Heads
7. Your Personal Practice: SoulCollage®, Sound, & Music

Books by Kylea Taylor

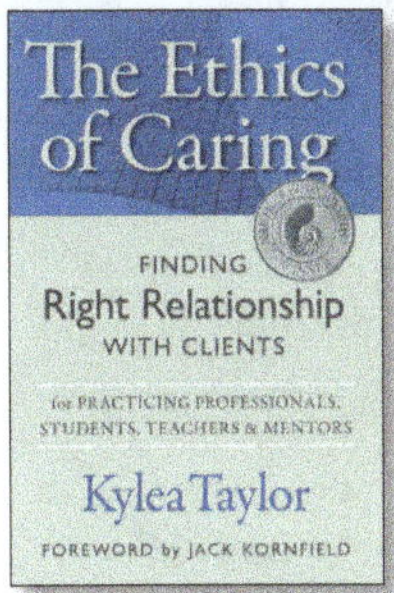

The Ethics of Caring

Finding Right Relationship with Clients

Kylea Taylor

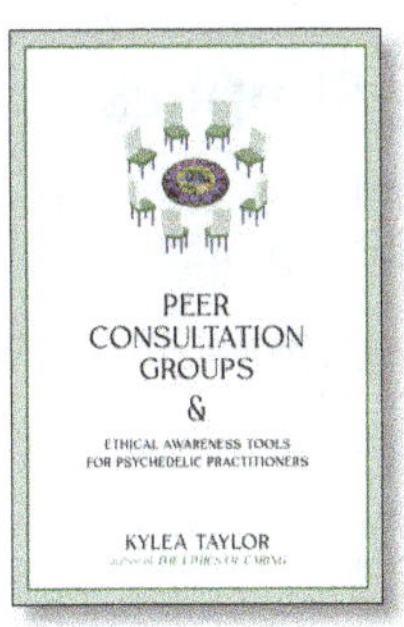

The Ethics of Caring was originally published in 1995. This updated, reorganized edition (2017) has an additional 88 pages and was written for all professionals, including psychotherapists, bodyworkers, medical practitioners, clergy, hypnotherapists, and acupuncturists, who want to become more conscious in their relationships with clients. It won a Silver Nautilus Book Award. The book provides unique help to volunteer and professional caregivers who want to sort out confusing ethical dilemmas, countertransference, and conflicts of interest in seven categories, including issues that arise more often in profound states of consciousness, like love, truth, insight, and oneness, as well as the more well-known ethical issues of money, sex, and power. It is so interesting to learn about what motivates us and our clients. These are the very issues that make page-turner novels and keep us binge-watching tv episodes. Ethical issues pertain to longings, feelings, and motivations which resonate at our very core. This book is available at Amazon in print, Kindle, and audio formats. 6" x 9". 360 pp. Softcover. ISBN: 978-1-59275-008-5

Peer Consultation Groups & Ethical Awareness Tools for Psychedelic Facilitators (2024)

Kylea Taylor

Practitioners working the clients in profound states of consciousness: grief, PTSD, addiction recovery, or sessions using hypnosis, breathwork, or psychedelics, often encounter amplified countertransference and other ethical challenges. Kylea Taylor, LMFT, describes the practical InnerEthics® Ethical Awareness Tools that are available to help practitioners identify their motivations and conflicts of interest and recognize, avoid, or repair precarious ethical situations. She explains the unique structure of an InnerEthics® Peer Consultation Group which is designed to help therapists and practitioners assist each other compassionately with the challenges and vulnerabilities that arise in working with clients in multidimensional states. Professionals working with clients in these deep states of consciousness can turn to this book to help them better avoid ethical missteps, increase client benefits, and create their own essential personal and professional support. Many therapists who encounter InnerEthics® are amazed that this approach to ethics can be so interesting and useful. They wish they had been able to include a compassionate, self-reflective study of ethics in grad school. This book is available at Amazon in print, Kindle, and audio formats. ISBN: 978-1-59275-047-4

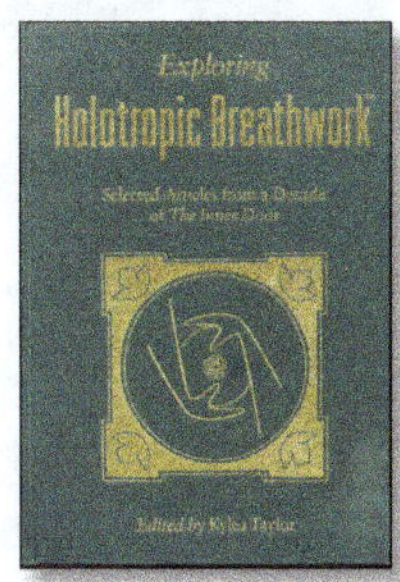

Exploring Holotropic Breathwork®

Selected Articles from a Decade of "The Inner Door"

Kylea Taylor, Editor

This anthology collects 144 field reports from a widespread practice of contemporary, non-drug, altered-state work. Virtually all this information is applicable now to psychedelic-assisted therapy. Holotropic Breathwork® was developed by Dr. Stanislav and Christina Grof. They pioneered in training practitioners to facilitate those experiencing extra-ordinary states of consciousness in a time when psychedelics were illegal. Any experience available in psychedelic states was possible also when using the Holotropic Breathwork® method.

These articles, by 85 authors who were trained in Holotropic Breathwork® by Stanislav Grof, M.D., were first published in the Holotropic Breathwork® newsletter, The Inner Door, edited for Holotropic Breathwork® Facilitators by Kylea Taylor between 1991-2002. Originally written to share their professional experiences and emerging theories with their peers, this collection of articles is a rich source of information, not only giving information about the practice of Holotropic Breathwork® and anecdotes describing psychological and physical healing in deep states of consciousness, but also discussing traditional therapy, kundalini, spiritual emergency, multiplicity, ethics, shamanism, addiction and trauma recovery, dissociation, astrology, and the integration possible in pairing extra-ordinary states of consciousness experi-

CONTINUES >

ences with many other theoretical and practical healing systems as well as with ordinary life in general. This is a beautifully bound collector's item and reference book for practitioners and experiencers. Hardcover. 7" x 10 1/2". 605 pp. ISBN: 0-0963158-6-6

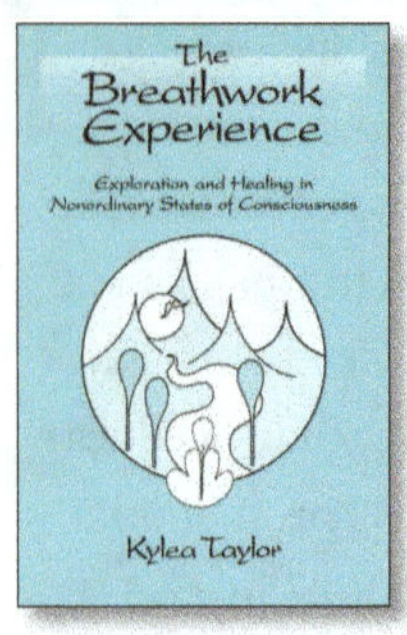

The Breathwork Experience

Exploration and Healing in Non-Ordinary States of Consciousness

Kylea Taylor

Using breathwork participants' descriptions of their actual experiences, documents and illustrates the power of the breath for self-exploration and inner healing. The Breathwork Experience takes you inside a breathwork session to see both what happens in the room from the standpoint of an outside observer, and what it feels like to be the person having the experience. It outlines the human history of using non-ordinary states to seek healing and wisdom. It also discusses the theories of Stanislav Grof, M.D., Ph.D., author of Psychology of the Future, and describes the sensory, biographical, perinatal, and transpersonal types of possible human experiences in non-ordinary states. Available in Spanish and Italian as well as English. 6" x 9". 172 pp. Softcover. ISBN: 0-9643158-0-7

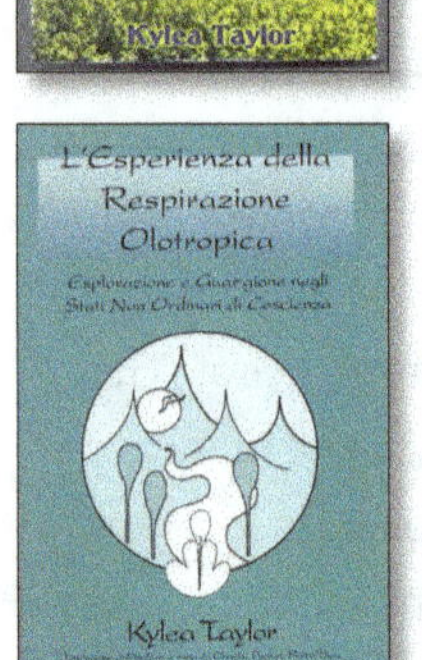

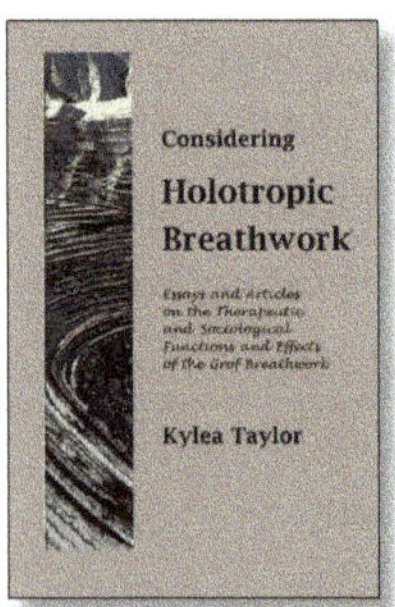

Considering Holotropic Breathwork®

Essays on the Therapeutic and Sociological Functions and Effects of the Grof Breathwork

Kylea Taylor

The book contains Kylea Taylor's essays and articles on the therapeutic and sociological functions and effects of the Holotropic Breathwork®, a non-drug method developed by Stanislav and Christina Grof that invites people to enter extra-ordinary states of consciousness and receive support for transformative process. Because any experience available with the administration of psychedelics is also possible with Holotropic Breathwork®, this book is recommended for those doing or studying how to be a practitioner for psychedelic-assisted sessions. It includes chapters on:

- What a therapist or a psychedelic psychotherapist can learn from being a Sitter in a Holotropic Breathwork® (or psychedelic) group sessions
- What is now the InnerEthics® Awareness Tool "Protection, Permission & Connection," which helps a therapist or practitioner assess and adjust the balance of risk, safety and support in a therapeutic container
- The research results from Kylea's facilitation of Holotropic Breathwork® in a residential substance abuse recovery program during the 1990s
- An analysis of the elegant design of a Holotropic Breathwork® workshop or training module for skillful facilitation of the elements of extra-ordinary states of consciousness and community to support the transformative process.
- Discussion about the Jungian Inferior Function as a gateway for spiritual emergence(y).
- Sponsoring the emergence and integration of previous 'Unexperienced Experience'
- Similarities in the treatment of spiritual emergency and multiplicity
- Yogic sleep and meditation states during Holotropic Breathwork® (or psychedelic sessions)
- SoulCollage®: An art Process to use with breathwork (and for the integration of psychedelic sessions)

6" x 9". 169 pp. Softcover. ISBN: 978-1-59275-007-8

SoulCollage® Card-Making Supplies

SoulCollage® Supplies available at hanfordmead.com and/or amazon.com include precut mat-board cards for collaging, SoulCollage® Starter Kits, Card-Making Supply Kits, and an assortment of tools for collaging.

www.ingramcontent.com/pod-product-compliance
Lightning Source LLC
LaVergne TN
LVHW061243100826
845148LV00008B/1010
* 9 7 8 1 5 9 2 7 5 0 5 0 4 *